T A H L

TAHL

JEREMY INGALLS

THE UNIVERSITY OF ARIZONA
POETRY CENTER

ACKNOWLEDGMENTS

This publication of Jeremy Ingalls' *Tahl* is made possible through the generosity of the Tahl Foundation, with special appreciation due to Marshall Fealk, Esq., executor of the estates of Jeremy Ingalls and Mary Dearing Lewis. Gratitude goes as well to Charles O. Ingram and Dr. Jimmye Hillman for their instrumental roles in bringing the gift of the Ingalls/Lewis estates to the University of Arizona Poetry Center.

Others to whom we extend gratitude are Joshua Wilson for editorial and archival assistance, Dennis Evans in the College of Humanities for his organizational wisdom and good sense, and Gail Browne as Director of the Poetry Center for her leadership and support.

The preface draws upon Ingalls' essay "The Composition of *Tahl*," published in the Summer 1952 edition of the University of Kansas City Review.

Tahl was originally published by Alfred A. Knopf in 1945. This edition published by the University of Arizona Poetry Center was produced by Stanton Publication Services, St. Paul, Minnesota, closely following the original typography and design of W. A. Dwiggins.

Printed in Canada

ISBN 0-9727635-0-3

The University of Arizona Poetry Center

Second Edition

FOR MY FAMILY AND FOR MY FRIENDS,

THE LIVING AND THE EVER-LIVING,

WITHOUT WHOM

THIS BOOK COULD NOT HAVE BEEN WRITTEN

TABLE OF CANTOS

Book Three

Book Four

"Reality cannot be interpreted in terms of continuity alone: within continuity we must distinguish certain individual entities. But these individual entities do not conform to the idea which pure discontinuity would give them: they must have extension, they are continually reacting on each other and, a still more surprising fact, it appears to be impossible to localize them with exactness at each instant."

Louis de Broglie. MATTER AND LIGHT.

"These ideas we inherit — they form the tradition of our civilization. Such traditional ideas are never static. . . . They are transformed by the urge of critical reason, by the vivid evidence of emotional experience, and by the cold certainties of scientific perception. One fact is certain, you cannot keep them still. No generation can merely reproduce its ancestors."

Alfred North Whitehead. SCIENCE AND RELIGION.

PREFACE

When Jeremy Ingalls won the 1941 Yale Series Younger Poets prize for her collection *The Metaphysical Sword,* she already had worked for a decade on her epic poem *Tahl,* the first edition of which was published by Alfred A. Knopf in 1945. She conceived the long poem at the age of twenty while walking through a stand of pines in a thunderstorm on Cape Cod where she was teaching landscape drawing at a summer camp. She spent thirteen years completing the work. The scope of poetic vision, range of formal experimentation and authority of voice she displayed in creating the work would be remarkable at any age. Springing from a young woman barely out of her teens, the work offers a strikingly rich polyphonic dramatic vision of the history of human civilization. Ingalls set out to answer the question, "How does it come about that, though we talk conventionally about the rise and fall of civilizations, we nevertheless can observe, in traceable forms, old ideas, symbols, philosophies, economic systems and theologies carrying on irrespective of the names of nations?"

Tahl, the young aviator-composer protagonist, was conceived as a new kind of epic figure, one not representative of any one nation, but rather one bearing "the major social conflict between man reflecting and man acting," an epic figure whose place in history is complicated by the indeterminacy of both the atom and the human psyche. This central figure is surrounded by a cast of twenty full-length characters, twenty minor voices, and ten choruses, all tied together in the formal symmetry of four books each containing five cantos, following the classic tragic pattern. Ingalls wrote:

> The old epic methods of character development are too solid in outline for our sense of the immeasurable corridors of the human psyche, of the lost line between the crystal and the virus, of the always to-the-naked-eye-invisible and

never wholly predictable behavior of a specific quantum of energy within the atom.

Her answer to this problem was to draw upon her own polyphonic experience, one that began with a richly textured childhood in Gloucester, Massachusetts. Ingalls saw herself as growing from Emersonian roots, and those of "vigorous women like Elizabeth Peabody and Margaret Fuller," in a New England that valued intellectual pursuit and cross-cultural influences. Gloucester, she described, was part of that orbit spinning out from Boston west to Concord and north to Salem and Cape Ann where, half a century after the death of Emerson, she found "something of the spirit of the old New England academy. By the age of twelve we were expected to be literate not only on the main aspects of European and American history but also concerning the most conspicuous events in history of Mesopotamia, Egypt, and Persia." Thus at age twelve Ingalls was reading Dante and at fourteen, Balzac, Goethe, Confucius, Sun Yat-sen and Nietszche. She explored museums and libraries, toured artists' studios on the wharves, attended free concerts given by visiting musicians from the Boston Symphony Orchestra. The exotic came into her imagination not only through formal cultural experiences, but in the homes of her family and friends.

"Lacquers and wood carvings in the cabinets of grandmothers and great aunts," she wrote, "were also reminders of a large world visited by seamen who were our ancestors." Her acquaintances included families, like her own, which had lived on that coast since the seventeenth century, and newcomers whose families retained customs, festivals and songs from Italy, Portugal, Greece, Ireland, Norway, Sweden, and Finland. Sicilian fishermen roared opera out over the harbor on summer nights. Voyagers from around the world came into port. "Long before any of us thought of serious, directed inquiry, we had acquired a sense of world history."

That learning which appears to have come so organically to Ingalls and so profoundly informs the poem *Tahl* may fall heavily on the contemporary ear, and yet epic vision requires the risk of largeness. When *Tahl* was first published Paul Engle wrote in the Chicago Tribune:

> It's a long time since anything as ambitious as this has been attempted in America. The contemporary tendency toward extreme concentration, toward metaphysical image and the

fear of sentiment, has trimmed poetry down to the shortest space. There has been a gain in intensity, but certainly there has been a loss of freedom, in spaciousness, in narrative.

Ingalls, like her contemporaries H.D. and Muriel Rukeyser, pushed the capacity of the epic poem to represent the oddities and intensities of human psyche, as well as the broad strokes of history, in an effort to achieve a sense of collective wisdom true to the complexity and violence of the twentieth century. As the twenty-first century explodes forth in conflicting cultural pressures, the epic task of achieving collective healing or wisdom may seem ever more remote. And yet the epic, as Ingalls defined it, though the literary genre most frequently half read and cheerfully neglected, still is the most durable phenomenon in the history of literature. *Tahl* is an unparalleled study in the capacity of poetry to represent the questing spirit of humankind as it moves and transforms through philosophies, religions, voices and cadences.

—Alison Hawthorne Deming
August 2002

T A H L

PROLOGUE

Of one tall man who walked the western world
We speak who were his friends, who knew his name.
He lives in us, the nameless, being names
Common as grass on graves, as wrecks on seacoasts.
A chorus reading anecdotes, old letters,
We execute a document demanded
Only in our devotion to the man
Whose passport read from no abiding city.
He knew, and we did not, his destination;
But we have heard his footsteps echoing.

The sea of memory we drag for wreckage
To tell the history of him we walked with.
We draw the net. We rinse the dreams, the gestures,
Journals, photographs, in light and sound
And thirty years of his mortality
And hers. We speak of Alison. We find them
Not as the royal twins afloat on seashells,
No children borne of swans with magic rings.
The sea of the world makes wrack of queens and heroes.
And for ourselves alone we speak their names.

He earned his bread. He went some years a journey,
Came home from Cairo and Jerusalem;
From Athens and Madrid with blood upon him.
His birth from somewhere northward and Atlantic
He made of small account, a changeling hybrid
Out of the tree of life, the sea of time.
We knew him. He was Tahl and a musician.
We knew her. She was Alison, a woman.
They whom the sea has claimed, now ever-living
In these our voices raised to their remembrance.

He was a man grown tall, the bastard brother
Of priests, perhaps, of prophets, mandarins,

Prologue

But he was a man among us, stood no higher
Than coffins, backyard bushes, six-foot doors.
His common day with us was like another's.
He did not speak with God in scatheless fire.
Some pages left of music, sound of thunder,
The while we wandered lost in a time of terrors,
Of tentative universes, roiling nations.
He lived and died. And we shall not forget him.

Of separate minds unanimous survival
In him we have survived, the accidental,
The late report, the sought-for recollection,
In many voices through our years assemble:
This man was born as a man is born — in lightning.
He lived as a man — drinking the bitter sea.
He thought as a man — troubled by wind and thunder.
He died as a man, as spring flood on the tree
Sucking the root, the branch, and straining under
The plunge of the riding earth, wrenching and raging,
Tears the trace at last. A man of questions.
The colt of God. And merely man. We knew him.

TAHL : BOOK ONE

CANTO I

THE HIDDEN YEARS

The Hidden Spirit

So much we knew of him as Alfred knew,
As Elsa guessed, as much as women's whispers
Eke public currency of private lives.
I watched him, eager always to set down
That mobile face where every muscle played
Its pertinence in portrait. Years I watched
That face far more than women I have loved
But could not draw it.

"So," I heard him saying,
"Incognito. My personal hibernation."

He dawdled with his breakfast, seemed to need
To empty out his throat of urgent words
And have no pause nor passage for his coffee.

"It's small events," he said, "which most assume
Portentousness, float threadlike, moult themselves,
Come stalking back as bogies. This has been
Just such a hexed and hag-beridden morning."

He paused for breath and butter for his muffin.
"Lying half awake," he said, "I notice
Wheels in the road roll inward like a wave.
Like that this morning, there with Margot lying

Asleep in snowlight and the lamp still burning
White as a ghostwatch. Grogged with sleep I saw
Like memory the grandfather of life,
That blind and viscid body through the sea
Searching, searching, till that quickened nerve
Quivered with light, the stricken cell and then
The sprout, the living eye. A muddled dream,
A memory of sounds, of noise, not music,
Like a reply in my ears, an answer, came.
I turned my eyes, my own, my living eyes.
I laughed. Why? Head in the pillow, laughing."

His eyes were almost closed. He might have been
Still sleeping. But his voice awake and steady:
"Then I was blazing mad. I saw myself
Short-snouted alligator bellowing
His slimy love, a bull-rut in a ditch,
And sweated. Did you ever think of murder?
I'm not joking. Murder? Take her up,
Two hands around her throat or jam your tongue in
Or smash that leering lamp, glass in her hair,
Rise up now, naked as Adam, smash her skull in?
Half asleep I laughed, head in the pillow.
She stirred. Could feel upon my back the cool
Appraisement of her grape-green eyes. And what
The devil's mischief in her soul to prompt her?
Seeing me sprawled upon the pillow, 'Tahl,'
She said, 'Tahl, turn over. Don't you know
Men who sleep with their faces in the pillow
Are born to be drowned?' And then she touched my arm."

I marked him set his knife upon his plate
With a most curious caution. Heard his question:
"Why should I rouse so blazing mad? I took her,
Shoulder and hip. I saw my straining hands
Ugly as talons, even saw her eyes
Grazed with terror, felt her shudder, heard
Her voice, 'Do you intend to kill me?' Quivered . . .
Yet baldly asked. Heard my own answer, 'No.'
What did I want to kill? The blood, the heart beat?

Did you ever think of a heart, pounding and pounding,
Lungs breathing and breathing, death in our hands?
I kissed her eyes, held her chin in my palm.
And what should haunt me, her two mocking eyes?
Or her two eyes that blurred almost to tears?
What do I want to kill? Myself? Not that,
Not drown me straight . . . break out this angry ghost
And wash it clean. Yes," his answer came
To half-born questions restless in my eyes,
"Yes, George, I've known the berserker before;
With Julian more than once because I loved him
Ached to crack his pale, his patient mouth.
Don't draw conclusions. I'd go soft for less
Than Julian. And no love's been lost in Margot.
For less than Margot, for the living eyes
Of birds, of horses, nameless men and women.
Before their eyes the furies fold their wings,
Because those eyes, that more than ghostly glance,
Are swift as light. You cannot kill that light;
Nor night nor trap nor hand nor death will hold it.
Save your coming witticism, George.
Someone died this morning. And not Margot.
This breakfast celebrates the funeral
Of one his friends had libeled, one 'Mephisto.'
Damn it, George, I think this coffee's cold."

There you have him. He could swear at coffee
And rip his soul out in so cool a tone
You'd gape as nerveless as a starchy intern,
Forgetting, for the master surgeon's skill,
This was no pickled and objective corpse
But flesh cut living underneath his hand.
I sat a connoisseur of the incision
As if he'd offered me no gift more solemn
Than my next meal. And still I could not smile.
It was like him too that he should know it,
Curse the coffee, ask me for a paper.
I watched him gulp and read until the silence
Irked me. Took the careless style, blew smoke rings,
Inquired, "Since when so avid of the headlines?"

And he, as dry as toast, his eyes still hidden,
"Dead men, George, return and haunt our world."

He raised his eyes. He drank a glass of water
And when he set it, ponderous and green,
Where feeble sunlight urged itself between
The half-drawn, sagging curtains, like a stain
A green light fell upon his crumpled napkin.

"Look," he grinned, thrusting his hand across
The line of light. "You'll say the napkin's white,
And I relentlessly insist it's green."

"But when the waitress takes the glass away?"
Embarrassed at my own sobriety.

"And when you steal the napkin for a paint rag?"
He countered. "Well, what then? We both have proved
That you saw white, that I saw green. And then
Time having passed, we'll filch this coffee cup
To prove philosophers can rise above
Their own conclusions."

"A cigarette?" I asked.

"Thanks, but smoke is not enough to choke me
If you will play my game."

"Then what's the wager?"

"I'll wager that you wouldn't steal a paint rag.
I'll wager if the waitress comes to stack
This clumsy glass among the crumbled rolls
You wouldn't have the guts to claim it's mine.
Yet so slight whims like termites eat the world
Till glass like cigarettes become an item
Anyone can beg, a noble guest-right,
As ancient barons smashed their lordly wine cups.
I choose for instance willfully to break
This coffee cup for devilment and racket

Against the wall. It wouldn't add more stains
Than stew already in the plaster's mold.
Or smash it on the floor among the crumbs
And watch the coffee soak among the butts
And blackened ends and spews of old cigars.
And yet this crockery's more dear than crystal
Since for fear of noisy words I'll spare it
Even though I know the boss would square
For a sizeable tip from two mad gentlemen."

"Yes," I said, feeling such sickly creep
As comes of having had too many drinks
Yet knowing he wasn't drunk and I as steady
As my own father. "Yes, your game. My ante?"

"Why, all your habits as a gentleman.
We well-bred colts don't murder, steal, nor spit
Nor call attention to our puny selves
By aberrant behaviour."

"Oh, for God's sake,
Tahl," I grouched, "talk sense. You can. What ails you?"

"My breakfast," his face gone sober, "won't digest.
This paper here I ate, this morning's journal
We take by habit, chaser for cold coffee.
I feel the helplessness of gentlemen
Facing in public those same facts of life
They can endure within their private rooms."

"Go on," I groaned. "Business here seems slow.
We're steady customers. We needn't move."

"That's shrewd to show your hand," he had me then.
"You're playing well. 'Please go,' they say. We go.
Or 'Business is slow.' We shake our heads
And eat stale muffins out of sympathy."
He scraped his cigarette along his saucer.
"All business is news. And news is bad.
There'll be a war in Europe, willful wolves

Gobble the sheep of all five continents.
The men with money bags have hired thugs
To break the heads of men who would prefer
A few more dollars or their children starve.
Although a down-east mother starved her child
For sheer disgust and mother's fed in jail
Where father's been already seven years.
Several fat and fed men lose their money
And jump off towers and bridges. Aldermen
Die and have expensive funerals
At which the paupers weep and speculate
On aldermanic incomes. Flowers they'll plant
On rich men's graves and never cabbages
Which are more nourishing. Although they say
The living die to feed the living, all the fed
Continue feeding. Other children die
Of troubles latent in unbalanced meals."

He coughed. His eyes had narrowed. "Just last week
The snow fell heavily. We praise, thank God.
There'll now be work for all the idle hands
At city wages. Snow has also fallen
Where fifty children coming home from school
Were lost. They dug the fifty bodies out
After the blizzard. With this heavy snow
There will be floods this spring and there will be
Another count of dead and others missing.
In every generation men write books.
'Beginning of the end,' the pages say.
End?" He ground his cigarette. "Of what beginning?
Read the news and take our compass bearing.
One shed of ink asserts the man in power
Preserves the state from all but acts of God.
Another sheet proclaims the now oppressed
Will rise and free us from the sins of men.
God, apparently, does not disturb them.
He'll make us free. They'll make us free. For what?
Since we must compromise with space, with time,
With temperature, with shibboleth, taboo,
And each man's need to eat his daily meal.

Some having grandfathers might listen to them.
I haven't, you know. Without a tribe, I talk
And wander far as I can turn my hand
To a cracked piano or a sleazy tune.
I read the books, the grandfathers of men.
Thucydides and Gibbon tell the news.
Tomorrow's paper is a poor translation
And all as current as the newest song
To tribes long lost in deserts, under seas.
The past is a piece with this old coffee cup,
Buried, broken, of dregs, of coffee none,
Washed by the ageless rain. The world is white,
You say. I see it green. The fat-hipped waitress says
It's dirty dishes, pictures on a screen.
And you and I and the waitress are the sheep.
The wolves, the long-toothed outlaws, eat us all.
We dare not own our souls. We dare not break
The tribal totem. Soft and generous,
We fight when the sword's already stolen, lie
Crumpled with blood on the fists of our bare hands."

Silence then. He looked at the clock. I said,
"Have we then souls to lose?"

But he had risen.
Shoving the coffee cup, he looked down, chuckling,
"It'd make a notable splash against that wall.
And what a lie you'd make to save our faces."
Taking his hat, "I have no cure for souls.
Anarchists seldom come to priests on Sundays.
No, I won't drive. I'd break my wind with talking.
I'll hire that tough old mare, take to the woods.
Better not come with me. It's fiendish cold."

It was March. A raw northeaster blowing.
Ice on the road so thick the spikes stuck, trotting.
Galloped and skidded. Paths were hard with snow.
The gelding stumbled often, but the mare,
That tough and ugly beast he loved and rode
As often as his hands could find her hire,

Snorted and cut out loose with Tahl straight up
Rocking the stirrups. Hurled his hat in a snowbank,
Flung himself at the icy branches, broke one,
Whipped it like a saber, charged and harried
A ghostly enemy. I couldn't pace him,
Trailed the spurting hooves, the jutting head,
And the rider swirling through the awesome silence
Settled on a wood long deep in snow.

Trailed him, frigid as I was. I saw him
Headed down to where the trees give over
To rock edge, to the coast. I still remember
A kind of woman's panic. Would he ride
Blind with his rage in the maw of the blowing sea?
Dug my heels and caught him up just hacking
The sea's edge, the wind tearing his hair.
He turned then, reined the mare, leapt off, and led
The horse and smiled at me and disappeared.
I shivered of cold and various apprehensions.

Suddenly he came. "The fire eater's
Tied above there in the upper gully."

I went, a docile son, but left the horses
And, bent in the wind, beat back along the shore.
His clothes on the glaring sand. I shook as hard
Of fear as of the cold. "You wild man!" howled,
Seeing him stripped there, diving in the surf,
The water curdled in the raging wind.

No answer. He came up stamping, took his shirt
Like rattling wire, ran off, came on again.
Never a glance, rubbing his back, putting his clothes on.

Then he spoke. "Come here," he said. I followed
Over a ledge where higher tide had left
A sea pool hardly troubled by the storm.

"Once," he said, "I climbed this rock in summer.
That pool was there and when the sun was shining

It was a mirror you could see your face in."
He wheeled abruptly, arm across my shoulder.
Wind at our backs, we struck across the sand.

On the edge of snow he spoke again.
"George, do you know the legend of the sea pools?
A man who sees his face there will be drowned."

Then he swung, shoved me into the gully,
A puppy wrestling, stuffed my mouth with snow.
"Just for luck," he laughed. "I'll keep my claws in.
You know you've got a soul," he spluttered, writhing.
"I'm showing you," he grunted, scrambling up
Mauling me, "a classic object lesson
In control, a pretty balance of
Body and soul. Now, damn you, since you chose
Chasing me out, you'll play it through. Come on."

Led the horses, hauled up, rode again.
Noon and the sun come out through mist, the kind
That comes with the quiet coming of the spring.

All afternoon we rode, the wind abating.
I couldn't hold my tongue, spoke out, said mocking,
"What are you playing? Faust, perhaps, or Hamlet?"

He smiled as one might smile appreciating
A phrase in music, brushwork in a painting,
Fingered his saddle, answered, "No, old lack-wit.
I'm the devil, the ghost. You have confused
The persons of the play." And then he leaned
Stroking the mare's stiff mane. "I tell you plainly
I'm no musician and I'm not a player
In tin-plate armor nor in tail and horns."
His eyes lit up with mischief turned upon me.
"You keep the secret. I'm a botanist."

I'd had enough of madness to be quit
Of any qualms. Said, "So?" And rode ahead,
But felt him waiting. Scamp, for sure he knew

I'd loiter till I'd finished out the question.
I stopped. He rode up slowly. As he had
A spell upon me, so the question rose,
"A botanist?"

"I'll tell you later. Come.
You have the evening."

Silence to the stables.
Watched him leave the mare, whacking her backside,
Pulling her head round, talking to her eyes.

That winter he'd been living near the harbor.
Three stories up, low ceiling and one window
But that one opened outward on the water.

"Can you light a fire?" he asked and left me
To foil the dark with paper, wood, and matches.
I knew him better later, then would cross him.
"No fag of his," I'd say, but not that evening.
To me, to Alfred too, he was the buck
We trailed like modest Bambis till himself
Had teased us from our first humility
And made us stretch ourselves to take his friendship.

He shoved me to the single leather armchair,
Lolled on the bench and leaned on his piano,
The big and battered grand. Leapt up, brought out
His bread and lager, served me. I could sense
His manner saying, "Here's return. I thank you."

Above me looming long and shirtsleeved arms,
Warm on my wrists his two big brother's hands.
"I want to talk."

Crackling in my throat
The words leapt up, "You've talked enough already."
But swallowed, having seen him in the firelight,
The tenseness in his face. He'd turned away.
Against the half-lit window I discerned him

The Hidden Spirit

Like a shadow, guessed his back was rigid,
Was a wall he'd set to hold himself.
"A botanist." The tone was like a challenge.

"I'd like to understand," I said more gently
Than I had known was in me.

"Understand?"
He took my word. "You'd like to understand.
I'd like to understand. That's why I'm talking.
I'd like to creep beside the whippoorwill
And imitate her crying. Be a light
Along the darkness. Be a voice. A seed,
An acorn springing to a tree and know
The function of my leaves. I'd like to say
What rises in me when I read the words
'The tree of life that is forever green.'
I'd like to know the ancestor of souls
Who could conceive that godhead lived in oak trees
And understood the immanence in forests
And named Poseidon father of the seas.
Now in the last of winter you have built
A fire to dry our boots with, built a fire
Of wood that smells of sea wrack; and we conjure
The demons in the lights and in the waters.
In March we here anticipate an August
Moonlight; the complaining whippoorwill,
My voice. I'd like to know the source of light
That car has use of, wheeling there below us."

He raised his head and turned it toward the window.
"You know," he said, "the story of young Bach
Copying his father's scores by moonlight?
I too would like to steal the father's wisdom
And make it mine to teach; but all the learning
I'd lay hands on, not so near as cupboards
For which attentive sons can find the key."

I told him then a story I'd reserved
As having meaning, as a parable

With meaning felt and never ferreted
Until that evening. "There's an Eastern legend,"
I began. "Old Doc we read our Greek with
Told me. Something maybe Sanskrit. Know it?"

"No," Tahl answered, "though he's liable,
Old Doc, for Julian's faith, my heresies.
Which shows the alchemy of words can make
Gold for him, long life perhaps for you,
For me a plague of gnats. Let's have your story."

As most who picture thoughts in mass and line
Come late to words and dread their faltering,
I knew perfection but the sentence stammered,
Feared of itself and stumbled in the phrasing:
"There was a man assaulted. He was led
With bandaged eyes into a desolation.
Abandoned in the desert he could tell
Not east from north, but when at last with patience
He had torn the bandage off he wandered
Village to village till he came by asking
To his own town." I felt as sticky hot
As any kid gone stage-struck. But he'd listened.

He said, "The waters on the jagged rocks
By devious paths rejoin the rising tide.
You give good counsel. Do you know its meaning?"

I didn't know. "It was a kind of muddling,"
I admitted, "like my searching out
The rubbish of my mind to find the makings
Of my next picture. Then it comes, is right
But I can't tell you why."

He took that too.
"Rubbish for a picture. So we enter
The desolation, searching, read the records,
All the rubbish, all the fathers' wisdom,
And all our recollections so to find
The other side of the sea, to find the seed
Of the green tree."

The Hidden Spirit

I said I envied him.

He laughed, "Thou shalt not covet, but what goods
Of mine would you have use for?"

"For your words,"
I said. "Whenever I am scant a pencil,
I'm just a dumb show jerking helpless hands."

"I talk too much," he said.

"That's not the truth,"
I stopped him. "Since the days at school, with Alfred,
Since," I hesitated, "since the death
Of Julian, you've had only words for women
And your dinner."

"Yet those very words
I've stuffed the air with, since I came this morning
To sit beside you in that greasy tavern,
Say nothing more than any day's reporting,
Say nothing more than you yourself will rant with
When you've a few more years to try your hands in,
Looking on men and knowing what you see
Is fooled with a light you can't glue down to canvas,
Something a shorter wave length than a star beam,
Something untranslatable as thunder,
Beyond your words and yielded up to music."

Stupidly I echoed, "Yields to music."

"Yes," the word-spurt upward like the flame
In a faggot wry or knotted, "George, I tell you
These books, this talk of mine is desperation,
My sour grapes, and yelping. Cannot snatch
More than I'm tall enough to manage.
The schoolman's dialectic, the device,
Is not enough. I am obsessed to go
Back of birth, beyond the death, expound
An apprehension that has haunted me,

A spirit that's besought me for its flesh
To make it living, make it serve the world.
I'd like to set out levers on the sun,
I'd like an Orphic music that could set
The sea and the stone and the snake to harmony."

He rose. The room was hot. He set his heel
On the solitary burning log and ground it,
Smoke about his ankles. "Let it roar?"
His voice, most gravely, "Flare? Stir up, incite it
Until it burns the houses of the world
As flat as in the time of fiery dragons?"

The room was nearly black and still I knew
That he was smiling. "Personal retreat
Into the past has built for me a language
Only mine. You make your vulgate version.
I'll tumble time. I'll write a symphony
For bagpipes, gitterns, clarions and rebecs.
The serpent, George, was once an antique horn."

Strode the dark sure-footed, sat him down,
Struck the piano, roused it to such storm
Of noise as set the neighborhood to swearing.
A knocking on the wall. He stopped, then idled
A kind of pastoral split wide with discord,
Placing a chord, a tremolo, a flourish
So light you wouldn't credit you were hearing
So much as dustweb fallen in a corner.

"I commit," he said, "an indiscretion
In various keys. You'll always catch the crowd
With any solo phrase on English horns.
You bounce them to their feet with three trombones
Loudly proclaimed. Bow up, bow down. Tongue trumpets.
I'd like to lay a fist on all their noses
And ape them with comedian bassoons."

"You're generous," I offered.

The Hidden Spirit

"George, so solemn?
You know that all this raucous *danse macabre*
Is so much mud I cake my boots with, riding.
Sometime I'll write you bells and flutes, as gentle
A passacaglia as April sunshine
That's now from me at least as far as Saturn
From the moon." He snapped the light on, blinking.
Shoved his bench to a table where the books
Were heaped as if a sober boy'd been playing
Soldiers in among his father's tomes
And set them thoughtfully to fort and bastion.
He swung his leg across the table corner,
Elbow on the nearest fort, his fingers
In his hair, and eyed me, cocked an eyebrow.
"If any of our friends report me missing
Search up here, among the heavier volumes."

"Joking out," I asked, my hand already
Finding the knob, swinging the low door,
"What do you hope with looking you may find?"

"A woman," he paused. "And several other answers."

Before I'd clattered half way down the stairs,
The door above let light out, sharpening
Patterns in the murk as I made note of,
Seeing light no surface but a motion.
Heard him calling, "Thanks." The light was gone.

I went regretting, did not wish to go.

Observe our faith who read in this our country
The weather signs of spring. The promising,
The bland and fecund mists of afternoon
Proceed toward night. Again the rising wind
And every road sunk hours deep in snow.

TAHL : BOOK ONE

CANTO I

THE HIDDEN YEARS

The Hidden Body

He was born in a night of thunder and no rain.
Came on the arc of the sea and into sound,
Came on the waters. Motion is a wave
And over the waters, thunder. Lives we live
Are born of the sea and the sound, the voice
Over the water, ancient word, the sound
Of threat, of promise, and of answering.

Begotten. The moon turns, thrice triple turning.
Borne. And the moon's wane. The sun uprising.

Under the thunder hoarse and dry, the wind,
The sound of the sea that breaks with a sound of breaking.
Lightning is scalpel-sharp, a surgeon's knife.
Mourn on the edge of the sea with the sea's moaning.
Thunder and lightning out where the sky comes down.
His mother died the night that he was born.

Cry against the dark, against bereaving.
Cry against the sun, the sound receding.
Bind him against the sea, against the wind.

Now morning sun and hidden in its light
Begotten and borne were no more palpable.
Four years of nights and mornings in the sun,

The Hidden Body

The sea all sun-fleck, rolling on the sand.
Death no enemy, the dead unknown.
Only the flowers at the grave in May
Forgotten soon. Immortal mother gone
Less than mortal, out of memory.

In four sun-smitten years, unfailing June.
The father's memories and not his own,
Naming the father's name, the figure prone
On sand, warning and watching voice, attending hand.
Dim figure, dim sea, tide on sand,
Dim with the omnipresence of the sun,
Dim in the summer-steaming sand. What brand
Out of the sun struck down a name, a man
Lying voiceless, unattending, lying
Prone? Cry sudden, child. They come,
The strangers surging sudden from the sea,
Trampling his well-built house, the sea-wet sand
Scattered with footfalls. Take him in the arms,
Struggling, bewildered. He is dead, your father.
Come. Do you remember? Do you understand?

Now and again a strange face bending down.
"I knew his father. He is like him." Then
He felt and fled from pity, memory,
The zealous stranger and the stranger's hand.
Do you remember? Do you understand?

Do you know, fatherless, motherless, do you see
The cloud, the symbol of the thunder reared
On the horizon? Having been once born,
Shall you be born again? No. Through fields
Running, a wary colt with the chestnut mane,
Sired, sireless, motherless, learning names,
Julian and Julian's mother of his blood,
Nearer than blood in nurture. Bless the names
At night with one 'Our Father, Him in heaven.'
Not to suffer. See. He laughs, he runs,
He goes to school. Like brothers, Tahl and Julian.
Fortunate son of the sea, now among mountains,

The Hidden Years

We who speak have loved him, questionless colt
Of the heavenly pasture. Do not weep for him.

Are not philosophers and prophets born
Of sorrow and of scorn? Thunder in the night,
He dreads it, says his prayers. Only when
Summer is black with thunder he will come
Whimpering home. He has never known
Terror but only this, no fear but sound
Cracking his ears. He loves a tune. He sings.
Follows a bird's song, thrush or oriole,
Watches the brook that runs below the field,
Watches solemnly the ailing bird
Master its broken wing. Julian talks
But Tahl has lost his tongue. And are you sad?
Do you ask of good and evil? No.
There's music Sunday, sure as supper and God.

Earth and heaven shattered, nations fallen,
Apocalypse of years, but not for him.
Thunder was a sign. And he could read,
But he was secret. Saw us searching down
The shouting print and pictures saying: War.
Julian, child of questions, tracked the breed
Of evil in lament, in all our words
Grave in the waiting nightfall. Level-eyed
Tahl there watching. Never might we know,
Save by the prophecy in retrospection,
The shape of the picture in the faithful mind.
Unknown the periscope of word will raise
Thought to the watching eyes. Seek the scar
Left, lacking a record of the wound.
The nations cringed and fled. The towers fell.
He saw the lightning and he heard the sound.

But there were other echoes in the mountains,
Sounds in the fretting roads, among the buildings,
Wheels, wires, and wind on long roads humming,
Crescendo of wheels and bells and whistling trains.
Sight and sound and singing, rise at seven,

Pendulum day swing, go to bed at nine.
Trucks in the night and street lights in the wind.
Under the song, with shivers in the spine,
Thinking of God, that He is Three in One.
And Tahl is one. And counting is a song.
Days and nights that never have an ending.
Julian sees. He talks. He plays with colors,
Tahl is silent. He is listening.

The lack of a word need not to lack a thought,
A record of remembering within.
There was the night the neighbor drowned herself
In the brook below the field. And Julian cried
Next morning, troubled with questions. She was good,
She gave them cakes, the two of them from school,
Julian and Tahl. And she was dead, was drowned,
She killed herself. And Julian could not go
For days to wade the fern pool. Tahl alone
Looked on the water with untroubled eyes.

And there were fires that burned the neighbors' cows,
And there were floods that gutted neighbors' farms;
But fires and floods from him seemed distant far
As words of wars, the news of kinsmen slain,
Or funerals for elders of the clan,
White-whiskered ancients, women very thin.
And nothing stirred him; or the music sung
In chapel solemnly, but only then
A sadness inarticulate. No tears.

What sea-born angel walked with him? We knew
Wear of disease. For Julian days in bed;
Never for Tahl. A hand's breadth and not harmed,
The day the elm tree fell, that mid-March storm.
Find no amulet, no charm for sorrow
And no scorn. No evil. Under the graveyard wall,
Hidden from eyes. The questions and the girls.
All without conscience, only the clear-eyed colt
Nuzzling. Julian was ashamed. Not Tahl.
No question. Of the world that it is round . . .

"That it goes spinning so you clutch your throat
Trying to think," says Julian. Tahl says little,
Says, "Do you think that all the gods are dead,
The gods in stories we can read at school?"

Twelve years tall, in his den below the alders,
Fondling fool-mad of a chance-found stone.
"This is blue, the color of sea at noon time.
This is red, and that is the color of lightning."
He made the words and then he made the tune
And blushed and ran away because we heard him
Under the trees. Fled with the flight of madmen
Till Julian for his dinner bribed him home.

Julian said, "I found him in the leaves,
Talking of bulls and stars and speaking stones.
But don't you ask him. He won't tell you. 'Blood
Is a magic,' he says. You must not ask him.
Yesterday he said he was a priest."

In the sandlot sun he flies, the arrowy runner.
He flanges and feints from the glozed bare breasts, the arms
Flailing, avoiding the blithe supple run-wet cottonlank
Thighs of the rallying boys on the ball that pursues him.
He flies. Is he caught? He is not in the thud of the bat
But the ball he eludes is pursued by the wing-flying seed
That rides on the air fluttered to current of bat,
The curve cut of pursuer pursued. And his need
Is speed as a ball, as the traveling wheel; but now
He is slow as the flow of the traveling seed that impelled
By the thud in the hot thick shift of the air's weight
Halts him still unhurt, for he has brushed
The lively seed unguarded from his breast.

Are not philosophers and prophets born
For making words of their long listening?
It was the music filling up his ears,
And teachers talked and books were full of words,
And he'd no stay with filling up his ears
To ask our questions or be answering.

The Hidden Body

The visiting relations, twice-removed,
In now how many years we have not seen him.
You are welcome. We'd not make so much
Of our few recollections. Years now. Gone.
Tahl, we think, was like his father, dark,
Quiet, common seaman . . . seldom saw him.
Tahl, we think, was like his father, held
Some blood's mistrust of all our reasoning
That kept him secret, as from snuffing scorn
Smelt in the winds of laughter. Years now. Gone.
They left us. Tahl alone; till Julian sought him.
Seeking himself and fled upon the tide-reach,
Tahl, alone, sixteen. And none of us,
None of our name who lived upon those sands.
As if he'd tasted salt in mountain rivers,
As if the sea had drowned us in our houses,
As if a tide we could not see had swept him
Out on a flood in springtime, he was gone.

TAHL : BOOK ONE

CANTO II

RETURN TO THE SEA

Julian in Life

Come in the morning. Listen to the horns.
The ships move in the mist with timorous bells.
The air is heavy with sleep, the breath comes hard,
Salt in the bitter wind and blinding fog.
Blind in the perilous morning, in the mist.
How shall the voices of the morning bruise
The ears of a man deaf? You alone
Blind to the shadow on the edge of foam.

Blind and deaf, dim the sight, the sound,
Dim the wave-sucked murmur, dim the horn,
Dim the prow, the men beyond the mist
Seeking the sound, breath of the quaking horn,
Shudder. The thunder's muffled. But it comes.
There was a night of thunder long since gone.

Morning sun will burn upon the mist,
But fog will rise on summer afternoons.
Baptize the child out of the sea's birth,
Bear him unction, wafer of your death.

The wharves are old, young stranger in the sun.
None remember when those posts were driven.
Old the spars and towers across the harbor.
Mind the lurking rope and guard your heels.

Julian in Life

Old the gulls. And mind the crooked nails.
Steady, balance on a gunwale. Will you go
For fish upon this sea? The sea is old.
The sea has the sound of bells, the sound of guns,
The sound of horns, the sound of dead men's cries.
The sea is a veil, a serpent, and a pall.
The sea is old, is deep. Upon the waters
A shape, a sound. A seaman's son needs know
Prayers for the dead. Remember. The sea is cold.

Down the misty searoads of his mind
Anchorless, adrift, he moved alone,
The derelict of any borrowed dream,
Until that day when not again alone,
A day without a name toward which he moved
Borne of his obtuse preoccupation
Unchartered, rudderless. His slight emotion,
Walking the harbor road an autumn day,
Scuffing the acorns fallen in brown dust,
Walking with Julian an old, afternoon way,
Idly pleased with the sun, the shore, and the seawind.

Now with Julian, brother as his own,
Julian with him. He was not alone.
Leading his brother to the three old logs
Beside the beach, the logs like sponges now,
Rotten with age. A day. It had no name.
Tahl. And Julian, paint kit at his elbow,
Julian sharpening pencils in the sand.

"How red the trees have turned, there on the island."

"I'd call it nearer orange," this from Julian.
"You with your music, and you see no colors.
Red. Green. A child with just two crayons.
You're blind, Tahl, and I'd not back your hearing,
To embalm that good man Bach with metronomes.
You know Italian, yes, but not *rubato*.
How can you? Seeing kindergarten trees.
What do you call a face? White, I suppose,

Since your professors tell you you were born
A white man. Still I guess a man
Of enough science would have sport with you.
You could not be a richer olive color
With that dull red. Don't all the women chase you
For that same darkness and your solemn eyes?
And what am I? White, too, as you suppose?
A Japan lily slightly striped with yellow?"

The sun was riotous across the searoads
Though through the mist Tahl caught but half the challenge,
And like a child adoring his own mirror
Said first, "How do you mean, I'm such an odd one?
I'm dark, of course. Is that remarkable?"

"Very," Julian laughed. "You are an odd one.
You're archetype, God's pattern for musicians,
Though mathematics freezes all your bones.
That rusty hair of yours that's got the yellow
Baby hair still in it. I recall
The night they brought you to us. You were four
And I was only six, but I recall
That yellow top of yours and how you lugged
My toy piano with you everywhere.
It's not your eyes alone that might suggest
Your ancestors were seamen. Lord, I've thought,
In some lights, you're a passable prince of Hindus.
And you've a Mongol in you in some shadows
And a Negro mouth that's nearly tempered out
By all our cool New England stock most likely."

The sun was riotous across the searoads.
Turning one sharp glance among the islands,
Tahl sat up, his face of such a brightness
That Julian felt a kind of awe upon him
Though what was said was only obvious.
"Your face is yellow and some red from summer.
You're like old tallow in the winter months.
And there's our family look about the hair

And you've my eyes, or I've got yours, I'd say,"
And Tahl stretched back upon the grass again.

Hear a horn and give the note a name.
Hear a bell strike. Will it raise the dead?
Shall that last trumpet hail us under sun?
Shall ghosts whine grappling in a final rain
Or spew out fathomless on fiery air?
This was a trumpet tone, a bell in a mist,
This was a doom, the birthright of a man.
Are you amazed? Of such simplicities
Make an epoch, find a Gabriel?
Shall the color of trees, the portrait shape of flesh,
Wake the shadow, the ghost? No words but these,
Himself seen shadowed on his brother's world,
And there rose round him all his memories
And he was one as when a hidden child,
Saw clear, heard answers, roused the deaf and blind,
The slumber ended, the awakening.
A seed of words. Shall he be born again?

That night, seeing Julian lie as he had lain,
Year upon year, the brother by his side,
Head flung back close under the window ledge,
The chastened strength, the consecrated face,
Hollowed, lined, and sharp beneath the stars,
There was a tide in the heart. He spoke the name,
"Julian!" But Julian slept. He spoke again,
"Julian, who am I? How shall I be born?
Julian!" But Julian slept. We cannot know
What we beget, what breeds in chance words spoken.
And Tahl slept, woke and listened, slept again.

Out of that night it came and Julian wrought it,
The luminous dark, the canvas dug to depth.
Julian, the master, Julian struck the oils in.
Julian composed the dancers and the child,
The infant idol with the fire-lit eyes,
That black, archaic nascence, living film
Ripped from a skull had lain with dreams abed

Return to the Sea

Before the ice and shifting of the seas,
Before the mammoths died, a witch's caul
Snatched from the very embryo of time.
We saw and brooded, envied or were still.
"But it was Tahl," he said, "who dreamed the dream."

Look at it. Let your mind to Julian's cave
Beyond the darks in darkness, to the heart
Of the man who dreamed the cave and loaned the dream.
Julian had known him. We would know him soon,
This tree with roots that asked of its own seed
Its first and last, its meaning and its end.

We who bandied words of shiny books
And raped all music pert with fingering,
We the brisk with chemistry of paint,
Packets of small and bright-wrapped information
We tossed as on thousand other evenings
Like jacks and caught them smartly on our knuckles,
We, sprawled in the north-lit room, besought
Diversion of his silence. "Tell us, Tahl.
Tell us your dream."

He said: "On that long night
White shapes as white as mist blew through the door
Dancing as slow as star turn. I was swung
Small as a child, round, smooth as ebony.
Then slowly, slowly, whiteness burned to flame,
The room in flames, the rafters melted down,
Curled over to the arches of a cave
That opened outward, opened down unending,
Groin upon groin of rock, the green-grown walls
Glossy with flame. The steepled sign long lain
Upon the sea floor reared as of itself
Out of a sea of flame. The white ones down
Fluttered to form, to dancers, and the sign
Shot root and branch and settled in the stone.
The fire blew down to coal. A river ran
Under the tree roots. Borne upon their hands.
They set me to the tree branch, called a name.

Julian in Life

The name was mine. My heavy head
Rolled. And I was cold, was frightened. Sound,
The feet of all the nations rocked the world
Till wall and tree and dancers wreathed around,
Till I, impaled and naked coal-dark child,
Saw myself the body of a man.
Then I heard voices. 'Fear the sword,' they said.
'Fear the sea,' they said. Then silence. Cold.
Mist from the sea swam cloud-like in the cave."

"That was not all your dream," said Julian. "No,
Not all," said Tahl, "but all your picture shows.
To make us small-talk, there's the gambit given."

The razor edge upon his silences
Cut to compunction till our tongues were bled
To his own silence. Till for courtesy,
Till for our torment, with his eyes ablaze
In that volcanic animation we
Would learn was much the nature of the man
As were his dryness and his silences,
He said: "Listen. I'll tell you. It was mad,
Madder than all the seven spirits sent
Upon the Gadarene. I'll tell you. First
I woke, was listening to the sea, was cold
With coldness of the sea and of the dead.
And then I slept again. Again I dreamed.

"Then I was warm. Warm, a colt in a hay heap
Nursing, could not find to suck, was lost,
Staggered, was in a forest lush to horror, fled.
There was a stallion. He was red. And a mare
Blue as the lightning. What had the stallion said?
'Beware the bull.' Let fly his heavy hooves.
I fled again and all the air was full
Of tears as red as teats. Now and again
The mare, sudden as wing-flight, come upon,
Came on me, grieved, and warned me with her eyes.
In the terribly green field . . ."

He stopped. The room
Was still as death-watch. Heard him grind
The dead ash of his pipe against his palm.
The muscles of his jaw quivered, shaped
Over the mouth the known ironic smile.
The lids dropped, the mocking mind erased
The coursing fever. But we would not yield.
"Tell us!" Like children cheated of the tale
Buying their bedtime clamored. So he gave
Baldly at last the sequel, held himself
To nonchalant address.

Said this: "The bull
In the terribly green field was like a god
Of bulls and shone to whiteness like the sun,
His eyes pale as flame in sunshine. Moved
Mightily. A woman came. Her face
I've never seen but saw it then, can make,"
He smiled, "no image now. I've tried. She came
She said: 'Love him,' and caressed my head.
Colt still, as you recall." He smiled again,
Twisted his pipe stem. "'He will kill,' she said.
'Love him. Love the tree branch and the sword,
The blood that drips from his offending horn.'
There I was slain. Died licking my wound."

Julian's voice, woman for gentleness:
"Tahl, that was not all." "No," as if grudging,
"No, The last words said. I heard them, lain
Sweating. These words, 'Love—nor comprehend.'"

His face changed. God and the devil blent
To shaken silent laughter. Took the cue,
All of us, murmured, smoked, and drank around.
Heard him observe to Alfred, "Julian says
There's meaning in seas and bulls and such strange signs.
He says the evil of the world's compounded
Of such bedevilment. And we're all children."

Alfred's chuckle timed our raillery.
Took our comfort, praised the craftsman skill

Julian in Life

For Julian's honor, heard a song of Tahl's,
New-done and flash with discord, glittering.
"Damned inconsequent." . . . the words his own.

No one has forgotten the great year
When Tahl and Alfred like twin princes reigned.
Their rooms were one address for all of us
Whose wit might give us entrance. Alfred brewed
The laughter, like a giddy effervescence
Around such tuns of words as left us drunken
With thinking that together we could read
The palimpsest of every hoary riddle.
Until that last and greatest night of all
When Tahl spoke best and Alfred seemed most subtle
And Julian was there too, come out from town.
We heard his words that night, or some of us,
But it was years before we understood
That it was just that night and Julian
Made Tahl thereafter like a man gone blind
Who'd lost his way. And even Alf was tamed
As if he were Tahl's dog and had to lead him.

All of us with Julian coming in
Talking of icy roads and skidding corners
And the color of beech trees in the moon and snow,
And huddling to the fire. He was sick then
And it was bitter cold. That evening . . . when
George was moaning for his pet Symposium
And Alfred had his memorable answer
And the easy surge of laughter.

"What about the old days?
Why should we regret them?"

"Respect is the word." Julian from the fireside.

"What about the old days? Why should we regret them?"
"George will tell us. They talked about love."
"He's no authority. What about love?"

"Tahl will tell us. He's the authority.
Ten more women than a week has days."

"This is the burden: Love is a power,
Love is a pleasure. Love is an apple.
Self is the core."

"We have learned it. We have seen
Love is the body and the joy of women
Paid with toys. And some ask nothing.
Is it not fortunate?"

"Let us have beauty. Lust is a good word,
Salt in the mouth and a heap of bones.
Besides, the wench is dead."

"Why not joy? Death is the end.
One small world. And then there's nothing.
So many nitrates sooner or later.
Girls love coolly underground."

"Who has seen a serpent, black and gold?
George, he paints them. Have you seen them?
They make pertinent designs."

Julian, meanwhile, with as much devotion
As an old priest about the Paschal flame
Fed his fire. Once he spoke and then
With a brief question. Softly to inquire
Just why his cousin's walls sagged down with books
And he was such a gourmand in his learning
When this so small careening world was geared,
Set and timed to meet its doom on schedule.

Answer him:
"Bright little packages, bright little pill boxes,
So many cokes and an opium dream."

"Let us have knowledge. What's your curriculum?"
"A shot a day makes good conversation.

Mix with gin and smoke four seasons.
Life will be easier bye and bye."

"What'll you do if you can't take it?"
"Hydrogen sulphide." "What's a sin?"
"What'll you have then, gas or drowning?"
"Dead or alive, who mentioned sin?"

"God's a delusion, psychopathological.
All neurotics. We have seen.
Religion, let us say, is a delusion.
Suicide's a kind of grandstand play.
The healthy mind adjusts itself to chaos.
Take your score and like it. That's the way."

"Is it fate or is it chaos?"

"Consider a million, million universes."

Laughter set at foils with eloquence
On that night of young man's arguments.
All our words had glitter;
But Tahl's were coolly chosen
And we were silent, listening to him:
"You will admit not everyone can call
A middle C without an instrument,
Nor name a tone though I should give him all
The harmonies. So also if you spent
Your days with some men's eyes you could not see
A portrait hidden in a nose and jaw.
Tune buries tone; flesh, the bones' symmetry.
So elusive is the simplest law.
For, call Fate or Destiny the name,
The atomic measurements rehearse
Star and amoeba, every one the same,
Man contrapuntal to the universe.
Like a perfect organism life
Fulfills its being. Every death, each birth,
The rise of great men, the recurrent strife
Of nations, take their rhythm with sun and earth.

Sin, therefore, is excluded. Did you choose
Your blood and brains that you must justify them?
Desires were not to take or to refuse.
How then, when once they're given, can you deny them?
Freedom is of all our words most hollow.
Our minds, which seem to choose, were long before
Set in the chain of concepts they must follow.
There's no alternative but to endure.
But it's all One, the Unity, perfection,
And that's the music of it."

Alfred parried: "There is zero also
And that's a much more modern mystery."
And he continued:
"Your law for nature I'm inclined to grant,
But man, Tahl, is such a small white ant.
Why should he need to run around in rhythms
With the stars and be the sun's small brother?"

Tahl replied: "If a flower move in the wind,
Are its leaves rigid? If you should throw
A fist of loose screws into a machine
Wouldn't you have a pretty mess of wreckage?"

That was most of what we said that night . . .
Something more about the fate of planets,
Energy's conservation or dispersion,
Phenomenal man among phenomena.
But what was most important we discovered
Some days after when Alf took to quoting
Tahl as if he were a modern prophet
And Alf his self-appointed John the Baptist.
It's well enough he took the doctrine over,
The little Oedipus Tahl was exposing
For any willing shepherd, had we known it,
Though he himself was not convinced till later,
And it was a harsh doctor who convinced him,
That this first child of his was really lame.

Julian in Life

Then it was that Julian mentioned friendship.
And Alfred said it was a choice indulgence,
Selfish, of course, for was not everything?
Tahl meanwhile was mute,
Searching Julian's eyes
Secretly. One must not
Betray the heart.

Then it was that Julian mentioned virtue
And Tahl said: "Loyalty, endurance."
And we said: "Comrades, loyal
And enduring." For one moment
A heart beating strongly,
Warm as Julian's fire.

"Alfred's a wit, but Tahl's a brain."
"Fate is an organism. That's a man's philosophy."
"Steel and experiment."
"Yes, and comrades. We have the answers."
"Write them in a book. Write them in a new book.
The old books are stories made to scare children."

When Julian rose as if reluctant still
To leave his fire, he had an odd, slow smile
Reflecting his slow words as he took up
The lamp cord that was caught across Tahl's desk
And said, as not intending we should hear,
"Was it so wise to strangle fire? Has not
The slave bound over his master?" Then he went,
Bent slightly, as with blows. Tahl was standing
With a great sickness in his heart and watching
The man go out and looking as he would follow
Somehow in the hope to comfort him.
But George still had his tongue and there was laughter.
Among us few to notice Tahl was silent,
That he was torn with questions — and alone.

TAHL : BOOK ONE

CANTO II

RETURN TO THE SEA

Julian in Death

Epistle, gospel, prayer, psalm,
And as in Adam all die,
Julian,
How are the dead raised up,
Julian?

He is reading from a book.
Do you hear the solemn words,
Julian?

The orchid lies beside your hand,
Silver, magenta, that you loved.
Take it with you,
Julian.

He was made a living soul.
Lay him down, the head, the heart,
With silver, magenta.
Flowers will grow where these are slain.
Make him a house to hide him in.
Why did you go alone,
Brother?

Lay down my brother's head and heart.
What is the name of him I loved?
He has no name for he is dead.

Julian in Death

The house is very damp.
Who will build your fire?
The house is very dark.
Who will bring your light?

What is the name of him I loved?
He has no name for he is dead.
Nameless men will shovel him over.
The peace of God. The peace of God.
 Julian.

They have smothered him, Alfred, there in the wilderness;
Down with the slaves of death, the imperturbable
Vassals of death, an acceptable sacrifice.
Feed the red earth. Feed the young crocuses
Better than straw of the leaves of last season.
Many the sauces and spice of that banqueting.
Some have been carved with the knives of the lightning,
Some have been washed in the snow-maddened rivers.
There is the exquisite service of battlefields,
Masterly butchers, excisers of entrails.
Fat fruits of disease and the charnel of factories,
Fire-eaten flesh, the olla podrida
Of vices and murders, the sweet immolation
Of earthquake and whirlwind and famine and pestilence.
The delicate relish which the assiduous
Servant of death has devised for his pleasuring:
Twigs of the gibbet, flowers of gunfire.
There are the tender, the beautiful children,
Back-broken laborers, child-bearing women,
All of the humble and all of the arrogant.
Death, the great swine fed on nitreous compounds
Out of the stench and the steam of his kitchens.

Death has two houses. That of the earth
Is crumbling and rotten with mould of the centuries.
The house of the sea has a cleanlier seneschal.
I and my brother will go there together.
Sods will move easily, night not yet over them.

Return to the Sea

I must go too. We shall go handsomely
Arm and arm through the quiet green doorway
Out from the beach where three logs sit forever.
Nothing is waiting, but Julian is waiting.
Before the first gate he will answer my questions.
With a red-silver orchid to the cleanlier seneschal
We shall pay toll at the soft green doorway.

The moon is coming. He is waiting. I am going.
He is waiting. Tide is coming. Moon is coming.
He is waiting. I am going. I am coming,
Julian.

So he met death and fought with him
Until the tide's turn,
Until the going down of the moon,
Until he went alone in the morning
To face the sky.

Out into the morning hesitantly,
A child, step and step, in uncertain courage,
Searching for something lost, something beloved.
He turned without salute from the tallow moon
That had been a candle to his desolation,
Its merciless beams plunging abysmal waters
Where soft amorphous festerings of the mud
Turned up their hungry sucking mouths to gape
At a face gone cold with madness peering down
That malice of light to the primeval damp,
Seeking the mother of flesh, beginning and ending.

He came with sick eyes into sightless hours
Of sunlight and of walking to no purpose
Half the day, until the lodestone set
Splintered deep in memory compelled him
Straitly toward the pole star of his thoughts.

Labyrinths of houses were resolved
To plummet avenues. The nervous crowds
Teeming at the curbside walked as still

As a procession on a holy day.
The shuffle and bark of horns, the shuttle of trains,
The racheting carts, the drumming rote of wheels
Were only as the plangency of tide
Come full again after the April storm.
His sharp misery took anodyne
Of his decision and he welcomed all
Landmarks coming quietly to meet him
Even to the last street, the bridge gone over,
And to the door and the familiar stairs.

The traveler knows this only and this surely,
A house he left upon an April morning,
All his maps and charts bound on his wrists
As surely as the thick blue veins that beat
His life along the paths of his one journey.

To come quite casually up high, dark stairs
For a morning snatch of talk. Quite ordinary.
George, had he been there with a scrawly drawing,
The morning's joke cribbed from the corner newsstand,
A commonplace would soon enough have ended
This mapped and charted private kind of travel
Through lonely convolutions of the brain.
Only there were no jokes, no commonplaces.
Only the bleak high room grotesquely raftered,
An easel leaning starkly,
And paintings like old tombstones
Lurching crazily against the walls.

This traveler without baggage, passport, visas,
Perhaps stood over-long beside a window,
Suffered too long the gouging incandescence
Of sunlight falling on an ice-choked river,
The desolate humor of sun on dirty snow.

Retreating from the paradox of light
And mud and soot and ice of a spring morning,
He found, so he told us, one of Julian's drawings
Lying as it were by calculation

For a cousin's window-wandering gaze to fall on.
A woman's head, in pencil, and a model
Whom he could not remember having seen
In all the days of four years Julian worked
In this bare room with river-looking windows.
A woman's head in pencil, somewhat handsome,
And eyes, like Julian's, holding an enigma
Of peace and fire, replies to several questions.

So he became upon this same spring morning
A new Diogenes of certain purpose. True,
A man might be a fool for even dreaming
That he might walk the world and find a woman
With eyes of peace and fire, a woman willing
To give a civil reply to his big questions.

Every man goes on his own journey.

TAHL : BOOK ONE

CANTO III

HOUSES OF WOMEN

Ballads of the Living

Every journey begun is full of endings,
Sometimes brutal. Prophets, gentlemen,
Philosophers may have their failings also.

His theory having been that every woman
Is adequate to just one situation,
Some served tea and some could cook a dinner,
Others were appropriate to the theater,
Some for play and some for conversation,
He kept engagements challenging all Byrons
With an efficiency that's mostly native
To young men brilliant at their mathematics.

Jan was tall and supple and long-legged,
With grace that grants peculiar compensation
To very young and awkward animals,
The kind of wiry slimness that grows up
To be a thin-lipped, country-walking woman.
We are not sure what day he first discovered
Music is something more than calculation
Vertical in seven, five, and three.
The girl of all among us who had known him,
His days with Julian in their mountain town,
The easy comrade, taking without comment

Obvious sunset, early rising moon.
We are not sure what day he last discovered
A heart may crack and melt though it resemble
An icicle to snap from a casual tree.

Elsa loved us all with a devotion
Possible only to warm-hearted women.
Opened wide her narrow courtyard garden
For talking, eating, looking at the stars.

  Alfred and Elsa dance a *pas de deux*.
  Bow the gallants to the winsome girl.
  Tahl may strum a stray guitar
  Or fiddle till the flagstones jar
  Or bring the moon down on his horn.
  Sing a ballad, sing a round,
  Sing the moon and Dipper down.
  Elsa in a green lace gown.
    Sing!

  She loves Alfred. She loves Tahl.
  Entrechat. Change partners. Bow.
  Perhaps she will not love at all.
  Chorus now, and treble leading,
  Elsa loved him, Elsa loved him
    Once upon a time.

That man with weary travel in his shoes
  Rested him for three months long,
Yielded at last to two small generous hands.
But three long months, with adoration,
Are three more months than give oblivion
  To most men out on journeys.

Elsa danced too long and loved too blindly
To see the charts bound heavy on his wrists,
To study the way a woman might compel
  That latitude and longitude
To close their compass on a courtyard garden.

Adoration is a small pond to see your face in,
No consolation
To him who's ordered out and over seas
Looking for something not his own reflection.

Alfred and Elsa dance a *pas de deux*
After some hesitation;
Tahl being called this time
To play at God as well as Adam —
Shutting the gates of one, this paradise,
Behind him.

Autumn comes splendidly upon the wild lands.
The clouds that carry time down every wind
Stream high along the blue and blowing air.
The bronzing ferns jewel each crumbling boulder
Handsome as if Cellini set them there.
Hard in the wind the juniper bushes lean,
Showing a dozen subtle shades of green.
Along the purple sods, the crimson rose haws.

Walk the road in splendor and exaltation.
Take the curve of hills and the color of clouds,
The sound of the wind and the fragrance of long-dry grasses.
Breed the senses mad with wind and sunlight.
Shout upon the hills and in the valleys.

Shout, and who will hear you
In the valley bottoms,
Among the creeping roots, the rotting trees,
Among the swamplands?
A voice among the waters
As bitter as Marah
Down where the road goes nowhere
Into the treacherous swale and ugly streams.
Come stumbling out and to the road and quickly
By any memory that gives direction.
The sun lays down its last light on the wheel tracks,
Out through the bruised, the scorched, the heel-torn grasses.

Houses of Women

Love is not the usual synonym
For the sixth commandment;
Love grown sib and cousinly to murder
Sired by lust and spawned by calculation.

This also is an answer and evoked
Consummately if you can have quick nerves
And with them too much weariness to ask
Anything as articulate as questions.

Art is at the root of the deception.
There is a kind of sanctity in Satan,
You notice, when he's sponsored by a Milton.
So arts, in any guise, are somewhat holy
And that's the devil of them.

"Dancing is essential. Let us dance
First a waltz. You return. You will always return.
You depart. You return from how many not Elsa or Jan.
But always return. I am Margot, the dancer. Return.
I have green eyes, small breasts . . . You will return.
Set your eyes that way again, Mephisto.

"But we cannot be waltzing, since Mephisto
Grows restless when we play *Dreivierteltakt*.
Shall we try something Slavic? Does it please you?
Or something Spanish, something like a tango?
I will not be impatient, mandarin.
I am not other women. You have told me . . .

"You say I have green eyes that can be yellow.
They will be yellow when this tango's ended,
Because you'll then set spin that savage moaning
You are so fond of. I have heard the rhythm
Before. I turn the lamp. But no one dares
To breed the senses wholly mad; he then
Would lose his pleasure. So you please to say
You like my shoulders. You will add a comment
Upon my hips as being somewhat wider
And say again that you are fond of slimness

Most when it's illusion. My teeth are sharp
As yours. And I have learned at least as much
As you of certain customs. Keep the light.
I like it too. I see your eyes. How else
Shall you see mine go blazing into yellow?
You know you like that. And to see my mouth
A little savage. You are handsome, boy.
The yellow in your hair's gone rather wild.
A ragged horn, Mephisto."

Take a woman
With imagination. Then oblivion.
Though one should break his back with his addiction,
This drug will give the retching and the sickness,
Invention finite, likewise repetition.
Snow falls, impedes the road beyond the window.

TAHL : BOOK ONE

CANTO III

HOUSES OF WOMEN

Ballads of the Dead

Snow in its white falling heals the wounds
Of trampled land, puts comfort on the broken
Shapes of houses. Upon the brutal shapes
Of outworn engines lays its absolution
Of design, the quarried earth cut clean;
Gutters run clear again, their throats unstopped
At last of the lingering refuse of the autumn.

Morning and Tahl out east against the wind,
Sped with flight and quick anticipation
Along one spectral road blind white with sunrise.
Blind white, for sun and snow make every moving
Figure on ahead a black abstraction
Plunging into gold. A man pursuing
Ghosts in snow and sunlight. Snow that's lazy
Spinning in the sun can raise a buttress
To a sagging wall. And spindrift dreaming
Builds a bulwark hard on desperation.

The days on the old white road he carried all
Our questions. He, the vicar of retrospection.
In his straining eyes the western country
Turned again upon the eastward ocean.
The old white road of the world where time blows backward.

Even to that far city he has gone,
To the habitations not to be upgathered
Until the last day. And to the rivers
That flow among the hills and little valleys
Of peace forever. There with God's light on them
Go Heloise and Donna Beatrice.
Even by secret ways among the reeds
To that still lake unstirred by any wind;
There, bright-haired Helen and the dark Ysold.
Even to that dim country at the last
That keeps the virgin of the javelins,
Artemis. And the Titan Mother sleeps
    Patient upon oblivion.

Far wanderer upon the way of visions
After the mirror of the vision in him
And saw no face nor eyes of fire and wisdom
Of all the fair and wise to be the woman
Who was the promise from the hand of Julian
Made with no words upon an April morning.

There in the glooming channels of great books
Where long-closed pages stand in verging files,
Within the walls of marble, the walls of granite
Where tiers of steel uphold their burden straitly,
The dust sifts back again on time-stained leaves
Two eager hands had shaken from their sleeping.

Then he told us what a sin it was
And how a subject for commiseration
To nurture up a large imagination,
So large that even Alighieri's dream
  Could give scant satisfaction
Nor all the dreams the Master Abelard
  Had dreamed in his young blood
Of her the lovely, learned, canon's niece
  With making songs in Paris;
Neither her passion nor her holiness
  Could have fulfilled him.
Only he said in solemn kind of jest —

For he most often had a way of speech
Would make a god himself apologize
  If he should much presume upon
    His spiritual station —
Only — and pricked the tone with irony —
She might have modeled for his cousin's vision,
She of whom the Druid prophesied
The sorrows that would be on Ireland
    Because of her great beauty:
        Deirdre.
The sorrow was on him now. Unfortunate
      That she is lost
Farther than even Fedlimid, son of Doli,
      Could hide her,
Even in a sod-green house within a wall
    In a garden of apple trees.

Then, also, the time some pretty-tongued young fool
We had along to salve her adoration
Began to moralize on compensation
And tell our doctor he should be content
Not to dissect the heart of the world.
"For you," she babbled, "make a keyboard weave
Tapestries soft as mauve and gray chenille.
You can take sound in the palms of your hands and spin
The clustering tones to shining bright and round
As if a troupe of young magicians called
Mimosa flowers from flame and empty air
Before their final curtain. Why is it, then
With fingers that have learned to comprehend
These pure and great abstractions, you must go
      After yet other learning?"

He sat with his long body lounging backward,
Only the tensing of his hands to tell
    There was to be an answer.
Speaking gently: "Yes, the great abstractions.
Our friend George can paint them rather well,
And you are kind to say that I can breed them
Out of my fingers. I have bred and slain

And cooked and served them all,
All your marvels of musical titillation.
Cocktail: brief counterpoint. Entrée will be
A vertical progression. For dessert:
A dissonant calculation.
Diagnosis: Just I'm fed geometry
Till I've got indigestion."

With that spring there was no hope of music
And one green leaf beneath a microscope
Gave him a better pleasure.
He would rather note the measure
Of pale gold bodies swimming spring and summer
In the green basin of a single cell.
Who can tell
The path of the man who goes on the road of answers
Or what the chance encounter lends him endurance.
Chlorophyll does as well as birth or death.
All simplicities bestow
Freely their benefactions.
Enough for him to have perceived
The number of men upon the earth
To be as the leaves of trees
And the thoughts of men upon the earth
As the gold swimmers in all the cells of all the leaves.
And the veins of a leaf are clear as any map
For certain journeys.

Then did the placid channels of his books
Hurl their perilous flood,
All of their dust and lava
About one head.
The sun went to the north and to the south
And the winds went over
While he slept season on season and dreamed of a road without milestones
Out through a wide country
Far from the houses of women.

TAHL : BOOK ONE

CANTO IV

JOURNEY INWARD

The World Renounced

The earth turns every hour her fated flight
True to the flaming harp, the awful lyre
That shall sing with all voices at the last,
And like a stallion yearning toward his mare
The flight, and the rider trampled under heel.
Nearer, each hour, the unthinkable culmination,
Star on star, and all of us seeing and going
Patiently, fearfully, faithfully always going;
And one there was observing this progression
Went over the earth to have an understanding
Of this unimaginable voyage not to be hindered.

Having asked the bones of the dead and the eyes of women,
He thought not even so to despair of answers
But only a shrewder way to deliver the question.
Before his days there were wise men on the earth.
                                        Therefore
Let the dead speak no words; the women speak riddles —
      The words remain and are living forever.
      Does not Sarasvati, the wife of Brahma,
      The goddess of speaking, the goddess of music
            Walk first in heaven?

But Tahl was seldom man for grave discourse,
Commanded to no concourse of savants,

The World Renounced

The record of his eastward wandering thoughts,
The sum of chance occasion's utterance,
The books that served him then and yet awhile
Only as catwalks swung in a void of faith
And disbelieving. We contrive so late
And with one song he called the Song Denying,
Sung to brass of trumpets, bronze of bells,
    Sea-born moan of trumpet shells,
To cross a bridge he swung toward ancient seas,
    A bridge few men saw building
        And no man saw its ending.

Among the honorable sons of Sarasvati
He sought the wise men coming from the north
Bearing the books of holiness across
    The great three-rooted Indus
  Into the valleys and into the plains,
    Their teachers going with them.

Enter then upon the way, Tahl, the latest son,
The way of the visible world and its governance.
The mother of fire stands in the east again
And Agni, the three-hearted, pours again
        The juice of remembering,
        The secret of the morning,
            The only truth.
Enter then upon the way, Tahl, the latest son.
Learn the legend of the lotus bud that is the heart of heaven.
Only the wise man comes to the teachers of wisdom,
The wise, the lotus-lovers, the honey-eaters,
  The free from longing, the free from grieving,
            The masters of death.

Pass by the bridge of knowledge, the arch that is finer than knives,
Travel the torrent dry-shod on the stream of illusion.
Come upon Uma the golden, the daughter of ancient mountains,
Under the banyan tree by the lake of annihilation.
She will teach what is more than sacrifice even with three fires,
She will teach what is more than knowledge even with mighty
    words.

Journey Inward

She will teach the ultimate concentration, the name of salvation,
The road of the fire to the heart of the fire,
The way of the self, subtler than subtle,
Flowing as hidden as water in water.
The vision of Manu who comes on the mountains
From the land that is west of the sun and the moon
And brighter than lightnings.

Tahl Arjuna, with heart cut asunder,
Who has lost his desire and grown weary of grieving,
Take signs from the East, from the blowing of conchshells,
From the rattle of arrows in the quivers of bowmen.

Deva: deus: that which shines
Indra of the triple dawn, sky, and tempest, day, and death;
Brahma creator: Vishnu preserver: Siva destroyer:
Who discerns, who determines
Whose creation, whose destruction?

But if the three-fired dawn shall give him no surcease,
Let him go onward till he find his peace.

Laboring heart and anxious, here surrender,
Here contemplate him in his silken garment,
The head made sacred with immortal curls,
Who is Siddhartha, teacher merciful.
Accomplish here Nirvana, unutterable.
Where shall he seek him now in this late time?
Beyond the grasslands and beyond the snowlands.
Approach: the answer waits among the mountains,
Within the walls, the gates with guardians,
The wing-roofed temples, the golden pavilions.

Upon the festival night of the New Year
Approach with us, the multitude adoring
The terrible masks. Slaughter with imprecations
Sorrow and barrenness, the primal sign.
Believe in us, the fires of sacrifice.
Beware. Look not alone toward contemplation.
Avoid the mid-pavilion, alien priest,
Regard our tables with bowls of silver,

The World Renounced

Regard our symbols of power and honor.
Rejoice in the demon-shout, the dancers' cries.

Within the mid-pavilion, alien priest
Standing alone before that sleek-skinned body,
That princeling slimness, the indolent guise,
The inward smile which sleep dissembles,
Beware the drowsy eyelids opening,
Beware, O uninstructed. He will speak,
  Gautama, Buddha, master of peace;
    The great throat trembles:
  Life is evil, my brother, and no kinder
  For going once more downward to the plains.
   You have observed no dawn libation,
     No three-tongued flame,
  No wine cup sanctified by incantation
     Not bowls of silver
   Nor ranging symbols of power and honor
     Bring you peace.
  Neither trouble yourself whether the round earth
   Swing eternal in the empty air
  Or plunge unerringly toward holocaust
   Or sit reposefully upon a tortoise.
  This only appertains, the only mantra,
  Desire — suffer — desire. This, the karma,
  The soul from death to birth, from moth to worm.
   And all the wisdom of the wisest man
    To find the pathway outward,
    The middle way, the one road
   Out of the pathways of death and birth
      To Nirvana.
Forswear desire but not by fire nor soma juice nor any use
  Of bell or candle or dancing or prayer.
  Keep faith, guard speech and resolve,
    By conduct unalloyed
By all striving and occupation upon the contemplation,
  The last abstraction, the perfect void.

    Then were the copper trumpets sounded,
    Brass of cymbals, bronze of bells,

Sea-born moan of trumpet shells.
Dance of the antlered Devil master,
Mask of laughter ring around
The Song Denying, drum and gong:

The gates of the eyes are as the gates of death.
Forswear. Forbear to rejoice
In the spring burgeoning
In the summer blossoming, heavy-petaled;
Autumn grasslands, straw and blue and scarlet,
Crystal winter in its nakedness;
Please yourself with the noble heads of trees
No more — the massive surge upreared,
Nor trace the lines of light on the tall hills.
Be glad no more to look on the body of love,
The breasts, the thighs,
Upon the face of a woman, the amber in her eyes.
Have no joy of barefoot children running softly.
In indigo have no delight,
Magenta nor in malachite,
Cadmium nor chrysoprase.
Let no colors nor forms of this bright world your heart assuage.
The gates of the eyes are as the gates of death.

The gates of the shell-formed ears are as the gates of death.
Forswear. Forbear to rejoice
In the multitudinous voices of the earth,
The morning stir of birds in the new spring,
The young men singing under summer stars,
The cries of cattle southward in the autumn,
The voice of the far-blown winds in the winter mountains.
Be glad no more in speech, the multiple tones — no more:
Neither the speech of old men dreaming in the sunset
Nor the words of a woman with her love to comfort
Nor children's murmurs to be sleeping soon.
Please yourself to hear the small tunes
Of pipes on evening hillsides not again.
Neither the instruments with strings shall give you joy
Nor low-toned bells
Nor many-sounding horns.

The World Renounced

Of all music be forsworn.
The gates of the shell-formed ears are as the gates of death.

Every portal of the flesh is the tiring-house of death.
Forswear. Forbear to rejoice
In mouth on mouth.
Shun the clasping of hands,
The bodies' communion,
Nor dance with long-haired women
In the light of the full moon.
Love neither the sharp wakening to love nor the long slumber.
Delight no more to hold the rinded fruits with idle fingers.
Swim no more with great strokes joyful in the icy waters.
Think not fondly of sands nor rocks nor cushioned grasses.
Cast yourself no more upon the earth with joy in the warm ground.
With abstinence confound your flesh.
It is the tiring house of death.

The hungering mouth is hungry after death.
Forswear. Forbear to rejoice
In the savors of food,
The flavorous oils of poppy and sesame.
Disdain
The tamarind juice and the wine of the palm tree,
Lemon and radish, the red-flowered honey.
After cinnamon think not eagerly, nor the green almond.
From the syrups of succulent fruits,
From sweet and from sharp and from salt
Abstain,
From tongue on tongue,
The teeth in the flesh.
The hungering mouth is hungry for death.

The nostrils are the quick twin hounds
That strain in the winds of death.
Forswear. Forbear to rejoice
In redolent pastures
Or holy Himalayas,
Their cedar nor their pine.
Pluck no lilac nor rose of the morning

Nor fruit nor flower of any vine.
Seek no more for sandalwood,
Bergamot nor oil of jasmine,
Perfume in the hair of women.
Leash the hounds of curiousness,
Devil hounds of idleness
Harrying down the winds of death.

Chant of the antlered Devil Master: Here is the red lord. Here is the black lord.
Neither suffer nor rejoice: Here is the blue lord. This world's guardians.
With the sorrowing have no sorrow: Here is Sumeru, great world mountain.
Starve the senses, the five gates. Guard the compass, eye of wisdom.
Flay the heart, the last abyss. And he that will not shall lament.
Here is the red lord. Here is the yellow lord.
Crown with skulls and crown with thunders, *Vajra* and three flaming treasures.
Shred your white brains: Here is the master,
Bull of the sky, lord of law, dark blue rain, the Lord of Death.
Grope for a word. Strangle with incantations.
Bull of the sky. Lord of law. Blue rain. Black rain. Lord of Death.
The antlered deer, his messenger.
Smite your forehead on the older answer.
The grave of your skull be death and laughter,
The black and scarlet rain, the rain of laughter,
The unremitting soft-come shower of cooling ashes,
And the eastward wind driving the voiceless sand.

The wind that sweetens grapes can also bruise them.
Husbandmen
Have this wisdom hard-learned
But he, returning,
As from a hill of harriers coming down
Weary with the tendons' throb and strain,
Held in his heart only the bruising,
Mindful of no healing latent still,
Of no sweetening well hidden.

The World Renounced

So were hard words spoken
Of liquors mulled in Eastern fashion,
So were all Eastern brews outspewed
As ill-learned recipes.
His lungs were sick with the thin air of strange hills.
His eyes blown blind with the gritty core of storm
Could see
Not the firm fruit formed,
Only the bruised vine
Quick-culled and pressed to poor wine.
And, the winds still thudding in his bleeding ears,
He nothing trusted
Of good measure in a year, and a good vintage.

But yet however sharp the day's mistrust,
There comes the still insurgence of clean air
That cleanses every festering day's despair.
The unpredictable season comes again.

Noble monitor of steadfastness,
Sagacious peace and heart dispassionate,
Self-conquering, at peace, and beautiful
In the remembering mind resides
Longer than death's lewd mask and festival.
The holy Monk's humility abides
Under the Bodhi Tree, the coral-petaled.
Of this he spoke, the wanderer returned
From first of many journeys to that land
Where time's return resides, remembering mind.
He came a road eroded, bare of death,
But love hewn down to keep the drought of lust.
He fled the order, "Acquiesce."
For him no blessed quietness
In self-concern, ascetic, isolate,
Impermanence excoriate
And Absolute assured, by man attained.
He fled a soundless joy, a moderation
On scales rejected by the living sun
And saw no light to weigh a balance beam
Of one come far with questions.

But light that shone upon the common road
Shone still a light of the ten thousand worlds
For all its darkness in the midst of shining;
  More than a witch-fire in a swamp,
More than a wing of flame upon a mountain.
It was that city shines without a sun,
A glory of light and there no darkness ever,
Its gates unguarded, all its swords renounced
And at its walls the same immortal waters
Washing the earth and all the sons of men;
That lordly city set upon a sea
Shining and that had shone
And that would shine for him again,
Its bright keys forged within his hands
Of steel no man could sever;
And in the city bloomed a deathless tree
Whose roots alone nurse thrice ten thousand worlds,
And though the city merge within the sea
    And he go far,
That tree's great shadow fell upon his road
        Forever.

The town that knew him never did apprise
   His place among them.
He earned his bread in ordinary-wise,
Loafed and skylarked more than most of us
And had sufficient coppers in his jeans.
They found him a convenient citizen,
Good at a fiddle or a Sunday organ,
        Versatile
To play at weddings as at funerals
Or to direct the Thursday evening band.

  That band was then his pet perversity,
  Excrescent irony of revolution
    From music that was all
    What he loved to call
   Esoterica and mathematics.

  He was made of contradictions.
   Though the years to come

Seasoned his bitter jests
Into a kindly saltiness
Upon his wisdom,
His just perceptions bore as yet
No consistent impress,
Allowed his public self its own career.
But negligence that seemed content
With vagrant minstrel competence
Knew its own freedoms and necessities,
Sure that a later-come identity
Would bring all his dissociate selves to fusion.

This strategy and shrewd defense
Spared him that hate whose chief affection
Is to assault whatever loves perfection.
It slept the while his strength was nourishing.
Among us few to hear within the deep white dust
The footsteps of his traveling.

TAHL : BOOK ONE

CANTO IV

JOURNEY INWARD

The World Proclaimed

His mountains as his deserts were his own
And none could dim what bright imagined moon
Led him, that Nicodemus, on again
To harry God with questions.
The sandy waste of recent desperation
Only so many easy leagues advancing
That same white road
By bridges slender as the wrists of girls . . .
Over torrentous waters, bamboo streams
Into the flowering marshlands.

The traveler is poor.
He has not so much as one yellow quince wizened in the sun.
But his heart is sober and gentle.
He has a packet of questions wrapped in a soft rice paper of
courtesy.
Not his poverty but his courtesy is worth a reward of rubies.

He is delighted with the golden heron.
He looks with joy upon the gleaming heads of the mandarin ducks
in the water-branches.
After the brown desert,
After the thistle and thorn of the long moors,
Many flowers are welcome as flowing streams.
He is glad to watch the yellow storks and the white pigeons.

The World Proclaimed

He is willing to walk in the path of the black crane
Wise in the ways of the Eight Directions,
Over the great east road,
On to the red hills.
At night he sails in a boat
Under the crystal wheel of the spring moon.
It is the night of the wistaria flowers;
Blue smoke of bloom fragrant above the river.
Lanterns swing in the garden of the admirable scholar.

The sage and honorable servant of his race
Sees with pleasure the boat that is moored by his river garden.
The traveler has his place beneath the murmuring white aspens.
He has his choice of thick and clear wine.
With humility he attends his host
Who has begun to speak of fame.

Fame is the son of a good mother who is very beautiful.
The beauty of these blue blossoms has borne them generations of
unforgotten legends.
The name of a wise man is remembered forever.

The strangers from the west in the very ancient times,
Though they were strangers and became masters,
They have not been hated.
They are now our fathers.
Music and wise words were their gift to us.
Wisdom was their gift to us.
It is good to desire to be remembered.

The scholar is silent.
An old woman carries away many lanterns.
There is a sleeper beneath the aspen trees.
The words of the scholar sleep against his heart.

See, traveler, it is morning again.
The dragon-sun has thrust his fire-fangs in the sky.
Your host, in silk as yellow as apricots,
Has brought a gift of wishes for your health.
He did not wake you with coming on soft felt slippers.

Journey Inward

He awaits your happy waking.
His boy has brought you a cake and a cup of rice wine.

It is pleasant to observe that the hoar frosts are safely past.
Rosebuds and blue blossoms are oppressed
Only with dew.
It is appropriate to remark the lotus pond.
How still it is.
The swimming crimson petals.
How palpable silence is
Among the green seeds.
Two can speak together many hours
Of green birth and white death,
Of frost and of seeds.

Death is a green seed fallen on still waters,
Yet is not stillness secure from the frost and the wind.
There is no harm in security.
Better a service of incense
Than a plague of importunate spirits.
It is better that seed should ripen.
It is better that evils should be foreseen.
It is possible sometimes to anticipate the maliciousness of spirits.
Caution is the womb of ripening seeds.
And my learning is no more than the words of my boy
Concerning the ways of death.
Better than seeds in the Yellow River are seeds in the black earth.
A melon in the earth makes a larger dinner than a river of lotuses.
This is not forgotten even by lovers of lotuses.
Therefore it is prudent to seek fame more than death and to burn
  incense against the dead.
We would be living names about our children's altars.
Only the temples of fame sit far from the paths of death.

The poet Po, gay with wine, perished suddenly.
While the moon came down to his pleasure boat,
He drowned in a flower-rimmed pool.
And Fu whose words were more mellow than orioles' singing
Died of much joy after his surfeit of sorrow,
Died with his friends at his side at a notable banquet.

The World Proclaimed

Can you purchase amnesty of death, traveler?
Then all men will learn of you.
Do you understand the secret of death?
Do you know a better gift than a gift of incense?

I have not that secret.

Friendship is the honorable friend of fame.
It is a treasure cherished even as a green bird on a gold willow.
Said Fu to Po:
There is the orchid fountain.
There is the soul's nourishment of trees and mountains.
They sat in the garden with joy.
They were two friends.
These have gone beyond the Yellow River
That were two friends.
They are two great names of honor
Because of their beautiful words.

Man is a blade of grass drawn with ink on white silk.
He is soon a yellowed thread.

A virtuous family is the best fruit of holiness,
The treasury of good tradition.
Idleness is a breeding maggot in the rooftree.
When children take their cakes and wine at dawn,
The family prospers.
When children learn the time-stick by their lessons,
When women pray to Kwan for many children,
That family is fortunate.

The scholar speaks.
His house has blue roof tiles.
His family are careful with rosewood
And gold cloth and green jade.
He smiles, his hand, slow arched over an old book,
Holding a thin page.

But the hours pass
And thoughts are best seen as birds

Flown in a picture of silence.
Shall we, then, walk in the hall?

Traveler,
Your thoughts are a noisy brood.
Hood them and hide them.
The still serene perfection of this place,
These ancient masks of godhood can endure
No secret question. They concede
Only the mask of the world's way,
Old and smiling men
Needing nothing of eternities.
So are these gods, these men,
So is he, wonderfully cut in jade,
This old and smiling man,
Humorous, subtle, kind, what words can tell
The thousand arts of him who cut this stone?
No man, but centuries of men have bred this face,
This kindly pride, this shrewd intelligence.
Here is no secret. Manifest, achieved,
Quintessent man, content here to abide
Mortality.

Conversation flavors fish and fowl,
But he has brought the silence of the hall
To dine with him.
A clamorous silence.
Will answers breed questions forever?

Here is an answer:
Man made perfect in his own concerns,
Plowman or peddler
Merchant or mariner
Something final
Not impossible
Self-created
Resident in space and form and line,
Examined, apprehended,
Held with hands.

The World Proclaimed

His host remarks the peace of evening hours
And summons flutes and two-stringed moon guitars.
How white the petals shine in the dark garden,
How eloquent the river under stars.
This is no sorrow.

This is a legend: A man made music cut from a yellow reed,
A man made music first for a wise king.
Small stream on pebbles flowing, a warm breeze.
This is enough, traveler. Let your heart come home.

This a legend: A man went out upon a high hill
And made a cup as clear as light
From white soft stone.
Clay has its own perfection.

The flowers shine in the garden,
Traveler.
There is music
And there are many legends.

And shall he comfort him with holy tombs
Who sees the shores of the world choked fast with sand?
A legend is a scant array for him
Who walks a single road in the broad sea.
Shall he trust tombs and legends who has come
Fatherless?
No progenitor of this his blood
More than a name?
What shame or pride they had he cannot know;
And where their ashes lie
He knows no more than what their rank or place
Or what food simmered on their breakfast fires.
No cloak of long mortality can shield
His shoulders from the swift immortal wind
That woke him on the night that he was born.

Farewell, then, scholar, for your courtesy.
I go again this night and go alone.

Journey Inward

Have you seen the wanderer?
He carries a package of questions.
He will walk beside you at the plowing
Or sit in the sun with you near the garden of melons,
Or stand a night long by the temple wall
Alone with the dim blue flying things
And the very ancient stones.
He sits in the noon's heat near a shadow of cypresses,
He learns of the priest of the Tao in the garden of plum trees.
He admires a dish of herbs and a cup of hot water,
He has grown lean on lettuce and last year's grain.

Traveler, I have no secret.
I am a simple man and follow masters.
It has been told me that great heaven is round,
Flawless, perfect, a white pearl,
Not to be seen.
It has been told me that men are sons of night
And poorer brothers to these cypress trees.
I have thought the honeysuckle bloom
Sweeter than men's dreams.
I have seen those long-clawed men who fail,
Straining their wrists against the height of stars,
Turn and root up devils.
We have small heads and the sea and the wind
Are stronger than all our houses.
I have lived many years.
A young man can be forgiven to defend his follies.
But I am old
And these walls older
And not infrequently I have seen death.
I have seen gentle men and men as cruel.
I have seen whips and knives.
Many words can teach few men perfection.
And who can murmur at the way of heaven?
I know that men are hungry and afraid.
I have seen skillful men make ivory sheaths
And handsome swords all delicately carved
With bees and humming birds and butterflies.
I have seen men who know that peace is best

The World Proclaimed

Go out to war.
Many men have known these cypress trees,
Scholars and thieves;
And they have shared these lettuces and herbs.
Men are hungry, traveler, and afraid,
And sick with lust.
And has it not been so
These thousand years?

What then is the venerable Tao?
Where lies the one white road that leads to wisdom?

This is the wisdom of the master Lao
Who went by the barrier gate to the northwest
And will not come again:
Live you simple men, unanxious, still.
See not, neither reprove,
Nor follow folly, be it hate or love.
Show mercy.
Learn that peace is best.
Endure. Be silent. None has conquered death.

Man of wisdom, is this wisdom?
This I shunned among the mountains
Speaks more courteously upon the plains,
Saying once more, forbear. Turn from the world's way.
Turn from the sorrow,
Turn to the shadow.
Staunch the breath.
Triumph. Overcome. Conquer death
With death.
Will the seed in the garden, father,
Hide from the rain?
I look for the sun in a garden
And the water that lies between.
I saw this water once.
Call it the sea.
Life was born there,
A single crystal flesh
Of dust and water.

Journey Inward

When I was a boy I tasted blood,
Sucking it proudly from some casual wound,
And there I tasted salt.
Shall the dust live without water?

In our days we have once more beheld
This miracle,
The pale amorphous single cell, alive,
Shudder and rend itself and still to live,
Multiple, torn, undying,
Whole and slain, and not to death but life.
One clear small miracle under the young stars.
And we, the sons of that small mother, bear
The pungent brine forever in our blood
And all our life is somehow going home.
And shall the flesh be living
Without blood?
I look for the sea, father,
And it is blood, not dust, that feeds my heart.
I will not yield me twice nor once to death.

Late evening when the curious self can shroud
Its head in darkness,
When the child
In every man will listen for a ghost
And loves a ghostly story most of all,
He spoke of the priest and the gray wall.
No demons now nor gracious subtleties,
But one old man's serenity
Saying: forbear. Die to the world's way.
Kindly patient priest,
Can a young man yearn
After your quiet garden
And still turn?

Shall we say
This is a child's story.
Then may the long-eyed dragon goddess pray
For those who go by water.
Then may an old priest stand

At night by the water's edge
And raise his hand.
Guard him, dragon goddess.
West and south he goes.
He looks for the lake where time was born.
Boat in the stream;
A burning twig set in the prow
Smokes and smoulders
In the wind.

TAHL : BOOK ONE

CANTO V

JOURNEY OUTWARD

The World of the Eye

Many people came. The halls were filled on Sundays.
The glories of the dynasties were there,
An emperor's collection.
This was no midnight phantom.
Only these tall young men
Come to laugh at a crowd and look at pictures.
And the least one like a mandarin was there,
A man in a gray coat,
A man with brown hair.
He was not always speaking.
Just a word between the doorway and the last broad stair:

This is a tiger merely.
This a mountain and a river.
You assume the plain between.
This is what you mean.
Abstraction is a higher kind of art
And imitation only craft and skill,
The finger's wit and not the shrewder mind.
Isolate the tree upon the hill;
That is idea, the absolute, the essence.
See how its bark is weather-torn and old.
See how the wind has turned it all one way.
A simple clever man can give you texture in the grass
And help you guess the season and the day.
Not they.

The World of the Eye

A tree. Or not a tree. A bird upon a branch,
A tiger with his paw thrust deep in silk,
The lunging shoulders and the angry eyes.
Here's a bench by the path.
Hot enough to wilt a palm tree there.
But the same old girls with little books
And families that stare.
Abstraction is a higher kind of art.
The peril is in making the abstraction.
A tiger can dispense with trees and grass.
The fault lies in the lack of moderation.
Abstract the state and you dispense with men.
Abstract the man and states go down to ruin.
Broken trees and tigers may have meaning.

See how we love the East.
We go and stare.
If they were Hindu idols we would go,
And all the same old girls with little books.
Odd it should be so.
Flesh abstracted . . .
Or isolate spirit.
Odd that it should be so,
That we should go looking and asking
And saying oh
Because it is strange,
Because it is art.
But look for a heart sometime.
Sometime when it's not so hot the dogs go drooling down the path,
When the crowd's away. When you needn't laugh.
Tell me if you find it. Mind, yes. Discipline, yes. Skill.
Tell me if mind and flesh with spirit are made whole.
Tell me, though,
If you find a heart.
Yes, the heart. Is there a word
Nearer the meaning? Surely some alphabet spells
The name of what's closer than blood and more vital than breath,
Born in the flesh and beyond it,
More than a passion or a pride, before the seed and the womb
And after the grave.

Journey Outward

Spend the summer
In a good cool grave.
Laugh your answer.
Forget I said it.
I'm not the Preacher.

Demagogues, painters, test tube shakers
All get at it.
When your girl goes mental
Or your best friend dies,
You'll get at it.
Talk of truths and particular treasons,
Sweat and die and laugh at hell
And buy and sell,
Nor add, subtract, nor calculus can tell.
Heart has, soul has . . .
Somehow.
I don't know.
Hearts have their own reasons.

Swear if you will that you want no answer
But girls and get drunk and die in the summer,
But go see pictures or read a paper.
Some more, some less,
They all get at it.
Old books know it, some of the answer.
I keep looking.
That's what I'm after.
The heart or something.
They all get part of it,
Maybe not half of it.
Not this world, that world,
But all of it,
Heart of it,
That's what I'm after.

TAHL : BOOK ONE

CANTO V

JOURNEY OUTWARD

The World of the Ear

"I would not believe that light could break
From sound. You saw it, Jan. You heard and saw.
He raised his arms, he struck the great electric
Arc prophetic, caught the ultimate trumpet
Spitting light. You saw it."

"I would not
Believe that sound could break from light. You heard
Up-plunging zooming diving, power come down
Two hundred miles of thunder, three trombones.
You heard it, George."

"And I could not believe
The antediluvial plains, the havoc of horses,
The huddle of bulls, the charging, the ramping, the hailing
After the burst of cloud, the sprung sword flashed
On a flute, the two swords scissored of harps plucked shrill
On the tympani's rumbling, horses alive in the sun.
You heard it, Elsa. The man is a demon. He's God."

"I heard and believed. And he is not God, but mad.
I heard. Did you hear? In the gallery crowds, in the lobby,
'Wild,' they say. 'Old stuff now,' they say. 'Superb.'
'Good.' 'New. ' 'Foul. ' 'Magnificent,' they say.
They say. They say, Alfred. They say. We heard."

"Yes, Elsa. He's not God. But we have heard him,
Seen the arc of arms and hailed the hundred
Praising on reed, string, brass, upon the drumhead
And over and over again those same five tones
He names, called fire, called horse, called tree, called sea,
Called thunder . . . those five tones . . .
Like bagpipe scrannel . . . like a Chinese mourning
Over a miming play . . . the old *naccara*
Of Marco Polo's prince before the battle."

What does he mean? They say. They say. They say.
They say, the shoulders, the heads, the elbows shoving,
The nodding coiffures, the mob in the marble foyer,
The tweed coats on the stairs, the faces bobbing
With anxious questions. Fair. Foul. Do they dare
To let this madman harry us here with lightning
Or hire a hall, they say. The critics say. They say:
Five tones, twelve tones, seldom diatonic, upper
Ranges, Oriental manner, stranger
Counterpoint on scales not indicated.

"Master
Of men who follow him. Yes. Yes, they followed
Like fishes gasping, hounds howling the trail
Of a wyvern. Scared, determined, following,
Capturing light and sound and the hooves of horses
Heard in the sandy skulls of the long-dead hunters,
Shattering air with shivers in false harmonics."
Applause. Applause. Heads shaking. Yes. Applause.

"I saw him biting that lip of his in sick
Disgust of the roaring herd. He'll say their guts
Rattle with rhythm. Guts can't comprehend
That string quartet he purls with bagpipe tones,
That wail called Bull in Thunder ended sobbing
On an oboe."

"What he means? Why that
You say, George. On an oboe. Rising question.
Bulls stampede in thunder. In an ocean horses
Shriek while drowning."

The World of the Ear

"Pardon, sir. Good evening."

"Our friend, the Doctor, professor of Greek! You also
Heard the great début. And you were saying?"

"I said, George, deeply stirred, more disappointed.
I understand he leaves us soon for Egypt."

"At seven tomorrow morning. Come. We're going
Now to meet him. We have eight hours left
To share him."

"He has gone. Who was he,
Alfred? He, the disappointed Doctor,
The ugly friendly head like Socrates?"

"A wise man speaking Greek and Tahl he loves
As a stallion loves a colt and bites his ears in.
He wouldn't come, old ghost. He's disappointed.
He wants the colt that's sired by hell to hobble
Like a spayed mare in classical cadenzas."

"Don't tell him, George. He'll hate to know the Doctor
Disbelieves his noises. Jan, recall him?
Taught us once. He's wonderful and wise
And would have wept to know our madman strained
His wits to write him tunes like Lydian moonshine,
Dorian goosesteps, Ionian perfections,
Fooled with nine-stringed lyres and all declensions
Conjugations, nouns and verbs made music."

"You two men, listen. Tahl is disappointed.
He and the doctor both. He says the merit
Lies in the hand lain light to the bridle. Only
The fool would raise the mob with galloping."

"Yes, Elsa, yes. Tahl sails tomorrow morning.
He took a plane tonight, rolled, banked, and pitched it
In air like glass as if he rode on thunder."

"Riddles, Jan. Explain."

"Remember, Elsa?
I told you once. He flew with me, remember?
A month ago, in March. I took him over
The city, taught him flying straight and level,
Hand light on the stick, foot to the rudder easy,
Easy. Heard him mutter: 'Yes, like this, to write
Air into light and easy, straight and level.'
I said: 'But, to learn, you fly it rough and sloppy.'
'That's how you learn,' he said. 'Like riding horses.'"

"But he's Arcturus, Jan, brighter than brightness . . ."

"Come on, you! There! I see him. By the exit."

A crowd. They say. But he's not listening.

We walk the dark in wind. The crowds at midnight
Stare at light whirling, skidding, blinking and blurring,
Moving the walls back, flaring on wheels, obscuring
The dim stars none will look for in this haven
Of motion compact of footsteps, cars, and voices
Taut with the midnight's tension, tightening, tightening
Avenues, streets recorded number by number, snapping
With light. Behold five tones together walking
The midnight city. Wind tonight. Hard weather.
But shall you surely sail tomorrow morning?

"Tomorrow Bermuda," he answered, "the far Azores.
Tomorrow sunlight on the Libyan sands.
And I shall sleep. They take a corpse tomorrow
Back to his eastern tomb. I'm sailing backward.
I shall retreat by sea to take new readings.
The compass heading's out and I've forgotten
The necessary magnetic variation
Between the past and present. I return,
Turn and return. My gyroscope is missing.
And I shall sleep and wake up dead in Egypt.

The World of the Ear

"The horns of ships cry eastward on the bay.
The horns of ships cry westward on the river.
Wind from the west bears promise of fair weather.
The earth turns east, rolls forward toward the star
In the constellation of last and probable fire.
I am impatient of sidereal time
And some celestial Greenwich, consonance
That lies beyond this day's cacophonies.
Between the paradox of D and E,
Between the paradox of sharp and flat,
The paradox. You know, my four good friends,
Way up is all the way down, way east is west.
And with this dawn I'm going east and down.
I go as one more rebel toward the sun.
And I shall sleep and wake up dead in Egypt.

"All day I have walked this city in the sea
Where men grope gutters, probing dung for money,
Where boys like wolves assault the pushcart vendors.
All morning one small child, a girl, pursued me,
Steady as fate she prowled before, behind me.
I stopped. She paused. She waited. When I looked,
Her eyes like dull blue pebbles met my stare
With idiot stare. Just once she smiled. I took
Her hand. And from a golden splay of tree
Among the chimneys fell the catkins dropping,
Driven by budding leaves to lie like toys
Upon the pavement. Leaning down I caught
A brown fuzz on my finger, spun it gravely,
Tendered it. She smiled. The stone-blue eyes
Washed alive with pleasure. Then she moaned,
Let fall the April promise. There beside us
Upon the curb a crush of feathers stained,
A half-fledged sparrow dead. I left her hunched
And mourning. Left her. When shall I return?

"There walked a man bent down with new-cleaned clothes.
There walked a boy who pushed a load of furs.
Wolves live. Wolves die. We cull their pelts. Birds fall.
And I remember quivering in my hand

Journey Outward

A wounded bird we found among the mountains
In a far-off earlier spring when Julian helped me
Tend it home to mend the wing that hung
Limp from a grazing bullet. In the cities
Go the lame, the paralytics. In the fields
The deaf and blind. I may come home alive.
A dead man sails tomorrow toward the sun."

And while he talked we turned him from the nightwind
To lights within, to lobbies lush with brightness.
Riding a car shot upward floor by floor,
We read our watches. One o'clock. Assembled
Ourselves about a table by a window
That looked down mountainous steel and saw the city
Recede within a sea wave-flecked on darkness.

We have not risen one mile above the earth.
Two hundred miles makes still a scant perspective.
That man, descending out of trammeled air
From wrought hard-patterned lightning into music,
Returned the nods of those who recognized him
Talking and talking on ritual champagne
For his first triumph. Listening to himself,
This man, and none of us who would deny him
Ears enough to make him think we followed
That spiraled vision wrestling with a demon.

"I find myself alone tonight," he murmured,
"And maudlin. But I'm looking for a tune
Appropriate to birds and reprobates,
Idiots, wolves and women, census take
Of all not me alone. The wind, the thunder,
Horse and bull, the dragon in the sun,
And my wild waters will not give me answer.
The microscope, the telescope deny me.
Today a stubby man in spectacles
Fitted glasses to a mirthless crone
Who glared at me like Nemesis for staring
Upon the operation. I must wear
A glass of magnitude, a box for hearing

Plugged fast behind my ear. I am alone.
A lonely man can learn no further language
Than webs he spins from out himself to talk with
And he goes thin and dies with weaving, weaving
Himself to threads that blow down waves to nowhere
Or else he hangs himself on his own spinning.

"Under this blackness and these lights the houses
Mumble with hands and eyes and I don't know them.
Among the iron stairs and cans for garbage,
The crumpled papers, the infectious flies,
The broken cigarettes, the wind-torn signboards
Lies a ladder to the moon and Mars,
Beyond the sun and to a rose of brightness
Toward which all music stumbles. I must find it.
But I have learned among my uncle's gardens
That roses grow in clay and need much pruning,
Must be cut clean or else the torn bark cankers.
And so at seven a.m. I cut me clean,
Break out the womb too dark for my attention,
And shall come home with eyes and ears to work with.

"Upon a glacial hill I look for fire
And dig reverse in time until I find it
Where still it smolders lost among the nations
That brought us here to stand between the oceans.
I too shall sometime go toward that Pacific
Which summons every man, but on that journey
I must have weather ways and compass bearings,
A dot and dash without night interference.
That music you have heard of mine this evening
Lies now around me like a cone of silence
And I retrace my flight to catch a station
Sends out its traveling beam toward all who voyage."

The clock turned round, the night propelled us eastward
To a primitive cavern called the House of Windows;
The clock struck three upon a hoary legend
He quarried for us on his hill of glaciers.
He stood now in his room, his bags beside him,
Telling us curious stories until dawn:

Journey Outward

"There was a mighty priest. His name was Manco.
He lived in the sign of the sun. He had three brothers,
Cachi and Uchu and Auca. Their wives were sisters,
Cura, Huaco, Occlo and Raua. I tell you
The story of Uchu first for, during their journey,
He put out his hands on a terrible stone and he perished.
They worshipped the bird and the snake and out of their wandering
They came from the sea of the east and upon the Pacific
Honored the bird and the snake which are signs for the sun
Which flies and begets and is life and is father and mother.
They came from a cavern. Its name they called Tampu-tocco.
They came from a country. Its name they called Paccari-tampu,
The House of the Dawn that lay in the House of Windows.

"And Uchu alone was lost on the westward journey.

"But Auca who flew with wings was commanded by Manco
To fly to the hill of the sun and the brother obeying
Failed of that flight and was injured. I tell you a story
Born of the race I have dreamed of, a myth of the Incas.
They carried a golden rod which leading them outward
Guided them on and beyond, from the center, the silence.
And as for Cachi sent back to the gods in the cave of remembrance
He was trapped by a rock at the mouth of the cave and he died
 there."

Tahl who was six feet tall at four in the morning
Stood by his bags and talked in a roomful of windows.
And all of us knew that Uchu had died on the voyage
And lay in his grave in the mountains, an orchid beside him.
But we heard a dim trouble of sound that made more than mere
 nonsense,
This pattern caught up from the past and pinned down on the
 future.
And our names that were Alfred and George,
Like the thumping of stones in the drag of a glacier,
Our names that were Elsa and Jan
Like the swish and the scar of sand in a melting water?
Might one have been Cachi and one have been Auca?
And who of us, two of us, where were the four of us,

Cura, Huaco, and Occlo and Raua?
And was it by chance or by whim or by fate and occasion?

Certain and fact that he left in the air of a morning
Clear in the east and the wind like the breath of an icecap.
Into the crowd and aboard . . . with a smile . . . but his eye-
  lids were sleeping.
The roar and the stir and the wash and down-river departure,
The signaling hand, the rider on reasons among
The reasons of strangers beside him transocean to Egypt.

Driving once more down into the city
Jan spoke most, as if the man's departure
Had been in truth his death and she his mourner,
Recalling all he had been in the flesh.
For she had known him longest, played with Julian
In that town little known of us, to northward,
The mountain town those years before he came
To school among us and to haunt the seacoast.

We sat like wakemen at our second breakfast
Till Elsa, kindly, putting out her hand
On those wired fists that knew of planes and horses
More than they understood of women's working:
"Jan, you love him." "Yes," her answer softly,
More soft than we two men had known she knew of.
"I loved them both, the cousins, Tahl and Julian,
And neither one is mine nor ever will be."

Then I put in abruptly, "You and Tahl
Were friends enough his first year there at school."
"We were friends," said Jan, "but he found others,
Dozens, perhaps—and Margot." Then I saw
Alfred look at his wife with sharp attention
And Elsa reach her other hand that lying
Free of Jan's across the littered table
Groped toward Alfred. And the dawning silence
Left me dangling in that cone he'd talked of.

Elsa, always tuned to every echo
Of harassed souls left kicking over danger,

Spilled the vacuum full of talk with saying:
"He always loved to stagger you with stories
Of Emperor Huang, the Islands of the Blest,
Of the Emperor Mu's eight horses that could trot
Ten thousand miles a day toward Paradise,
Or there was some such tale of red-blue hills
And of a royal mother in the West.
He said such yarns to him were roads toward music
And marked frontiers between the sound and sense."

Elsa talked. I was concerned to shape
Within my mind the hands that lay before me,
Elsa's, small and subtle-fingered, twined
With Jan's square-axled thumbs and Alfred's paw
Taking them both around, alert, on guard.

"I see them both," said Jan, "at night with books.
Julian reading with a troubled forehead
For every unknown word, his lips just moving
And asking questions with beseeching eyes.
Tahl beside him. I can see him plainly.
His eyes were clear and on his cheeks a down
I liked to touch. He'd sometimes take my hand
And tell me stories made of dreams he had
Of horses, ships and birds. I think his talking
So much of birds it was that made me go
To flying. He was with me when we saw
Our first, a plane that soared above the mountains.
His uncle came to call us, waving his hoe
And shouting. And we watched until it dipped
Eastward. Where? 'Across the sea,' said Tahl.
His uncle laughed and said the sea would drown him.

"We must have been just six that year or seven,
Perhaps. I know already Tahl was playing
A strange thing called a zither. Do you know it?
Was his father's, I believe, though where
It came from no one seemed to know for certain.
I used to argue with him, take the key
And tune a string or two to chime the note

With our piano but he'd shake his head
And say it wasn't meant so; there were sounds
I couldn't hear. And he would go off singing
And strumming like a minstrel out of lands
I couldn't find and do not know the name of.

"When we were nine or ten we made a play
Out of a book and talked it over and over.
I found it. Julian showed us how the brook
Could be the river, but we always chose
Tahl; he was the leading character,
The fisherman Wu Ling upon the stream
Peach Blossom flowing west to T'ao-yuan.
I was all the village Wu Ling left
And Julian all the folk he came upon
In the very wonderful country just beyond
The pool of ferns. And I remember, I remember . . ."

The words fell on my ears like the hour's chime,
Over and over. My train. Nine o'clock. Time.
But still we sat and she said 'I remember.'
I rose to go but stayed. For she remembered
The day that boy aged ten, the fisherman
Wu Ling — insistent of his newest name —
Out by himself on a raft in her father's pond
Came poling back to where she stood on shore.
And I could see him there within her words,
The boy that lived immortal in her mind,
Sun in his hair and on his shirt that shone
White in the wind. He held within his hand
The tribute he had brought of water and slime,
The long stem dripping mud and in his palm
A water lily for her offering.

I said goodbye and ran for trains bound west
Along familiar rivers, sprawling lakes
Indifferent to way-signals in the leaves
Which signed him voyage eastward over oceans.
Impatient with him then, as often . . . betting
His all and prize-take, going down . . . to Egypt.

TAHL : BOOK TWO

CANTO I

COMING FORTH BY DAY

Katabasis

All the brothers of the western world
Go to the mountain or the yellow river
Or wherever
Blood of the world has made them brothers
Seeking the first river, the great mother,
The warren of mud and wattle set to sun,
The clay and reed torn
Out of the matrix.
Take your boat, all passengers, and go
Down to death, to the desert, to time's answer
Which, if not first nor oldest, surely older,
By that great muddy undividing river,
Down to the lake where some say time was born.

Take the white man on your patient shoulders.
Get him a camel, a boat, the fat black mud to walk on.
Is there a white-skinned man who has not dreamed nor seen
That vast mute head in the desert?
Manhead, womanhead, body of the lion,
Beyond the pyramid, the man-made mountain,
Assertive first intelligence in the stone.
Lord, king,
Athenian, Roman, Frenchman they have come;
English soldier, American traveller,
Rich man, poor man,

Katabasis

To see what sand has caught and never conquered,
Dead stone more live than any man's cadaver.
Sphinx intransient out of living rock,
Named and nameless still, still undefined,
Transient symbol still intransient,
Irony of transient resurrection,
Commonplace of all antiquity,
The usual thing to see,
Crumbling in the centuries of sun.
Ride your donkey hot and thirsty,
Come. Stare.
Great silent affirmation there,
And what affirming, what asserting,
Saying yes
To which of many questions?
Emperor, soldier, monk and martyr
And many a young man growing older
Make hegira there.

This was the place to come to. On these walls
Among the scribblings holy and obscene
Of generations, here among the tombs
Are words, the words of priests
Concerning the hearts of men and what they mean.
The latter-day late scholar may discover
The sorrow of evil hearts that weighed against a feather,
Were dog-consumed, died utterly,
Devoured of the Devourer.

Here are the hidden sepulchres. Within
The clear-faced, clever, much-commanding kings
Enshrine
What must be kept eternal out of time,
Bound with basalt, granite guarded,
Since the dead live long.

Silent fellah holding the steady torch, lift up the light.
Read the recording walls.

This is death in which the happy prince
Shall have his garden, hunt the wild goose on the marsh,

Pushing the boat among the leaning reeds,
And with his wife shall watch his children play
Forever with silver fish and mild white doves,
The boy, his small gazelle; the girl, her butterflies.
In stately towns his governors shall rise
And bring him Khesit wood and bronze and gold,
Papyrus, linen, incense, copper rings,
And raise him monuments with glassy eyes.
Rowers, butchers, masons serve his whim,
The corn to be winnowed and stored,
The quail to be fee to his table,
The ro-geese and crane,
The orange and date to his hand.

Where is he, the happy prince who shall return
Within the hingeless door
And claim
These unremitting joys?

Open the gaudy cerement, expose
Under the turquoise, emerald, vermilion,
This happy prince
Sealed with a hundred perfumes,
Bathed in wine,
The yet unrotted skin, the perfect bone.
The holy scarab where the heart has lain,
The great ungendered beetle born of sun,
The promised resurrection.

Here rudiment and chemical
Among the shadows of his windless tomb,
He is not dead, he lives, this prince,
This here assembled bone.
From the double-doored horizon
He ascended the stair of the sunbeam,
He has come on the lake of rushes,
The friend of the green falcon,
The morning star.
In the shadow of sycamore trees
He lives, the son of the father,

Katabasis

This prince, the son of Ra.
He shall have his everlasting joy.
He was a just man. He cannot die.

He was a just man. He raised his hand
Against no child nor widow, served the state,
And did no murder nor no sacrilege.

He was a just man. And shall the just men live
Who lie in these broad cities of the dead?
And shall they live,
That multitude
Who burst their hearts to build
These giant pylons, manheaded rock colossi, cliffhewn tombs,
These great straight majesties of strength in man?
That multitude
Who had for their rest no linen nor ivory pillow,
But tossed the hot night through on mud and sand,
Rising, father and son, to daylong labor
In yellow unshading shadow
To cut out sandstone, level thickets, bring down limestone,
Tunnel tombs, and die embalmed
In mud and sand,
Dead where the last blow fell, the tool laid down,
The flesh unrotted in this thirsty land.

For them no monument
But where each highcrowned palm
Proclaims all life resurgent,
Forcing opulent fibers still to fruit
Out of the dry earth,
Osiris, sacred palm branch,
Tree in the desert,
Under the parching sun.

The women have wept for Osiris.
Planters of barley, watchers of corn,
Stonecutters, roadmakers, drawers of water,
All of your women shall weep for Osiris,
His justice shall judge us

Coming Forth by Day

Who die in the quarry,
Who faint in the sun.
His name is green tree, fresh water.
For him we do justice.
The great tree will save us
Who look to the west and remember the grave.

Who are these gods?
This poem shadowed on the life of man?
Can we love gods who always hated kings?
What is here but innocence in them,
And we too knowing for these godly kings?

Can we dismiss it so
With a large term
Like anthropomorphic?
Will learning be enough to whittle down
These mighty gods to ancient righteous kings?
Is something here that time can not adduce,
Out of our measure?

Something is answerable beyond the myth.
These men who would be righteous
Not in the death of sense,
Not for the shrewd convenience,
But for the life forever,
Palpitant, sensible, generous,
For the life that knows no end.

Prince's god or people's god,
What matters on this rolling dustball,
This small world?
Ask, one not-so-young man in a sunhat,
Thinking man
Taking his night beneath mosquito netting,
Walking the day among the beggars' cries
In the city of all the world, the slave of the king or the caliph
Or the latest oppression of peoples,
And only a mile away from the Sphinx of Gizeh.

Katabasis

What are the words for God?
It has been hardly decent,
We have not been used
To speaking of him.
What prince and servant now can trust in justice
That it shall reign whatever god's in heaven?
And to the just shall gods still give their peace?

Give a penny to a mewling beggar,
Man in a sunhat.
And the beggar said:
"Go with God."

Where shall I go with him?
Who is he?
Think of the God of your childhood,
The whitebearded man on the ceiling,
Great glorious God of the starlight from your bed.
Great God.

But all god's men were sniveling
Long-nosed pinheaded creatures, melancholy.
What have I to do with dreary men?
The handsome men were gay and godless fellows.
God's men are dreary. He's a dreary God.
What had God, this prince's myth, this beggar's legend,
To do with me?

Is it fear that makes us dream that there is God?
I heard in Egypt that God was to come.
This has been the world from the beginning:
The brother falls by brother and brother deserts him,
The traveler dies at the knife of the highway robber,
The slaves have died like flies on the public works,
The sick have been thrown from the dikes to the hungry fish;
Sedition, rebellion,
The rich inventing repression,
The poor resenting oppression,
Both wrong, both violent.
When the great are kind, the humble are more greedy;

Nor any generosity assuage
Ungraciousness,
Nor patience make the powerful more kind.
Who eats your bread will lift his heel against you.
Is this a good man's masterpiece,
Is this God's world?

Why do the clever skeptics always go
With faces as of men who've been in hell?
Whose world is this
In which there is no peace?

Is sense the sum of evil? Then deny
All joy, all sorrow . . .
Rot to nothingness.
What have we to do with nothingness?
Whose world is this
In which there is no peace?

Here live these ancient men; they, too, have spoken,
Pyramid men and those who lived to see
The pyramids succumb to time and sand
And still were ancient man
Though Gizeh was gone down to dust
Before their kings were born:
We have no death,
What have we to do with nothingness?
We still shall live by the grace of God
And lay our hearts to rest.

What to him, the weakling
Subject to sunstroke and lingering tropical fever,
Are the halls of Osiris, seas of flame?
Fallen is the temple, rifled the holy of holies,
The blest bread molded, the white sandals stained,
The hounds of hell but the figure of poets,
And the goddess of justice:
A small lapis lazuli image
In the national museum.

Katabasis

There was a king in Egypt talked with God.
The strong and the weak were hating him together.
He made the craftsmen poor.
He forbade the servant's amulet, the peasant's comfort.
The men of God go spitting on each other,
Calling the names of God against each other,
Breaking, defiling the holy altar,
Burning and slaying and crying out
In the name of God.

That king in Egypt never deified;
A young man saying God, that God was one,
That He was good and loved all men
All living creatures;
And the priests of God and the people of God
Who said that God was good and loved all men
Denied this king in Egypt.

These were the men to say:
In the day of death the deeds of a man
Are set in a balance beam.
And will the heart of one young righteous king
Swing in the balance?

These were the men to say:
None know the day
And in that day
Eternity shall meet him.
And the spirit of man that is born in a man
Shall go there before him.

Where is the wisdom, what is the wickedness?
Sun, great hawk, green tree, bright disk of Aton.
Still is the city of God the burrow of jackals and rabbits.
Many the kings and the men of God who were slain in Egypt.

Beyond the colonnade, the fallen pylon,
Still, from slayer and slain, the affirmation.
What is the wickedness, where is the wisdom?
The sun shall rise as a falcon
And all shall worship him.

Coming Forth by Day

Man, woman, child
The many living and the happy dead,
The humanheaded birds with mighty wings,
All shall raise their arms and worship him.

Shall these bones live?
These bones shall rise again.
The words of an old song
When did I hear it?
Not first in this land.
And the name of the Book of the Dead
Is the COMING FORTH BY DAY.
Shall these bones live?
The words of an old song.

This was the news we had of him at last.
He said he'd caught the fever, dreamed of tombs
And all the kings of Egypt come again;
But what he said the more was fever-bred
Of more than parasites along the veins,
A rising heat of anguish in the self
Not blood, the nameless inner stream impent;
His private ague to be dared or dodged
As we our own who dare our own or not
Somewhat to season or the state of mind.

"Here," he said, "I'm grubbing in the bones
Of music: market catch and peddler's cant,
The singsong of a harlot; can as soon
Stretch me a drumhide, gut a sheep for fiddles,
Stealing tunes.
I'd go to hell or Jericho.
I've owled it in the house at Port Saïd.
Those cursed mirrors. The face the beldam has.
I sleep nights when I can.
If it would come. But will it come?
A lot of paper full of straight black lines . . .
And a plan."

The plan was never quite articulate
In words or music, but its major theme

Was so much his obsession we'd have been
More than the dolts we were not to have seen
At least its shadow. What he most believed
Was we were all of us the sons of men,
All men, the final nation bred of seed
Untraced and so more traceable to every tree
Has put out rod since Adam; so the heirs
Of every race, all myth and music,
Every art, all wisdom. And our weird
Was on us, having now the soul, the heart,
Accumulate science and the massy truth
Of generations, now to make us wiser myths,
More mighty music.

This was the demon kept him up of nights,
That sent him out for hell or else to go
The world around to find the best way in.
He even went that road to Jericho,
To southward and beyond in search of brimstone,
Liking a grim joke and having heard that hell was over Kedron,
Supposing that a wilderness that spawned the prophets
Might spare at least a dream. The curious
And anxious self-appointed, there we joined him.
He was himself half-demon when we came,
Two of us the world around. We cured,
Perhaps, the pip of our own ignorance . . .
Who could not purge the fever that possessed him.

Then we came to the ultimate valley, to the hills of Judah, to the
    mountains of desolation,
To the home of the owl and the wolf, to the house of the whip-
    tailed scorpion.
No man should look with opened eyes upon that valley.
No man should remember forever in sleep that terrible hollow
    snarling with heat,
More cursed than a land that is cursed with a ravin of locusts.
We walked on one white road. We came to a dreadful land.
We set our teeth in the hairy apple of Sodom.
We puckered our mouths on the sand and the ash of the fruit of
    Gomorrah.

Coming Forth by Day

We took small comfort of thirst among terrible waters.
We sat in the desert of salt. We looked to the southern deserts, to
the northern whirlwind, to the mists that rose with the sun on
the summits of Judah.
This was the valley cleft like wax in a fire.
The earth was rent and the rock vomited.
The depths of the earth spat out flame.
And the flame blew cold
And the rock lay cool in the wind.
And in the silence the sucking waters,
The sea of the dead, the terrible waters, the sea of the plain.

Look for a fish in that fatness of waves.
Look down.
Look for a lotus bloom in that brack of blue water,
Look for a long-stemmed wide-leaved lotus flower.
Look to the sky that was burned in the fires of the furnace.
The mountains of Moab rose and bent upon us over water,
We saw two suns in the sky.
The mountains of Judah writhed and leaned upon us over water.
We saw the evening conflagration in the west,
We saw six corners on the setting sun.
This was a place for tearing your hair and groveling in ashes and
crying a great cry.

We were three young men who stood there gazing down
Where driftwood lies like bones.
We were three young men staring at clear blue water,
Smashing the crystalled salt with idle heels.

Was this the cleansing of Sodom, the purge of Gomorrah?
Salt is harsh on a wound.
This was a terrible purification.
Did men here writhe with fire?
Did men here slit their throats when God came down?
Are we more kind or only less than God
Who can be merciful to fornications?
We do not flee our father's houses;
We do not turn our backs upon our neighbors.

Katabasis

Tahl said: "Surely if there were sin and God
And God decreed a punishment on men
For such as sinned the sins these cities name of
This were the punishment appropriate.
The very earth is scabbed with sores of sin.
Yet not all met that death.
Some unregenerate son of Siddim
Survived to bring his city's secrets to our cities
And country lanes are not unlearned in ways
Malodorous of brimstone."

We were not unaware how each man's brain
Opened its privy and the dreams crawled out
As vermin out of rags that face the sun.
Not dreams but dim remembrance not disdained,
Taking some joy of retrospect upon our follies.
We were three young men, three white fools who aggravated fever
Born of the heat we waded in,
We were three white fools who drowned in a jelly of heat
Till we were maudlin.

Then we sat down in the shade of a rock.
Then we sat down in a field of pock-marked grain.
He said: "It must discourage God who could throw out
So much hell from his reserve supply
To see the sins of Sodom still about
And not all paid for."

He was tearing an olive leaf, paring the spearhead down to its finest
strand.

And we thought our thoughts in that stinking smell
And the sun.

Funny to remember again and in this country
How we'd lain with our girls together in one bed,
How we'd lain in corners together with music playing.
Funny to remember a lot of things you might as well forget.
Funny to remember that this was a far country.

Coming Forth by Day

Tahl there sweaty and gaunt and tearing that leaf:
"What do you think they thought, those Sodom guys,
When the earth started coming apart
And the rocks started spitting fire
And the mountains cracking around?
Do you think they thought it was God
Or just had one last hell of a good time?"

Nobody but a black-broiled Bedouin could stand that sun.
Silly enough we looked with handkerchiefs under our helmets.
You had to talk but it was hard talking.
We'd been away. We hadn't seen each other for a long time.

"Who said God pulled this act?
How'd the story get around?
Quite a town to stay notorious all these years."

We came three heathen to a holy land
And found it nearer hell than holiness.
We came on a road in a powder of limestone dust.
We saw the sunrise on a sea of nightmares
And fried our skins in the hour that follows dawn.
We heard the mule hoofs click and our own thoughts saying:
We will go down with dawn and come again with the night's
falling.
But it was a month of nights before we rode
Out of that valley.
Was holiness in hell that we should find it
East of Engaddi?

We came three heathen to a holy land.
We watched the men dig potash out of Sodom.
Common salt from Sodom,
Magnesium chloride quarried from Gomorrah.
We heard canned music in a polyglot cafe.
We eyed the wealthy ancients taking cures.
We damned the heat that stuck to khaki helmets
And read by smoky lamps
And slept on lousy beds.

Katabasis

Once we saw a hermit let his dirty face
Out of his personal cave.
Once we saw a monk upon a mountain
Who sighed for the world's sorrows.
We popped slingshots at black goats to make them run.
We had a look at the walls of Jericho.
We talked sign language and cigarettes.
We ate rice stew and bean stew and bread and onions.
We blistered our eyes at night over fires of thorn
And waited and chased our fleas and swatted mosquitoes.
He always came back, from wherever he'd been,
In the cold toward morning.
We called him the wolf boy and other less well-bred names
But he'd just grin
And toss the thistle or reed or whatever he had in his hand
On the fire
And say nothing
And sit down.

What do you think, you Moses on the mountain?

No, he's Dante come to hell but missed his Vergil.

The thing that got you down about that man
Was he would always talk when he was ready
But kept his mouth shut till the stars or his brother, the devil,
Called his time.
One night he said:
"I was thinking about the walls of Jericho
And how we say an earthquake brought them down,
And how they say the lord of hosts decreed
And the walls fell.
And the dwellers in Jericho were drunkards and harlots
When Herod had the town from the queen of Egypt
Long ago.
And the town is wattle huts and sad eyes
Now.
Dull eyes for the heaps of mud we call
The trumpet-vanquished walls of Jericho.
Here are three cities gone to mud and salt

Coming Forth by Day

By accident or by some law on sins,
Which sinning needs a God to make the judgment.
I've looked for God
Since that hot morning when we first came down.
I've walked these hills like mountains in the moon.
I've sat on the beach, I've stuck my feet on pitch and slime,
I've looked in the narrow doors of leaning boulders,
I've listened to hear in this country without grass,
I've listened to hear God walking.

"Mountains look nearer here, the sky bends down.
The prophets of Israel saw him in these valleys
And something mighty walks among these hills.
But if there are signs in the sky and words in the hidden rocks,
I cannot read them.

"All that I know, this wilderness is not
So strange or alien as you might suppose.
You see bare rock where you would like a tree;
And, seeing trees, forget the rock is there
Under the crumbling soil.
Hell is earth with all the trees away
Perhaps.
It may be hell's an attribute of God
Since it's disaster sets us looking for him."

Once in the cool gray windless early hours:
"I've taken their book with me upon the hills.
Words more hot than a rain of living coals . . .
And in the words of prophets there are words
With promises of mercy on this place.
Fishermen shall once more set their nets
Where fifty miles of salt suck north and south.
That in a day comes healing on this place.
But when shall the tree spring up?
When shall the grass take root about Engaddi?
When the sons of God on earth have made repentance.

"What sin shall we repent and what repentance?
We say that war is murder and a sin;

And murderous wars have rolled among these hills.
Were not the innocents of Jericho
Slain by the men of God and in his name?

"What sin shall we repent and what repentance?
We keep
Neither new moons nor sabbaths.
We have condemned both greed and wanton crime
And as we judge expedient have kept our hands from sinning.
Why should the words of prophets, sharp reproach,
Be more than history between two boards
For us who, did we see the devil walking,
Can find no God to make defense against him?
The law of the lord in this valley,
The sin in Canaan,
The cancer in Sodom,
This is the sin we will not grant . . .
This is the word that scratches the heart as the brier the hand.
This is the word we read and resent and resist.
We will have no repentance.

"Men believed in God and were afraid
Of his great anger. And this angry God
By the mouths of prophets set the deadly sin
To be the sin of foulness in the flesh.
This was the doom of Sodom, the damnation in fire of Gomorrah.
This was the foulness found in Jericho
Betrayed by a harlot.
Its gods were gods of fruitfulness appeased
In the shadow of oaks, the laying together of flesh
In the shadow of trees.
The angry god forbade
The male and female symbols most accursed.
This was the message written in rock in a desert place.
This was the word of God on the holy mountain."

You do not look at a man when he says these things.

"Fear is the power he wields who so condemns.
We fear no God.

Our wars and earthquakes we'll put down to luck
Or just our own poor wit for having been there.
We'll die in a worm's way
When the worm's ready.

"Who shall purge us, who will hug our sins,
Who trust the ecstasy we know more sure
Than all the promises of holy men?
What ecstasy is more than this we know,
Which sought more often, sooner set upon?"

He stopped.
He propped the fire with sputtering twigs.
He said as if to himself:
"If you're bound you'll stay in this ugly hole with me,
I'll hush my mouth or we'll all three be out
To bark the moon."

We didn't look at him.

George said: "Damn you, I'll find a cave
And wear a haircloth shirt
And talk with God myself, if you aren't careful.
I often do not like the world we live in.
But all your talk and this God-blasted place
We chased you into
Has made of all my best diversions
A kind of suicide in evil."

And Tahl's rejoinder:
"What I know is nothing if I do not know myself
For no ascetic — nor afraid,
Looking for God in thunder . . .

"And did not God's own men against his laws rebel
In this same valley? But still they bowed
And wrote in their books: He raised his hand
Against their lecheries and owls have dwelt
And wolves howled all the night among their houses,
The leopards watched over their cities.

Katabasis

Because they assembled themselves in the harlot's houses,
They have written, of themselves,
They gave up water to the salt of tears.

"They have written in their books: Jerusalem
Was saved by righteousness and lost in sin.
All this is problematical, indefinite,
Probably beyond the mind of man."

Once when we walked the hills George drew a sign,
The double triangle in sun-caked earth:
"There is the sign of wisdom, the amulet
Attributed to Solomon, by old wives said to be
A charm against fever. What do you say, philosopher,
Will it serve?"

"Not for a charm against fever in the brain,"
Tahl's answer. "Though disdaining this great Jinn,
This God who rules the wilderness we mourn,
I cannot yet escape this double sign . . .
That gods are somehow relative to man
Since men have made so many words to name them:
The god of hosts, the god of righteousness,
The god of the fertile field, the god of love.
Call it the fears of ignorance, the manic mind;
I cannot but find false the one surmise
That there have been no wise men on the earth
Before our time
And all the white-haired books remaining us
Speak madness."

We had not gone from the world who had gone to a far country.
We saw the water channels red at sunset.
We saw the palm trees black against the sky.
We were acquainted with desert light and the grumbling of camels.
We entered into a wilderness.
We counted lizards.
We were amazed that the race of men who live on locusts
Had not died out in the caves and dens on Moab.
But the burden of vision was his, not ours, in the valley.

Coming Forth by Day

Though something we took more than sunburn,
The stars were not ours;
And if there were voices,
They were for him.

Once in a swift white-travelling dawn he said . . .
Over a cup of coffee . . .
"You know there's something wrong with power lines
And railroad trains. I like a camel at the plow.
Women in blue robes and sheep and goat talk on the hills.
I didn't like Jerusalem,
Typewriters, big cigars, and chromium plate
In the city of Zion."

George said:
"I was thinking,
If cars and electric wires conflict with God,
Maybe it's God himself's a period piece
In an antique shop among the Roman coins."

Tahl said:
"But it wasn't the chromium plate, the big cigars
That drove God out of town.
If God is anything at all,
I think it's peace of mind.
But there's scant peace in his Jerusalem.
Hate's the enemy and bitterness.
Not a holy day but we saw noses
Punched, a knife in the ribs, a little gunplay
For the glory of God who's left his squabbling nations."

George said: "It's much too small a town for God to live in.
Ten minutes barring the mob at Jaffa gate
And you're from end to end.
But it sure has lots of religion.
Pilgrims and pictures and rosaries and priests
In sunhats
And lots of monks in black and white and fancy colors
And all the dowdy fathers looking glum
At the dressy Armenian prelates flashing by

In red and gold and gaudy decorations.
And don't the sons of Mohammed and the sons of Jesus Christ
Go chalking scores up like a game of ball?
Seems so God must need police protection."

What did we go to see in God's own town?

We saw Jews and Germans and Syrians and Greeks
And a lot of red hats and oranges and cucumbers
And artichokes and melons.
David's street was dark and cool and full of steps.
We saw American schoolteachers, Mohammedan sheiks, English
    tourists and two French nuns.
The Arabs, we noticed, walked the streets like men.
And there were lots of cats and lots of smells
And all the world was kind and full of smiles
Till God got mentioned.

Tahl said:
"Some impudence may be a fair reply
To squabbling priests' competing pieties,
But not all's answered in the flippant jest,
Neither the pilgrim not the honest priest.
Some are honest, I believe.
Answer for me the chapel's trance-like hush.
Answer those great scarred hands that lay
The reverence of centuries upon
A slab of cracked white marble, on a stone,
A stone made sacred in a burden of bones
Held once, a prophet dead, a holy man.
In that labyrinth of murky shrines
Beside the gape-faced dolt, the gawking eyes, the idler's stare,
Something unwavering, some exaltation,
Something was there.
Those two French nuns were there."

"Yes," said George, "those two French nuns.
I know I ducked like a kid and cleared the stage,
But damn it all, don't grin.
To me it's meeting ghosts to meet those veils,

All black and white and soft.
I'd face a raffler or a bayonet
But not that floating blackness and those eyes."

Tahl said: "I think I always did despise
Those smug perennial virgins in their twos,
Or speculate on how it feels to rape
That blackness, excommunicate the ghost
And make the woman yield.
But something in those eyes you wouldn't meet
Made me less sure the woman could be won.
Most I would say were plain or smug or merely scared,
Safe in a dream,
But not those two French nuns."

"You'd better be a Jesuit," said George.
"For me, I'd rather burn.
That Easter evening when the big bell rang
And the turbulent muttering pious people swarmed
To get their cut of fire at the little door,
I thought it better most of them had burned . . .
If praising God is cursing half your neighbors,
If greed and strong-arm's what they make hells for.
Weren't there busted jaws and pulling hair
To get the blessing? Holiness, I thought
On Easter evening,
Goes to the guy that's got the toughest head.
God saves the guy who's got the longest arm.
No little brush of holy water splashed
Across the mob could wash those faces clean
With all of them mad to get a singe of fire.
It's not the fire I'll burn my fingers on."

Tahl said: "We look for a light
And now and then I've seen
On some face not my own
Illumination.

"I saw such faces at the wailing wall
One Friday evening.

Though surely the old world's sorrows have assailed
Those long unanswering stones to no avail . . .
Perhaps the answer's, 'No.'
To cry a litany of woe
Answering woe.
We sit in solitude and mourn."

George said: "No.
It's just a national case of blues.
Sit and be very morbid.
Tear your hair and say a prayer.
But where's it get you
Where?"

Tahl answered:
"The scraggly-bearded men,
The hoarse, the somber chant,
The yearning women and the solemn girls,
The scraps of paper in the broken stones,
I do not understand.
I heard a sound,
A patient steady tone.
I heard the sobbing women and the men.
I think such sorrow mourns against that wall
As we three have not known."

"If it's not God in these unhealthy hills,"
Said George, "then you've caught something.
Is it a pox you've got or just more fever?
When do you think it started coming on?"
Always he would take a riding well
And tie your tongue in your teeth with your own free rein.

"Remember," Tahl said, "that hill through the city gate
Out of that net of nerves, that tense and violent city?'

"We saw it. We went out."

"We came to that garden in the outer hills
To the hoary ancient olives and the monks,
Brown little men

Under tremendous trees.
They said to us, God prayed before he died
There in that garden under the olive trees,
Before he died, God prayed.

"Though one man pointed down the dusty range
That goes out south and said there lay
The grave of Israel, Ezekiel's bones.
He said the bones would rise
That God would stand once more upon these hills
I don't believe it. But that God is dead,
I got that much.
That's the fever and the pox
That's turned me solemn."

Melodrama suits a wilderness.
It is appropriate to feel quite sad.
It is something grand and black to say
So let us say
That God is dead.

George said: "If God is dead, will you come home?
Will you deprive us of this stinking place?
It smells.
I've got a notebook full of seedy natives,
Every phiz, each lean and hungry face.
We're tired of chasing goats and mangy game
And speculating on mirages and the rain.
I want where the sun stays single round and sane
And doesn't skip a beat or do adagios
Afternoons. We want out.
The bones won't rise, Ezekiel.
Will you come?"

That night it rained. He stayed inside and slept
However the rattling thunder reached his brain.
All night he slept although the sky hurled down
A great inverted sea and lightning snapped
And spun in balls of fire along thc ground;
To fool the jitters George and I laid bets

Katabasis

On the rate of recurrent flashes and the time.
The stove gone nearly out in the sneaky wind,
The ground already to heave and swooping fire
Worse than a mess of shrapnel bursting round,
Felt like the world itself would go off shortly,
One final belching bomb.
It lasted hours. That was a storm.

Morning came with a scrannel single cock
Crowing his drenched indignance at the sky.
Nothing is lonelier than a cock
Vocal in desolation.
The sleeper in thunder woke at that thin cry,
Woke and was writing and neither lines nor notes
But regular abc's that he put down.
Matching our own comments to his grin,
He said: "My unrepentant friends,
Here is a bedtime story.
It could do with illustrations
When you've time — somewhat erotic
With a subtlety of line.
It happened. I don't believe it was a dream
But for your business it is much the same."
He stood at the door. He said:
"I'm going after the horses from the khan
So we can shove up north to cool our brains
And leave this hell hole to its rightful dragon —
Unless you've changed your minds."

This was his vision in a valley of vision
Born of a desert and thunder and one man's dream:

Out of the thunder I saw the riders,
A roan-red horse and a rider not a man.
I saw him once in a smoke ring. And he cried:
"Who will have water?
Water will drink up a desert.
Water will put out a fire.
When the needy seek water,
Who will deny them?"

Coming Forth by Day

He had wings. He rode on a roan-red horse.
And under the wings no semblance of a man.
I said: "I and my brothers grow madmen after water.
We choke in the desert, we parch in the fire
For water to drink, for water to drown in.
Where is the cup and where is the stream?"

Last night in the time of thunder while you slept,
I went by the margin trail to the nearest hill
That looks on the sea of salt, the ancient death-hole.
There was a light not lightning in the east,
A steady glow that grew to be a moon
In crescent though the time is the moon's dark
And it was midnight. Yet the line
Of light, refracted, followed to the shore
And shone on a clump of myrtles by the lake
Where trees had never grown. And there the horse,
The rider's roan-red mare without a rein,
With quivering nostrils and with straining neck
Watched with an anguish of anticipation
The path of the moon. Upon the calm
Unshifting surface suddenly it came
Up from the black, a boat, and blacker still
Against the light the form of a man alone,
Hand to the tiller with a course aligned
To the space of myrtles coming on, though how,
By what propulsion not the more appeared
Than how he should not with the boat go down
Since he was all awash, unbaled and filled
Up to the gunwales. Nor no more I know
Why I ran anxious at his unconcern,
Swearing and shouting. I remember as I ran
I saw the sand was green and damned myself
For a spooking gutless fool that knows as well
As you do that the sand is always green
In moonlight. Getting a spasm for a boat
And a dunderheaded stranger was enough
Without the gooseflesh for a common trick
Of the desert. Getting prickles in the feet
And fingers, let alone a crawling spine

With the cool unwindy silence. I'd have prayed
For a thunder smash to crack the soundless air
Between me and the trees and the horns of the moon
And that approaching.
I could not hear the sound of my own running.
Not so the mare. With flattened ears she pawed
And curled her lip, disdained attack and turned
Again to the nonchalant boatman coming on
To strike his keel in calculable time
And give a horse her master. There I stood
Like a laboratory tyro spinning schemes
To weigh the weight of salt against its buoyance
And setting up the probabilities
Against his landing
And all the time aware these speculations
Were poor defense against the growing blight
Of some profound disorder in the world.
This moving fantasy of sloshing boats
Beached in a lawless unpredicted moon
No more resolved than sets ashore a man
Black with a gleam. No more I could discern
Except the foot set from the dripping stern
Released no moisture to the dusty ground.
No more except his eyes' indifference
More clever and more cool than makes a man.
He made a sign.
The roan-red mare in the space of myrtle trees
Turned with her long neck downward and was gone.

Thunder was west, the moon was east, and he
Had come. And not the first but a recurring dream
Of boat and man, but I had never gone.
Now was the going sure. The moon was wrong.
The thunder wouldn't drown it. We were gone
On the oilgreen halfdark water gurgling in.
And he with his eyes. And then I felt it come,
Known in my heart and bones before it came,
The arc of ascending prow, the settling stern,
The backward flying plunge, the awful swoop,
The rising gorge, the scream like wind in the ears,

Coming Forth by Day

The wracking spine, the headfirst down through water
Unfathomed, down and down.

Last night in the time of thunder while you slept
I was the guest of a stranger in his town.
I was the guest of a man who owned a boat,
He in black. He took me down.

Surely this was the city built by men
For man's fulfillment, here their promised land.
Here were no starved and ragged. Clothed and fed
They walked the dustless pavements, shining spans
Of faultless engineering, tier on tier,
Their towers' aerial magic shaped the air
In most ingenious metals, curve and plane
An infinite device. I saw the arms
Of ceaseless engines, majesties of power.
I saw unmurmuring people, suave and cool,
Bred by design to bone and blood's perfection.

The stranger said:
"Man may master himself or master man.
In either problem one man is the master.
I am the man who masters men.
I am the master."

His were eyes without shadows.
"The deaf, the lame, the blind, to take an instance,
Create expense, make sickly servants, yes;
Pain being no discourtesy to pain, the blood runs cleaner.
Adequate flesh survives to house the minds
Agile to grasp and execute the order.
A discipline from birth,"
Said the stranger.
"Dreams and rebellions are the major crimes
Eliminated also. One survives,
One dream and they its servants.
I am the dreamer."

Assuming irony, I mocked his eyes.
But voice alone, the eloquent, replied:
"The primal factor of administration

Required by force of total demonstration
The classic, static ideology.
The arts are yet imperfect. In the spawn
Still agitation, but majority
Disciplined and docile soon retrieve
The trail all rebels leave.
Sanitation, distribution, transportation
Exhibit even now efficiency
Unparalleled. Of our priority
In mob psychology, mass recreation,
Our scrupulous society
Suspects the solitary his dissension."

"Finally," he said, "since all terrains
Of government acknowledge my dominion,
International diplomacy
Is non-existent. Military factions
Rise, invade, reconquer at command.
I do not frown on civil insurrection.
Recurrent cycles of the mass destruction
Can mitigate the dullness of perfection.
Everyone within his favored time
Believes in me his friendship is forever.
All emotion serves the dominant mind.
Their feeding pride evokes the proper answer.
The least erotic subtleties seduce
The few who passionless might think too shrewdly.
That aristocracy is never dull
Though for that reason dead men shortly."

I dined with the solemn lord of that, his town.
Never were wits more supple though the theme
Was just a cut above my comprehension
Being the wit of money and machines
With all appending legal stratagem.
I, the poor provincial, the visiting kulak,
A pert irrelevance in repartee
On bureaucratic items and statistics,
Admired them, ate or dozed, or hardly listened
To these designing dozens of his women,

Coming Forth by Day

Lithe, with most shapely buttocks, firm of flesh,
Breasts you could put your hands to, redder lips
Than pomegranate seeds. Mohammed's snare
For all his holy warriors is a cheat
Beside this black one's heaven. He in black
Watching the trained, the trigger-lively brains,
Watching for heads to fall
On all the shining shoulders trained and waiting.
Sating the rout of soup, of nuts, of capons,
I thought to bait him on official murder,
But "Come," he said, "Come! Come!"
"The festival of dancing," said the stranger.

Confused and amiable, I still perceived
This festival engendered no rejoicing,
A kind of gallant silence. "Come,"
Was a proclamation without answer.
Walls removed upon a terraced mesa
Three sides precipitate. The moon
Was full nor why no more I know nor how
The tables went or when the sliding walls
Accomplished landscape, sky spring-violet blue,
And lawn-smooth grass and shaggy trees
And no wind.

Then the voice of one
Upon an elevation like a throne
Of natural eruption, like a tor,
I saw him stand.

Walking at first, just walking,
Hardly a sound.
Walking, all of us walking
Around.
Eyes, his eyes
And all eyes turned
To the one.

Turning now, turning,
Turning in circle
Slow.

Katabasis

Deciding, returning,
Going about in twos,
Steadiness all
And slow.
Humming now, humming,
A tone, a kind of moan,
Humming, all humming
A tune of my own, the girl
In my arms
In the eyes
In the moon.

A drum
From under,
From way down under
And he sat down.

The circle
Wound,
The night closed in and was warm,
Wanted it warmer,
We all closed in, swung
Eyes on the one.
Heat from the drum.
No horn to cool us,
The horn that came.
Whirling, reeling
We spun, heads cracking,
Our flesh cried out,
Burning and moaning,
Breath caught screaming.
And the eyes of the one.
Our bones swung,
Swung in the sockets,
We all bowed down
To the drum
Cloven together
Hips, tongues, loins,
Crawled for mercy
And heard no sound.

Coming Forth by Day

We saw them come,
The flying silent stars without a sound.
And then the pounding, the running feet,
The fleeing, the mighty-headed men
Under the silent coming,
Broken on the precipice,
Struggling on the plain.

I was held by the hands of two women.
Pinpoints of fire came down
And wheeled them in, the men on the plain
Like a dancing circle, a herd of cattle.

Then the sound, the quiet thud
And the beautiful flame.
Wings of an army of bats went by.
The air was sick with fire
Of burning eyes in the skulls on the plain.
But the eyes, the unshadowed eyes, his eyes
They did not burn.

Then I was given a gift of parsley and vervain.
Then was I set on a red horse with two women.
I rode in a valley of stone.
I saw great fires of alder and of fern
Embracing human bones.
I saw blood, the great wine.
The moon was wasted thin.

The bones sang:
"By eternal silence, by eternal creation,
By the serpent, by the long-polluted bread,
By fire and blood
The sign of man weds the sign of God."

What I have written is what I have seen.
Whether immersion or illumination . . .
Whether the asking answers, riddle ravels . . .
I have come back from where I have been.

TAHL : BOOK TWO

CANTO I

COMING FORTH BY DAY

Anabasis

Forget it.
Shove a paper in a pocket smudge of crumbs.
Shove it in
With old tobacco, chocolate, and dust.
Mist blows eastward on the sea of salt.
Ride the rockpile upward west and north.
To hell with Abraham . . . we haven't time
To look at bones of any friend of God.
Leave the bones of Joseph in his tomb.
Ride.

Stuff your ears against the sunset voice
Of Islam calling from the southward towers,
Scorn the pub that sets its waterpipes
To catch the gawking tourists; close your eyes
To blue-green mottled flagons, grapes and wine.
Ride west, ride north. Get going.
Swap your horse for a tin machine with engine trouble.
Ride.

Irony, that hand grenade of fate,
Swift overtaking malice that assails
The man whose road outrides his destiny,
That cuts the wires or blows a ditch or kills a horse
If so the man go scatheless . . .

What less contriving genii could prevail
To set three wheels at once upon their rims
And so compel that fugitive from God
To spend the night where some say God was born,
A most illustrious, much neglected Child
In Bethlehem.

Starlight in the lanes of Bethlehem
Betrayed us to the shrewdest devil's imp
Who ever wheedled three poor aimless men
From pocket money.
Consequently we were shown
The manger grotto and the dusty cave
Of Latin's latest master, old Jerome.
The latter's woman-shielded hermitage
Aroused some powerful sentiments in George.
"That lucky son of God," he said. "See what you get.
The pious way of life has its reward.
We need his Lady Paula while we sit
With nice fat lions nuzzling on their paws
And pretty holy dames to knit our socks
And feed our bellies while our minds go free
For idle matters like theology.
If Lady Paula loved us guys right now
We wouldn't have that tin anomaly
On four bum wheels to take us out of hell,
But ride chauffeured and with some useful boys
At seventy miles an hour to where we please.
It's trusting heathen patronage that puts us
To counting dimes and dinners."

"Said like a holy man, good Brother George,"
We two replied with ribald gravity
And would have made an evening on the jest
But that our grinning guide had faced us in
Upon another cavern in the stone
And said one word of English pointing down:
"God."
Not knowing what the courtesies required,

Anabasis

Three men saying nothing stood
One minute near the spot where God was born.

Then on a starlit night in Bethlehem
We leaned against a window ledge and smoked,
Tahl saying:
"The seaman and the woodsman still can name
More than the Pole Star we're uncertain of,
But we are a people unfamiliar now
With stars.
We build us skillful whirligigs to show
Upon the arch of well-built lecture rooms
The flight of aeons, but we seldom learn
To match the expert's darting torch, the diagram, the key,
With this light-dazzled vast reality."

George inquired:
"Aren't there serious scientists who claim
The legendary star that marked this town
Will bear investigation and be found
Because the zodiac was changing signs
A not unlikely sort of situation?"

Tahl answered:
"Some such mystic rigmarole
I've heard and sounder speculation too,
But have you noticed how the central arc
Of radiance the star is fixed upon,
The point in time it lights upon this earth
Is hard to come by with exactitude
And that one star reflects with equal light
In more than one deep pool?"

Our pet particular devil's imp who lay
Asleep behind us on the window shelf
Awoke and, with the gift his blood bestowed
In reading men to springe their weaknesses,
Beckoned and bowed to where a ladder stood
Ascending nearer to the night with stars.
We stretched ourselves upon a level roof.

Tahl, with the imp asleep against his knees,
Spoke after some long looking in the dark
That was not dark, being the East with stars,
And as in answer to inquiry grown
In all our thoughts that none had given words:
"Whether a light of more than stardust made
Drove all shadows from these simple planes
These repetitious rooftops on a night
That, some men have it, altered history —
Whether or no, and we do not believe —
Whether or no — I never see a wick
Floating in oil before the gaudiest shrine
Or crudest icon that I do not feel
What Adams felt at Chartres,
A veracity
Older than records which may tell us lies,
A primitive essential sanctity
In these antique madonnas with the child."

George, whose pencil drew a little row
Of roguish virgins on a smutty card
The while he listened, ventured finally:
"I'd rather guy you for a mother's boy
Or recommend psychiatry or Epsom salts
For sentimental drool about the mother,
Mother of God or first eternal paps
The old ones called the mother of the world,
But fact is, damn it, that I get your drift.
If nothing else it is a loss to art
To lose that great design. There's none of us
Can fake enough religion now to draw,
Paint, carve, or model that immortal pair.
It always turns out satire and obscene.
The naif Byzantine, the early glass,
The Gothic stone
Comprehend what's now forever gone
Or gone for us . . . for us forever gone."

Tahl said: "The Mater Dolorosa now
Is something alien. Do you recollect

That flaccid waxwork in Jerusalem
Stuck to the heart with that enormous sword
And all hung out with rings and colored glass
And half a thousand medals?" He paid off
Our Midas cub
Persuaded to depart in sleepy grins . . .
"When I see that mummery of bleeding hearts
And beads and blessings, makes me wonder, then . . .
These pious seizures over candlewicks
Smoking before a virgin and her son."

George said gloomily as we turned in:
"You'd think we were three dirty shaven monks,
There's so much God in all our conversation.
I'll be glad to quit this Bethlehem,
Jerusalem and all its smelly tribe.
Let's make it quicktime through that Galilee
And show old rolling Jordan our behinds.
And," he concluded with dramatic moans,
"Anyway you shouldn't have reminded me again
About madonnas.
Every primitive we see until next year
Will make me bilious."

Time-honored endless compliments exhaled
With gasoline and grease attended us,
Good health and peace with calisthenic bows,
The gifts and all the blessings of great God.
"Great God again," said George, jamming the gears,
And swung us perilously out of town —
Steering among six camels and their calves,
Nipping two dawdling boys in sheepskin coats —
Pedal to floor careening north to make
Jerusalem and far beyond by nightfall.

That city's far-stretched roofs and spires and domes,
All contours flat with high noon light, deceived
Our month-long absence into a surprise,
Remembering no such fine placidity;
Surprise dissolved as soon to memory

Coming Forth by Day

With cattle market cries and moiling crowds
And cars and camels, porters with tin cans
Erupting inward through the Jaffa gate
To meet the shrieking women selling grapes
And nectarines, bananas, cauliflower,
Our own noise less than all the dinging bells
And blatting horns. You had to yell
In concert at the stall for roasted eggs
And then give up and hail a coffee tout
Who banged his cups in raucous sympathy
With all this glorious noise unto the Lord.
"Fourteen times destroyed is what they say.
It must be noise that keeps this town alive,"
George megaphoned around two halves of bread.
"There was a fellow named Gamaliel,"
Tahl shouted, "said whatever was of God
You couldn't overthrow it anyhow."
And grinned and took the wheel and chased the signs
That said Damascus highway, Nazareth.

Who has not known nostalgia for old names,
Swift Indian polysyllables for home,
The hedge-rowed English hamlet of the sires
In antique peace beneath a footworn stone,
Some classic hidden valley, satyr's spring,
A Mantua among Italian hills.
The world is his who owns no native town.
The maverick of the west can most assure
His heart's Jerusalem, his secret Rome,
And deeper than iron can burn he brings a wound
Of memory retrieved of disbelief,
A singular emotion dark with years,
Brushed from the dust of childhood glossy clean,
The history, the legend now retold
In signposts leading inward to old dreams.

Out of Jerusalem the road is north.
Ramah is north, a voice is crying in Ramah,
Rachel weeps and is not comforted.
Samaria is north. And then he came

Anabasis

To a city in Samaria.
Now Jacob's well was there.
There was a man who from Jerusalem
Went down and fell among thieves.
A certain Samaritan upon a journey
Saw him lying beaten, bruised, and robbed
And had compassion on him.
The plain of Sharon's west, the rose of Sharon,
The mountains north. The sea is west of Carmel.
I will cut wide Lebanon's tall cedars.
And Og the giant which was of the race of giants
Reigned in Hermon and over the country of Bashan
And him they smote, the servant of the Lord,
And now there are no giants in this land.
Out of Jerusalem the road is north,
Desert and mountains, quiltwork of new trees,
Scarlet and purple lilies under thorn,
Snow and heat and dust and mustard sown
Brighter than sunlight. Warpath of the world
Bloody with empire, still the shepherd's stile,
The stammering patter of hoofs, the herdboy's pipe
Stumbling a tune along the homeward trail.
Armageddon's got no murder more
Than grasshoppers will make with their small noise.
North is Nazareth, Cana in Galilee.
Hell's gone over; north is Hermon's mountain,
That gentle upland white with sanctity.
Placid a rabbit sits upon his heels,
Sparrows at sunset gossip in the wheat,
And there are running brooks among these fields.

Three young men come riding into Nazareth,
North of Samaria, south of Hermon,
Four hours west from the inland sea.
Guides and beggars and petty hucksters.
What did they come to the town to see?
Plows and yokes and old blue cradles,
Fountain named for a girl called Miriam.
What did they come to the town to see?

Coming Forth by Day

Man named Joshua,
Man called Jesus,
Jésu, carpenter in Galilee.

Three young men came riding to Tiberias,
East of Cana, south of Capernaum,
Four hours east on the inland sea.
Mud will batten on a marble column.
What did they come to the town to see?
All of the spawn of cities fallen,
Rags and eyes and flies and fishbones.
What did they come to the town to see?
Man named Joshua,
Man called Jesus,
Jésu, fisherman of Galilee.

Three young men set sail at evening.
Who with a boat would stay on shore?
Water's black and the bottom's stony.
What did they sail at night to see?
A hundred gorges seethe with whirlwind.
Oars bite deep in the eastward running.
Thunder walks on the waves at midnight.
What did they set from shore to see?
Man named Joshua,
Man called Jesus,
Jésu, prophet of Galilee.

Three young men ride over Jordan,
Mean little muck stream down to the sea.
Summer's thick and dust lies heavy
On almond and thistle and evergreen tree.
Steep and barren's east of Jordan.
The hills were cool in Galilee.
Roll Jordan, muddy river,
Thousand years and more gone over.
Wasn't ever a deep river.
Wasn't even a wide river.
Wisest brother, what did you see?
I heard thunder.

Anabasis

Thunder's an accident of midnight.
Roll Jordan, muddy river.
Turn your back on Galilee.

They spoke in Nazareth:
Nail and hammer and saw was Joseph's trade.
Hammer and nails devise an evil death.
On every timbered shaft his plane essayed
Was Joseph's son betrayed.
He crossed the wood he was himself to bear,
Apprenticed son, the oldest, silent, with brown hair,
And that high-headed calm so like his mother's
Who pampered him, the prince, among his brothers
And bred the renegade.
Not a gossip spared her sneer when he
Came to his hanging on a gallows tree,
Joseph's son of Galilee.

And in Tiberias,
Now the lorn dark town inhabited,
All monuments of old Hellenic grace
Garden and villa, both untenanted,
There once that high-held head.
The wonder-worker from Capernaum,
Preacher in synagogues, friend of fishermen.
What alien foments or what ancient scores
Survive that young man's hardihood of yours
So hardly forfeited?
Levantine, Greek, and Roman came to see
Wide-eyed yokels pledge him fealty,
Joseph's son of Galilee.

        That night upon the sea
They said: He blessed the merciful and mild,
Brown-bearded rabbi out of Galilee,
He blessed the humble-hearted and the child
        In knowledge undefiled,
So served our darkness, shamed us in our pride,
To every sane man's searching still a guide
Pre-eminent. But the ages' wonder,

Coming Forth by Day

Wave-walker, faith healer, son of thunder,
        We are not reconciled,
To feed our quaking hearts with cups of blood
Nor fortify our seed in Jesse's rod
Nor name him son of God.

        Beyond Jordan river . . .
He was a man of peace unjustly slain.
Grant it so. Then where's the riddle, brother?
Will you question more of the world's pain
        Or more than Israel's stain?
Truly the wounds he held in his wounded hands,
Those were the wounds he had in the house of his friends.
The world runs, blood in its mouth and blood in its maw.
The priest grows fat who blesses blood's own law
                Invoked again.
Ride and fight and lust in the blood's fever.
Let the sword to the heart in the last danger.
Ride, brother. Ride with your answer.
        Campground's over
                Jordan river.

Ride the gray green breathless waste, you riders,
Ride to the old white tombs, the sunburnt lava,
Ride on the rocklip road of the horny ibex,
Ride the drifted hills, on the rutless sand.
Strike for the broad red clouds on the northern marshes,
Ride on the blue-cropped weeds where the sheep have scattered,
Ride in the sleet and splash to the dead volcano,
Ride on the ghosts of hearths in the mapless sand.
On mud and boulder drive your horse to water.
Take your brackish best from the sour goatskin.
Throw your date stones wary at the well curb.
Commend your gritty bread to the guardian Jinn.
Ride in the blistered noon, the long gold evening,
Praise your mounted shadows in the moon.

Tribes are up for a fight. Then fight, you fighters.
Horsemen meet in the hills; the jaw is shattered.
Fight for the watering well more dear than fruit trees.

Anabasis

The curve of a bullet is harder than wind-cut sand.
Fear nothing. Life is today and death will find you,
Quails more than hawks and antelope sooner than huntsmen.
Shall the mare that eyes you at night repent of her master?
Trust your gun or shut your mouth with sand.
Steal his bridle, slash his woven skullcap,
Throat-curved sword of the booted camel driver.
Saddle-sweat mares on jaded hoofs retreated.
Clean your gun and swab your sabered shin.
Horsemen met in the hills make truce at evening.
Water your mules, you naked herdboys under the moon.

Lean on your huddled rugs, you hungry eaters,
Guests of the nine-poled tent of goats' hair matted.
Peace be on you. Here's no camel's porridge.
Feed your stomachs hard; the mutton's killed,
Bread's to the skillet, birds wade high in onion,
Curdled soups, no poor man's rusk of barley:
Hold your wind and hide your delicate noses.
Roll your rice ball fat in the flesh new-killed.
Roast the iron-spooned beans and pound them singing.
Pucker your lips in the purging coriander.
Bitter the brew in tarnished urns unnumbered.
Hold your head in the smoking reek and grin.
Shout with your hand in the bowl and laugh in your belly.
Good men feasting see the third night's moon.

Talk of the evil, talk of the good, you talkers,
The names on the desert rock, the ageless murders.
The long white sleeves of idleness are folded.
Smoke your cigarette and think of God.
Talk, eternal people, God's beloved.
Ascend your smoking talk to farthest heaven.
Vent your guttural scorn on mighty liars.
Invoke the utmost name, the name of God.
He is least wise who fights against the prophet,
But he is a fool who soils the name of God.

God is east and west, you gaping strangers.
Paradise promised warms the death-cold warrior.

Coming Forth by Day

The owner of bleating sheep shall come to judgrnent.
None shall escape his destiny in God.
Hear the lies of the worshipers of devils:
The giant of the world's end when man is shrunken,
The prey of the worm of the dust and the seven waters . . .
When Christian and Moslem and Jew shall come to God.

Rake the fire. Refuse no meat to beggars.
Who calls our name shall have his answer, "God."
Ride from the desert. By God, you can not endure it
Ever to live in a country gone naked of trees.
Damascus girdled with fruits, her apricots sugared,
The corn on the market stones, the salted pistachios,
The hyacinth potted, the rose of the garden courtyard.
Trade your horse for a book, you city-dwellers,
The parchment close-studied in gardens, the painted, the mellow
brocade.
And dearer than words is the shade of a tree in a garden.
Praise be to God for the olive, the date and the orange.
Never draw breath in a country long barren of trees.

What are the words on the blades of sheep and the sayings on palm
leaves,
The ancient wise sayings on vellum, tall stranger, the antique
brocade?
The words of the righteous are faith and the words of a fool are
destruction.
Never a wise man lived long who was lost of God.
We who want nothing will pray in the morning and evening.
Answer the thousand towers and a thousand years will answer,
Prostrate the doctor in silks and the prosperous dragoman's master,
God is great. Come to the prayers, to salvation.
The aisle of the temple, the roof of the sky shall answer,
Praise him, the desert and sown, almighty, compassionate God.

Devil take lambskins dried, the plague of books, you lovers.
Lust for the cup of the lips, the plump thighs waiting.
Plunder the narrow well, you young men waiting
More taut than well-cords drawing the cup of peace.

Anabasis

Like to the water-green grass is the hunger of women.
Not for the empty wind you ride, not for the stars of God, you
 riders.
Under the moon you ride for the cup at the well-spring.
Books burn a colder fire than the scald of peace.
The tongue of the stranger lacks naught in the language of darkness.
Go with God, tall strangers. Go in peace.

Depart, but not in peace. There is a woman
Whose lion loins will make a madman sooner.
Gizeh, Damascus, Antioch hunt him down,
That one of us, insatiate of riddles,
Plaguing the past of the world for a Sphinx's answer.
See him in red-roofed Antioch pursue
Beyond the iron gate the fabled hill,
Beyond the cave the lean cat-haunches waiting.
Carven in rock again the Sphinx is waiting,
Sphinx of the east, her eyes on Babylon.
The single syllable muttered once in Cairo,
The one word wrung with jests in the hills of Judah,
Single assailant word by Jordan river,
Cant phrase, priest chant, over and over,
Eyes of the woman, voice of the man give answer,
Sphinx of the east, Sphinx of the west give answer:
God is the word. God is the word.

Ride the gorse, the muddy gulf, the bridge on the torrent
The westward-ranging hills.
 See, it's a Judas tree.
Yes, that's the name.
And now the green slope westward to the sea.
The water's west.
 The blossom's paler than blood.
Syria's full of them north.
 Yes, there's another.
They call it the Judas tree.
 God damn your answer.

The boat for Cyprus in and Greece up over.
You easy-hearted fool, she's just a beggar

Coming Forth by Day

Handling you out of bakshish with her fiddles,
Plunking her one-stringed tune. Sure, God made her.
Suppose you think you bought that tune she's playing.
God made that too, old boy, and all the lice
You caught from the pipe-boy for that lizard charmer.
Come on. Last call. Boat's west from hell gone over.

TAHL : BOOK TWO

CANTO II

VOYAGE BY SEA

Symposium of Seven

TAHL:
This sea is ours, this sea, the land enclosed, the cradle of men,
But still dissociate, thirst unquenching, salt and wet,
The enemy of land and useful fire.
This flowing dark unstarlit wet and dry
Of sea and air, as when first out of chaos ocean poured
Hot suckling seed on naked oyster shells
And bred the world.

ALFRED:
A midnight watch will breed philosophers
And they breed worlds or poems so I hear
With tunes appropriate, if somewhat drunk,
And two white girls to give you all four ears.
Pretend you mewk your dinner and so scram
And have it dark with all the women too
To practise up your hastily reviewed
New Ovid, his creation of the world.

TAHL:
Drown it, Alf. You're drunk. Alf, you and George
Display less decency than makes it wise
That even these two women come on board . . .

GEORGE:
The sink of Tartarus! It's got my foot
Tighter than hell, this stinking rat tail here,
This God-damn rope.

TAHL:
What, George, no more spaghetti? Alfred here
Insults my education which beside
Those phosphorescing classic tags of yours
Is most a grunting peasant. This way here,
You bandy-legged blindman. Sure it's dark,
Darker than deserts. Darker than Tartarus, sure.
And you be Tantalus. Be miserable.

ALISON:
No Socrates to lend so much as half
A ragged coat to Alcibiades.

GEORGE:
Hark, a voice . . .

TAHL:
Your manners, George. Two women here tonight.
Alison. She goes toward Athens too.
And so we're friends. Her cousin has a name,
And if she pleases, likely she will tell you,
You hawk-faced young Apollo. Like as not
Alfred is falling off the bowsprit now.
I doubt if Elsa'll Aphrodite up
For all he looks so sickly on the waves.
Seems now he's caught a boat that's nosing home
He recollects he has a wife and child.

GEORGE:
And you've caught blues again. I hear you moan.

TAHL:
Ideas, Apollo, sought these many weeks.

GEORGE:
Well, lose them. Leave them back in Jericho.
Alison, kiss him. Excuse it, but I mean
When Tahl there gets ideas, they get him bad.
He's best when he has vine leaves in his hair . . .
And stony Aristotle when he's dry

Or lonesome. He can get you scared
Aboard a boat. He's whacky over masts
And higher up the muddy dark it is.
When human beings hang themselves on ropes,
That leaping satyr's on the masthead crowing
Or crooning that damn fiddling Traveler tune
And orchestrating on that damn guitar.

ALISON:
What was that about the oyster shells?

GEORGE:
Alison, don't you ask him questions, see.
He thinks you want to know.

ALISON:
But George, I do.
You missed it. It was — well — Vergilian.

GEORGE:
Vergilian, my God! Him, you mean Dante.
He gets the pangs of hell and no mere ghosts,
No bloody-drinking wandering shades, that hearty.
But all right, boy, let's have it. Oyster shells?

TAHL:
You couldn't get it, George. Your classic brain
Is tired and you don't read the dictionary.
Anyhow this kind of oozing damp black dark
And us afloat is like that early world
Before land was but only dark and motion,
As Alison was saying.

GEORGE:
So you started this.
And on so short acquaintance may I ask
Did you know that you are dangerous, my lady?

ALISON:
I've not been told before.

GEORGE:
I'm telling you.

TAHL:
And so am I.
Though maybe George will give
An odder definition of my peril.
But see here,
The old ones had it right, as she was saying.

GEORGE:
I've heard you say it too.

TAHL:
And so you have.
I told you Tahl and Alison were friends.
My friends are hers and you, you seem to find
Her little red-haired friend agreeable.

GEORGE:
Is that red hair that I've been chewing on?

IRIS:
Excuse the wind.

GEORGE:
So you can talk! Ideas? Like Alison?
Can you make sagas too
Of wind and ocean and the god Apollo
Abroad with Dionysus? Hermes there
Has hung himself to a bowsprit.

TAHL:
George, you're drunk.

GEORGE:
But learnèd, Tahl. I read the guidebooks too
And ponder on the universe at twelve
Of the clock the while my neck is very warm
With hair I'm told is red. Is hers red too?

TAHL:
Seems not. But rather honey . . . of Hymettos.

GEORGE:
And where'd you learn such words?

TAHL:
She told me when I half remembered it.

GEORGE:
I see she tells you much.

TAHL:
She does.

GEORGE:
What's all this talk of hell, then?
Isn't this your kind of heaven?

IRIS:
Nor rain nor snow and cloudless days rejoice.

GEORGE:
Well, red hair, who said that?

IRIS:
A man gone blind, Apollo.

GEORGE:
Homer, by my sacred arrows, red head, yes.
But here's no heaven. We're come straight from chaos,
And there's no peace nor oneness anywhere.

TAHL:
But we are like this darkness moving on,
Formless, mutable, and like the wind
Impetuous, unresting, wheeling round
The earth, becoming always, never being,
Always going, never somewhere, never home.
Just Alfred's going home.

GEORGE:
Yes, home to stick his fingers in the land
And get so fagged with rats and beetle bugs
He'll never know upon that cussed farm
Till Elsa's old and all the kids are gone
That he's a wandering man.

TAHL:
He hasn't got a home.
Christ-truth, you talk in blues.
Hot-blue-purple blues is what I've got,
I'm making moan. And I'm not going home.
Blues or no blues, because I've got no home.

GEORGE:
Stop those sneaking crazy chords you, shush.
Take it away from him, Alison. Hold his hands.
He makes that noise and calls it quarter tones.
That antique lyre he mauls he made himself.
A clever lad. Too bad he's got no home.

TAHL:
Only the sea. The sea is where I'm home.
I make a path like a boat. Now look behind.
The waves roll over and the path is gone.
All roads are undiscovered on the sea.
The white road reefs and turns, rolls under, drowns.

GEORGE:
Tahl, you're drunk.

TAHL:
That's true. Myself I taught
My brother Greeks the nurture of the vine.
I read it just today. It must be true.
Such wine will make the fools who drink more wise . . .
And that's a kind of oldish wisdom too,
Isn't it, Alfred? Hey you! Thought you'd drowned.

ALFRED:
No, I've been comforting the strayed and lost.
They call him Paddy. Kind of sailor guy,

Tanker, or some-such. Missed his boat at Haifa.
Found him below. He's coming up. A bruiser,
A breathing Hercules, and full of beer.
And Andreas — not drunk — the very guy
You chinned with down at dinner, Tahl. He runs
This horrid sieve, Piraeus bound from Crete,
And knows his stars as well as antique flowers.
He wants to spar some more on asphodels,
And pro and.con that Judas branch you brought
From Antioch. You, Alison, you know
You've got a madman with more passions strange
Than twenty Juans and Werthers. Watch him, girl.
He fancies leaves and ladies and high masts,
Philosophy and half a dozen trades,
And writes loud music in his office hours
And runs amuck prodigious in despairs.

PADDY:
I'm feeling low myself in this damn mist
And all that stinking Noah's Ark out behind.
Of all the scows I've rid since I got weaned,
I never yet was bunkmates with no cows.
Aw, quit your grinning. I don't mean no frails.
Though I don't ship them neither. Frows ashore.
Not you, excuse me, it's them other kind,
Them fishes' flippers, not the likes of you.
Him there says I should come, he says you ain't
No eyeglass dames, excuse me, so I'm here.

ANDREAS:
Good evening, ladies, and to you messieurs.
And as I said before, the asphodels. . . .

PADDY:
Them's nothing, mister, did your eyes behold
An orchid from the Amazon. I went
With lots of four-eyed guys to bring them home.
Pretty as Jesus they were, all red and gold.
We banked them wherries stem to stern with blooms.

TAHL:
And were there none at all silver, magenta?

PADDY:
No sir, mister, none at all.

TAHL:
Of all the loveliest, magenta, silver . . .

ALISON:
Yes, I know.

TAHL:
And do you wonder how
The years will bear the one, the destined seed
Borne multiple, but every seed its own
Nor orchid seedlings blossom asphodel?
What will not wonder do?

PADDY:
That's it. Lookit, mister, who knows who
The guy that thought up boats now, who was he?
Sailing like angels, beefs and sailor guys
And all us here.

TAHL:
True, Paddy, very true.

GEORGE:
Affirm it, jack priest, ring the bells at mass,
Chiming true, it's true.
And what is *isn't,* sophist. Isn't *is.*
Let's have it, Tahl. What is it? What is true?

ALFRED:
Hullo! Apollo's turned Protagoras.
We've got more Greeks than listed bunked tonight.
And dawn's not yet, perhaps not ever. So
Protagoras, expound. And what by you
Is true?

Symposium of Seven

GEORGE:
No, Alfred, no, you Socrates. Quiz Tahl.
He'd preach orations at a funeral
Tonight. He pickles truth in alcohol.

TAHL:
You gadflies.

ANDREAS:
Monsieur, regard. By torchlight here I show
A book, the flowers of heaven.

GEORGE:
And do you know
A book on heaven itself to show him, too?
He goes over the world to find one.

ALFRED:
Quit it, George.

TAHL:
No, Alfred, let him be.
He tells the truth for all we're gawky-shy
Of all that's true. Enough we measure out
Our mortal day with lies, but here's a night
That's dark enough to shrive the devil's dam
And hide her shame in — and a sea
That's deep enough for drowning — and the truth
Under the sea tied up in George's ropes,
The braided hair of gorgons. Here are seven
Devils or souls, but seven of us at least
To serve one Perseus or Odysseus well,
To slay a gorgon, set a lady free,
Or sail
After a much-beset Penelope.

ALISON:
And is truth double then to need two names,
Two wives, two heroes?

TAHL:
Sometimes, Alison,
A metaphoric accident will cut
The sea as well as any other keel
Built for an old adventure never done.
Doubles are god and the devil; truth is one . . .
And all the serpents in one hairy head
And all appropriate atoms in one sea.
Pollen in orchids hides coagulate;
Stamen and stigma make one asphodel.

GEORGE:
And spathe and spike, skunk cabbage in the spring.

TAHL:
Cynics, George, being dogs, are fond of smells.

ALFRED:
And cabbages having but one head to lose,
Shall we then cut him?

TAHL:
No, he'll wilt himself
Some fatal spring. He'll mulch and rot away
To nothing or to atoms, as to say,
To split the atom fair,
Being to end with guesses in a vacuum —
That is, in nothing.

ALFRED:
And nothing, hypostatized, is one again
Or something.

PADDY:
What do you mean, *hypostatized*?

TAHL:
He means is *isn't*, Paddy, isn't *is*.
The whole damn world's a riddle or a dream
With all things loony and yourself insane.

And one from doubles, zero. Is that plain,
Whiteness absolute, absolute silence, then
Featureless, formless whiteness like sea foam.

GEORGE:
And like white water out astern we blow
Bubble and burst.

ALISON:
At least the ship can go,
And sea-burst bubbles serve a voyage home.

GEORGE:
But being home, where is it? There you find
The house needs painting and the grass grown long,
A thousand sorrows passed and you unknown,
Nor hearth nor house nor housewife quite the same.
The world gets dizzy turning aeons round,
And you'll get dizzy watching it too long,
It turns and it won't stop. The clutch is gone.

ALFRED:
But, listen, George, there's something stays the same.
The grass is long, but cuts and comes up green;
And Elsa in a year is still my own
And not my neighbor's wife but Elsa still;
The heart, the mind, a something that's the same.

ALISON:
The sea is deep, Ulysses, needle, star
Nor bag of winds, perhaps, will get us home.

TAHL:
But Alfred, Alison, . . . he has a home,
Compact and irrefutable, a wife
Who's something like ideal Penelope
Weaving a hearth-rug, and Telemachus
Aged two, whose name is Buck, and he is real
To papa there although his teeth are in
And he can walk since he left Alfred's arms.

ALFRED:
Of course he's real and there's what's real for all
Your guessed-at vacuums and your flux of time
And planets whirling. Though the boy will change,
The grass come new, the rug wear out, the name,
The thing, the person is, rug, grass, and son.

PADDY:
Thank you, mister. Boats and women, too.
By Jesus, I had to think I'd damn well foundered
With all them five-pint words unless you'd said so.
And boats is boats and if you ship a thousand,
And so is women.

GEORGE:
Plato's come on board as twins tonight.
It seems his noble state has gone awry
If tars and farmers are his only friends.

ALFRED:
But tars and farmers have their hands to thank,
Since grass and sea-salt reek and taste and stain
For us as for Odysseus. An immortal
Call it something, call it form, remains
Ten thousand years returning — only the dream
Is change, the music maker's, puddle-painter's
Change who dabble sound in floods of time
And flowing oil, forget their bread and fish
To feed on dreams.

TAHL:
But whose dream is it, Alfred, whose the dream?
Where does it live, who named it? For your names
Are only dreams of what your hands have held
And, thought of, fade again. Where is that wheel
Wider than seas and starlight you can ride,
What mounted rocket breast the Milky Way,
Moor to a mast above the gods at home
Where all seven thousand orchids bloom as one
And seven patterns cut for asphodels

Around one sea rim? Who shall surely find
Whether the pattern's flower, narcissus, lily,
The stamens one or six, the ovum under
Or over? What will do for seven, what
For seven thousand? Where is bred
The protic grass, the paradigm of spring,
What paleozoic flora gone to rest
Your hands have never marked nor sharp eyes seen?

ALFRED:
What need to find what's found — for I have come,
Whether by love or Elsa or these dreams
Of yours, upon a cogent world
To live in. Listen, Tahl,
You taught it me yourself that night at school,
You and your Julian, priests of this perfection.

TAHL:
What Julian dead discovers I've to ask,
And what he knew alive is more than mine,
And I have still to find it. Fortune, Alf,
Is yours, you've found a world that works,
Makes sense, gives answers.

PADDY:
And don't the world make sense except you're drunk?
It looks some different in the morning, mister.

ANDREAS:
Surely the world's well made, monsieur, that gives
Life for death, the orchid, the asphodel.

TAHL:
Alison, chorus please. I need a tune
Alfred sings his round and Paddy's with him
And Andreas, as courteous captains will,
Honors this sea which drenches all the world.
He mentions land and flowers, but I know
It's sea and wind all over to the void.

GEORGE:
But, Tahl, — excuse me, Alison — it's light,
Not dark, not wet, not wind, it's light, it's fire
That's real. Hell, don't I know? We're all
Chameleons crawling the earth. It's sun we need,
Not sea. I'll watch one hill a blistered day.
What is the color of grass? I've painted waves
Under and over, mast and bowsprit, down
And up. Look from a porthole. Glass and glare
You'll never see from topside. It's the same
Wet water — but it's change. It's change we live in,
Tanning, burning, peeling, losing our hair,
Life for death, but not the captain's kind,
Just brighten, blacken, accidents of sun
That blazed this whizzing ball of ours to being
And bimeby — Pouf! he'll singe us black again.

TAHL:
Alison, what are you saying?

GEORGE:
Alison, what have you saved
From my big fire and Tahl's so dirty sea
That you have words for? Alf, he doesn't need them.
Paddy and Andreas got a ship they trust,
Red head's asleep. We're cold. And dawn's not yet.
Save us. Hell! Save Tahl. His sea will drown him.

ALISON:
What did I say? Why, hell, of course, since you do.
You've got both kinds of hell with these your fires
And waters. Whether for streams of gulping flame
Or gurgling Styx or deadblack Acheron,
The Greeks will serve you and your prophesying,
Raging of wind and fire and cracks of doom
To let the sea in.

TAHL:
Whether we're prophets or philosophers,
Either or both's not likely. We make hell
Or hells or draw or drink or scribble music.

ALFRED:
He's lying, Alison. He calls it music,
And so it is, but what he says is thunder;
And that's a prophet's business. He goes round
Like smooth-chinned Dionysus, but he's got
The beard of prophets smuggled in his coat.
He syphons music through philosophy.

ALISON:
I've heard of men who tried to drink the sea.

PADDY:
Yes, ma'am, and what you get's a case of vomit.

TAHL:
Paddy, you aren't a sailor. You're a poet.

PADDY:
Luvva Jesus, no. But I been thinking,
When some while back that friend of ours was saying
Of ships, that is. Why not? And don't it prove
We're getting somewheres? Them old bark canoes
And floating tree trunks and them handsome shells,
Them big black curving Norway boats — I seen them —
Went across the Atlantic. Jeez, and now
Sails is gone for square and schooner both,
And shame it is, white as the Mother of God,
So clean and handsome. But there's tons of steel
Riding out gales now, riding on oil. Why look,
This little one-smoke boat and then, canoes.
We ain't yelping savages no more.
We're getting somewheres.

ALISON:
To a city west of all the seas perhaps?
Or under the sea and lost since gods were young,
Fed by the rivers of hell and come upon
Unlooked for?

PADDY:
Huh? I don't know, lady, how you mean.
I mean a ship's got a course, the stars got lanes

For no collisions, and the world runs steady,
Captain'll make Piraeus, barring storms,
The sea's a road for riding, not to drown in.

ANDREAS:
You spoke, monsieur, at dinner of the tree,
The little branch you carry, how the seed
Of trees can purpose, sprout and come to bear
Ultimate twig and bloom.

TAHL:
And barring storms, yes, captain, it will bloom.
Matter will render form, the life will win
Seeded in purpose; Judas trees will bloom
Pink blossoms always, never asphodels
Yellow or gray. But what's the end of purpose
More than a spur of honeyed juice to glut
The heavy-bodied pollen-bearing bee?
Was it a seed of purpose set the tree
And were its arms grown strong for hanging Judas?
I'll make a dirge for Judas so entrapped
If trees were set before the man was born
Intent to hang him.

ALISON:
Alfred, at least, sounds out your purposes
If two philosophies will make one dirge
And Judas' fate is last to read in music.

GEORGE:
But that's no purpose either, Alison.
Play it on dice the same; to paint the tree
Is mine; to Andreas for notebooks;
Tahl, he'll make a tune for dying men
Hanged by the neck in springtime. It's the same.
So much sunshine, so much guts and glands,
Then nudes or notebooks, tunes, philosophies.

ALISON:
You take the guts and glands. I'll keep the music
Or even a picture if you've one your glands
Have just secreted.

GEORGE:
Help! A woman's tongue . . .

TAHL:
Is fine as a dagger, quick and beautiful.
It will let blood or air.

GEORGE:
Save it. I know it's air and hot to burning.
I wasn't born to bait philosophers.
I think it takes a tidbit rare in worms.
No, Alison, don't knife me. I can feel
That look cutting my throat. He knows I'm harmless.

TAHL:
At least I've never killed him.

GEORGE:
You won't. You know I'm useful. But, oh God,
I'm lots more use at keeping ladies warm
Than wrestling Plato. Will this one come to,
Will she wake up, this red head?

ALISON:
She's known to kick or scratch or bite your hand.
You'd better leave her alone.

GEORGE:
O little red tiger, red tiger my love,
I will leave you alone.
How's that for a tune?
Come on, Alf, starboard watch and ship ahoy,
Have a smoke, have a drink, better move . . .
Red tiger won't budge, Dionysus in love . . .

TAHL:
Shut up, George

GEORGE:
Shut, locked, and barred and hardly breathing.

TAHL : BOOK TWO

CANTO II

VOYAGE BY SEA

Dialogue of Tahl and Alison

TAHL:
The night grows blacker now their eyes are gone.

ALISON:
Where's Andreas?

TAHL:
The captain? He bowed out with hearing how
To hang a Judas. He has work to do.
I wish I'd a wheel that I could set my hand on,
A stinking machine to oil, a rope to haul.
This sinking nets in seas of sound gets eerie.
Nothing to hang to . . . waves, more waves . . . then drown.

ALISON:
And is it sound or silence sucks you down?

TAHL:
The sea floor's silence, but the waves are sound.
Or maybe there's no silence. Cunning sound
Strikes thousand-leagued and ricochets on stars.
Maybe it's air I'll drown in till I come
Beyond the margent dim blue atmospheres
To breath and sound's extinction, to the grave
Of Tethys, ancient mother of us all.

Dialogue of Tahl and Alison

Who says it's harps and cymbals over seas?
God's dead. There's perfect silence . . . like the fog
That chokes the North Atlantic, white and still,
Stuffing the throats of horns. A year or more,
I'll meet that fog again. I'll walk at night
Muffled in whiteness, all the water gone,
Merged in unmeasured silence. Not a sound
In fog . . . or snow, there's silence too . . . but fog
Will blur, will mute, will bury the sound of waves
That's sounded in my ears since I was born.

ALISON:
Silence is numinous, is ghost-enchanted,
Blurred in the fog or snow or piling seas
But waiting, whispered, echoed, and the floor
Of God's pavilion . . . harps, and lyres, musician . . .
And whistling reeds, flutes, eloquence of drums.
If God's alive, not dead, he fathers sound.
Sound is a ghost, a spirit, it will raise
The walls of Thebes or break a fortress down,
Shapen, will smite a devil to his knees.
This scaled and measured sound's the child of God
Eternal like his own divinity.

TAHL:
Sound is the child of God? And must he be,
Young sibyl, so immortal? Can't a mad
And savage father eat his children, eat
This sound or hide him in his thigh or serve him,
Sliced, to unsuspecting relatives?
I've heard
Old Zeus could serve such feasts. I'll make him vows.
He'll make a feast of sound and gobble him.

ALISON:
And when the bones of sound well-chewed float down
That stream you're drowning in, you'll strain your arms
To scoop them, save them, nurse them into flesh
For very love.

TAHL:
Is it your sibyl's wisdom that contrives
Such hardy answers to my mystery?
Well, let him live, then. Let's not drown. Let's live.
Let's let this sound have his eternities.
A god, at least, and not a book of rules
On metaphysics in the minor scales
Where no acoustics answer. Grant him godly
Cousins. But see here. I'm out of depth.
If I can't drown tonight, best make for land,
Escape the doldrums and the mystic calms.
I'll prick my ears for tone and time and tune
And only milder brands of ecstasy —
Entelechy and accident, large words,
I will disown them, charter in the trades,
Founder the golden galleon, take a ship
Small as my hands can swing in — find accords,
Write pretty tunes with polished sequences,
Build me a ship for only inland seas.
I'll plant a tree won't grow too far toward heaven.
I'll fix a formula to calculate
Sound's ratio within a six foot grave.
Take what's in my ears for real, believe.
Take the "as if" for real, eat it, a fowl
To feed you. Leave the sterile eggs of reason
In logic's tepid gravy. Or to say
I am a chemist. I've no mercury
Or not enough to render solid gold
From brine though I've a spitting-salty sea.
I'll be astronomer — I'll number years,
Yet will not catch those gone since Sicily
Went dry-shod over Scylla from Charybdis
Nor when Euboean mountains overtopped
A Greece unislanded, unshattered land.
I'm a musician. I shall name my friends.
George, now: a jig, a dirge, Crusader's hymn;
The three together make the oddest catch
That ever was both fine and ludicrous.
Alfred's a tune played cleanly on a flute,

Graceful and grave and fit for pastorals.
But what am I?

ALISON:
I think you're like a fugue. You run and run,
Chasing yourself to fetch up harmonies
And all your modulations, every key
Will come out sure at last, disclose the plan —
The hunt well ended and the quarry won.
I think that you and George and Alfred too
Are all musicians as your names pretend:
Apollo, Hermes, Dionysus, these —
These are the three musicians of this world . . .
The eloquent, the graceful, and the mad
Bacchus, master of orgies, mortal myth,
Breeder of life, hierophant of graves.

TAHL:
That they are good musicians, that's the truth,
Though one cuts paint, the other pumpkin vines,
But are my somber titles all deserved?
You read the fates, not I.
Though there's some neatness in the metaphor,
Even if reeds, young Bacchus'attribute,
Are not my forte so much as Hermes' lyre
Or what's more ancient, old Poseidon's horn.

ALISON:
But you've forsworn the gods, will have no names
But time and tune and tone and formulas
And nothing godly for your life belt. Can
You swim now in your sea? What's music when
The god is gone?

TAHL:
What is the music? These commensurable
Sensations, jungle drums, renascent time,
A trinity of matter, motion, law.
It is a dance, a leaping blood, a stark
And elemental horror pedaled bass,

A shrieking, heaving, unappeasant horn,
An exaltation, an obscenity of
Indelicate tubas snotting at the strings.
It is the step-child of Pythagoras,
Brother of physics and astronomy,
A baby's pastime counting one, two, three,
Thomas Hobbes and Euclid, Plato proved
When good is three-four-seven, chart and sum,
A monochord, a string stretched on a frame,
A leitmotif, elusive overtone,
A scientific partial, oboe, horn.
An elegant trick, a Byrd or Ferrabosco
Playing a plain song forty ways to show
How intricate and skillful *miserere*
Contrives in agile brains to praise themselves
Who ask no mercy being so contriving;
A barmaid's tune would do the Church as well.
Yet is not all of music. Why it is
The music men have made, the nameless songs
Will live to feed a Beethoven, a Brahms?
What in the memory, ear, and centered mind
Needs steadiness and sanity, resolves,
Rejects the scale that grants no anchor tone
To hold the tune in harbor, nor no star
To calculate the course by, must assail
The gods to bring each lost Odysseus home.

ALISON:
This is wonder, fiddler. This is not
Your bandstand tune. This scents philosophy.
This is that fine Platonic music makes
Beauty, consonance, goodness, ripened nature,
Harmony, rhythm, precepts to the soul;
This is a wisdom fled from ignorance,
A universal voyage, a request
Of underworlds and overworlds, of seers
Wise as Tiresias from harp-born Thebes,
A Socrates by plane trees of Illisus,
The seven wise men by the wine dark sea.
You dive on ultimates like pearls or pennies.

Dialogue of Tahl and Alison

TAHL:
And so I do — and cannot stuff my ears
Or put on helmets, but go naked down.
Alfred is right, I gulp philosophy
Morning and evening, graze me on abstractions,
Truth and reason double-jawed to catch me,
And weight of water squeezing breath and blood
After a something never here nor there;
A tempered clavichord all keys adjusted,
Is that what I want? A germ for perfect trees,
A teleologic mathematic cycle,
A pulse to calculate, a tractable breed?
Or is it I'll elucidate the wave
I dive in? I'll augment, diminish waves.
I'll make a pond and in the midst a tree
Safe from a hurricane distortion, saved
From discord, incoherence. I will make
Unargued, sure, sonorous lines. I'll save
The universal harmony. I'll hold
Sound to itself transcending sound. I'll make
Cohesion of a hundred men. I'll find
Some soft viola, second violin,
Subdue my brass, make less ecstatic strings.
I'll make a theme that's stated, rendered, proved
Cohesive, cool, not passionless — but clear.
What if I write for men? Thev cannot sing,
Nor men nor women, their three octaves more.
The roundest human breath is strangled cries.
And what's a heaped-up orchestra but more
Of yelling, crying, talking, saying: Here!
Listen, we speak. We listen. Answer. Here!
This is the truth: What truth? This? There? Or here?

ALISON:
And will it answer, madman?

TAHL:
Answer? I'm a fool,
But not so mad to bruise me on ideals.
No men at whistling, tooting, sawing strings

Will give you ultimates, realities.
I said I'd live as if the world were real.
I will. I see how much, what kind, the near
The far, the where, the when, the sound, the silence,
So many violins and drums and horns
And subtle shift crescendo strings to wind
And sudden hollowed oval chasm dug
In silence out of sound. And this is real,
The sound. It fights: it will not; but we will.
Our minds shall drive it; we will demonstrate
Ellipsis bridged. We'll cage reality
That Aristotle stole from Plato's sky
And brought it back to earth where it belongs.
His father was a doctor. He was wise,
That Stagirite, in medicine of herbs.
Yet he'll not heal me staggering at night
Battered and cut from searching ugly seas
To find the drive, the will, the energy
Will shape out sound; he will not teach the mad
To look with still eyes on the heart of God.

ALISON:
If Byrd and Ferrabosco only asked
In forty variations, you have made
Four hundred *misereres* to this God.
Will he at last have pity?

TAHL:
I cannot know and do not know. But you,
Your eyes are clear. I see them now.
Dawn's coming soon; your eyes are clear to see
This madman bellowing mercy. Does he live,
The God who'll give him mercy? What's alive?
This broken twig I carry — once it shone
Glossy with juice; it's crusty, withered now.
All I have seen is mutable; a Judas
Was in his time an eloquent disciple.
And yet I take the common chord of C
That I can orchestrate a thousand ways
And that same chord retains its thousand forms

And can be found. I tell you that I drown.
But that's all melodrama. I can swim.
Whenever I remember that the sea
Has edges, beaches, shores, and then that tree,
I make a yielding edge against unknowns.

ALISON:
The beard of prophets flutters from your vest.

TAHL:
That beard of prophets' been well aired tonight
And waves its banner in the coming dawn.
Nobilities impinge on petty hours.
I heard one afternoon an organ played.
The church was closed. I sat outside. I heard
The Hallelujah — Handel's — and I heard
The Kyrie — yes, Bach — that mass would stop
The sea from rocking, bring a traveler home.
A majesty, an oratorio,
A mass. There's something said, a certainty.
I have believed
God might create an oleander tree,
Adapt a yellow reed to rocky walls
Or rear a purple-bodied green-necked dove
As gaudy as a Persian tapestry.
And wing dips cut the air convex, concave.
But holy dove descend and cup behold,
Convex, concave, cut trees for crosses, rend
The flowers for carpets soft on Christus' way,
Hail the Messiah, Lord, Hosanna. No,
I cannot whip my instruments to lies
Nor can I reason it. A prophet so,
And no philosopher; and if I come
By mercy, as you say, or fate or chance
On what is good and beautiful, serene,
I think there'll be no blueprint and no inky
Course surveyed, but just a blind man swimming
After a sound he's heard until he finds it
Or slides up near enough until he's learned it.
Then he shall make

A mass in honor of the sound, a feast
Of music.

ALISON:
Such beauty lives to haunt imperfect worlds.

TAHL:
Beauty's a name I've shunned. She is a whore,
I say, to make me braver. And I say
God is a name I've shunned. I say he's dead.
But, so you are a sibyl, I will tell you
That there are furies, winds upon my sea
Restless, avenging, wrathful, drive me on,
Necessity which is the name for night
Will blow them on me out of Tartarus
To somewhere that's called beautiful or God.

ALISON:
I'll wave a flaming thyrsus on the shore,
Calling you, Dionysus, from the sea,
Dionysus were-wolf, winter-born
Devourer, master of worlds, the wanderer.
India, China, Egypt, Greece, you've sown
With blood-ripe grape. Your sea's a sea of wine,
Deva Nahusha, Bacchus, and Osiris,
You tree of names, you water fresh and salt
To succor or to poison; Dionysus,
You who have made so many women mad,
Look at the sea for it can bear your eyes.

TAHL:
I'll look at the sea. The water'll wash out dreams.
My grandfather the sea, Poseidon, rides
His horses against the sunrise. What has come
Upon us?

ALISON:
Not drunkenness nor lust nor weariness,
This lightness.

Dialogue of Tahl and Alison

TAHL:
This lightness. If we rose into the air?

ALISON:
There's something far
Too strange about this morning.

TAHL:
I could hear, almost, that sound I'm wanting.
I see your face quite clearly now. Your eyes . . .

ALISON:
Cool them on mine or else you'll burn you blind.
Sunlight would be more cool than what I've seen.
Look at the sea.

IRIS:
Alison, look at the sun.

TAHL:
Awake at last?

IRIS:
Awake and seeing sunrise. Look, a fire!

GEORGE:
Coming. I'll find a fire. I like a fire.
I like a sun. Hey, Alfred, sunrise, you.
Explosion in vermilion. Here it comes.

ALFRED:
More sudden than a cockcrow. How it burns.

IRIS:
It runs like blood on water.

GEORGE:
Tigress, no. It runs like wine.

ALISON:
Like fire it runs — and all the oceans burn.

TAHL : BOOK TWO

CANTO III

VOYAGE BY FIRE

Acropolis

And sunrise past, a day till that sun's setting,
From sea to land, though sea on two horizons,
Up from Piraeus, smoke-held, triple-harbored,
The five gods stranger-faced with native names
Came to the sacred hill.
The citadel of gods, a stone enchantment
Mellowed in mildest sundown toward us swung
A myth made tangible.
Dark elder silence awes young yelping sound
When night comes in on Athens, violet-crowned.

So leave the sun. The offspring of the moon,
Young Dionysus, son of Semele,
With entourage chance-summoned now commend
Each swelling curve of stair.
A half-believing jest of mummery
These five blithe aliens wear,
Hermes, Apollo, friends of Dionysus,
With red-haired Iris and Persephone.
His mother moon up eastward from Aegean
Sets sandaled light to welcome his ascension.

Here on this sacred hill, Athena's mountain,
Precipitous home of owls, the olive tree
Long dead that was its honor, home of Nika,

Acropolis

How shall we dedicate this victory?
Where has triumph flown?
Who raised this fallen stone?
What grave this great hill marks to bring us solemn
To cry out suddenly, "I see Salamis!"
And sea fall eastward strain as to descry
Fantastic moonlight on lost walls of Troy.

This is the grave of man. To west and southward
We saw the grave of God, but man lies here
Where gods were men triumphant, bold, austere,
Or more than manly maddened, but as men
Hellenic tribute had
For fighting, loving, ruling, holding council
To humble human pride.
And now all's fallen. Shall we once again
Reset the drums of wisdom, hoist upon
Lost chastity a new-raised Parthenon?

What is the house of man? Achilles' shield
Immortal measures his mortality —
Who fell himself, beside a town besieged —
As heroes must their arrows breast or heel.
The god of fire annealed
The glassy blue of ocean circled full
On towns at peace, at war, the earth-black field,
The grapes their yield,
On quarrels, judgments; moon and sun's bright ball,
Though central, set against us rather small.

This is the house of man; blood's sacrifice,
Antigone, the wrath of brothers slain;
The phantom host of furies circling down
Upon Orestes, Agamemnon's son.
How read such auguries?
Untrammeled violence, man's heritage.
Why guard the golden masks of tyrants dead?
What crumpled portents these?
The blood-wet legends salvaged countless years
From fortressed hilltops scaled by buccaneers.

Voyage by Fire

Look southward through the dark. Bold mountains rise
Black over harbor lights and down beyond
There lies Mycenae, Tiryns ringed in bronze.
They swaddled kings there soft in whitest wool,
The long-haired princes, golden-helmeted.
Look north and west. Those heads
Of hurtling hills hide all the sins of Thebes.
Here suckling earth has bred
All wanton glories, reared her restless hordes.
Now wheel ruts only, chariots of dead lords.

Here on Athena's mountain who shall say
The race of man's foul ghosts? Their mortal wings
Have overflown their tyrants. We have found
No castle cherished as this temple's crown.
Their tall Athena here
Carried the head of gorgons. Must she wear
Also the shield and spear?
For what defense? No owl nor serpent serve?
No aegis guard, no victory atone
Man's folly, turn his Nemesis to stone?

Speak of this war. Not gods' nor Titans' shout.
What fathers, brothers with long swords assailed,
What Golden Fleece the Argonauts have won
Beyond the clashing rocks by magic spells,
By trick and ruse, the lie, this shrewder shield.
The wind-wracked ruin of Cyclopean walls,
The rust-brown fallen pillar moonlit clean,
Old ash of fir and cypress guard our own.
Who long adventures dies
To win what dragon's prize?
Who were not frogs nor mice to battle gone.

Now comes the choric thought to its full turn,
The circuit of the marbled memory
Wakes at the rattle of an iron key.
Unready dreamers on the stumps of pain
Take short proportion of eternal passion
Charneled from the gossip of lost time.

TAHL: BOOK TWO

CANTO III

VOYAGE BY FIRE

Hotel Aesculapius

Go down. Go down.
Exaltation such as single heart
Can seize on sags. A company invades
Its contemplation. Joke the crone
With her impatient keys and tease the beldam
Of stony virgins holding up the moon.
Pygmalions to rape the moon's illusion
Depart with their two women. Crack the trance
Of holy wonder, cock keen eyes upon
The engineering of the stairs, the mind's delusion,
And sight beyond the slums old Theseus' tomb.

Go down. Go down. The moon is setting
Over the mountains. Let us be hungry and thirsty
To pass our idle time. The idle men,
The amiable and unobliging women
Sit down to heavy coffee, to sweet wine.

In this cafe beneath the midnight trees
Where all the well-brushed world foregathers we
Find him waiting, then to now transported
By time we have avoided. Push our chairs.
Say what's commonplace. We are surprised
To see you here. Indeed we are.
Doctor "Socrates," you used to smile

Voyage by Fire

Under your flattened nose at boys impaled
On conjugations, boys in rows. Suppose
You've come to chew the beeswax of Hymettus,
To reconstruct a town, to find a kylix,
To excavate the shards of the pluperfect?

Let us be witty over omelettes,
Let us be clever over new-plucked almonds,
Let us mock Alfred running to his master,
Good humpbacked owl, and listening jowl to jowl,
Grave young Hermes learning Father's orders
For the Olympian day. What does the Doctor say,
With his deprecating smile? There'll be a war?
Is that the news? And what's the fighting for?

Frenchmen talk to Irishmen in corners;
Ouzo lingers on the German palate;
The Hungarian is growing ill on cabbage;
The Portuguese drinks liqueur *abricot;*
The girl from Ravenna is raving over the olive
Groves of Colonus; the Londoner is saying
That boys with brushes and boxes
Accost one for a shoeshine on the street.
Alabaster and pearl, silver and shadow,
New-leaved willow, blossoming thorn,
Thyme for a salad, motorbusses grinding.
The express howls on, Salonika, Vienna, Paris.
The plaza shakes with reliable underground trains.
The five Americans consult a doctor
In this café, the precinct Aesculapius.
In the children's ward
Eating small preserve with small spoons,
We contemplate the stars above the willows
And ask if war is coming soon.

If not to this white city with long walls,
City of brilliant exiles, of all cities
Inland from pirates, if not here,
Then where, for money and for need of air,
The need to build a stronger wall than spears,

For guns that sneer bareheaded citizens
In tunics, gold cicadas in the hair?
Breeding mother of demagogue and tyrant,
Son of the shell of ostracism, find
Her new fecundity, now prove, invade
A cause than Romish Goth more renegade.

Go down. Go down. When royal Spartans speak,
Will Socrates be more laconic who
Consults his demon in the rising sun
Until the sun's gone down? Go down.
The world like Oedipus has skidded off
The precipice of pompous mind.
What do the papers say? Consult the market.
This oracle, this scholar turned a statesman,
Will drink his honorable hemlock of ambition.

Drain the glasses. Kyrie! He comes
Wiping his forehead in the lush air
Of a spring evening. Speak, Doctor:

"It's down the doom of ages coming on
Since first he rose, six feet against the cave,
For rumors of the northern men come down,
The gruff and guttural voices through the trees.
With filth and sacrilege against his walls
To bury him and bones of all his sons
Against his hearth and altar. Heard them come,
Later, the last Minoan in his room . . .
The northward voices growling on the stair,
The stately bull last hunted caverns down,
The blue and red enamel in the ash
Of pirate fire, assault of angry men.
And after Crete, great Priam where the prey
Of harassed Greece, Achaea's tribe, they come,
The bright-haired giants at the gates of Troy . . .
The northern seed is breeding. Where you saw
The eagle of the legions by the Rhine . . .
The death is coming, not by Caesar slain.
The long boats coming and the horde by land . . .
Open the mountain passes. They will come.

These gods will have no twilight. See them ride
Black over Europe. In the seed of time
Recover still the older gods of men.
Listen. The sharpened stone, the sword and spear,
Saber and gun split shock on fouler war.
The minutes of earth are shorter by the stars
And cold breeds evil. Guttural in the night
The battle shout out of the north once more."

How many quires of amber-colored goblets,
How many spikes of anise on the tongue?
To squint-eyed dames how many hushed appointments
With Doctor "Socrates" whose ribs endure
The elbows of diplomacy, uniforms
Of other cut among the starched *evzones.*
You hear the priming of imported planes.
Fustanellas swing and bootblacks whack their brushes
To military tunes. The world turns
To a cypress moan. The tears of the world are running
In the bed of the beautiful river Eridanus
Which is now the city drain. The wise men
On the hill of old men say: "They come."
Man is the measure. What is his measure?
His ashes neatly fill a half-pint tomb.
Ashes need less room. There peril lies,
That men and states reveal analogies.

TAHL:
Now gentlemen are soldiers once again
And small men can grow great with stolen bombs.
The clock says three a.m. I say the time
Was clocked when Plato went abroad for laws
And made a myth of states with lungs and hair
As if they lived and could be friends of ours.
That ghostly state still stalking on the Danube,
That skeleton still prowling on the Rhine,
That marvelous structural robot as fallacious
As ever turned the ivory gates of dream,
The terrible state, the false two-footed word
Like well-set columns with which we delude

The dream of the straight line; the justice which
Wrapped in the garment, wearing the long sword
Of hoplites wrecks all realms below the moon,
Tumultuous realms too ready to abhor
All metaphysical perfection, sure
In mass arrayed, the military power
Of arms distributed to citizens,
Not for life; for profit, tax and trade.
The prince-philosopher of ivory dream
Died on the page that praised his lovely face,
A portrait of illusion's resurrection
As Theseus' bones in their Pentelic glory
Survived the middle age because the Mass
And Christian company secured his corpse.

DOCTOR:
The mensurate recurs, the measured man
Recapitulates reality.
Barbarians, learned in the antique tongues,
Take airplane pictures with a cloudy screen
And raise salutes upon their false conclusions.

GEORGE:
Syracuse, sweet pride of Sicily,
By Plato's skill reduced to bankruptcy.

ALISON:
The props of the cave forever in the rains
Of heaven assaulted lurch and tumble in.

IRIS:
How could we think we might escape the hutch
And live immune on vitamins and sun?

GEORGE:
How shall shadows ever show us truth
Out of shadows leaning aeons long?

TAHL:
The lying unity of tribe and state
Which out of unity makes unison;
Harmony lost in the tyrannic one.

ALFRED:
Can we not new appraise our platitudes
Or find a Daedalus once more to read
The map of any labyrinth he made?
Plato, the man of common sense, descried
Death out of life, life out of death delivered,
The pregnance of the great contrarities,
His conscience, conscious and political,
Saw the little in large, the great in small,
The substance allegorical,
The parent of the beautiful.

ALISON:
The sky is wide and missiles fall as deep
Dropped from that height to bury us who hide
In the dry drain. Who is the plow and who
The plowman in the day of Jason's pride?

ALFRED:
The cultivated plant is known to show
Great vigor and yet seldom give a seed.
Freed animals upon their native soil
Reveal no law why they are slow to breed.
Why peach tree buds will burst to nectarine
Or rose to moss rose raise a variation
After a thousand buddings; shall we see
More simple the budding of nations, the cleared screen
Of our intent, to know what we defend?

TAHL:
Our lost Acropolis a second time
With wooden barricades.

GEORGE:
There is no fathom mark nor level line
Can trace our future in the past.
We shall not brag
To the disillusioned engineer
Of the straight column, the level stair.
The world returns and turns upon itself,

But we cannot be sure
How far we are from there to here.

ANDREAS:
Messieurs, mesdames!
Monsieur le docteur! We have met before.

GEORGE:
The doctor's ribs will ache for many weeks.
His hands will tremble with his hearty greetings.
But come, captain. Come sit down, for we
Discuss the fate of Athens.

IRIS:
I note the year

ALISON:
When the willows bloomed and the thorn blossomed.

ALFRED:
From the independence of America
One hundred and sixty.

DOCTOR:
From the fall of the Roman empire
Fourteen hundred and sixty
According to customary calculation.

GEORGE:
Too many to count from the date of original sin.

THANASIE:
From the Greek revolution
One hundred and fifteen

ALL:
Strike the glasses all from base to rim
To the Frenchman and the Irishman,
The German and Hungarian,
The Ravennese and the Portuguese
And the gentleman from London.

ANDREAS:
This is my godson, Thanasie,
Lieutenant to his Majesty's forces.
He will call with a car at seven
For Monsieur Tahl.

THANASIE:
I am an airplane pilot by profession.
Planes are prohibitive during the present tension.

IRIS:
Who recounts the history of Athens?

ANDREAS:
Not gauge of height, not breadth of city walls
Reads the proportion of a city's honor.
The Parthenon does not obstruct the sky.
Grant us all such grace of the just measure.
And grant to my oration such design
As the pebble of Demosthenes could treasure.
Solon first commend whose wisdom gathered
Farmer and merchant, carpenter, cobbler, trader
To court of commons with our princes here.

DOCTOR:
With the sausage seller, his defect of breed
Unfortunate, that such a wretch could read.

ANDREAS:
Peisistratus next whose slaves new-rendered Homer.
Athens to Homer, Homer of Athens bore
Beyond the pillar of Corinthian coast
Polis pre-eminent and praises far
As our colonial clemency uncurst
While Cleisthenes' shrewd banishments had care.
Recall Salamis after Marathon,
The skillful sailorwise Themistocles
Serene against the blandishments of Xerxes.
The empire eminence of Pericles;
Praise the model of ages, sacred whole

To none allegiance and to all allied,
The demos dwelling by the holy hill,
To every infant nation realized
Adulthood, duty's grace in man deserved
To serve our state whose glory we desired.
The world subsists for Reason rules the world;
The state, not man, achieves the perfect form,
The noble state the function of its man,
Not company but compact unison,
Not to himself but to the state belongs.
Philosophy, the temple and the town,
Poem, pageantry and least amphora
Not skill alone but reason has designed.

TAHL:
Creep to the womb of state; Jocasta hanged.

THANASIE:
I interrupt. The bold Homeric hand
Holds Athens, Hellas. Sooner shone and longer
The Peloponnesian glory
South and beyond that same established pillar
Of prosperous Corinth, earlier, later story.
Argos and Agamemnon's hundred ships
More mighty than ox-measure of Mycenae,
Further than acres' breadth the sea-flung power.

ANDREAS:
I quote, the observation of our most
Distinguished statesman, Pericles
Renowned: That courage Athens never lacked
But needed never scant her festivals
With marching Spartan multiple rehearsals
For the tentative moments of battle ecstasies.

DOCTOR:
Quibble, quarrel, trick, no truce forever.
Athenians nor Spartans would have peace
Either between themselves nor with another.
The Spartan doted on stupidity.
Athenians paid fraud to keep them free.

IRIS:
The alma mater of democracy,
The proper industrial society.

GEORGE:
Hark the Lacedemonian helots cry.
The ruthless logic of sobriety.

ALFRED:
The act of the past is past. Like children we
Suck dew from grass nor care to ask what god
Or gardener granted morning liberty.

GEORGE:
As simply suck up poison in our broth
From fouled kettles soiled by the cook's breath.

TAHL:
The clear drop fallen on the tainted vines
Will beverage poison from the gnawed weed.
Such temperance the sophists' fee defines,
Mutates, confounds, defiles the first-found word.

ANDREAS:
The happy sons of old Erectheus' line
Lived nobly. Who would stain this lucid air?
By Zeus' command did Hermes render men
Justice and reverence and ours to bear
The fault if we disdain the paradigm.

GEORGE:
And fallen generals alone opine
Whether the Spartan treasons were less fair.
The world's on chances toward a racetrack doom.
The law is stake but in the running time
Pays small exchange in the hand of the dead man's heir.
I quote the speeches of ambassadors,
The twist-truth models of diplomacy
Whose heirs we are. Thus says Thucydides:
Athens growing great, proportionate
Alarm increased among Athenian neighbors.

Lacedemon sought hostilities,
Battles at sea, a Macedonian skirmish.
Complaint alleged, the present enmities,
Corinth versus Corcyra, over the matter
Of the quite unimportant affair of Epidamnus.
Megara by the democrats betrayed
From oligarchs received a second jailor.
Alas, alas, Megara, Megara.
The tyrant ever professes his love
For his country's honor.

ANDREAS:
Not vicious man but law's divinity,
The proper subject of philosophy.
Zeus the just made Athens priceless prize,
Justice, the law, the visible form of heaven.
The happy, just in justice, this
The god's gift to our good fathers given,
Glorious goal in statehood's great assize.

THANASIE:
The great Olympic of our history.

DOCTOR:
Through cyclic demagoguery
Libertine blackguards trample dust
In the eyes of the mob set free;
Degenerate democracy
Finds Aristides much too just;
And Phidias with too much skill;
Socrates superfluous
In his insistent honesty.
On men and states the moralist,
Idealist, and realist
Compose a single tune,
Ineffable of harmony,
Resolute, absolute one.

IRIS:
Out of the gentry, out of the commons
Always arrives the single dominion.

GEORGE:
Parties are of nature treacherous.
The intellect plays poker with the state.
Poker chips would be less dangerous.
The misanthrope is an aristocrat.
No cast of dice will ever cancel that.
His propaganda is a cynicism,
End of all idealism.
The bolshevik, no less, each age despising
The mob upon whose shoulders he is rising.
From Myron to great Phidias' Parthenon
To indolent Praxiteles the span
Revolves, shudders, returns
From the heroic to the simply human.

TAHL:
Five a.m. in Athens. I see the waiters stir.
Music upon the violins, dawn in the eastern air.

THANASIE:
Dancers now prepare
A circle in the square.
Their music very old.
Handkerchiefs unfold.
The leader swings in the brightening air.
Heel and toe in triple time,
Circle, circle, turn and twine.
The dance is very old.

ALISON:
Phaeton whirls in the sun's car.
All the world is set on fire.

ALL:
The Frenchman and the Irishman
Find the five-tone scale is charming;
The German and Hungarian
Declare its dignity disarming;
The Ravennese and the Portuguese
Find solemnity distressing;

Hotel Aesculapius

The gentleman from London has retired.
Applaud in the brightening air.
Stars fade. Willows shine.
Stately measure, alien tune.
Dancers sing in unison.

ALISON:
The heart weeps for lost and ancient grace.
A holy rhythm every wall assails.

GEORGE:
The express to Salonika, Vienna, Paris
Syncopates upon the western rails.

TAHL:
The five-tone scale rebels against its own
Tyranny of tone.
Unison strings remembering
The future they disown.
Only by falsehood we return
Upon the native town.
Restless heart and ears assume
A wider range of sound.

ALISON:
The time of wakening birds. In this strange sky
Like hard-blue detonation, prescient hawks
Ascend the quartering wind.
The goldfinch hovers in the plaza fountain,
Rooftree swallows murmur, doves venture
After our least crumb. The pigeons choosing
Hawks for kings make dinner of their kingdoms.

TAHL:
Voices of birds have range above this music,
This pallid clowning of a village dawn
In city squares.
And we the gapers practising on cowbones
Yearn with nostalgia for the holy syrinx
Blown on Helicon.

ANDREAS:
Before the season of new wine

TAHL:
The new spring. The winter cask
Sours for the old wine to be drawn.

ANDREAS:
You are a very young man.

TAHL:
A judgment, captain, or an observation?

DOCTOR:
A truce to metaphor and myth. The watch
Of night nests birds upon our brains, nets
For finches. We have other business, captain.

GEORGE:
May you breakfast with more useful company.

ALFRED:
Gently, gently, George. Gently.

ALISON:
What virus here infects the gentle air?
Perhaps this Athens for such pox of reason
Quarreled with Corinth, badgered Lacedemon.

GEORGE:
Lack of sleep, no surfeit of the air.
My bonny head gone wandering on a star.

PADDY (from a distance):
The hotel Aesculapius! You'd think
You was the sacred, orthodox church, by Christ.
Barring my clothes, I'm as white a man as you are
And washed my face a lot more recent, waiter.

GEORGE:
Our lovely brute, good morning! Friend, come closer.

Hotel Aesculapius

PADDY:
Boy, I ain't got nerve to sit down here.
See you later, Tavern of Young Bacchus
Down the Piraeus, busses every hour.

GEORGE:
Don't be so vain, sweet Hercules. That shirt
Sails well in a breeze.

PADDY:
The Biarritz, that's me — and the Hotel Astor.
I ought to on the northern tack, not here.
North where hens pick pantlegs and the sows
Without no wings collect the family garbage
The other side of that handsome Acropolis there.
After you seen your marble and gold museums,
You better go see this moldy Athens ain't
No goddess country. They got districts here
Without no Hebes hired to sweep their floors.

THANASIE:
Tribeless, lawless, heartless one who foul
With your pig mouth our country's courtesies.
Observe how stupid pride and swagger seize
The man by freedom set from out his station.
We lack the ancient style of education
Which graced Thermopylae and Marathon.
Master and slave made mutual distinction,
Nor chattered all like sparrows in a midden.

PADDY:
Who blacked your eyes, kid? Don't screw up your mug.
There's sun enough without your glaring eyes.
And fight enough in the world without your quarrels.
We guys got passports grabbed from the same barrels.
Don't have to turn our overcoats for labels.

THANASIE:
I am an officer to His Majesty.

PADDY:
And I got papers signed for the Lord God's sea
To grease machines on anybody's barges.

THANASIE:
Entitled to salutes from common soldiers.

PADDY:
Easy does it. You're welcome to your salutes
So long as I ain't required to lick your boots.

THANASIE:
I will return at seven, Monsieur Tahl.
My car is yours to judge the roads of Hellas.
We shall discuss
The Peloponnesus.

PADDY:
A trip through his important head, that's what.
Juno's peacock couldn't match that strut.

IRIS:
The fault of his education?

ALFRED:
But no indictment of his nation,
Though holy justice, once the gift of Zeus
To us, the hoofless and unhorny tribes
Who earned the pity of the famous Titan,
Seems somewhat scanty in his disposition.

PADDY:
Justice ain't no lack of education.
I think fat brains got less of it than most.
They waste their time with laws and regulations
To keep our paws from off them leather coats.
The more they got of starchy tablecloths,
The less they like all other guys to use 'em.
Them oriental rugs they'd sell to moths
Before they'd have us hobnailed guys to visit —

Which don't mean I ain't leaving here this minute
And ain't the same as saying if I was
Dolled up like you I wouldn't gladly damn 'em
And fight like hell to sit here at my ease
And put my paws wherever I damn please.

GEORGE:
Aristocrat is democrat is Greek.

PADDY:
Listen, son, that's fighting, what you speak.
There's fighting in the wind and there'll be more
Before you're five years wiser. Pull your oar in.
Don't be asking who's a Greek.
Don't ask a German who his uncle's wife was.
Don't ask a Frenchman what is sauerkraut.
Don't ask Italians who just bilked their boss.
Don't ask. Chew marlinspikes or shut your mouth.
See them museums, take your little drive.
I'll see you later. Take the busses south.
I'll feed you octopus and lion's gut.

IRIS:
The waiters offer us commiserations.

GEORGE:
Upon whose education? Who determines
The collar and tie that tables a man's measure?
A demi-tasse, a postulate in ermines
Finds backyard company in other pleasure
Not commensurate with clothes it wears.

IRIS:
Cardboard mountains on so blue a sky
Invite us to a balcony. The smoke
Of cigarettes drifts with a curious pallor
In this halcyon air.

GEORGE:
Factories also smoke in the halcyon air,
Breweries, pottery kilns and chemical works.

Business is busy with cotton, busy with beer,
Marble and leather, carpets and capital cognacs
And prosperous tanneries here.
Piraeus, I quote, is a model of city design.
Octopus spearing, a picturesque scene.

ALISON:
Conventional mind can never long contain
Athena's vermilion goatskin stripped of hair;
Dotes upon wharves where solemn black-prowed ships
Unload their purples from long-fallen Tyre
And board the golden oil in perfect jars.
Does not remember, does not care
For citizens'corporations, surplus store
Financing Salamis with the silver owl
Of Laurion where myriad coffined shafts
Bound silver slaves whose lamps with scanty oil
Burned the scantier air and who died there
For the greater aggrandizement of Pericles.
The present yield is lead, unlovely ore.

GEORGE:
Dear Tahl, for Diotima, if you please
Expound the truth of ancient treacheries.

TAHL:
Eat your cigarette. It will illumine
Your wit, perhaps, or clear your brain of vermin.

GEORGE:
What demons prance in this too placid air?

IRIS:
Upon a balcony we lounge and smoke
And consider the glittering distance very fair.
But what of relevance detains us here
Deluded like the eyeless eidolons
Imported from a world that was not there?

Hotel Aesculapius

ALISON:
Entrain, embark, pack deep the tinted glass
Guarding our painful eyes from this bald sun.

ALFRED:
Roots of ours will never fix upon
This sulphurous rock.

GEORGE:
Nor strike the heroes' pass beyond those mountains.

TAHL:
We, the distracted tumbleweed, are blown
In orient autumn. Together we roll down
The unreal plain of the past, anachronism
In the new spring.

ALFRED:
Tomorrow we turn home. We have been gone

GEORGE:
Too long from the Gothic arch, the further forest

TAHL:
Beyond the Gothic nave, grandfather's barn

ALISON:
To what cottage? To what duty to which dream,
This night shall determine and tomorrow's morning.

GEORGE:
Write this prophecy on leaves of the forest.

TAHL:
The sure future shall be our ferret.

IRIS:
Plausible ferret. For which rabbit?

ALISON:
We shall not yet yield up humanity
Nor fit our flesh to the skin of the fleeing hare.

TAHL:
Our immediate plans, our brief detention
Is not the circumvention of our past.
At six we join you, fit for Paddy's tavern.
We shall set our watches fast.

TAHL : BOOK TWO

CANTO III

VOYAGE BY FIRE

Tavern of Young Bacchus

ALFRED:
Welcome to seven gallons resinata
And equal rye to cool your travelers' throats.
I'm told the Greeks returning home from Troy
Fired all Hellas, blazing with revolt.
Tell me, did you walk on dying embers?

TAHL:
Achaia lives. I drink to all their wars,
The weathered shepherd on Taygetus' slope,
The seamen shipping for the eastern isles,
The crones who tend the railroads, their stout arms
Minding the crossing chains, to all the farmers
Tending the young corn. I will not drink
To Lieutenant Thanasie. To all else, drink out. A health!

ALISON:
Thanasie, the toy Achilles in his tent,
Sulks for the compliments our company
This day denied him.

GEORGE:
What's his grief? That we did not salute him?
He is dead. The world is dead and laid
In bright museums shining like old skulls.

Pasted well with gums of the well-dead fishes,
The broken pots; Apollo dead in marbles.
We've walked on glistening roads to bordered tombs.
The plane trees mourn for every dead Achaean.
Silenus lives. Look at him, happy drunk.
No water rinses garlands in his wine.
I drink to Paddy. Health! Drink out a health.
I drink to the fishes flopping on the platters,
Drink to kebab, the lamb more soft than butter,
Drink to our host, Silenus. May great Pan,
The father of revels, Bacchus, the brother of orgies,
Bless us all. A health! A health! A health!

TAHL:
Drink to the mighty race, noble Achaeans.
Not to the battling ants nor the dogs barking
Beyond the door. To violent beauty and glory,
The fortresses of rude and restless men,
Turbulent glory's memory, mud and death,
To the bull, the lion, the wolf.
I am sick of boulevards and pepper trees
And solemn elms and decorous pale poplars.
I'll drink. I'll shout. I'll eat my goat's flesh raw.
I'll fill my pockets full of bread and bullets.
Rage with the wrathful. Devil take tin soldiers.
I'll have my warriors roaring. Let us sing
A battle song. Am I a beast? A god?
I am sick of all the marching pygmies.
Greaved in bronze, great breathing battle line,
Thunder of hoofs and wheels and the gods laughing,
The vulture gods who perch on cloudy mountains,
A health to them all, a health! A health! A health!

PADDY:
Drink to us and to no damned Thanasies,
The snoopy shortpants kid, the tin lieutenant.

GEORGE:
Drink to the girl more lovely than Aspasia,
To pomegranate-sweet Persephone.
It is the spring.

Tavern of Young Bacchus

ALISON:
Above the lizard in the poppy fields,
Above the myrtle and anemone,
Above the cobbled streets, the honey tiles,
Above the crescent of currants, the olive and cypress,
The gods hang weightless on the peaks of snow.
Churches are red-blood rock, the water runs
Purple in misty Langada's impregnable crag.
O river Styx, O Chelmos and Kyllene,
In this, the year of the ox and the dull donkey,
The divided heart of Tahl lies dead in the long tombs.
He comes as a god from the lions of Mycenae,
His brains impaled on a bronze Achaean spear.

GEORGE:
Trouble, trouble your heart, Persephone.
Dead. Dead are they all. The workmen labor
In sweaty pinstripe shirts, their rubber toes
Tumble the potsherds in their dirty pans,
Fumble the broken marbles in country baskets
While frizzle-head scholars eye with inquisitive glasses
The bones of the dead. The white-armed goddess of Corinth,
Fair Aphrodite, has not head nor thighs.

IRIS:
The hares are crawling in among the lions.

ALISON:
Where are their teeth? Who cut their claws?

IRIS:
The hares hang by their feet in the covered markets.
The skin of the Nemean lion is lost from Mycenae.
Lost is the golden-antlered stag. We burn
The ninth head of the hydra. There is fire
In the cask. Listen. The flames sing.

NORTHERN SAILORS:
The world is shaken as the sea. The fires
Of the world sink down, sink down, before our coming.

Voyage by Fire

This is the day of doom. Drink out!
This is the day of doom.
The engines turn, the fires are ours who turn them,
Under the waves the well-oiled wheels are turning.
Fly shaft, turn wheel, the wires, the wires shall blossom
Power, power. Ours the day.
Cargo the day of doom.

SOUTHERN SAILORS:
The world shatters. The sea will vomit islands.
We have seized them. Ours and we demand them,
Cyclades and Sporades, Skyros, Chios and Cos,
Ours on the day of doom.
We are the lords of the isles, the kings of navies,
Rhadamanthus speaks and Minos rises,
The fleet sails. We sail in the new spring.
Drink along. Drink along.
Hurry the day of doom.

WESTERN SAILORS:
Autumn maize will ripen in the springtime,
Western gold will jingle and jangle, crumble and crumble,
When the sand of the west strangles your throats. Your ears
Are hearing the avalanche. Tear your hair for the whirlwind
Come from the west. The rocky mountains tumble
Into the sea's midst. Drink. Drink
To the day of triumph
When we shall rise on the western whirlwind,
We shall sit on the topless mountains,
We shall laugh with a western laughter
When the skies fall down on the day of doom.
Our wings shall fly on the terrible whirlwind.
We shall be lords of the sky and shout when the world
Drowning
Cowers in the sea.
We shall leap from the sea and laugh at the crying
Lost, lost in the water's tumbling,
Leap, spin, and leave you dying,
Laughing, flying.
Ours is the day of doom.

Tavern of Young Bacchus

THANASIE:
I enter this den of yelping dogs with some disdain.
I am impelled by duty to your service
And all I owe to Andreas, the captain.
The city is very tense tonight, the piers
Crowded with restive men. You are not safe
In this tumultuous company. The news
From the north implies some grave disaster stirring.
You will be more secure in your hotel.
The cordon of police is most attentive
In your own quarter. I am armed. We five
Can move with more security before
The evening darkens. It is not right the ladies
Should be so long among these louts and rowdies
Roaring drunk with the custom of the sea.
The world trembles. Soon you shall retreat
Farther than Athens. The planes mount.
There are shelters. We shall travel underground.

PADDY:
Crawl, peacock. Pull your pretty feathers.
Creep in the dirty lanes. Look at the peacock.
Think of a peacock toting a gun
Uninvited to this here tavern.
Who invited the peacock in?

ALFRED:
The night grows warm in the new spring.
The glasses steam. Consider with how swift
Transformation water springs from ice,
Water leaps to steam.

SOUTHERN SAILORS:
Glory, glory, glory of old when Theseus slew old Minos' bull.
Shudder. Shudder. Terror and Fear
When Theseus slew the Minotaur.
Glory, glory, glory of old when Perseus stole the magic shoes,
The helmet of hiding. A Gorgon slain.
Shudder. Shudder. Terror and Fear.
Look, look in the mirroring shield.

The head of the Gorgon will turn you to stone.
Shudder. Terror and Fear.
May the devil take your father, May your wine
Make you spitting-sick as a sour sea.
May the mother of the devil break your bones.
Shudder. Shudder. Terror and Fear.

WESTERN SAILORS:
Give him a goodboy kiss and sneer.
All of us are gentlemen here.
His father wore a bronze wig; his mother was a stone.
Who let the little lad out late alone?
The sea is very near and the sea is very large,
The sea is very deep for drowning.

NORTHERN SAILORS:
We serve the officer who comes
Now unattended on our common foes.
We'll teach this rabble honor.
We'll roast our host like a blushing prawn,
Lieutenant, if you'll draw your gun.
We'll teach this rabble honor.

ALFRED:
The competition is most keen among
The allied forms who share the common living.
The weapon is the foe of isolation.
The Delawares fell tribute to a gun.
The hills of Megalopolis this spring
Are sown with many hills of Indian corn.

THANASIE:
The vile baboon who crouches by the table,
Hairy baboon who hides behind a chair,
Twice this day intrudes his doggish snout
Upon my proper business. He supposes
Gentlemen enjoy his den of apes.
Their courtesy alone has brought them here.
To slaves and apes no courtesies are due.
My friends mistaken in their condescension.

Tavern of Young Bacchus

PADDY:
O the baboon on the bank and the tadpole in the pool.
The baboon owns the river bank
And the tadpole is the fool.

NORTHERN SAILORS:
We walk where we please, we recline where we please,
But we tip our hats to our betters.
Let the baboon beat on his hairy chest
And yowl in his horrid voice.
We know our strength in the letter of the law
And the officer is our choice.

WESTERN SAILORS:
Now tadpole crawl while your tail's still whole
And your gills are free and breathing.
Soldiers are known to get sick at sea.
Soldier, the sea is heaving.

THANASIE:
The law of the land has rules for drydock seamen.
My friends, be at ease. With trigger cocked we shall
Retreat and leave this ship to its own vermin.

ALFRED:
The single man is not the master when
Many men have otherwise intentioned.
We shall not escape to peace with triggered thumbs.
The will lies not in steel though accidental
Dooms impede the decent road of reason.
Must we succumb to barbarism, cut
The tongue of the host who asks the right he owns
In his own tavern? Here is the wonder how
Peace has ever attained, and not that wars
Have been so frequent, vengeance being always
Dearer than preservation. Whose the right?
Shall citizens all stand at the gun's point?
Matter enough is here for arbitration.
We are destroyed by terror. We corrupt
Ourselves in the ready anger of these present,

Chronic with civil wars. Shall we deceive
Ourselves? We are not tribeless here, not polyps
Swimming a savage sea. This is no matter
For violence, for massacre, Lieutenant.

ALISON:
The evening darkens. Through the door I see
The ocean restless in a rising wind.
The night comes on.

IRIS:
There is a gun

GEORGE:
In the angry hand.

IRIS:
A circle forms.

TAHL:
A stranger might mistake the pirate here.

ALISON:
Silence lies like oil upon a sea
Before the storm.

ALFRED:
Let us consider. Let us go while time. . . .

GEORGE:
If your feet tremble, your knees shake,
I'll knock you down. For I shall loose this fist
That I have held too long.

THANASIE:
I will not be set upon, not trapped,
Not shamed in a den of drunkards.

IRIS:
What can happen in this peaceful town?

Tavern of Young Bacchus

GEORGE:
There is no peace but truce for treacheries
Berserker for a fight. We stagnate here.
Strike! Shoot! Earth, shake!
Shatter fear! Thunder in this spring.

ALISON:
Alfred, do not walk within
Those circling wings.
Those are not men moving
With heavy boots that hardly murmur
On the sanded floor.
The furies have risen out of the restless sea.
Their wings crowd the hardly opened door.
The lanterns shudder.
The terrible vans
Crowd the tense and locking arms
Of the men trapped
In their own trick.
Alfred, Alfred, do not walk within
The retributive ring.
Nemesis is blind. She cannot see you,
And her words not yours.
Return. Turn away, Alfred.
Her justice is not yours.

TAHL:
The lifted hand . . .

SOUTHERN AND WESTERN SAILORS:
We are the spire of the whirlwind turning,
Wound from the terrible wind of the sea.
Pity all in the vortex churning.
There is no mercy, no mercy, no mercy
In the path of the whirlwind, the maw of the sea.

PADDY:
Give him a little quarantine.
Haul those spits from the open fire.
Whittle them fine.

ALL SAILORS:
Tear. Spin. Rock. We are two companies.
He has one.
Blow wind. Blow sea. Blow Gabriel. Almighty God,
This is the day of triumph, this is the day of doom.
This is the march of blood around.
Muscles dance in our merry arms.
Rutting bulls, we strut and cover.
Crack, ribs. Cry, skull. Melt in the loving hand.
Bristle, club. Stand, hair. This is the whirling.
This is the dancing
Doom! Doom! Doom!

ALFRED:
George, go. Take them. Alison, Iris.

GEORGE:
You coward, stand! Drink the beautiful blackness.
The heroes comb their golden hair.
The gods laugh. Hephaistos lights his fire.
O beautiful fearnaughts, charge!

ALISON:
The earth rocks from its orbit.

IRIS:
Stop, Alfred.

THANASIE:
I have raised my hand . . .

TAHL:
Glory to great Apollo,
I shall put it down.

ALFRED:
Out of the arms, legs, hands, knives, staves.
George, let go. I'll get him, Tahl.

GEORGE:
I'll strangle you, you fool. God, let them at it.
Yes. Yes. Yes!

Tavern of Young Bacchus

ALISON:
Alfred, Alfred, Nemesis is blind.

IRIS:
The trigger-hand

SOUTHERN AND WESTERN SAILORS:
We are the spire of the whirlwind.
We are the hurricane.
Fly, glass. Fall, roof. Sky, fall down.

ALISON:
Alfred! Tahl!

GEORGE:
Shot!

ANDREAS (entering):
By what man's hand? Who falls?

TAHL:
Proud and clumsy hand, lay down your pride
Upon the knees of love. Lay down your head,
Alfred, on my guilty arm.
My hand must needs
Staunch the blood of my friend's wound.
Shattered foot that ran on a just errand.

DOCTOR (entering):
How is the pattern froward of itself
Beyond our first design? It is not time
For friends to stagger on through crumpling lines
Of broken heads and arms, carrying fallen friends.
It is not time.

ANDREAS:
George, Monsieur George, be kind.
Be quiet. None can talk
Of nothing known.

DOCTOR:
Speak, that we may understand.

ALL SAILORS:
How does the whirlwind rise?
Where does the broken branch
Fall?
What mast or boom will founder in
The unpredictable storm,
Who can tell?
One with words, one with a mighty wrist,
One with a gun.
A fire shone on the mighty shoulders,
A fire shone
From this great wrist that turned
The hand with the ready trigger,
The hand of Thanasie, the hand of Tahl.
What hand shot down
Unaimed the willful shot
That struck the heel of the man of words
And laid him down,
All shall whisper. None can tell.

PADDY:
God of mercy save us all.

TAHL:
I shall carry my friend.

THANASIE:
A most unfortunate occurrence. I
Am reassured to hear the wound is clean.
I did not propose to shoot, only to awe
This overbearing scum, that ape
Taunting me with his lordship in his tavern,
Teach him whose world, whose world . . .

SAILORS:
This is the world belongs to men
And Christ pray for us all.

DOCTOR:
We shall have time to consider the rights of taverns.
We shall have time. Immediate concerns
Omit philosophers and theologians.

SAILORS:
We shall sail tomorrow, nursing broken heads
And a curse on the quarrels of gentlemen.

THANASIE:
The sea is not without the locking land,
And this is not the end.

DOCTOR:
Let this be end of what this night occurred.
Rumor talks but facts unregistered
Blow down the wind.

ANDREAS:
Accident. A cause to a sorry ending.
A gentleman shot his friend.
No recorded intention.

DOCTOR:
The records are choked with news from capitals
And great events. A tavern quarrel
Needs no mention.

THANASIE:
But not the end.

SAILORS:
No end, no end forever.
Port and ship, ship and port
Forever and ever.

ANDREAS:
Many the tales in taverns,
Many to tell on the sea's margin.

TAHL : BOOK TWO

CANTO III

VOYAGE BY FIRE

Return from Sunion

IRIS:
At the core of sorrow levity
Lies and laughs and mocks itself. I saw them
Leave us, that tall man and there beside him
That tall woman antithetical
And yet his own and she still unaware,
As I was not, of his determination;
She who as a child said often sadly:
"Iris, when do the columbines bloom? I found them
Once beneath the hedge of arbor vitae
There by grandmother's fence, by the white pickets.
Will they bloom? And when? And do the blue bells
Always grow on the grave below the garden?
Do you love the maple flowers, those green blossoms
Before the leaves bud silver and in rain
Glisten? Iris, always is there spring?"
I was a red-haired child and often sullen.
She was Persephone with hair like corn.
And she strode now beside that tall musician,
That desperate Dionysus full of angers,
Plotting alarms to trouble her amethyst eyes.

Spring has come, my darling, spring is coming,
Has come upon this land we sought together,
Suspecting no Dionysus full of angers

Return from Sunion

Who carries a grave in his heart for his friend who lies
Beside me now, stricken and lame. His wound
Aches. He shades his eyes from the heavy sun.

These matters I contemplated having chosen
To be their servant and to scent damnation
And urge it on as he did, that tall man.
The heart that has dreamed of the beautiful covets destruction.
That he knew. I also. And that girl
Careful of flowers, child of the wheat and sunshine,
Was not unacquainted and never afraid of the dark.
I sent her out so, knowing, let her walk
Beside that six-foot traveling Dionysus.

These matters I contemplated having chosen
To be their servant, comfort and companion
Of this man, lying with his aching wound,
Who talked of Elsa waiting in the mountains
And of his son and murmured without anger
Of how he'd drive his plow though walking lame.

I sent them out so, knowing Tahl would leave him
Only with my assurance, seeing how
The grave of Alfred's wound had gouged his heart
And hard beside it like a martyr's fire
Burned Alison. I watched them from the terrace.

He wounds, he saves, the angry Dionysus,
I thought. Whatever men may say in taverns
Is less than I know, stranger in this Athens.
Whoever shot the bullet, Tahl walks guilty;
His madness wounds the heels of lesser heroes.

But she grown ripe in fields is not less willful
Than spring's returning, takes in her two hands
Enchanted pomegranates when they please her.
She who bends as a lime tree rich with blossoms
Fears no oak though summoned in terrible thunder.

At the time of young corn's coming into ear,
And fodder not yet bruised from the stalked wheat,

Voyage by Fire

They went from the sea-god's city to the high road,
Toward myth-scarred rocks crowded with carts and lorries,
Making a path through poultry, fish, man's luggage
Above which crows and kestrels, hawks and starlings
Swung in signs to the left, devouring seed.

I watched them dwindling, lost among the plane trees,
On through the laurel groves, the yarded olives,
The gray sloped ways burdened with traffic bearing
Honey, cheese, barley and wool among the stone
Houses pummeled with weather until I lost them
Headed to seaward torn shrubs on the dunes,
Out of the city struck by the sea god's trident.
Lost with the berried ivy, the hyacinth curl,
With the past like a name cut deep on an ivory comb
For the hair of the dead, with the antique tigers,
The ponderous horses that once in the pebbled rivers
Fled with the shifting winds. And she straightforward
Steadily walking, he with his head turned often
As if his guilt laid ambush on the high road.

Alfred talked to the sun. I waited watching
The hawks shift with the wind, the smoke turning.
Darkness came up late and lastly midnight.
Alfred long ago with George to help him
Had stumbled off to nurse himself with sleep.

I sat in my chair and waited. In the night
And dimness suddenly against my knees
Her head, her shoulders shaking: When I dropped
My hand upon her hair I felt the damp
Salt still clinging. Said, "You have been swimming."
There in the dimness thoughtfully I held her
Caught on one knee, her head upon my breast,
Arm to my shoulder. And that long bright hair
I could not see shuddered like tide at the turn
With every stammered breath. She talked of seamen
Along the beach, a barrel of wine, a fire,
Of music, dancing and swimming, a holiday tumult
Out by Sunion, the broken shrine of Poseidon.

Return from Sunion

"And yes?" "But no," she answered with a tone
Clear as a smile. "But no." I dozed and wondered.

The soul is breath, a motion as the wind.
The soul as a bird descends the shifting air
Turning the thicket to dust, the rigid dune
To whirling sand on the last precipitous fall
Over great Sunion's death-leap, a king's doom.
All who die in the sea are sons of kings,
Princes seeking wives in foreign towns.

Little enough I know though I had known
This girl as long as my own memory
Dandled us both like helpless dolls upgathered
In one grandmotherly lavish lap that held us
Both as surely as our fate in time.
She gave me her "But no," and a scene to work with,
A fire and his guitar, Aegean waters,
Fishermen, holiday crowds and a barrel of wine.

Little enough I know. The line that passes
Between my dreams and her reality
Has dimmed with later talk, her reminiscence,
Her answers to my "Why" the while we journeyed
Westward leaving Tahl to come with Alfred.
For George from that month on has seldom left me.
And I have rigged a moonshine on that night
I could not share as she has not shared mine
For all our many honest words together.

Tahl I saw next morning. He was broken
And still and tender as a new-cut sapling
And all his rage drained out as if he'd had her.
And still I knew that she who told me freely
"But no," endured one only assaulting kiss
To pledge her for a next encountering.

From Athens on to Paris. There she left us.
Across the Atlantic, news in many papers
Before she came. And all we saw in taverns

Had fired the continents before he claimed her.
I saw her ripen and I saw her waiting
As I would not have waited and I loved her
And feared a majesty that made me tease her
And call her mighty queen Persephone.

She took the pomegranate in her heart
And let it work there while her body lingered
To its own season. Yet indeed I knew her
As seldom woman ever knows another,
As I could not know him as George, as Alfred.
But who knows more? She wrote to us from Spain.

But when I speak of her, my words are riddles
And poems. Only so she lives for me.
Much I can tell you plainly of her marriage
As I can tell of mine, but mostly carry
A vision grown that night she lay against
My shoulder all that sea-damp hair and trembled.
And whether false or true that night I saw them
As I speak now, as true as every legend:

By Sunion swam the fish as visible
As figs on fig trees and the bearing earth
Blew with a rosemary calm. The shepherd's bells
Rang blessings on the crusts they dipped in wine.
And the man to the woman said, "Blessing is peril."

By Sunion the ashen adder, the gall of vipers,
And a ready knife to clip the shells of snails.
At noon he walked within a woman's shadow.
The sun and wind tied lightning in her hair.
Soul in the breast, a small white bird that loiters.

By Sunion men with traps and hooks and creels,
Lines of the hair of horses stirred the sea
That lay like the eyes of fishes, treacherous liar,
The water, home of the silent shark and the mullet.
They cried, "Beware of the seawrack, the black snarls."

Return from Sunion

By Sunion they said, “Look not in the dark pools.
Beasts will seize the soul of a careless man.”
By Sunion they laughed, “The whistle of a woman
Can save the soul as butterflies return
Safe on dolphin ferries. Guard your souls.”

By Sunion ride the dolphins, men transformed,
King’s purple, violent gold and red in death,
Following ships which inhabit desolation,
The dolphins, friends of the son of the moon, Dionysus.
Moon shadow, follow the dove. She flies unharmed.

By Sunion light the blaze and blow it higher.
This is the man whom Hermes from the char
Of life preserved in childhood. O my mother
Laying the sleeping child upon the hearth,
A peril to all straight line is curving fire.

By Sunion it is forbidden, O king. Look there
On the pomegranate’s broken flesh hurled down
Out of the dance in fire where ankles twined
Like snakes with firelight soon unbound
With ashes. It is forbidden, O king. Beware.

Speak no more by Sunion, men of the sea,
With your continuous flute and Phrygian strings.
We shall seek out the fabled honeycomb.
Dancing is old as love and one desire.
Speak no more by Sunion, men of the sea.

Caryatid of the sea-wrought raging fire
Unhellenic, all-consuming, bear
My golden stave, the sleepthorn spindle rising.
Blessed go all who in the hollow earth
Have looked upon the thyrsus without fear.

Caryatid of the sea-wrought raging fire,
Amazon out of her time upon the mountains,
Out of Athenian tombs since the years of Deucalion,
The feet of gray goats tread the sweet jocund flower of Adonis,
The fragrant Thessalian apple-bloom blows in your hair.

Voyage by Fire

I seized the burning pine to cleanse the air.
I searched the cavern of serpents, I opened the ear
Of wheat before the harvest, fearful of famine,
I the insatiate seeking the wine-dabbled juice of the pine cone.
The fragrant Thessalian apple-bloom blows in your hair.

Hecate, mother of furies, come down from the moon.
Bull father, ram signet, raze us the zodiac, come.
I am caught as the bee in the cup of the orchid sucking
And dragging with pollen, the orgiac huntsman.
By Sunion it is forbidden, O arrogant king's son.

The anemone of the earth,
The anemone of the waters
Are not of single nature.
The anemone of the wood,
The anemone of the waters
Are not one creature.
But the land wind
And the sea wind
Are one wind blowing.
He sought a woman
In many women,
And that woman to be wise
And that woman to be knowing.

And she was as knowing as fire knows timber;
A courtesan wit and a dancer's thighs.
And she was wise as his brains were limber
And she rode a witches' Sabbath in her eyes.
But she would not be won as a sop for anger
And she would not be won as a syrup for despair
And she would not be had for an arrogant banner
Whipped upon a lance with its mark too sure.
Wisdom of feast and wisdom of hunger,
Terror and tenderness, fear for the fearless,
Tripping the arrogant traveler wound with a brightness,
Bound with a salt damp strand of one girl's hair.

TAHL : BOOK TWO

CANTO III

VOYAGE BY FIRE

The Wrath

ALFRED:
Only the tune survives, most often sad;
The movement, the emotion from that depth
Below mind's motion, more profound than strives
Toward architecture and the measured string.
Only the tune survives, most often sad
With weight of world made audible impressed,
A vast preponderance on vaster deeps.
Each new-made man makes measure of his scales
And each new scale an airier apparition
Of reasoning flesh; but the continuum
Is skeleton, the tune, most often sad.

So had he often said and now he stood
Hour upon hour beside me and his eyes
Most often turned upon the road where last
Alison, Iris, and jaunty at the wheel,
George had whirled to the north, to Salonika,
The sun but barely risen on the smokestacks.

And he would not go with them though I urged him.
"I'll wait," I said. "The bone at last will mend
And I shall come alone." But not to him
And his continual "No" could I make match
With any tune more confident, less sad.

Voyage by Fire

And so he stood, his eyes upon the road
As if assured that Alison's bright head
Might come by metamorphosis of wish
Out of returning wheels or from the sun
Burning at least as hot as in his flesh
I sensed unslaked beside me fire that burned
Until the flame leapt kindling in his words,
Speaking of one night past and Alison.

I laid the cards out patiently enough
And he smoked pipes enough and all I heard
Was not enough to make me quite forget
That splintered bone, that damned spliced heel that takes
Its spasm still with every muddy spring.
And still and through my solitary game
And through that paroxysm shot with fire
And through encroaching sunlight from the east
His stinging smoke of words burnt on my face
And stung me from the lull of that placebo
Of laying red on black and jack on queen
And made a metaphor of sick man's pastimes.

"Alfred," he said, "you lay the knave upon
The queen too readily." The smoke that steamed
Out of his nostrils curled around my head
Enough to suffocate me while he leaned
Over the chair and pointed with his pipestem.
"You should be chary of your knaves and queens.
You've lost a king there underneath that seven
Of hearts and every ace still hidden in
Unopened future careless chance sets down."
Then his long fingers angry in my hair,
Angry against his hand and self-condemning.
"I'd shoot myself," he growled, "if that could heal you."

My wits smudged out of somnolence by his
Attention caught upon the cards again,
Switched and placed and caught a king and ace
Before I answered: "Neither is the past
A chance nor more the future. Whether you

Or that lieutenant spavined me or just
Our own fool meddling and too much on board,
What's done is fixed as Alison's refusal.
And you'll not alter either with your growls
And self-damnations. I am still the pip
That, red or black, the red or black ace trounces."

Just about then it was the message came
From Andreas with his three courteous clauses:
"That I should be the guest of his own household;
That he and the lieutenant left for Castri
Before the night; that Tahl might join with them."
But Tahl was obdurate to my persuasion,
Was done with milord Thanasie, done and doomed
With going, always going, was determined
Not all Parnassus and Castalia's spring
Would have him out of Athens. Not until
The captain as a guest-right shoved him on
Was he compelled and not by my prevailing.

Once was the time he'd honor my request
And there were times thereafter he would listen.
But on that day his heart was blistered rough
With burning care for me and fire he'd held
To scorch himself before he'd let that girl
So much as wince at singeing. Pain, I know,
Like fear, both physical, can sour the tongue,
But men afraid of God grow sooner savage
With fear half apprehended; and the man
Sick with a metaphysic ache more harsh
Than men with wounds a surgeon swabs and stitches.
And all that day he probed the wounds that ailed him.

His silence prayed for some deliverance
From thunders heard, some burning bush he'd seen
In the Piraeus first and then on Sunion.
But talk of Elsa, gossip over George
Whose sudden love both real and slightly comic
Another time would make him chuckle, tasting
The spice conjoint of human ironies,

Palled on him more insipid than my game
Of cards, my maundering on fate. He stood
Groping Trophonian caves for Gygian rings,
Visions and apologues, ladders to beautiful good,
And farmer's common saws could only prick him.

He called me Hermes, thief of other's wits,
Of Aphrodite's girdle, Zeus's rod,
Of purloined tongs and tridents, pilfered swords,
Advisory to athletes, gamblers, trulls.
He blew malarial, both hot and cold,
Reviled to pity, melted blame to praise,
Dubbed me fool and wise man in a breath
But blew his heart with bellows on himself
For a stove-in drumskin feckless even in hell,
For a plague upon the beautiful and good,
For a blundering insolent jack, a clumsy axe
Felling the tree to choke on the apple's core.

"Your fate feeds well enough for fools," he stormed.
"I tell you all your fate-fed still adore
A supernatural hope of miracle.
I've swaggered: Nothing for nothing. God is dead.
To hell with women. Other wind-belch fit
For colts and year-shaved bulls. Or said I looked
For God and the beautiful and strength that holds
The saint assaulted stalwart, poor men proud,
Sick men valiant. Now amazed I fall
Plunk as philosophers in puddles or wells
Upon the holy, strong and beautiful
And come up gawking at a woman's will.

"Whatever is blinding in beauty, the sun's effulgence,
Whatever is terror to hear, the harmonics of thunder,
Whatever is wonder to read on gold and the perfume of leather,
Whatever foretold in Chaldea, remembered in Egypt,
The flesh of the seraphs, ineffable satyrs, Messiahs
And miracle-makers, I impound like a brat going vain
That he plays with both hands and so plugs his piano with masters
In conceit of his own variations; a drunk Alexander

Razing with orgies the palaces built by his betters.
I play at a cock. The sooner the throat slit and spilled
Blood on the stone of a house I am witless to live in,
The sweeter the foulest of worlds for one less bad musician."

I laid my cards on, cursed my throbbing foot.
He plunged and yet stood still as if he struggled
Upon a leash attached within his soul.
"Jan said once," he grumbled, "every plane
Had its own will. You have to know each one
And one by one; no general rule can handle
Planes or women. Love is singular
And double like those double decks you're dealing
To solve a single game played solitaire.
It is complexity's anticipation
I tug at and a wonder at her will.
Your forgiveness poses other problems."

The waiter serving lunch served also, gratis,
Lieutenant Thanasie followed by the captain.
And Andreas digested hours inveigling
With kind ingenuous ingenious stories
Of Delphic ruins and the Phocian hills
The man whose morning had renounced excursions
And further tours antique. "Though I should find,"
Said Tahl, "the necklace Helen lost or yet
The golden foils of Orpheus in the rocks,
Pythia herself and every bribe
Of kings, you must excuse me." Andreas
Beguiled him still. Thanasie sat unsmiling.

Thanasie sat and stern as he had bowed
To us, with a reserve and deprecation
At odds with sympathy. He made no mention .
Of obvious evidence which in my bandage
Thrust out like challenge recollected recent
Unfortunate scuffles. Neither did he urge
The captain's arguments. I might have known
His silence threatened, but that afternoon
I only knew his silence. Fugged with dope,

Voyage by Fire

I seemed to sense the room recede and saw
In telescope the captain urgent, Tahl
Recalcitrant, a taciturn lieutenant.

As over fields and very far away
I saw them. But upon my ears the words
Of two, the silence of the third imposed
Exaggerate as mountains over cloud-banks
Looming. A fantastic talk like words
Gone walking on their own along my eardrums.
'Music is moral. Beauty ethical.
Man is Titanic. Incarnate Dionysus
Of man and Titan renders rude salvation.
Near the Pythian tripod once he lay.
The ashes of Dionysus in an urn.
The god of trees and water.' Rampant words.

'Sublimity. The grand. The terrible.
Promethean man. The evolute Apollo
Out of the wolf to subtlety of light.
Beloved Pan and all ye other gods.'
Words like giants walking on my eardrums.
'Water, vegetation culminate
In music blown from reeds. Folly and pride
Must cool to harmony. As ivy wreathed
About the skull will calm the brain and cool
Its discords. Seaward, mystae. To the sea.'
Words like giants prowling on my eardrums.

'The relevance of trees. The photogenic
Miracle. Evil. Pythons. Oracles.'
Anthropomorphic rhetoric enchanted
Bore like a Sphinx's riddle on my ears
From over fields and very far away.
Then focus staggered. Then garrulity
Gasped for breath. We ate in foursquare silence.
The telescope reversed. They lunged upon me.
At last the soldier spoke. "Permit me." Stooped,
And Tahl to help him, bore me not ungently
Stairward to the car. We drove, not speaking.

White wall, courtyard, basil and vine enclosed me,
A window on the Peloponnesian headlands.
Tahl to stow a knapsack for the journey,
Thanasie gone to coddle tank and tires
Of his Mercedes, vanity egregious
Of trimness such you'd think the robot steel
Would rise on its rear axle and salute you
Or fire a ritual salvo on its pistons.
Meanwhile the captain, to anticipate
A more gregarious satisfaction, summoned
Our diplomat dubbed Socrates, persuaded,
Another passenger for the lieutenant.

Andreas' month on shore meant summoning
All talkers to his talking. I discerned
Thanasie, angered at enforced assignment,
The clan code clamped upon him as attendant
On godfather's entertainment. I knew later
What cause he had, unwilling chauffeur set toting
His innocent kinsman over-enamored of strangers
Whose naïveté the soldier well mistrusted.
But now I gave his sulks more simple occasion
And, reviving with action and air, had no qualm but concern
For the doctorly diplomat's suave causerie with the captain.

Of Thanasie we suffered a pompous godfatherly praise
From Andreas whose dotage middle-aged
And childless could perceive no nature in him
But model courage, statehood's citizen.
In me a not quite conscious apprehension
Supposed that godson one wise men escape
As from a tyrant or summarily kill him.
The crossbreed of a dam from princeling Hesse,
And sired by a prosperous Peloponnesian burgher,
Arrogance grafted on a martinet,
A Dorian decorum, an Athenian danger,
Such sprouts as seed a thousand years of darkness.

An hour we spoke of Tahl, that other hybrid
Whose father claimed no nation I could name,

Voyage by Fire

The vagrant sire of a peregrinating orphan
Mothered by the northern Appalachians.
To Andreas this chance young man he'd found
With a sprig of redbud in his fist purported
Some kind of collectible natural aberration
Offset to his whims, the curious seaman
Of botany, the past, and definitions
Attic, well-supported, but at variance
With altars of fire in far inaccessible valleys,
Some rending of gods that befuddled his new-found musician.

"Dreams and madness, sum of false perceptions,"
The pontifical Doctor asserted, "are all of his burden.
His music some cat's cradle noose to catch
Impossible suns, a mumbling shaman luring
Phallic and fertile rains. The rock of reason
Slithers in his brain like Agamemnon
Gargling and gulping infernal tides of tears.
He'd rather break his wits on Thracian runes
Than master useful verbs and common nouns.
He plays at biology, catalogues wind-eggs for value.
Disdaining a parity world and a plain man's appraisal.

"Some brave and burly midwife, Phaenarete,
He needs to let the spawn from that good womb
That was his brain before hermaphroditic
Dreams deranged him, he a proper bow
Strung for a sound Greek tune now ever fiddling
With dissonant diabolics Oriental,
Drunk with *somas, haomas,* Hindu dragons.
Now he'd exchange Hellenic demonstration
For any apostrophe to asphodels.
A boy, he was not so, rode, thought, and fought
As sound and sane as Euclid's propositions.
He was part genius that is now all madman."

Late afternoon cut shadows on the headlands.
Andreas studied his watch but I detained them
Enough to hear me, feverish with a day
Too long for ailing bones, make protestation

The Wrath

I would not of my usual mind have ventured
Against the Doctor's callous disposition
Of Tahl's vagaries to capricious madness.
"Whatever he wants," I charged, "is nothing simple
As fool romantics over asphodels
Which stand for death. His sanity comprises
A life your Euclid's squares have never measured."
I felt the Doctor's patience in annoyance.

And I annoyed to tantrums like an infant
Spluttered on, resentful of his patience:
"Worlds at parity and compromise,
Pygmy fears and pussyfoot adjustments,
Pygmy minds with pussyfooted reasons
Are microscopic in that heart he carries.
I'll never say that I can understand him,
But he'll know more of love and good and dying
Before he's dead than either you or I will.
He isn't cool. And your hermaphroditic
Buckshot wouldn't scrape the skin he walks in.

"If he plays Dionysus, he has reasons
Which wear a comic mask to trick your eyes.
His botany takes wit your own can't answer,
Misprizing energy for posturing.
If he assails the verb 'to be' and functions
As on a day of judgment ever present,
He nurses embryos determinate
Of himself the borne and the begotten.
Your wind-egg absolutes, your logical being,
Are crumpled weeds before his living engines.
His noose can tuck you in, but his emprise
Engages men you diplomats don't meet with."

Shadows on the headlands reached the sea.
The Doctor's patient annoyance, the captain's strained
Attention on our imminent explosion,
Prevented by the cause of conversation
Appearing at the door, were sublimated
To a military promptness in departure

Voyage by Fire

Of all but Tahl who, dangling at his back
Kit and guitar, stooped, linked his arm with mine,
Solemnly promised me a daily physician,
A postcard to Paddy, presents for Elsa and Buck,
Letters. Man of boyish loyalties,
I knew he'd keep his promises. I slept.

TAHL : BOOK TWO

CANTO III

VOYAGE BY FIRE

Journey to Delphi

ANDREAS:
The large bright stars of my own land, the bells
Of restless sheep, the hoofs of donkeys slipping
The loose red stone, spruce-flavored taste
Of country wine, a young man's singing,
An old man's meditation over meat
Restore those large bright stars that bring me home
Perennially from Haifa and from Cyprus,
Home from Crete, reminding me no longer
Young of growing old. I sit between
The stars and meat this year as I sat then
Between the bells of sheep and country wine;
But then was Andreas who now am no one.

More hard than rock the donkey hoofs have cut,
The inch-deep track in Delphi's living stone,
My God, and more aloof than seaman's stars,
The Great Unmoved removed from any world
So small as this that has its navel there
At Delphi where we sat that week by fires.
What says the Great Unmoved because I grieve?
What being grows to God because I grieve?

I grieve, exist, and dread the coming on
Of wars that my own godson put his hand

Voyage by Fire

Upon to pull them near as a bargeman tugs
A broken coaster from a bar of sand,
And hauling overturns it till the spars
Make weight and tip, until the hulk careens
And settles and the careless bargeman bound
To the flying rope himself with booty drowns.

Delphi lives no more. The village leans
With houses ever scantier of wool
That once heaped snowdrifts in the new-sheared spring.
The name itself long gone for all except
The learned and the stranger, two such men
As they who there beside the fires with me
Posed paradoxes with my countrymen
In herder's woolens ready for the hills.

Whether the stars love God or God, the stars;
Whether music owes astronomy
Or man's progression most, or whether now
The just men dead may come on Chronos' tower
To halcyon coasts and islands of the blest,
Such speculation often touched my heart
When first I learned among Aegean isles
And reefs the skill of rudder and of sail,
Lolled at taffrails, looking backward, dreaming
Of seeing running ships transformed to islands
As in Phaeacian worlds no man can claim.
I then was Andreas who now am no one.

My heart I rendered to that thankless son
His father gave to me in God to guard
Has fed the motor of that brigantine
Sailing without a clearance from my harbors.
Those nights around the fires below Parnassus,
O irony of names the past transforms,
For plunder more than brass purloined by Nero,
Or the Christian Byzantine who stole Apollo
That pirate had already shipped his anchors.
Whether the stars love God or God, the stars,
All paradox is nothing now. Now nothing.

Journey to Delphi

You ask of other men. I have no sons.
The young musician. Would he were my son.
I found him on the sea that I shall drink
When my last voyage fails me home from Haifa.
But whether by storm or cool deliberate fire
From one man's will, his hand upon the levers,
It is that other son too shrewd for me
Who lays my death, who mines defenseless harbors.

Before some voyage fails me home from Haifa
When I have looked upon the large bright stars
I shall perhaps remember boys and, dancing
Arm and arm with them, the young musician,
And recollect and lastly understand,
And then be Andreas and shortly nothing.

Before that time the time for recollection
Recurs but not the time for understanding.
The first of those seven nights on which the stars
Which seemed so surely mild were crossed with fate
We slept. The three first days we walked on ruins
With that young man, an octopus head for seizing
The infinite possibilities of question.
I'd say, perhaps, some years ago *Prometheus*
Was played again among these fallen stones
And he would spin my head with speculations
On man, on fire, on exodus of tones
From choric dances to liturgic psalms.

Thanasie was not with us. He was gone
Three days. But that fourth night when he returned
And we among the shepherds by their fires
And dancing children and the women's songs,
That night they quarreled, he and Tahl, or better
Say their paths were crossed like gunners' aiming
To trap a target in a cone of fire.
Our words, as soft as oleander blossoms
The country boys wear saucily, broke open
To poisoned juice. Code of the Pythian games;
Observation on the circles dancing —
Burst and spattered burning in our hands.

Voyage by Fire

"The oaks that held our hills have fallen away.
The hymns on marble none know now to sing,"
I said. "The acorn, I am told, remembering,
Can still restore the oak," the young man murmured.
"And we decipher even now notation
Cut in stone," the doctor added, polishing
His glasses busily as if expected
Antiquities sat ready on his lap
For his regard. Fire crackled in the boughs
Of spruce. Hillmen awkward on their chairs
Talked of their herds and sucked their thin cigars.
Until my godson shot his declamation.

He called me captain always. Now he ranted:
"Captain, you, your friends, are rotted oaks
Weathering sooner than rock. You, even you,
Pickled for years in Mediterranean brine,
No more than a woman fussing and clicking her needles,
Piling lace on lace of uselessness,
Busy with music no man comprehends,
Busy with learning even fire must work
To make a smoke in. Rotten all. You'll learn
Soon a brisker way of living. Slaves
With lily feet out paddling in the past.
A newer boot will set your toes to wincing.

"Speak of the Pythian games. You're winded even
In speaking of them. Speak of warriors' dances
These goatish boys so badly imitate,
And ogle them with your degenerate glasses.
Mumble of God, some delicate and meek
And mewking foreigner who needs his candles.
Yes, Lord Apollo. Yes, the blazing sun
That needs a man with guts of fire to face him.
This alien vagabond, your latest dotage,
No doubt assumes the sun god totters on
Humming tunes to titillate the ladies
And pruning laurel trees in lovely Hellas."

The village men, alert in sudden silence,
Drank their wine in gulps and turned their eyes
Like questions larger than my mind could span
On me and watched if I would knock him down.
I rose half from my place but felt a hand
Commanding on my arm. I heard a voice
That stumbled at the gates of alien language.
The stars shone large and mild. The air that stirs
With coolness always in those westward hills
Seemed suddenly more thick than any fire
Of scattered boughs could heat. A crack. A choking.
"Look!" A boy's shout. "Look! a fight. They're fighting."

The men, no longer awkward on their chairs,
Slapped their thighs and laughed, drank hard and chuckled.
A boy somewhere beyond the flickering light
Whinnied and scuffled off behind his mother.
Not angry, not amused, I watched. My cub
Lieutenant solemnly mopped his bleeding nose.
The long-poled brown-haired stranger gently swung
The splintered neck of the wired guitar he carried.
The Doctor's head shook general negation
Of laughter and of bloody snouts. And then
Startled to unbelief, I heard the stranger debating,
Thanasie assenting: "With me. Very well. Tomorrow."

Tomorrow has been long for me. The night
He earned his bloody nose the last of nights
For me. Although the Doctor drove us home
With our unlucky passenger to Athens,
I waited out my furlough, sure that car
He loved or money he loved more
Who from a boy had fattened best on pennies
Would bring him rather promptly. I am sure
The accident among the mountains owed
From him no motive. He'd a righteous pride
Of courtesy for all his rant and temper.
His mother is dead. I have a ship. No sons.

But you've no care for him. You ask me always
Of your musician who has not returned

Voyage by Fire

Since one long month he lay within my house
Guarded by his friends. I cannot say
What happened in the hills. The Doctor found him.
I liked to hear him play, to hear him singing.
He said Greek tunes were crossbreeds like himself,
Turk and Slav and more than half Egyptian.
I liked to hear him talk. He said the Greeks
Were saved in mystery, betrayed in reason,
That man and God were Hellenes but the poisons
Of Hellas were her heartless politicians.

Do you know what he meant? I do not know.
I stand my time at the wheel. These are the years
Most dangerous for seamen. There are planes
That fly from nowhere over us. The sun
I'm told will soon be syphoned into engines
By parabolic mirrors, clever vacuums.
The sea, they say, will soon be mined for metals,
The air disgorged of atoms, that the leaves
Which I collect for my amusement give
Us soon the secret of a solar power
More terrible than armies of tyrannous nations.
Seaman and ship subside to the common jetsam.

Was he a great musician? Meeting strangers
We hesitate in judgment. I am sorry
He and his friends came over-late to Athens
Once a moderate city full of sunlight.
"Philosophers are perilous politicians,"
He said. "Their absolutes," he said, "are false,
Treacherous to statesmen and musicians.
German or Greek," he said, "Russian or Frenchman,
Like body wrenched from soul and heart from reason,
English, Italian, name your nation, leap
To suicide on half-truths, half-truths being
In measure tractable to generalization."

He went into the mountains with a plan,
I think, for quiet hours above the tree line
Where tumbled stone has fortressed level grass

To sheep and herder's huts, where he might stand
And watch beyond the heads of pine and olive,
Beyond the shining rocks the sails come in
Toward Corinth and to Patras, quiet hours
For some musician's problem. Bandits, yes . . .
Thunderstorms . . . along those hills. I did not know
What quarry called my cub lieutenant hunting.
That cub. He said I'd wind myself with talking.
I am not young. I have a ship. No sons.

TAHL : BOOK TWO

CANTO III

VOYAGE BY FIRE

The Wound

DOCTOR:
By chance, I followed Tahl. But I pursued
Of purpose other business. Andreas,
Generous, simple, melancholy friend
Over-abused by those his heart misjudges,
Supposed I sought my ancient petrifactions.
He knew me years when one incrusted scribble
Might take me weeks out walking on the past.
But what I read upon Parnassus slope
This time was a more present public business
Though private and not unprofessional.
By chance I followed Tahl. But clue and cause
Which I pursued were far less personal.

A cult upon those hills prepared a shrine
With rituals more harsh than a musician,
Within the solipsism which invested
His wits until he had it fairly shot
Around his ears, I thought, could take account of.
And yet he listened. I observed, involved
In cults more recent than Olympiads
Have clocked, gymnastics international,
A prize colossus much outstriding Rhodes.
I've no pretense, no pretext, am compelled
By curiosity far more than zeal
To excavate the substance of this world.

The Wound

Although the past accumulate *in petto*
The present implicates more public action
Which takes its sum from private enterprises,
Piracies and banditries assembled
Before revolts and pageantries of war
Come catapulting into private faces.
The piracies of Menelaus pale,
The banditries of quaint Odysseus tremble
Before the gale and current of cabal
Faction, junto which may predicate
Portentous future in the present's little
Swarming which the sharp attention traces.

Reports to Metaxàs on Crown Prince Paul,
Ciano's notes to Franco, what Laval
With Ribbentrop consults of but subsume
The cuneiform in Provençal cafés,
The hieroglyphs in Andalusian taverns,
The midnight whispers on the quais of Bergen,
The bubbles blown on Munich beer, a small
Incursion of Vlachs with meat to sell or yet
A little lieutenantish hunting where the rabbits
Have periscopes, some guns, a little wire
And grass for prompt celestial landings. All
A bloody nose can't scent is my commission.

Research requires at first a proffered question.
If you go after God upon Parnassus,
You might find answers good for theologians
Or even, God knows how, for one musician.
And looking after God or after peace
From over-heat in absence of a woman,
You might omit the delicate perception
Which sights a tripod not obtained in Delphi
And water can and hose for other function
Than sacred leaves for munching priestesses.
You might have visions but the python lurking
Might mark catastrophes beyond Deucalion's.

He went before me but I followed soon,
Tracking other footsteps than the Muses

With herders and their dogs upon the mountain.
In the streets the women at their spinning
Called after us and clucked the donkeys bulging
With panniers, bread and olives. Morning waned.
The cries of ewes, a charge of flare-horned rams,
Clatter of mules, the herd bells clamoring,
The bearded goats, untragic, galloping.
I do not know, am not a man for dreams
Of cygnets on my knees, ascending swans.
Bawl and bleat. A lizard rustling. Bells.
He climbed that morning also, heard these sounds.

I do not know, am not a man for dreams.
My ears do not accommodate my brain
With musical distinctions. Bawl and bleat
Are goats and sheep. The tinkling chime of lambs,
The wether's clang are plain pragmatic sound.
On such a pastoral morning I had climbed
Often enough, heard hoofs and bells and cries.
My eyes see much. That morning first my ears,
Piqued to emulation of that boy
Whose art was listening, took sharper note
Of tone. Lounging among the sheep around
A well in noonday glare, I thought of him.

Student of gesture, of betraying word
And twist-tongue meaning, now myself betrayed
By sound. His voice before the sunrise saying —
I could not see his face — he said: "I'm going
Hunting for sound. You do not trust Thanasie.
Neither do I. But I shan't need your gun.
One gun can't quell his army." Did he know
More than my eyes had seen? When I insisted,
Again that non-committal voice in darkness:
"Neither does he trust me. And he has game
Too big for fireside squabbles, though he'll watch me.
He flies for hawks, he thinks, and not for men."

Lounging around the well in noonday glare,
I pondered, summoning for recollection

The Wound

Our previous noons among the fallen marbles.
"Here," he'd said, "late Europe would restore
Apollo's temples, but retracted time
More crooked than the trail Apollo's priests
Ascended, sure of oracles, deceives us.
Old gods will not restore by scrubbing clean
Their ancient characters on weathered stone."
He called me "Socrates." No compliment.
Indicting irony. An antic cloud
From Aristophanes; a peddling sophist.

The women of Parnassus store a cheese
As white as innocence. Upon the slope
Where mules can graze untethered, icy springs
Send water cold as virtue. In the sun
The hills like domes of chastity lie still,
The summer air as calm as Plato's reasons.
I contemplated, rinsing out my throat
With homely sour wine. The shepherds dozed,
Their black caps nodding. There above the almonds,
Above the last of olives, hardy laurel,
The hunters gone before already prowling.
"Unarmed," I mused. "The devil's mother take him."

Then figures swinging cross-strap from their shoulders
Such sacks as farmers sling for seed in springtime.
Summer now. No seedcrop in these hills.
Delicately they moved as wise men handle
Loaded mortars, volatile grenades.
Silently they moved. The shepherds dozed.
Among the pines the gentle figures laden
With burdens. Not a sheepdog stirred detecting
A stranger's scent upon the summer noon.
By night I found the fires and held discussion
With several hounds less subtle than their master
Thanasie, gallant and not quite surprised.

'Malaria in summer.' 'The sirocco.'
'Yes, a hut here. Oven by the cave.'
'Thorn burns hard. Olive chunks burn longer.'

'Dried figs. Nothing too much. A stew of lamb.'
'Know thyself. Ah yes. Old Delphi. Tourists.'
They trenched me, wired me in with commonplaces.
Bequeathing Tahl for company, they left me
For other conversation. I was patient,
Abiding the laws of hunting. Tahl at last
Addressed his cryptic comment to the firelight:
"The priests of Delphi interdicted iron.
A broken sanctuary's unpropitious."

"You think it odd," he added more directly.
"I too have patience. Here below this cave
Which has no primal sanctity I know of,
I excavate an argument to bring
God from the tombs. The maximum of men,
Who left us now for other conversation,
Proves and disproves the measure of a man.
His lordship at his fire is culmination
Of tribal purpose, all his schemes ingeared
For mightier domination than subscribed
By this one mountain. Here the python lurks.
The fables lie that say Apollo slew him.

"The sophists' tracts and Pericles' orations
Foreran this officer and he has read them.
And he is right as navigators' angles.
Conclusions follow from his premises.
Man is the measure? He has measured man,
The wiliest of animals and proud,
Athletic, spry at triggers and machines.
He trusts his reasons and his intuitions;
His blood and brains co-operate fulfilling
The purposes of nations. Nemesis
He scorns, spilt guts and chance indignities;
Sure of praise and posthumous deification.

"He is correct and cleverer than meekness.
His vanity endures humiliation.
He sneers at you. He's right. His premises
Have guarantees and adequate ammunition.

The Wound

If you outtrick him, you may also ride
In triumph since you operate with reasons
And causes implicate to his conclusions.
You are hunters confident of tribute,
Terror of farmers, dangerous to herdsmen."
I gnawed his argument. My angers choked me.
His fist grazed at my chin, an impudence
Not insult. In the dimness he was smiling.

The night blew cold. My words came hot and froze
To useless breath in starlight. "You intrude,"
I muttered, "beyond the range of your profession."
He rose. I saw him loom against the starlight,
A man in silhouette who hauled his coat
Against the wind. A thorn branch burning cracked
And smoldered. "Doctor, men light fires on mountains
For orgies, campwatch, festivals, and warnings,
For rites which have survived their first occasion.
You fear superior men and you have chased one
Into his lair. I mean good Andreas' godson
Who's neither good nor godly but a chieftain."

He moved. "I'll go." A statement. "Hope you trap him."
"Sit down," I snapped. "This hill's too cold for boys
To stroll around in. You may meet what's colder
Than my strained friendship." "I have business,"
He countered, "also for this evening.
Two years ago you didn't like my music.
And you made no mistake. Your taste is perfect.
But it was clever though you'd not admit it.
I've been out hunting too. I've caught a prize,
A bird invisible, a remarkable phoenix
That may outfly our airman, your lieutenant."

I would not stop him then. I'd had sufficience
Of double-talk. The ashes of my anger
Smothered concern to gray indifference.
But I did not ignore him though his words
Were conscious monologue anticipating
The icy fog that blurred our conversation.

Voyage by Fire

"In this country much is known of God;
In this country much is known of men;
Conjunction of the marketplace and mountain
Set in the circling waters. Here the crisis.
Dénouement south or north or east? Or westward?
The range of choice drags tide from all professions."

He turned away, flung off his final sentence
To hang like frost, a blur upon my glasses.
I wiped them with my handkerchief and watched him,
Another silent figure going onward
Out of the trees and to the rocks beyond.
Within the cave a continuous grumble of voices.
The night came cold. I examined the dark and waited.
I slept, persuaded the greater inconvenience
Of murders not on schedule might defend
More than the laws of nations could have salvaged.
I did not hear the shot. Next morning found him
Bloody and dazed a mile above the campfires.

Next morning. Not a herder in the mountains
But honest men. The hunting party swallowed
Upward possibly. I walked at random.
He lay on his right elbow as one fallen
About to rise, the left cheek crusted, blood
Along his sleeve. He'd caught a straight shot bullet,
Not a wildcat ricochet, I thought. He'd live.
Shock and loss of blood. But out he was.
Hung like a corpse long-leggèd, rather a carcass
To manage. Along the southern slope the hoys
I commandeered rigged sheep poles, stripped the coat
From my comatose adventurer. We lugged him,
As hunters swing a kill, upon our shoulders.

"Bandits," I said. Sagacious bearded men
Discussed old mischief on Parnassus skyline.
A sizeable cortège, a shepherds' pomp
Of curious men and boys with several women
Offering water to bathe him, mugs of wine,
Bread on cloths still hot from hillside ovens,

The Wound

Gabbled, wept, and stared, admired his length,
His mussed and bloody hair, that towhead wisp
Above his temple. "Look! the sacred horn
As of the gods." A woman touched his hand
Limp as sunburnt putty on his chest:
"The wounded god." Whatever you are, I thought,
You're not the son of luck. That bloody gouge
Was ripped by a slug out gunning other targets.
That shot was meant, I think. But not for him.

TAHL : BOOK TWO

CANTO III

VOYAGE BY FIRE

Let None Profane Approach

CHORUS OF YOUNG MEN:
Let none profane approach. Poseidon's youngest son,
Stranger from the gulfs of earth and through the gates of iron,
He who danced among us in the fires of evening,
He who walked among us in the glare of morning,
We who in the crimson meadows pledged him,
We were not deceived by his disguising.
His sire, the godly brother of the sun high mounting always over Skyros;
His dam more sorrowful, the moon in dark, who rises always on Hymettos.

CHORUS OF OLD WOMEN:
Let none profane approach. For him our mothers grieved,
Out of the mortared urn restored, in summer drouth received,
The winter god, bewailed of women, now returning.
Reverse the jars. Dash out the torch. Give over mourning.
The son of the tree restored to us before his season,
Immortal visitant from alien seas,
Brother belovèd of corn and vines increasing,
Our withered breasts were quick for him who danced. We laughed. We bound our fading hair
Once more with ivy bud, the bryony of virgin guilt our willful daughters wear.

Let None Profane Approach

CHORUS OF YOUNG WOMEN:

Let none profane approach. Our hot and anxious hands
Claw and caress and drench our prying fingers in his wounds.
What fiery messenger compels us toward him?
Who taught us so to rend him and devour him?
We looked for a sorrowful wanderer wound in goatskin
Borne of winter feasts by drunken throngs
With shouts and prophesying. Many springs
We have watched for the crow in the wood, the raven, the wolf and the hawk, the frightful, the pestilent
Births. We have broken the cradles with prayer in the grottoes. We have brought from the caverns the stranger, the perilous serpent.

CHORUS OF OLD MEN:

Let none profane approach. Here sleep and neighboring death
Debate the soul of a man for the soul of a beast. His waning breath
Condemns us in our guilt, our massive fear
Outpressing justice. Silent we conspire
With loud conspiracy, his death which we in ignorance desire
In our endurance. This recurring grief
Of wounded sons, of fallen guests, our angry fathers bore.
Evil and retribution. None have named the hidden cavern. All have known
Nightly fires and dancing. Darkness. Morning lamentation. Lay him gently down.

TAHL : BOOK TWO

CANTO III

VOYAGE BY FIRE

The Burning Ocean

ELSA:
Alfred's letter came in June. The sun
Clear that day. I'd spent the morning chasing
Buck with the camera. And here you have him,
Buck and his tree, both much taller now,
Clustered berries red before next autumn.
The alder bushes were much sparser then.
Yes, he holds a blueflag in his hand.
The postman brought it from the marsh below
The hill. And Buck was playing with it, throwing
The leaves like spears at the ash tree bole. I caught him
Like that, very small, back tense, ready to hurl
The leaf. The garden since, above the rocks.
The ground's all stone, you know. Yes, glacier soil.
The trees, the rocks, gigantic to a child.
Perspective alters. Mine did, that June morning.

Buck with his blue flower, babbling, shouting to look.
The green leaves lanced around. The sun the same.
Still there. The sea. The land breeze warm. My hands
Were cold though. Buck came scrambling toward me, laughing
That wild ecstatic gurgle of his and clutching
The helpless petals, purling about them, mad
Alien that he is. Then somehow felt
As children do, my anxious cold attention.

Sobered. Pulled his fingers shyly down
The camera lens. Peered in. Ran off to sit
By himself. Yes, here he is. The little wise man
Under the alders. Then I lay there reading
These pages and pages. Somehow bruised and limp
As Buck's discarded flower in the grass,
I stared at the sea. And read the words again.

The curving world. No camera, no lens
Nor any ash tree high enough to climb
For such an Athens. Or as if all sound
Flowed into Piraeus and off to the crags of Parnassus.
A mountainous interference mocked my ears.
I might have wept. But the child there wily and still
Like a cautious chipmunk watched me from his lair.
George, he wrote, had abducted a red-haired girl.
Clear as air. But the other, the beautiful woman?
Remembering. No secret. Alfred knows
That Tahl alive or dead is still my love,
Though I was mere bicarbonate consumed,
No slow volcano in serene disguise.
Words. More words. A woman, yes. But wounds,
Riots in taverns, conspiracies on mountains?

Death for myself. Why not, with bearing children?
But Alfred. Alive. And Tahl must also live.
Now we encounter sudden willful death
Stalking friends and husbands. Then? Perhaps
An accident. Even a stalled plane.
But feverish tales of sickrooms, drunken sailors,
Treacherous soldiers, puppet Machiavellis?
Strawberries ripening. Blueflags in the marsh.
Meals to cook. A caller or two on Sundays.
No print would come of such a negative.
Glaciers shaped this earth. And fiery lavas.
But this world slipping? Alfred ominous, warning;
"The fuse is lit," he wrote. "I'm glad of an ocean
Between our house and hell." And Alfred lame.
And then. Read for yourself. Articulate madness:

Voyage by Fire

ALFRED:
Athens, yes. Still here. It's five in the morning,
Elsa. His fever's worse. I keep on writing
And stroking his restless shanks. Doesn't know me. Snarling
The sheet into knots. Wild as a voodoo. Cursing.
I'm using a flashlight now, but the sun's coming.

He's crazy with dope, I know. But more with pain.
Yells that his head's on fire. To hear him scream
Like a sick horse, Elsa, makes me hot like shame.
He wouldn't want me here. But here I am.
When the spasms come, somebody has to hold him.

He's sopping, drenched with sweat. The bandage drips.
His hair a lanky amber horn that droops
And oozes in his eyebrows. Have to hold him. Rips
The gauze and claws his skull. Then again drops
Limp. He's glaring at me now. He's shouting:

TAHL:
Ride to judgment, hunter. Goatfoot! Prancer!
Thrust at the sun. Now crouch, very cunningly hidden,
Poison and point in the delicate shells of my pollen.
Ride on the sea. Flame vault. Hoof clip. Water.
Thrust at the sun. Very dark in the cavern of judgment.
Wave after wave. Ride the fire. My skull on the saddle.
Sparrows fly hard. They pursue me. Ascending and falling
In flutes and in trumpets. Thunder. A drum in my skull.
Pluck, brains, pluck. A vibration of women. Dancers
Shriek in the seawind. Hunting now. Hunting the tree roots,
To strangle the niddering dragon. I know you. Thanasie!
Liar! Gnawtooth! Squirm now. Tides of fire.
Lotuses. Listen for music. Rehearse it. Rehearse it.
I leap on the worm from years upon years of this riding.
A hunter. A hunter. Now listen. The breasts of a woman
Pillow my skull in my saddle. I'm knotting this ravel
Of brains to bind heaven, throw hell to a fire and a tangle.
This beautiful fiery orchid. It sprouts in my eyeball.
Red and blue. Red and blue. I am riding. And falling.
Sparrows. Their wings. They are dangling. The lotus is singing.
I blow in the wind. I howl in the pillars of judgment.

Ai! Thou dead god. Julian. Julian. *Ai!* Julian,
Hiding his head in the terrible plumes of the lightning.
Now, slime of a snake, spitting soldier, old ground-worm,
He is watching us both. See his plumes and his hands and his whip
Dangling, curling, swinging, biting the staff
In his hand, his immovable hand. And the knives
Pure in the needle of flame. Bow to the jackal, the lion,
The wallowing one in the mud, to the gullets devouring.
Judge with plumes, what have I not done?
I thrust this worm in the womb of the earth for my sin.
I whistle this froth of my seed to the winds of the altar.
Joined. Joined. Head with plumes. Blasphemed.
Slay. Betray. I have not done. Torn.
Ride in the pluming wind. The silent cone
In a forest of lights. She hides in the burning green.
Venerable people. Unclean. I climb the long vines of her hair
On a team of white doves to my mother, the virgin. Now come.
Here. My wheat in the veil of this foam. I have found
Red and blue on the moon. The leaf-green flame.
The tree. Honeydew. How it burns. Water sings.
Now the hordes and the thousands of heads. Falling.

Flute now. Trumpet. Tambourine.
Hide my sister in her silent cone.
I leap. The spine cracks. It is broken.
I kneel before her, lowering my horn.
Watch. She moves beyond the flame-green sea.
Cradle in white to wash. Fleck. Falling ash.
A fountain. Hush now. Watch.
She bathes the unicorn.

ALFRED:
He rides, he says. Pulse at a canter truly.
Under his ear it pumps like a swollen brook.
Lies there rigid, Elsa. Knees in a crook,
Stiff as a corpse, as if his spine were broken.
His breath comes hoarse. But still his pulse goes surely.

Several people here. It's now high morning.
That seaman, the big guy. A dragnet for every physician

In Athens, it seems. Not the bullet alone, they are saying.
The fever again, as in Cairo. Or the headpiece is cracking.
I swear at them. Drugs. God, I hope so. He's groaning.

ELSA:
You know as I do that he lived. And Alfred
Came home that year before the sweet corn froze
In late September. Yes, the apples bloom
As usual. We always have a crop.
The sea? They're sheltered. Sea wind doesn't harm them.
That was a cold year. But a warm June.
Evenings I'd stare at the stars and toward the town.
Obsessed with time's divisions. As if trapped
On another planet. Nights by other clocks.
What camera might catch their distant star?
Vega high in June. When I knew Tahl —
Nineteen, I think, before I married Alfred —
This earth, he said, would smash upon that zenith
Beyond blue Vega in some fabulous summer.
Fire troubled him. And here again. The letter:

ALFRED:
He's broad awake now, Elsa. Calls my name
But all his talk is nonsense still. He thinks
He's in a plane that swings around the globe.
He tells me what he sees. I have gone mad
Myself perhaps. And he most cruelly sane.

Out of his sleepy drench the molecules
In unpredictable couplings rise, dissolve
In gaseous marsh; and meteors coalesce
In monstrous copulation. You devise,
If you can, a rudder in this streaming chaos:

TAHL:
Men and boys are dancing in the fire.
Yes. Alfred, I'm awake. I know I'm here.
The room is hot. A fortnight I've been lying

Here and you've been sitting there. The fies
Are moving on the window, always buzzing.
I saw the moon at dawn between the curtains.
I'm in two worlds at once. I know the captain
Has gone to sea, the Doctor to Vienna
You and Paddy sit there speculating.
But there's this other world below the eyelids.
Very curious. I see you. Still I'm straining
Out of my cockpit, swaying toward that firelight.
I bank and turn, fly down cascades of flowing
Hyacinths and plumpest grapes transforming
Dozens of goats and cocks, very black and swimming
A crystal beach beyond a fossil sea.
Down below the ice-green surf is burning.
Women sweep the cities, Paris, London,
Rome, Jerusalem. And geysers. Falling.
The whole world swings. And four bronze unicorns
Sit on the jungle, the sand, and the glassy poles.

Now the men and boys are going hunting,
Carrying fire in their hands. No, Alfred, listen.
I know you. Cooler now. And I am thinking
As steadily as you can. But I see
Another world that moves between my eyelids
And my eyeballs. Keep on writing. Tell the girl
I love her too, you bastard. And the boy.
When I go home. Go home? Go home. Just tell him
I'll kidnap him and make him a good musician.
Now they march again, the holy huntsmen.
From this height they look most strange, like carving
Lacking depth. And there's no sound. Processions
Far below and I above them swaying.
I dive in close now, skimming on their cheekbones.
They come to crossroads. Countless in their silence.
Mist of stillness. I can't hear you, Alfred.
You know I won't go deaf. The surgeon said so.
They march in silence. All the roads are burning.
Men with heads of bulls and goats and rams.
The women. Alfred, if you can, imagine,
A woman, a horse's head and a blond mane.

Glory! A white bull slopping the filthy ground
With coiling seeds, sharp scarlet. High above
I read a map well-marked with asphodels
For flying solo this celestial Nile
Nights and nights awake. A cake of wheat
And honey and cheese they leave for the sleepless man.
Naphtha, niter and sulphur. The star burns.
I'm pulling close again. And now I hear them.
The bull with lowered horns has turned. They're moving
One by one before him. Let us loose,
Suffering, suffering, suffering. Now. I know.
Lúo, lúein. Eluso? Could gut
That beast, let down and make him spin. I can't.
I can't head in. They're coming, eyes and hands,
Too close. God damn you. Let those people go!
I'll light a fire with water sooner than
He'll listen. I am far away. But here.
Alfred, the whole damned earth is boiling mud.
It gulps and bubbles eyes and heads and hands.
My father. And my mother's hair in flames.

ALFRED:
He's quiet, Elsa. Lies there like a corpse.
It's coma though. Not sleep. And on his face
A look both mild and awful. Drugs, of course.
But what subliminal skyway has he flown:
What frightful darkness scattered in that flame?

Paddy says that we're all born for hell.
Queer cuss. Hiding his reverence in a hood,
A salty kind of monk. He smells a devil
And calls Our Lady down to help him. Would
Have called a priest. Tahl would've have died . . . of laughing.

An odor on him now, like smoke that drifts
For days from woodfires. Like a hypnotism.
He struggles and mutters now, over and over,
"The burning cone." As if he wept. "The burning cone."
Paddy's washing him. Good guy. The fever's gone.

TAHL : BOOK TWO

CANTO IV

VOYAGE BY LAND

Power

Vienna

ALFRED:
To the forest, the guardian of nourishing water, by fire and iron
Ravaged to weed of hard power in cities, peninsula Europe
And now in the navel, Vienna, we entered a wood for the waltzers,
Beech and the tremulous birch and, beyond, the dead rats in the Danube,
Bubonic, the night of long knives as a warning to every fair Sunday
In every terrestrial city, though walls girdle Danube and Tiber,
Iron and glass as the temple of Set who was lord of the desert.
In this forest above the abyss, the lips folded thin as negation,
The brisk financier, and eyes sharp as glass, rimmed in metals, the lawyer
Beyond simple law unresolved as the nuclear riddle of atoms,
Hiding his birchrods of power and his axe in his summertime coat-sleeves,
Traded with us in the light morning air the sweet oil of the gossip of cities.

To the forest, reversing the road of the Celt and the Goth and the Scythian,
While great Paddy the seaman shipped westward for Spain, the late Hercules seeking
The fabulous daughters of Atlas, we had roared to the north, barely glancing

Voyage by Land

Olympus beyond the Peneus, the blossoming valley of Tempe,
Still ripe with that stream in the land lying parched, the green
breath
Of a land lying senile, beyond the red roofs and the ruins of Roman
And Turk, Salonika brash with her crowds by the sea in the twilight,
And turned from the islands unseen, the inhabited world of a lost
Alexander,
The riverside filtering sandpools, the pantalooned farmers, from
stark treeless ridges
To mountainous woodlands, the train whistling on through the
bowmen and archers,
Past Charlemagne's lancers, Tatars and janizaries, werewolves and
vampires,
And far to the east and the north of and twenty-two years past the
bullet of Prinzip.

To the forest far northward of Oedipus' sorrows we shook with the
screeching
Of wheels the oblivious bridges of Buda and Pest that have spanned
The desperate deaths of a massacred Israel blandly, the man-world
River of conjugal nations, the Danube we wound upon glimpses
With cornflower and poppy, through copulate Rome and Byzan-
tium to come on
The flat land, the smokestacks, potatoes and barley, the stenches
of sulphur,
The slums and the gasworks, the arsenal, slowly and slipping, the
tunnel,
The vast vacant station, the Doctor to meet us, the drive dipping
downward,
Past Belvedere gardens baroque and so buried Apollo. And Tahl,
The plaster still streaking his face but now smiling and saying:
"We came by a tunnel and downward to visit the world on a
headstand,
Its feet on Parnassus. Past gunracks, through tunnels we seek for
the country of freemen."

To the forest where panic and fright, the vast secret gods of old
empire,
No longer assailed and bewildered the powerful, leveling bastions

Power

To a Ringstrasse congress, a dance to exhaustion for Metternich's
  hundred
Of years light as tunes of the men he despised in the streets and the
  vineyards,
From Kahlenberg's height, after coffee and *schlagobers,* eyes were
  instructed,
Our barbarous vision benignly requested: beyond the bright
  suburbs'
Green distance the city of spires to the dagger-thin tower of St.
  Stephen —
Have faith; in its rubble of catacombs huddle imperial bones —
River-coiled steel and stone Iliad, haze of Hungarian plains,
Palace and Opera, Parliament, power's abandoned emplacement.
Cleanse as with oils any barbarous question of carbines, barbed
  wire and grenades
On the Ringstrasse. Who hanged a mayor? A chancellor bleeding?
  This fort of brave buildings.

From the forest return. Let the leaves rear a screen on Walpurgis.
  No lightning
On serpents that fornicate over the breasts of the mother of harlots,
No lecherous saraband howling nor Faust on the haunches of
  Moloch
More visible Sundays at noon than a ghostly Huang Ti, Amenhotep,
Or sullen advance versus Pompey or Caesar nor any dour Apis
Plotting a death for the archdukes and kings from these placid
  green avenues
Leaping. Breaking all winds from the mountains, this forest pre-
  serve us,
The Teuton, the Slav and the Latin, here merrily kinsmen. High
  noon.
But retire by noon of a Sunday the fairer and wiser from strolling,
For now to the beech trees the crowds pouring up from the street
  cars, odorous
Sausage and beer of the barber and shoemaker seize on the forest.
"Beggars in Hellas," said Tahl, "were with caution made welcome
as gods in disguise."

WALTHER:
In the garden on that afternoon? Their words still as clear as her voice might be calling me Walther;
Their faces more clear than the maid in trim black and the gold of her earrings then coming with tea
Always at five. For Stephanie's British relations, my business in Spain and the Austrian trouble —
Though I was well over the border by then. Her mother was French. And with Stephanie's eyes
On the West three Americans snared on one Sunday were marked for remembrance. Though after the business
In Spain my wife, I might say, grew less cordial. But then, one's attachment for women. It lasts
For a night, for a year. Even several. She had much animation, was never demanding, most clever,
A wit in flirtation. She spent several evenings, I think, with your friend. They came late for the season.
The concerts were over. July, I recall. Poor Schuschnigg, that next more deplorable Sunday,
Conceded too much to von Papen. I think of that monument there on the Graben set up
For the plague. Let us now, I say, put up subscriptions again for a statue, a prayer against death
From American bagfulls of cures. The third one was lame and most silent. I think he owned property.
Stephanie's gone there, I'm told. She had eyes on the West and a fondness for farmers and cooks,
But might miss Kaerntnerstrasse, no doubt, and her tailor. However, that summer in Spain . . . and the woman
Full of fantastics, binding up poor broken heads. We must now break them twice for that folly.

In the garden that day I had set most Praetorian guards to my tongue. I perceived
Your Doctor tuned into my business an ear rather finer than needed for merely a visitor's chance.
Had met him once only, in Paris, but since much too often. They spoke a most passable German,
Though Stephanie treated her German to maids and spoke French. She was strange. But all women are strangers.

Power

That day we spoke often in English. Had gone for the usual stroll
in the morning. I gather
Your friend, the composer, is rather a man of the people, but
shrewder. He deviled with questions
Among his admiring remarks on the lawn and his love for my wife.
The tennis we'd thought of
Abandoned. No ballboys that Sunday. I spoke of their troublesome
absence and smelled like green wood
His burning in smoke of an altar offended. Not clumsy nor gauche,
but the young nation's fetish
These years to make love to the caddy and plumber. I think of that
garden most often, the chestnuts
And lilacs. But I am content. Hold the market in tungsten and cop-
per. Though pleasanter then.
Our divorce? Very easily after the Anschluss. Nevertheless . . .
have a Clerical heart . . .
Stephanie I have not seen in six years now. I brought her to France.
And indeed, as you guess,
We saw your scarred bravo again and too often that summer. Now?
Austrian woods . . .
A lance corporal's madness. Tree stumps from Steyr to Graz. Soon
dead land. A Spain or Croatia.

In that garden with trees he made jest of that iron stump standing
or stood in the City, that studded
Antique in the corner nearby the Cathedral. "Two Richards," he
called it, for Wagner and Strauss,
Iron for sperm in facsimile, music for deaf men. He'd impudence.
Said we heard howitzers,
Shell-thud, truncheons of thugs in the classrooms, uniformed
princes and prelates and crashing
Of bodies flung down, but walked cotton-eared past shattered
houses, torn with a February wind.
Universities have their traditions, I said. The lies of the rabble. And
Jews, I admit,
Are musicians. He'd met them. He said that an Austrian blond was
a devil in curls. That only
I grant him. I saw them that day of the fire at the Courts. Every
mob is a yowling of devils.

But implied tail and horns for us also at tea. I disliked him. That scar on his face. But adroit,
I've no doubt, and above a mere commoner's quarrels. It's Spanish to me. That old phrase,
Though I've business in Burgos and Vigo, grows truer. Write *hic anthropophagi.* Add *hic dracones.*
The mines there are ours and the ships and the money. Much saner in Lisbon. Composers, I think,
Have scant urge to protect their investments. Poor Mozart. How Stephanie mourned for that young fellow's troubles.
A matter of patrons and money. I think Esterhazy, Lichnowsky and Waldstein were rather
Our sort, or whose table fed Beethoven, Haydn? Now? Faugh! A vomit of Schönberg.

In that garden your young merry-andrew had sport with the thrushes and merles. He whistled-the yellow-beaks
Into his hand for the cakecrumbs. "See, Herr Direktor, they're hungry," he said. "These wars . . .
And blackbirds can't feed as the vultures." The Doctor meanwhile talking Freud and resources of power . . .
I overheard Stephanie jibing at men, "You are sadists," and laughing. A joke about bagpipes
In death and in love, rather broad, and because she had dubbed him, "*Dudelsack.* Dear *Augustin.*"
Three airplanes went over. They labelled them too in a long triple eddy of laughter: *Ein Volk!*
Ein Reich! It rang in the garden. *Ein Führer!* with Scaramouch gestures and laughter. He pounded
His fist on the chair arm: "Freedom! *Tovarich! Genossen!*" Your Indian whooping. But harmless
As Stephanie mimicking Starhemberg's prancing, his plume of the osprey, his boots and his medals.
The Prince and the Major meant well and it paid us to keep them. And more than once up at Kobenzl
Your Doctor had taken their sherry. One figures a charge on the books, a percentage to chaos,
The gangsters, the strut, and the slogans. Bavarian tortures? Dachau? Died there, my friends,

Very many. But for Bauer against Mandl, red against white or the brown with the black, merely wolves
Against boars. I have hunted them both in the Dobruja swamps of the Danube. Heimwehr or Shutzbund,
The power of the best will not read in the ballot. Wit and skill. If one must, then banditti, the grooved bayonet and the bullet.

STEPHANIE:
Evenings Walther would read his Lucretius, *chacun à son goût,* and pronounce:
"Stephanie, nothing will change." And will not, for him, till he dies.
Or not then? Tahl used to say as a joke but half sober, he'd met him
Before and below the Dead Sea near Engaddi. And Walther in death
Would retire and rule there until the world burned. But for us the world changes.

Evenings, those few in Vienna with Tahl, the chaise longue, the red leather,
His hands on my thighs, the long fingers caught under my breasts. I am used
To speak frankly. Conclude, if you will, as he did, that I play the ingenuous,
Changing perhaps but no more than *que sais-je* may shift to *quién sabe.*
Perhaps for more dire inhibitions I blush, but not for a lover.

Evenings he too very forthright. Though Elsa lived then but in words:
"A sweet violin, an Amati." Alison then: "A viola,
Sordino, a troubling enchantment." Music transposing with time,
I struck as a tritone upon them, a demon, and only resolved
By the beautiful terrible seraph she was. But you know. You had seen her.

Evenings we talked. Also. Of course. And read much of his music.
Haydn of devil-may-care in the horns, a Mozartian scherzo
Or Beethoven turmoil. The chuckles were his though, intruding

Voyage by Land

A syncopate core in the missa solemnis. Those ladders in sandheaps
Essaying cohesion. His Genesis foiled with a Don Giovanni.

Evenings we wrestled for synthesis. "Listen," he'd say, "to Vienna,
Old forms in new tones where the east and the west here have met
and the scales
Are still writhing. How long have we played a chromatic on horns?
But a hundred?
Stephanie! Less than the years of a grandfather since we have
learned them.
What river will run to what sea when we've cut through the
seventh harmonic?"

Evenings he'd put on his most solemn face and proclaim: "I have
heard
In the coffee house rumors. Your music men whisper that harmony sopped
Full of counterpoint saturate drowns our profession. Dead men
still talking."
He'd gather me up in his arms and then earnestly: "Gnädige Frau,
Dead men breed death. When they rule, all the living must bleed
for their silence."

Evenings he'd listen. He said the air tangled with sound. A neuralgia
In Europe, blows on the head and a fever, paralysis creeping
The ganglia. Physicians have eyes but the ears find the klang of the
partials
Electric. Composers, he said, cannot live without flute-makers,
cutters
Of skins for the heads of drums. And the sound? The slow crushing
of hands.

Evenings, a creature of moods, from eclogue to dithyramb
whirling
And always vibration as if in continuous thunder. Yet he would
Listen as mild as a boy to a story twice over. He treasured
My tale of the fiddler so poor that Our Lady took pity, bestowing
Upon him her fine golden slipper. And then. You insist? I shall
tell you:

Power

No man I have known I could fear except Tahl. I was never afraid,
Not Madrid nor Vienna gone mad. And he could be gentle. That
 nerve-primed
Musician's adagio of grace as I've seen among dancers, the Negroes.
And also their brio with appoggiatura of Don Juan deviltry
Mounting and daring. He himself named it. The last *morbidezza*
Of beauty. Suspended from viciousness only by some hidden
 nerve-end
Of tenderness. Under the rasp of his breath it is true all my body
Conspired to snap it, to break him. He knew it. And knowing he
 knew,
I could fear him. To uttermost man lives the woman compelling,
 to smother
In tunnels of power and rend, if she will to ride farther than
 conscience
Or innocence, mistress of mastering. But in the thunder of
 wracking
Compulsion he ever minister, tempting the swamp with all tortures
 of sense
And the throbbing arpeggios of entrance, I never could rip that
 last filament
Holding his heart. And I at the last who must wrench to a deep
Purpling torpor of sleep as a suicide drowning. You asked. No,
 I shall not forget him.

Fiesole

ALFRED:
Supposing we had found the perfect city
Anemic banks need never further bleed
The milk of wars with sugar-rags of pity
For indigence in artists. "But they breed,
The continents," he said, "new Ricimers
To crown new puppet Caesars. All I need,
The fishwife cries and tunes from donkey drivers,

Voyage by Land

The barrel organ ditties, I must snatch
In haste. The purse is thin. Of other rivers
To the sea we must go scant. We'll catch
The Arno. Never Tiber." So we went
Under the mountains swiftly. Struck a match
For one last glimmer at the past. We'd sent
The Doctor off for Moscow and Shanghai
With drinks and cheers. Aware of his intent
But dimly. How he'd read the Orient sky
With his astute bifocals we might guess,
But his report came later. Tahl and I,
Now gossiping cadavers saying yes
And no to Rachel and the British Father
Austin bound for Rome. Purposeless
Enough we seemed to them. Eschewing neither
Rome nor Leningrad, upon our bench
Divertimento, playing idle traveller,
We baited them, young dace and aging tench,
By San Francesco's wall and parching green,
Fisherman's luck of strangers. Since that wench
Called Margot, dancing succubus, had seen
News of her long victim, she must waft
Fata morgana; and as if her scheme
Were a nun's innocence and not the craft
Tahl knew as well as I, he must to Paris
Quickly. Gulp Firenze. Then abaft
All voyaging save westward, so to snare his
Doxie of ballet. Fiesole
This evening only. True. He must repair his
Purse which fed him short. And Stephanie
Had left him randy. In his sweating seasons
Restless more that Alison might be
In Paris also. Aggravating lesions
Multiple. The ladies of Boccaccio
Were not, it seemed, more anxious for good reasons
To flee the livid pest. Palazzo Vecchio
Remote from him beside it as upon
The crag that night the bell-tower of Giotto.

But still his wits were in him. Said: "Each gun
In your Piraeus and on my Parnassus
Slays us but to life. The powerful sun
Of future's infinite each day must force us
To death or revolution. What grandee
From Spain in Borgia's time though daring glorious
Poisons, so to bulk the Holy See
From summer rot, could stop this sun from turning?
The living turn from death. Among them we
Turn also. Now each tongueless anger spurning
Posters 'per il Duce' by the Arno,
Though Black Shirts march, prepares again adjourning
Guards of death. And now runs up the Ebro
A sour tide the Doctor says will call
Boys from Arno's turbid green to go
With fouler Inquisitions to install
Death from Barcelona to Seville.
He may be wrong. Or traitor heads may fall
In the first thrust. Whatever happens, still
The same that shone on Leonardo's vineyard
Up here among the roses, sun that will
Brown with age some later flimsy placard
Proclaiming power for death. The cyclic bull
Of violence, the adder's guile, canard
Of fear, with all the timorous to pull
The sun to anchor, will no more avail
Than props to leaning houses. Though the whole
Earth become one junta to assail
With leopard, wolf and lion this one motion,
The struggle will not end. Though he prevail,
Walther, and his cool ingenious notion
In sons of Walther after him, a law
In act not yet recovered from the ocean
Of whirling gas we call the world will draw
As sure as Galileo drew from out
His clumsy differentials every flaw
In Greek dynamics and as clear without
The finer calculus as we watch here
That rigid cypress. Split your lungs to shout
This steep to *bel Giovanni;* not an ear

In Florence will be troubled, but the sound
Travels. Santa Croce holds no bier
For perfidy so old as sins that wound
This stony path before false Catiline
Was routed down by Julius. None will found
In briar and olive, oak and ash the shrine
Unharmed, the peaceful city. Yet this knoll
Is vestibule, via the devil's spine."

Sunset. Yellow. Dense. He heard the toll
Of angelus and stopped. But his emprise
On devils caught that vicar of the soul
Who sat beside us. Votive lights, the fireflies
Winked before us. Austin spoke: "In spring
You'd find it milder. Now the almond dries."
"Again we come too late," I said. "We bring,"
Said Tahl, "reprieve after the hanging." The girl,
Rachel, laughed, "You watch the dead men swing."
No more the Father needed to unfurl
His heart. He'd held with her, it seemed, a stern
Debate. And now she watched the evening curl
Up the precipice of sun in unconcern
Well studied. This he marked and promptly made
Among us no distinction. "You will learn
The truth," pursued the priest. "That balustrade
Upon the nearest villa is less wide
Than our divergence, you who cry 'Blockade!'
Transcendent, immanent, two truths divide
But are conjoint, the truth of God and man,
A railing crossed but with a single stride.
Unto the city of our God the span
Is ours to build serene as Ambrose' hymn,
Te lucis ante; Christ our partisan.
As my own saint replied amidst chagrin
Of Vandals sacking Carthage, Rome abashed
In Visigothic shambles, libertine
Nations bear the sin. Not God. Encased
Again in license, 'freedom' an abuse;
Forsworn that Law Saint Peter once embraced.
You speak of law, young men. We can make truce.

But hopelessness," he bowed to her, "your hope
That builds salvation in a word's misuse."
Out of summer dusk Tahl's voice: "We grope
In coldest space. Though liturgies may move
Our ears, the eye defaults your telescope."
"The truth innate among us shall behoove
Belief," persisted Austin. "Triune Host
You shall proclaim and triple hell reprove."
"And so shall I," said Rachel, "but the ghost
That you call Holy is a brotherhood
Of comrades and the power of the most.
You priests deny our power. And your good
Excludes us." On the bench her hand
Clenched to hammered fist. "I've understood
Your sermon very well, but your demand
You know won't rescue Antichrist in skirts.
You memorize no prayers to save the damned."
"*Ego sum qui sum,* the Lord converts,
Not I," replied the Father gravely. "All unchanged
His Being still shall move. And who averts
The will from heaven chooses. The estranged
Exist within him still. Irradiation
Still a light though dark for light exchanged."
Below us as to make him affirmation
Valley and city tumbled into night.
Then Rachel's voice in strenuous negation:
"I've watched a woman climb this cobbled height
Aproned in strength and burdens on her head,
Her burly man in shirtsleeves, dynamite
That will in time explode your words. You dread
And so repress their fire. But tell me how
Survives San Marco? Tourists watch the dead."
I saw Tahl take her hand. "As then, so now,"
He said, "the new Rienzis rise,
Savonarolas follow. Both avow
Salvation. Yet their boasting fructifies
Destruction. Both most innocent in dream
Become in action criminal allies."
But she ignored him. "Bishops most esteem,"

She said, "those men who steal from rebel sheiks
Their wells of rightful water. I blaspheme,
And not the priests. They blessed the shrieks
This winter past in Kobbo when the black
Christians burned. And what avenger speaks?
You weigh us patience, generous with your sack
Of lies. But," she concluded, "there's a fuse
Will gouge you from your snuggest bivouac.
Whom tyrannies abuse remember whose
World this is." She whipped away
Lithe as a minnow swimming. "Whose world, whose?"
I heard Tahl murmur. Like a virelay
Of rhymes I heard once more Thanasie bark:
'Whose world!' My foot twitched then. And does today.

The circular city in the eastward dark
We eyed as monks impelled to keep the rule
In silence, barely stirring to remark
The marble campanile in a pool
Of wavering lights. The heat abated with a spice
Of pine and dew-drench mercifully cool.
We heard old Austin sigh. "By what device,"
He asked the air, "may we persuade? My sin
I know. And yet he lives who failed Him thrice."
We rose to go. I still can feel his thin
Old man's fingers steady on my arm.
We left him at the bus. "The heroine
And hero both are right," Tahl mused. "The harm
Perhaps is mortal." "But," I asked, "beyond?"
He grinned. "God calls them both for man's alarm."

We caught a midnight train. "The vagabond
New Ptolemies have found each satellite
Of Jupiter. But seeking God," he yawned,
"We founder on similitudes. I'll write
In music, if I can, an Almagest.
At least I've learned as Dante's proselyte:

The voyager Odysseus travels toward the West."

Paris

ALFRED:
That nineteen six and thirtieth year
A more than fortnight now declined
The sun from Europe's hemisphere
Retreated toward the day enshrined
To dungeons broken, all confined
Uncoffined, justice to unseal
With summer mercy and unbind
The martyrs of the last Bastille.

But in that year, upon that day,
Though still in glacial provenance
Starvation's summer hid away
Its creeping dearth, we came to dance
Reunion's last extravagance
And sauce our meats with gasconade,
The restless freeman's sustenance
Upon a Gallic promenade.

A woman at climacteric,
The frantic world still cried,
While brain and womb retched deathly sick,
That who should doubt her health implied
She was not honest; to deride
Her anguish many, few who heard
Her stepsons praising matricide,
A kind cold cure administered.

Few who heard the glaciers crack.
There were five of us, and three
Heard nothing. In their almanac
A fair July. Minority
Of two were Tahl and I. And he
In his impatience to be gone
Misjudged in his anxiety
Who sought for more than Alison.

Voyage by Land

Yes, he went. That day he read
A day-old paper while the guard
In plumes and scarlet marched; no tread
Of turbaned lancers, battle-scarred
Colonials, no boulevard
Quake of tanks nor crowd's sensation
Of guns nor racing camels jarred
His eyes from his preoccupation.

The news was brief. Someone in Spain
Was shot. "Last night," he said,
"I heard another died. The slain
Were enemies. Upon that shred
Of land I think they test the dead,
If ghosts will rise." In his behalf
I spoke. Not George. "A maidenhead
You want. No corpse!" He joined the laugh . . .

But left us nonetheless, misjudged
By George and Iris, Margot more,
Who having lost her kill begrudged
Even her wit as a lovely whore
To hide chagrin. She could adore
On Monday and on Tuesday hate
With equal brilliance. I forebore
More words. She would not arbitrate.

He had enough from Friday on
Of Margot. Under the mountains steaming
He'd seen her as the paragon
Of all he'd left to go on dreaming
Journeys so to fill his teeming
Ears with antique tunes. But found
His obvious demon unredeeming,
Hostile to elusive sound.

Friday his purgatorial walk,
The penance Margot had declared
To pique his ardor. All his talk
That night upon Montmartre aired

His chafe, of course. Ensnared
He might have been most surely if
He'd been a usual ass. Prepared
For colts, she lost the hippogriff.

At twelve the primary assignation
With coquetry. But first the bar,
The brandies; then a demonstration
For us both of her bizarre
Inventions to a lewd guitar,
And recognition still surprise,
This moon-girl and the singular
Yellow sapphire of her eyes.

I left them, Tahl as if bemused,
Now bending over the guitar
Himself, the heavy night suffused
With wilder chords, his jagged scar
Blazing in the crepuscular
Smoke above the saucers piled
Like sacred pillars, tawny Ishtar
Dancing. But he had not smiled.

Alone till dawn I ruminated
His words upon the parapet
That evening past. As satiated
With his wanderjahr, he'd set
Himself accounts. His alphabet
Of 'power and love and God and death'
Cosined with logarithmic debt
To the flying arc of human breath.

"Power and love and God and death,"
He said, "have risen from this hill
With ever-multiplying breath.
Name it for martyrs if you will
Or hill of Mars, the meaning still
Eludes while Baedekers inter
The bones. A ghostly codicil
Swirls above this Sacre Coeur."

Voyage by Land

Below the floodlights on the dome
He'd stopped. "This Sacre Coeur concludes,"
He said, "Byzantium and Rome.
Here the double desuetudes
Of east and west, the longitudes
Converged. The flying breath has bound
A wider arc, the latitudes
Of igloos with lianas wound.

"Gargantuas with wingèd shoes
Have heard the pirate aerogram
Of greater booty. Who would choose
To steal mere bells from Notre Dame?
Upon the Amazon the qualm
That turns the current of the Seine;
The tortured Yangtze never calm
Troubles Limpopo and the Cambridge fen."

His old familiar pounding on
A tympani of names. We stood
Again above a city. "I have gone
Vertical journeys," he said, "as should
Not rouse geologists but would
Have excavated every last
Shard of music's livelihood,
Sorting this present from the past.

"This journey ends in crisis here.
No more I'll stand upon the hill
Of retrospect. The Atlantic near
Not yet recrossed will soon fulfill
My second grist upon the mill
Of time." That second grist would come
Later than he hoped and still
The grind of husks within the drum.

He had heard the revolutions
Of the bruising grain. "We've dug,"
He said, "new resolutions
Out of simple sound. The smug

Academies deny or shrug
The news. But plainchant though declared
Liturgic felt the westward tug
Of voices while the Pope despaired."

Along the terraces, the stairs,
Perhaps a hundred strangers passed.
"And every one," he said, "prepares
A voice, Down there the city's vast
Confluence of light will cast
Motets and symphonies, a sound
Construed of many voices, heirs
Emancipate upon this Gothic ground."

I lost him there. But vaguely grasped
He meant that orchestras somehow
And oratorios unclasped
The ancient unison; the prow
Of Tyrian voyage and the plow
Of Celt, the Mongol pony's quest
For sweeter air to us endow
The free descanting of the West.

He saw me frown. He laughed. "I'll give
You gratis, Alfred, the retort
You want. Just say you could forgive
Old Guillaume de Machaut who wrought
Polyphony to an Arabic knot
Of mystic numbers. Not my drool
Of symbols, burblings of the sot
Of freedom and the muses' fool."

His voice was sharpened on the edge
Of his own persiflage. "There's drool
Enough," he added. "Scholars dredge
The mud of libraries. Each rule,
Each medieval note's a tool
Now bludgeon, as the latest fashion
To thump the little snobs to school
With counterpoint as iron ration."

He went on: "It is enough
To save Josquin and all his peers.
They may constrain the nervous fluff
That's blown confetti in our ears,
A pointillism of sound. The dears,
However, now like Hitlers strut.
Pure-blood counterpoint! Who fears
It not . . . the bastard of a slut!"

We'd left the parapet by then.
"You see," he grinned, "that music makes
As good a road as any when
Every sea and mountain shakes
With screaming demagogues. The stake's
The same in art and war. To snare
The power by lies. The man who breaks
Ground these days must own the air."

Leaving him with Margot, you recall;
Lying awake, I cursed that dank
Old singing school, a rodent's brawl
Of moldy stone that dripped and stank.
There's no St. Jacques that I would thank
For that address. When he came back
Next morning late I swear he drank
Pantagruels of coffee — black.

His mood was blacker than his brew,
And so till afternoon I had
Scant company. I watched him chew
His pipe. Then double dose, the mad
Shout from George and Iris, glad
Spill of Brittany, a ton
Of tales to make him sad
To sickness. Where was Alison?

Her absence's sharper ailment caught
As fatal as thrombosis. "Left
Some days before for Spain." The clot
Pressed uglier that this his theft
Of hope his own. So less than deft

He'd wired to George that Margot was
The loot that lured. Of clues bereft,
Who'd look for an unwritten clause?

I speculated on his saying
That previous night his journey's end
Was crisis here. A past betraying
Present peace this day had penned
The private citizen. Amend
He would. But first to George he owed
Courtesies of a decent friend
And gamely played the episode.

Two nights we watched while Margot danced,
And left him sober but intent
To make of hours with her as chanced
His lingering devils. Days we spent
Idling the quais and slow ascent
Toward Montparnasse. His night's divan
Of dervishes toward churches leant
His days. And most, St. Sevérin.

I think he liked its legends, read
Villon and Dante and Verlaine
In parody himself, bestead
By heaven, the hapless denizen
Of various hells. His regimen
Also included the gravelled square
And crumbling walls of St. Julien.
I still can see him lounging there.

Sunday we met him there. He'd known
We'd come. Buffoon of nonchalance,
He waved his pipe, he skipped a stone
In the public stream *de convenance,*
Handy to urchins. None to glance
Him at his antics would have guessed,
Skimming that gamin's countenance,
The solemn heart behind his jest.

That Sunday started well enough
With Iris always artisan
Of stories moulding from the rough
Power of stone in Morbihan
And Breton Carnac tales outdone
Only by George's fantasies
On migrant worshippers of sun
And Celtic dolmen's mysteries.

Well enough, but talk of power
Bred danger. How old Goya laid
With fixative of carnage dour
Cartoons to violence, betrayed
The naked bawling renegade
Under the brag of empires. "Still,"
Said George, "the braggart thieves have paid
The artists, not the common will."

Up boul Mich the chancers spun
Their wheels, the quacks and bagmen cried
Their mangy wares, the roaring fun
Of sidewalk Sunday up the tide
Of Mass let out. "But who defied,"
George shouted, "Rembrandt, but the fools
He painted? Who was it denied
Leonardo's *Anghiari*? Fools!"

Iris watched in young dismay
As if his anger were a knife
In the public street to lay
All Paris gasping and his wife
Cut down beside. Margot rife
To all intrigue saw Iris, Tahl,
Intended victims and the strife
Pleased her like a carnival.

She abetted him. "They'd choose
For wits, these gamblers. That Sorbonne
Above them is a bore. They snooze
In cinemas who used to snore
In the Luxembourg and Louvre

On cold December days." "But time,"
Tahl countered, "whose the fault will prove
With moving pictures of the crime?'

Iris, hurrying to retrieve
With her quick steps his stride, her hair
An auburn glow against his sleeve;
Margot, mischievous, aware
Of triumph, dragged us like a pair
Of suitors. But Iris' voice came clear,
Insisting, "If people were taught, they'd care."
Tahl answering, "First the deaf must hear."

George pushed on like a knight at prick;
Margot, abiding her lost ally,
Gallantly waited my hobbling stick,
Heard George protesting, "Of course they'll buy
Scrummy postcards, but not a sky
Of sulphur and cobalt, the true Van Gogh.
No clinics cure them, ear nor eye."
"Here, 'yes,'" said Tahl, "plays stakes with 'no.'"

By cab we left the gamblers' stalls,
The argle-bargle of the street
Toward futures run on spinning balls.
Still truculent, George would not treat
For peace, and Margot to repeat
His japes, their wit joined coterie
Soon *cagoulard* for heart's defeat,
Coquille against community.

"This holiday the first, I hear,"
Said Tahl, "all Paris *sans culotte,*
Who put the Ganelons to fear,
Heirs of Danton and Lafayette,
The laundress and the midinette
Join *haut monde* and Weygand's crowd
To watch the long parade." He stepped
Last from the cab. The driver bowed.

BALLADE OF MARGOT:
I dance all tragedies, the pain
Of all dismembered gods, the dance
Orgasmic, healing flesh with sane
Redemptions. I advance
The measure of intemperance
Tempering steel to the princely gun
Will rape our antic ignorance.
Of love's two names I know but one.

The sad aggressive saints who strain
Out of their bondage must finance
Lustknaben ever, and the bane
Of magdalens is vigilance
At price to keep the consonance
Of earth for every chosen son
Of the coiling whip's inheritance.
Of love's two names I know but one.

But darker mysteries disdain
The common purchase. Arrogance
In slaves can buy them no germane
Alliance. Beauty's sufferance
Excludes the multitude, the prance
Of gutters. I shall yield to none
Save the initiate countenance.
Of love's two names I know but one.

ENVOI

He was that prince. O my mischance
And sorrow. He is now undone
Who turns from my deliverance.
Of love's two names I know but one.

BALLADE OF GEORGE:
I am the last proprietor
Of light, invest El Greco's old
Prime of ocher with a sure
Profit, both Islamic gold
And fretted sunshine, have not sold
My eyes to junkmen. I'll debate
Their darkness, shoddy's manifold.
My love, for caution, breeds with hate.

Who challenge me would rather pour
Subtle Dégas to shimmered mold
In common drains. They will abhor
Picasso more than Hitler, hold
For housepaint. By which art enfold
More light? Do I exaggerate
With squirming oils? The blind grow bold.
My love, for caution, breeds with hate.

I mistrust the orator
Who touts for charity. I'm told
I owe a debt of love; to shore
The forts my Dalis best enrolled;
My knives to bullets; nor withhold
My last Sassetta; subjugate
Myself the people's legator.
My love, for caution, breeds with hate.

ENVOI

He was my mentor. He condoled
My angers. Shall I vindicate
His hopes and find my own cajoled?
My love, for caution, breeds with hate.

BALLADE OF ALFRED:
I am a man of words, the squire
Of others' wisdom, prosperous
In learning, ready to admire
My masters, love the valorous,
Myself unvaliant. Credulous,
I'm told, that I could not foresee
All tunnels to their terminus:
That love is hate's first enmity.

I learned his words. He said: "We fire
The mountains open, clamorous
Beneath the Alps of fact, inquire
The shafted earth, the nautilus
Encrusted; valiant, villainous,
Together toward one jubilee."
But I'd not learned his abacus:
That love is hate's first enmity.

He knew and I did not the dire
Sands, false rock, slipped prop and truss
Attending miners, gulping mire,
Ganelon the treacherous
With Roland in one perilous
Indifferent grave. And toward that tree
Of his, one marsh most hazardous:
That love is hate's first enmity.

ENVOI

My friend and honor's syllabus
I loved but read most tardily,
My glosses now superfluous:
That love is hate's first enmity.

ALFRED:
That Iris lagged as slow as I
To catch his meaning can condemn
Neither her zealous heart nor my
Good will. And he could not contemn

Power

Our too much trust; nor stratagem
Of George and Margot whose quick fear
Of hate was honesty in them;
And all four answers most sincere.

We saw a bright ascending road;
They saw it ambush; he alone
Foresaw the future as a node
Of intersecting orbits, lode
Of hate with love magneto bound.
This planet's wire alert he strode,
Each stopped string tested for its sound.

He marked vibration of the air,
Empiric tunnel in the wind.
"Now flight's a paradox. For where,"
He said, "on roof or hill the thinned
Breath came hard no longer lair
Secures the fleeing from the flier.
Under sea and from the glare
Of light we hide our saving fire."

Epitaph and Roundel

From every past the future flies
With fire and sound. Who shapes the wind
To music and who glorifies
Raw light with color, who'd rescind
The sprawl of chaos, disciplined
To dance, must hoard his breath.
Past danger's preterit implies
Recurrent present tense of death.

Who dig a grave for power and pride
Must trust all neighbors. None can choose
Alliance. Some of us misuse
Angers; others themselves deride,
Their purpose never; but we ride
A common chance and risk a bruise
To dig a grave for power and pride.

Whose graves these are we open, whose
Worlds these are we close abide
A future judgment. Others died
Before us. We must chance a bruise
Who dig a grave for power and pride.

ALFRED:
Of eastern books and western towns
He made his music. He'd explored
His past. But fabulous man who drowns
On purpose in this sea will board
Renascent Icarus. He'd stored
His helicopter resurrection
In thunderdromes that called him toward
Himself with lightnings for direction.

He took his plane upon that day
I've spoken of, the long parade
Racketing Champs Elysées
With bands and camions' cavalcade.
He'd gone before the searchlights sprayed
The spider night from Eiffel tower.
He'd gone from dream to act. He'd made
His leap to test the webs of power.

BALLADE FOR THE END OF POWER

Time, distance, space, and altitude
With earth's electric dragnet we
Compute toward hope. The ancient feud
Of flesh with spirit, each decree
Of priesthood's war with laity,
Baron's vendetta with his bondsman
Sets joust for love with enmity.
Both strength and frailty are human.

The Celtic cromlechs with all rude
And weathered monoliths agree
And every tumulus accrued
From Chaldic Ur to Brittany:
Not one good man for fealty
Survived the death of his coward kinsman
And time is death's community.
Both strength and frailty are human.

No isles beyond vicissitude
Receive this body. Agony
Is every actor's habitude.
Man's Atlantic is to be
Infinitive, our pedigree
Of mortal trouble. Every merman
Fears his immortality.
Both strength and frailty are human.

ENVOI

Power is strength. And frailty
Is sometimes stronger. Choose now, freeman,
Between the thunder and the sea.
Both strength and frailty are human.

TAHL : BOOK TWO

CANTO IV

VOYAGE BY LAND

Wisdom

Wind and Fire

Crisis in time recurs. And ever wars,
Fury of desperate men opposing, ride
Death's hurricane. The horizontal air
In voyage spirals inward and returns
Revolution counter-clockwise, burns
To lightning, bursts cyclonic. We have named
The violent winds, in prospect have determined
Their imminent occasion. None has named
Beyond the ruse of language other names
Than time and war, destruction, which are names
Which are not causes and resolve no questions.

Crisis in time recurs. And all the names
Of Mongol, Hittite, Persian, German, Russian
Resolve no more than Trojan with Achaean
Or who fell lately on an ambushed mountain.
We who know this bear no title, wear
No badge of chancellor or marshal, lean
No photographic heads on hands that write
From London, Paris, Washington, Madrid.
That which moves and that which moves not turn
Recurrent cyclone. Calendars and clocks
Mutely attend the gaseous air's eruption.

Wisdom

We are not hopeful people. We have lived
Long years in Shensi and ten thousand years
Retreated to the valleys of Szechuan;
Long years on shadowed Ararat and fled
Northward; Titicaca, Tanganyika gone
Westward, eastward, bearing cautious children;
Lake to mountain southward, grass to sand;
By Nile and Danube, Indus, Ganges turned
A wind against a wind; our voices blown
Beyond the Volga and the Lena; sound
Of riders struggling, wind against a wind.

For us no single name, no habit, tongue
Nor trade. We are eternal motion blown
Against the temporal wind. From masters learned
Who learned from masters none can hide
The flesh from torment. And the death
Is various only in a ruse of names.
We are no single nation. Every son
Unpredictable Abel, murderous Cain;
The dead at Chichén Itzá with those struck down
At Jericho; the stumbling, harassed throng
Of yellow turbans, rebels of the Han.

Whose sons were loyal sons in Jericho?
Which partisans rehearse the cause of Han?
Where on eternal winds of yesterday
Search out the crying feathered words? We fell
In that fair Indian city. We shall fall
In cities still unguessed, not nameless more
Than those forgotten. The eternal wind
Encounters time until a voice can still
The wind of time. What then we shall be
Lies nameless. The immediate hurricane
Bears private death a multitude of names.

Crisis in time recurs. And we have fought
A mesa that remembers east and west,
A house of many nations and a ground
Of keels let down to every ocean. Speak

Voyage by Land

And who shall name us? But the air records
The black char of Irún, in Badajoz
A shriek, and in the Guadarrama hills,
Toledo, Teruel, the listening dead.
Bilbao crumbled also. And the fires
Burned in Barcelona. To four winds
The spider towers spin voices from Madrid.

Crisis in time recurs. And all our names
Are chalk scar on a planet. We were here,
Madrileño, Andalusian, Basque,
The Navarrese with flowered bayonets,
The fifty provinces of every name,
Iberian and Celt and Moor and Jew,
Roman and Goth. We the Frenchmen came,
And Saxon, Bavarian, Austrian, Czech and Finn,
Italian, Pole and Swede and Turk and Greek,
The Adriatic and the northern Slavs.
The air spoke. By fire and air we came.

We were hopeful people also, came
Bringing our charters from the northern isles,
Bringing our creeds across the western sea,
Dreaming of Arthur and new Albions,
Dying for Lincoln and for Whitman's shout
Learned young. And with us also came
And they will come again, whose fathers saw
Glories of Delhi, wonders in Ch'ang An.
For us no single name, no habit, tongue
Nor trade. Upon this scarp of earth to learn
Our sore defense, a wind against a wind.

Whose sons were loyal in Irún? Who now
Rehearses Albacete and Getafe?
The counter-clock Alcázars hold their dead
For judgment with Durango's ghostly choir
Where in the chapel of Santa Susana they lie
With Father Rafael, where in the Santa María
With Father Morilla they lie in the rubble, the crushed
Vineyard of God, mounting a bloody sea.

Wisdom

Out of this crisis in time the hurricane
Digging the grave of man with fire and wind,
The thunderous air records our many names.

We said, "Love." We said, "Fear." We said:
"Remember death." "There are powers," we said, "in the air."
"Fly then, son. Flee, daughter. There are powers
Above us, behind that mountain, in the parching ditch
Below that olive tree." The winds have met.
The compulsive hurricane has caught
The north, the south wind with the east and west.
The fires make charcoal of the oak and pine;
The gorse, the maize burn down. Our sons have gone,
Their shoulders scarred with rifle straps; the girls
For virgin's belts wear bullets. Vineyards burn.

Two there were came running through the vineyards;
Their names were Federico and Miguel.
One there was came running down the mountains;
His name was Tahl. Upon the sea they came,
Paddy, broad as a bear, and Jim. He came
Out of the air, his wing-tips signed with blood,
Felipe very young. We give you names,
Felipe, Federico and Miguel.
We loved, you feared them. All of us were Spaniards.
And these most alien, naming us as brothers,
Tahl and Paddy and Jim, we loved and feared.

You shot at Federico and Miguel
Fleeing north beyond Granada's vineyards.
We fed him, running by stars through rock and fern,
Tahl running southward by night and the Dipper and Scorpion.
At Alcalá de Henares they shared news,
A shadow of red-tipped wings on apple orchards,
Larch trees, pitheads, foundries in Bilbao,
Young Felipe, riding October clouds.
All of us were everywhere; our arms
Closing for death, open to love; our hands
Dexterous with living grapes and death's grenades.

Voyage by Land

Draw no lines on maps, for all of us
Were everywhere. The rolling earth provides
No wired trench between the me and you.
Air collides with air. No tower guides
You away from us or us from you.
Babel's tower fallen that had failed
Above Euphrates and a world of rivers
Lurched as loud as thunder once again
Upon the Tagus and the yellow Ebro.
No temporal noise of words can so divide
The heart as power and fear dissever love.

From Alcalá de Henares to Madrid
Came Federico and Miguel and Tahl,
Riding the trucks, walking the treeless road.
And riding from Albacete to Madrid,
The slow trains pasted bright with shouting words,
Hulking Paddy the seaman, who had lived
The world around. And restless with him came
The lanky man called Jim with idler's sun
Browned on the beach at San Sebastián.
For them no common habit, home or trade
Converging on November in Madrid.

"Some," said Tahl, "have feared the sign called red."
"The sign called blue," sang Federico. "How
Has Christian blue become phalanx of danger?
We now divide the scarlet of Navarre
From stars these truckmen honor." "Who unbinds
The prism of time," sang Tahl, "when blue and red
Make truce together?" Sang to the rising wind.
The truckmen sang. Miguel can tell you. Sang
Up from Valencia, running the rice and bread . . .
Rojo-azul, both red and blue. They made
A deep song rolling forward toward Madrid.

The flags we hung three winters in Madrid
Blew crimson and yellow with purple, the *rojo-azul.*
The flags you hung three winters in Seville,
Burgos, Pamplona, blood with gold. And still

Wisdom

You said your sign was white and ours was red.
The purple berretta of Father Morilla opposed
The purple berretta of Don Tedeschini. The girl
Called Jan who came among us said he sang,
This Tahl, a *rojo-azul* in other hills,
A boy of signs and sounds, like Federico,
That sea was blue and red the color of thunder.

The girl called Jan came up from Barcelona
From over the sea at the time of the summer games.
She saw the dead in the Plaza de Cataluña
In harsh July under the torrid sun.
But Rachel who helped in Moncloa and Cuatro Caminos,
Who had covered the dead in the Plaza at Barcelona
Those days we fought the barracks in Madrid,
"She hated," says Miguel, "the man who played
The ram's horn reed from Vizcaya they call the *alboka;*
Tahl who," says Miguel, "had not declared
That white was white and red the only red."

Paddy said red was red and Jim said good
Was good. They screened and sodded the ground and slewed
Muzzles, found range, fed drums, slid bolts and held
Gentle the triggers, trolleyed north and west
To fire hell's hob across the Manzanares,
The concrete ditch that buckled against a city.
Federico, Tahl, and our Miguel
Never said red was red. But still we heard
November nights a stir in vultures' nests
Among the rooftops, rattle and fire's burst.
We saw dead vultures, mornings in Madrid.

The earlier vultures dead, Goded, Sanjurjo,
The graves had flowered blood beyond Alhambra,
The matadors in the reek of Badajoz
Cut roads for wings in cargo crates at Vigo,
Shouted at Salamanca, "Long live death!"
After our courtesies had lost Toledo,
The broadcast speech from the balcony in Burgos.
Magnolia-fragrant summer froze. We saw

Voyage by Land

The leaves fall early in the Guadarrama,
The pine woods move on wheels and from the south
The sulphurous plain coil upward like a Jinn.

Monday in Madrid in harsh November
"We guarded Federico," says Miguel,
"But he was there and Tahl. And Paddy worked
With Jim to brace the great square schools to northward,
Packing the sand with books for barricades.
Rachel, and Jan, they passed me running, wearing
Stains of iodine and other's blood
After the Sunday bombing. The fair-haired woman,"
Says Miguel, "not yet, the Austrian with her,
Came to us before that Christmas evening.
But we were there that Monday in November."

Thousands of us that Monday in November
With kitchen knives and naked of a gun
To the copper-glint parabola of shells;
The homeless ones, crouching upon the curbstones
Around new hearths, cut beams from no man's houses.
After the bombs at dusk a fortnight past,
Children we buried like mice, the women limp
As doves. The moonlight warmed our clumsy burdens
Tumbled in aprons, bundled in Friday's papers.
The radios chatted, the pictures gabbled. In busses,
In trolleys, in beds, on the blistered rafters, the dead.

We had swept the streets one Saturday. On Sunday
After the men had marched who came to save us,
Slicked in the morning mist, their helmets banging,
On that Sunday, flying no higher than trees
The white ones aluminum-winged had knocked us down
Like pigeons. With Monday's sun the craters gaped
In oozing laboratories; law books crackled.
Tuesday the sky fell down, the subways gulped
And spewed before our snubnosed planes, our eagles,
Came to save us. Wednesday, Thursday, Friday,
Saturday again, the long white vultures.
We died on streets, in doorways, afternoons.

Wisdom

Sunday again. At three o'clock we died
By hundreds. After shrapnel we cut plasters
Mending children's faces. Night hung starless
But out of earth the blue stars, red stars rising.
With cords, with fuses set, six bridges shuddered.
The clanking worms tracked north and screwed and tripped
On the Bridge of the French. The tanks blew up.
On Sunday. We cleaned the streets on Monday, poured
Asphalt with stench of ether, flesh and tar,
Were sick, made jokes. We trim the vines in autumn
Down to the inch. They grow again in March.

We expected noise on Monday, tocsins,
Sirens on the motorbikes. We counted
How many steps from us to the nearest door
And eyed the balconies for walking vultures.
An embassy filched bare of tommyguns
Might have heard them playing two pianos,
Federico, Tahl, performing concert
To treacherous parapets below Atocha.
We expected usual death. Miguel
Expected usual death. He walked the markets
And day and night wore ears like telephones.

On Monday we heard the flying vultures, none
Sooner than Tahl perhaps with ears of owls
Surer than telephones. But he was busy
After a sniper's nest behind the chimneys.
And we were busy thinking, washing clothes,
Waiting in line for fish and milk and coal,
Mocking Mola's bluster over beer,
Checking ammunition in hotels,
Chasing Moorish lizards over boulders
In the park, or fighting wind that blows
Six ways on car-tracks, crossing Puerta del Sol.

Miguel, he knew. And everyone knew in Madrid
The wind blows hard. And everyone knew it was cold
In November. And everyone knew that whoever is hit
By a bomb never hears it; and that it is very much better

Voyage by Land

To lie down and cover your head in a very high wind.
Some of us knew when winds come up from four quarters
At once, from the north and the south and the west and the fourth
Wind fights, the barometer measures a cyclone. We knew
That men and women and children and birds are crushed,
Cars topple and houses might burn in a hurricane wind.
But nobody looked for apocalypse on Monday.

Night. High clouds. No rain. And bombs might come.
But look. The skyscraper. There. On the avenue. Gaping.
God, great God who first made light on Monday.
The smell of fear blew thick. The street stood still.
And then. The city opened. Opened green.
The buildings stood like day. Our faces haggard.
It bloomed. A tree of fire rose up. Green.
Green. Green. The houses blanched. The windows
Withered. The coned head rose. It wavered. Bloomed.
The hovering vultures watched with shadowless eyes.
The fiery branches wound about us. Green.

It was not night nor day. The pregnant woman
Under the naked acacias cried: "Child,
Never come out of my womb." The vultures eyed
The city without defense, the standing dead.
Avenues floated on light. The lamp posts writhed.
Red-tiled roofs were pale as sand. Our jaws
Ached with death. The tree of fire bloomed.
Ran. Shedding its hungry orchids, striking earth
With burning light. And then. The gouts of flame.
The coiling market spouted. Houses squirmed.
Where shall we run from light when the world burns?

The tree transformed to rivers and seas of green.
Water was fire. Air was fire. And earth
Leaked poisons. In the sewers footsteps.
In the air men walking, dragging wings.
The air rocked. Our bodies stripped and hurled
Spun on flame. The wounded, the sick, the dead
Vomited sparks and burnt in geysers of flame.
We heard the cocks at midnight. Monday burned.

Wisdom

The men on rooftops strode like prophets, heads
Distorted in blazing air. The whole world came
To this peninsula and on this mesa
A city. The tree of fire. In our time.

"This night," said Miguel, "burned history."
His shoulder under a cornice, he lifted the woman,
The pregnant woman who cried. The markets burned,
The hospitals, the libraries. The air
Laid down a fog on mercy, bread and truth,
Sifting the smoulder of green. "Upon this night,"
Said Federico, "hell's epiphany;
We opened bolts and blew to cool the barrels,
The muzzles bent with harrying the planes.
We hid the guns and fought the fire with sand.
Tahl did not speak a word. He worked till dawn
Silent as trees grow, covered with soot like sin."

Valiance

JAN:
I have lived through war but seldom thought
Of war. Tahl called it hurricane and when
The house is falling, patterns of the weather
And diagrams are not our first concern.
After the games were canceled in July,
Crowds stampeded the boats. The dead lay still
In squalid Paralelo. Rachel said:
"Jan, I think we'll need you in Madrid.
Come." I came. And I could swim and fly.
But here I learned to crawl on broken stairs,
To handle bloody lint and headless children.

The men in overalls and canvas shoes
Crowded us more often when October

Threatened. Scolding women, dark hair shaking
On pinched, aggressive shoulders, marched with shovels,
Cursing whatever husbands hid in taprooms,
Unread in diagrams, but smelling wind.
Youngsters shuddered with rickets and pellagra
Before they shivered in fire and first explosions,
And after October they slid long-leggèd in scrabble
Of bricks and tipsy beams and shrieked — with laughter,
Like stillness at the core of hurricane.

But legs and tunnel of evil closed around
Madrid, a foul and frightful consummation
Slower than hearts could grasp. The spurt of fire
First in Moncloa and Cuatro Caminos, later
The palaces west, the tenements toward Atocha,
Fire in the Prado burned accustomed night
And usual day. The boys gone wild with guns
Frightened duennas. Gentle girls were locked
In shuttered houses. We by habit running
With splints and iodine, we hardly stopped
To look that Monday night at the green flames.

Those flames belonged to charts and diagrams.
We slipped on gelatins of flesh and dung.
Our frigid minds ignored the bowels and brains
Already burst. We ran immediate wind
Toward agony articulate, the woman
Holding her skull together with bare hands,
The boy who brought the stump of a burned arm,
And were too occupied for indignation,
Having been tamed to death's indignities.
Tuesday, Wednesday we coughed in smoke like blood.
Thursday on litters they brought us wounded men.

Jim I'd never seen till then. They brought him
From out melée of bayonets and bombs
And ricochet of shells from room to room,
A corridor's skirmish in the habitation
Of plentiful sun and continental learning,
The institute for cancer now a fort,

Research insured with acrid ventilation.
He lay with revolver and pockets of cartridge papers,
Hunched in a stripèd rug, like an Indian brave
Fallen on strange hunting. I wrote him down
On lists and did not wonder at his name.

On that anxious Thursday Jim was no one.
A man with fingers smashed, a broken leg
And a recognizable face is no one when
Men die of bullets in the groin and scream
Through a violet streaming gash where mouths had closed
On love or desperation. I've forgotten
How many days went by. But Rachel came
One morning after the daily breakfast pounding
Of ugly low-winged planes, the black ones, saying:
"The man on crutches mentioned one you know,
Your friend I met in Florence." That I doubted.
To Spain that year came few men from my country.

I would not ask. But fog again and snow
Gave respite. And he trusted me as strangers
Trust familiar words in alien cities.
We talked of planes. He told me of Felipe
Practising eights in August. Then the message
Come somehow from Bilbao, names like cyphers:
'The German consul. Papers. Captured. Shot.
Walther closed the house in Lequeitio.
Skipped. But Stephanie and Alison
Still here,' Felipe wrote. 'Find Tahl and tell him.'
Jim read that name I knew. All else said nothing.

And yet myself conspirator. From screams
And lint and pails and sticks I walked as calm
As busses still rolled down the Alcalá.
The yellow embassy, the hidden shaft
Relayed the words toward Tahl through Federico.
But when I named to listening Miguel,
"Federico," his long wild pony's face hung rigid
As monuments that rear on the Paseo.
I seldom thought of war. But this was battle

Deadlier than spattered brains. His eyes
Shouted like 'Raid'and warned like a world of signals.

And from Miguel no clue but this. And Tahl
Stayed lost till Christmas. But a sick man talking
Heals his soul. Though Jim at last went back
To fight while raids still shook us in December
And bombs burst like bouquets of mud and snow,
Nights Jim had talked made Rachel restless, rolling
Cotton, counting lists of dead. She twitched,
Looked up beneath black brows like four-foot anger:
"You and your renegade. Your what's-his-name!"
And shook us like barrage. Then silence. Jim
Looked at the wall and nursed his broken hand.

Tahl those days was fighting in the schools,
Taking death on chance as if he held
His papers and a name on muster rolls.
But still unregistered, a prowling bat
Because of Federico. Rachel said:
"Federico! A man should hide his gun,
Steal food and smokes to coddle some Andalusian
The whites will catch, be sure, if they're looking for him.
Before this winter's over we'll make armies,
Proper brigades and loyalty to parties.
Your what's-his-name shall choose or we will shoot him."

"You will shoot him, Jim?" She took his silence
For corroboration. I had heard
Artillery ripping air and seen and heard
Tanks, and men with more than broken hands;
But war in the eyes of Miguel and war's alarm
In the words of a gnomish girl I called my friend
Racked me more than bones thrust raw through flesh
Or stubbing my foot on pulp at bleeding thresholds.
"If red is not his color, why," asked Rachel,
"Does he crawl in beside us? Or perhaps
He pipes in code to teach our loyal generals?"

This scorn she'd captured out of all Jim's story,
That double pipe, *alboka,* Tahl had carried

Along with rope and knife for guard and weapon
Crossing Iberica and Guadarrama,
Freezing to granite, stalking among the pines.
If she had heard him further, she'd found scorn
With further reason. But to me alone
Jim told his story of the night of fires,
How Tahl next day in choking soot and fog
Smuggled the tommygun to schools besieged,
Giving the bat's cry under the propped door.

"That high thin call," said Jim, "a password learned
In dark July. San Sebastiàn went mad,
Casino and the Nautico conspired,
And red bandannas, toffs with pearl-set pistols
Fired at us impartially, like sea gulls.
Knowing he'd left the coast, I'd set my ears
To hear that cry again. We blacked the light
And ready to lob at treason, let the door in.
The floating wick sent up an oily shine
Glossing his rope, his knife — that ammunition
And — we nearly spilled the Molotovs — that gun.

"Assigned to hold that hall, we'd just two rifles.
Grenades. The Lewis gun we'd had surrendered
To a sharper team. Most sad. We'd nursed it,
Gave it syncopation. My revolver
Hardly'd serve for time to die. We fought,
Till Thursday, mostly smoke and cold *frijoles.*
The building shook. We heard the Riffs out yelling.
But this was ours to hold, for me and Paddy,
And two milicianos, plucky bastards.
And not our job to hunt in other graveyards.
We cleaned Tahl's gun with sardine oil and quizzed him.

"Paddy coddled the barrel and bolt like girl friends
And set and aimed and growled like a bear in love
And seemed to talk to gunsights but he shot
His words at nearer targets. 'Look at him,'
He purred, 'This punk. He squirms on his long belly
Straight through hell, he does. Some pony face

He calls Miguel gets news. And so he comes.
Howling to God he was in Athens, fighting
Before the shooting started. Playing pianos,
Fiddling. And he is now so much as a colonel? No?
Him with his brains comes whistling by like nightbirds.'

"Tahl knew already," said Jim, "and Albacete
Taught me Paddy's heart recoiled like cannon,
Backing to fire. The two milicianos
Caught his tone and grinned. Those handsome eyes
Of theirs alive like four salutes, they watched
The gun and Tahl, Tahl and the gun. They stuffed
His hands with smokes. And dead now both of them.
Those nervy long-chinned kids, God damn it, spoiled us
As if they'd been our fathers. And what'd we give them
But a lot of words without a dictionary
And a few more hours alive before the gun jammed?

"Paddy," said Jim, "there shaking his head like grief:
'Whyn't you roll a drum of oil?' says Paddy.
'The slope's kind of pretty outside. Could run it easy,
And a couple of detonators while you're at it
Could blow them Sacred Hearts to Mary and Jesus.'
The sardine grease ran down his quirking eyebrows
Set for a laugh. 'And why we mustn't use 'em?
Kids got tender heads. Them slick explosions
Would jar his ear for fiddling.' Tahl took turn
At listening post, played dead while Paddy ribbed him.
He stretched and waved at me across the sandbags.

"The building rocked. 'May pigs die on their graves
And God forgive them,' says Paddy. 'But, you lunk,'
Fetching Tahl by the ear across the sandbags,
'I'm solemn. This army's not so short on brains
But never say brains still whole is one too many.
You got a head for figures. Go join up.
They got telemeters and calibrators
And don't just guess like me by skin and elbows.
You got ears. Go ride that telephone tower
And sing high C for Heinkels. Sign your name
And stop this traipsing like a goddamned gypsy.'"

Jim stopped for breath. "But, Jan," he whooped, "to see them,
That bear's paw yanking him up like a dangling hare . . .
And Tahl, by God, he does look like some crossbreed.
But then," Jim said, "we are. My mother's Dutch
And won't give up New York for all the acres
South of Richmond. And my brother's like her.
Just Dad and me, the F.F.V.'s, God help us.
And even Dad's converted to Manhattan.
But Tahl . . . with his molasses thatch . . . and yet,
That darkness . . . like a Moor. Who was his father?"
"I don't know," I said. "I never saw him."

Nights for us were also days. I worked
With Rachel, hardly thought of Jim, or Tahl
He'd left in Paddy's grip against the sandbags.
And then one morning, sun. And then the bombers.
We called the men to keep away from windows.
And then, Jim suddenly: "Look there, those shadows
Like inky T-squares floating." They went over
To pound the schools again, the western suburb.
The day that Jim checked out. That night, to shells
Slogging Gran Via, we measured talk and beer . . .
And Jim I've never seen since that next moming.

But I can see him still as I see Tahl.
Jim was lankier but somewhat like him,
Steadier, I think. And Alison
Sent Jim as she sent Tahl to fight a war;
But only one came back for further battles.
That last night of his though, Jim was mellow;
Repeated, "Floating T-squares. Little ink spots.
When we saw them first along the Concha
Tahl said 'crosses,' great black flying crosses.
Tahl. He thinks too much. But I won't kill
Those poor old Riffs he left tied up like turkeys."

I skipped the Riffs and crosses for the moment.
I let Jim drink his beer. And then I asked him,
"What does he think about? He's always thinking."
"Thinks about fire," said Jim, "just eyes and fire.

Voyage by Land

You remember. All that freezing Wednesday,
Before the scrap that conked my leg and fingers,
Talked about fire and tunnels. Eyes and tunnels.
Jerusalem and all the little cities
Like Madrid a guy can run in lunchtime.
Fire-damp. Fire-clay. Fire-bombs. Sure. Just fire."

I was impatient then. "Must I remember
All you haven't told?" I counted shells,
Heard three explosions, wondered guiltily
At staying there with Jim. But must have known
Somehow I couldn't leave him. Not that evening.
He rambled on: "Now, Jan, you put out fire.
Now here's the formula. Just take some sugar,
Potassium ferrocyanide . . . parts water . . .
Sulphuric acid, chlorate of potassa . . .
And blow. The one sure gun against cremation.
And fire," he hummed, "is the source of civilization."

He smiled as reasonably as if he'd talked
The best of sense. "That's Tahl," he said. "He knows
All about tunnels and fires. And so do I.
Hannibal was a chemist too. You heat
Rock and pour on water. There's the crack
And then you dig it. Then you run a railroad
Or dig a lot of copper like Phoenicians
Or, if you're smart, let Spaniards dig it for you.
Greek fire . . . naphtha, sulphur, resin, nitre.
It burns like hell. And blame it on the Greeks.
But it burned my great-great-grandad up in Charleston.

"That's me," he said. "The rest is Tahl and me.
That hall was cold to freeze grenades to duds.
We talked a fire. And how we'd wash our clothes
In dynamite and turn the rest to butter
And cure our gripes with tear gas and set up
New tables in that institute for cancer.
God, what a place to fight in. See? And turn
That punch-drunk oxygen that eats you silly
Up in airplanes, runs amuck inside you,

Gives you cancer. See? Into a power
To burn all hell. But Paddy said, 'You're screwy.'"

"Jim, go douse your head," I said. He went
As mild as sheep we'd find that bawled in alleys
When the herders drove them through that autumn
Running from the guns. I tossed his words
Like anagrams but could not make an answer.
But it was beer. He came back nearly sober
And made replies like good boy's recitations:
"Fire? It's good and bad. And nitrates blow
Your head off. Better keep for fertilizer.
Glycerin? Choose. It comforts and it kills.
The sun in Charleston's hell on the Sahara."

"Are you quoting yourself?" I tried to tease him.
"And Tahl," he laughed. "He says I'm Don Quixote,
The headpiece whole but patched with strings and pasteboard.
I want to take apart uranium.
And if I could, you'd have a nonstop airplane;
Though if I did, you'd likely stop in China.
But Tahl rides fourteen hundred million years
Reverse to find who made the gram I worked with.
Whoever heard of a guy who went to Egypt
Because he looked at a leaf with high-power lenses?"
"What about Riffs?" I asked. "And flying crosses?"

"I'll tell you. But let me finish. I would like
To take apart uranium. Instead
I spend July in Spain and also money.
A girl named Alison you haven't met
Says, 'Still you think that good is good.' And so
I fight and catch a broken leg and now
I'm going back to offer up my head
That isn't worth the kissing. Four long weeks
And what'll you have of me? That damned musician."
But before he left me that next morning
I also had the story of Riffs and crosses.

"Tahl," said Jim, "he heard them first. And then
The bombers' shadows showed. And then we knew
Our number really called, the Riffs, the Tercio
Lurking the cover of planes. Right on us. Smash.
Smoke. Smash. Then mouseholes gaping. Paddy packing
The tommygun. Let militia have the rifles.
Lit for the corridor contact, eastern corner.
Tahl to run the rear for interference,
We fanned like a football squad when the pass is zooming.
Tahl shouting, "This is for us!" I guess it was.
I came to, lifting a staircase with my fingers.

Dragged them out somehow and kept on running.
Deaf as a fish. This fool revolver flashing.
All like dreams. No sound. Saw Paddy pointing
That nozzle square at my chest, milicianos
Sighting my ears like rabbits. Not a sound.
Then out. I guess they cracked my legs with gun butts.
Left me for dead and got the boys with rifles.
The rest is Paddy's yarn. That lovely gun
Jammed with still two Riffs alive and shooting.
Tahl came pitching down that busted stairwell,
Kicked their behinds and noosed them with a clothesline.

"I came to again, still deaf as herrings,
But judged from Paddy's face he was condemning
All Tahl's ancestors to broil in stink bombs;
And read his jaw, 'You goddamned acrobat,
Whyn't you kill 'em?' Holding their irons and frisking
Their pantaloons for bullets, turbaned guys
Trussed like turkeys, big eyes bulging and rolling.
Tahl then pointing at me, 'You didn't kill him!'
Paddy too mad to spit. I watched him mouthing
'Prisoners! Goddamned prisoners!' Tahl replying,
Shaking his head, 'Their eyes,' he said. 'Their eyes.'

"That's all," Jim said. "Just Paddy blasting my ears
To make me understand that bitch of a gun
Had saved my life and also Tahl's twin turkeys.
I was still grogged. We made the corner. Tahl

Toting me like a babe. I likely shouted
'Whyn't you kill 'em?' meaning it a whisper.
And Tahl yelled back, 'They looked at me, I tell you.
Their eyes, I tell you. Eyes.' The last I saw,
The orderlies bundling me off with the other ninepins,
Was Paddy booting those Riffs but glaring us down
Like a father embarrassed by an idiot son."

I'd seldom thought of war. No one had thought
To teach us. We among the Appalachians
Fought for power with elementary toys,
With jack-knives, balls, "lassoos." Our education
Primary. The algebra, the rules
Of games we learned. Planes later. The idiot daughter,
I sometimes thought of eyes. Of idiot sons,
The grave and skeptical eyes of Tahl at school;
Jim's eyes before he left me that last morning.
Though war moves space and works by diagrams,
Last 'x' may factor 'eyes' in last equations.

Victory and Defeat

MIGUEL:
Rainy December's turn and longest night
He called me from the dusky Metro shelter.
He hid a laugh obliquely in his eyes.
The smuggler's habit and the street guerrilla,
His cigarette he held beneath his hand.
But nothing else betrayed. A new "reporter"
Hurrying toward a crowded subway car.
"The shaft, Miguel," said Tahl, "and pronto, please."
No more. I slid our camouflage and found him
There before me, spruce in tourist mufti,
A tall American, visiting a war.

Also transformed like wonders out of Ovid,
Federico, once on nightly forays
In cords and broken shoes, but now as trim
As I had seen him months ago on Sundays
Strolling Alameda in Granada.
"Salud, El Tahl campeador. He prays,"
I joked, "with sandbags for a loan. And now,
Behold, we shine like bishops. Shall I raise,
Señor, your elevator? Straw and water
And broken ropes will vanish at your hand?
Permit Miguel to share such mysteries?"

"Comb your locks, Miguel," was all his answer.
I asked no more. I followed, walking blithely.
We moved the door October had secured
And dared December stairs to cross the lobby.
With all my questions pumping heart and tongue,
We bowed at ease to someone's secretary
Who bowed to us as normally as breathing.
Once I tried: "Do you expect to die
More gracefully in neckties?" Had no answer
But jest about distemper of St. Francis,
That we should mourn our sweet, lost poverty.

His promised Austrian just three days later
With Alison arrived from Barcelona
And I could trace his stories wound in stories
As would have graced hidalgos of La Mancha:
A draft that followed him, for "studies," sent
By one named George, Tahl spent, each last peseta,
To force a wise retreat on Federico.
"Investment," Tahl said, "in the arts of Andalusia."
But catching one disease to cure another,
Being identified, a man of papers,
"We lazars," he said, "must chance it toward Bilbao."

Three weeks later they had gone. They said:
"Come too, Miguel." "You think we should expose,
I asked, "the consulates to speculation
On missing Austrians with Spanish noses

Or give our Stephanie a second son?"
We laughed together. I did not refuse
For valiance. They would jump the ship at Vigo.
To join the Basque, Felipe, slip the coast,
And, Federico safer in Vizcaya,
Fight for the north. And we would hold Madrid.
I still believe they made the sterner choice.

We fought that year alone. The partisans
Our friends, not then our masters. And we fought
Our battle as we saw it, still to win
A common freedom from the common hurt.
I have seen neither Tahl nor Federico,
But I have ears. It was no mine that burst
Up there beyond Bilbao. We had talked.
I knew that Tahl fought later on the Ebro,
A year with the brigades before they marched
In Barcelona's last parade. Though lost
In victory, we shall outlive defeat.

Jan can tell you more perhaps, or Rachel;
Though none but Tahl the fate of Federico,
Our private hostage in the public battle.
I know they reached Bilbao. And I know
That Federico saw at Guernica
One further mask of death. And you will do
A kindness if you know my friends are dead
To tell me so. I have a tale or two
That ran the winter alleys of Madrid
Will make you smile. A prisoner survives
More gaily who can brace himself with heroes.

From shop-girls and the boy-milicianos,
When I walked free, a courier of alleys,
Tall tales of Garibaldis, later Byrons,
From lottery-sellers, toothless women, stories
Over chess and dominoes, the whispers,
El Campesino and our tall Dolores,
Rumored among the sickles, stars and hammers,
Murmured among the rosaries and crosses,

Also the righteous Moor, the mighty Russian,
Or called him Greek and named him Dionysus.

That last walked everywhere. He came to save us.
He lived in the ground and rose at night on wings
Or played strange music, lured a thousand planes
To sure destruction, owned a thousand guns.
As tall as the Hill of Angels in the east,
That Monday night the city shook with flames,
He saved us in the west against the Moors,
With a ringing *irrintzina* and his hands
Thrusting the Riffs beyond the Manzanares.
And those who saw him knew him by his signs.
Yes, you will smile — a scar and an oryx horn.

That scar to them the sign of the gored man,
Fighter of bulls. The kabbalistic horn
Evoked him also horse's hooves. You smile.
The stories blew with wind-drift, common sound.
That unicorn, a rhyme of Federico's,
His hair, the ram's horn reeds, and every totem
That curls its notions into common campfires,
Makes Moors, renascent Greeks and mighty Russians
To shake the drinkers from their iron chairs.
Of all the legends seeded on a war,
This sprout, a man who rode their subway cars.

At Alcalá de Henares when we met,
I did not trust him. Why he came alone
Out of the north I could not understand.
Our flight had purpose, fleeing from the guns
That chased us through the vineyards that hot morning
To break forever every mouth and mind
That questioned hate triumphant. But he chose
His coming as to choose a boy's adventure,
So I thought. He found the shaft, though. Found
Our nightly business, fighting for Madrid.
I soon forgot to ask him for his reasons.

Wisdom

Rainy December. We had now assigned
To the committees our last gun forlorn
Of ammunition. Plutocrats of time
Those few long nights as freemen, till I bound
Myself to sergeant's orders and they walked
As if toward kinder countries with the line
Of aliens crowding glossy cars that ride
Through vulgar war like old enchanter's islands.
I would have cursed them if I had not found
In those few nights the tunnels of his mind,
And heard his heart, more cogent than his reasons.

Reasons need no music. I remarked
To Jan that winter after Tahl had gone,
I'd never known a man could shout so loud
And keep so fast a secret. "Yes," said Jan,
"On strings and reeds and horns and like a prophet
When he pleases. But his cousin Julian
Who knew him best was never good at guessing
What Tahl thought until he chose to tell him.
I sometimes tried to swim the sea he walked in
But gasped for breath. And George could never fathom
Nor Alfred either, though they tried, his ocean
Until he brought the wreckage up and showed them.
He walked alone or else with Alison."

"Miguel, you do like Alison?" She asked
As if she feared the answer. I debated
My reply and countered to amuse her:
"I confess I am not acclimated
To such women. By her hair and eyes,
That maize and amethyst, I am distracted.
But power like innocence all-knowing walks
Too tall a stride for ponies. I have slept
With women who thought of bracelets, children, God,
But not also of schools and manuscripts
Depicting the creation of the world."

And there I give you one of many reasons
Brought him toward us southward. She had heard

Some Mayan picture-book she sought endangered.
He was, you'd say, musician; she, a woman;
Yet both the race of vagrant scholars bred
To honor past occasions. But he had
Commissions closer I had not descried
In three months' company. I knew he held
Some underground or overseas direction
That wired him to Bilbao. But I learned
Only his indirections in Madrid.

I was myself a runner. I can hold
A secret. Though I caught Felipe's name,
The air force north, hard-pressed and needing aid,
And Tahl appointed ears for battles turned
In rooms with maps and brusque decisions made
To save or lose the north, his grave will hide,
No doubt, or air absconding all his words,
The fight he lost for one more pair of wings
Out of Madrid to clear the Nervión.
That fight he lost; but fought. We fought and lost,
But have not lost those few December evenings.

Those nights he gave me reasons. He had come,
He said, because an officer in Athens
Challenged him; because he heard a noise,
Not music, in Vienna; and because
Of Italy and France; because of visions;
Because he'd dug the past and heard a sound
Of crying. "But, Miguel," he said, "too late
To hear the cries go past on years of wind."
And so I think he came that year on time.
He fired a gun but said no war is won
By guns, devolves on clear communications,
Needs ears and sounds, profession for musicians.

We watched the tracers of the planes. We watched
The waiter's eyes for trouble. Federico,
One murky night, said, facing us, his eyes
Black as olives, "Tahl, the planes will come
One last time. If we escape the waiter,

If we and your friends start off as if for England,
Death in a mask goes always on before us.
I can fight in daylight in Vizcaya
And that is better than to fall on slogans,
The touted effigy, the poet murdered.
But who kills whom at last? Who owns the world?"

"We do not own the world, that's sure," said Tahl,
"Though some of us perhaps would pay arrears
On rent if we could find an honest agent.
I would, for one. I doubt if God is dead.
But who kills whom? The whites would like your skin
As artist. And they'd have a use for mine
As alien; and the reds, for non-conformist.
The whites will hang Miguel to Nevergreens
By ears and tongue if they should hear him." All
He said cut never nearer truth than this.
Though I go free, I still expect my hanging.

Our enemies I know more close than armies
Employed to sack one country. "Hate," he said,
"Prepares its noose not only in Madrid.
In every city where our fears have made
Entrenchment, tribes will march in lawful dread
Of us, the outlaws. Call them white or red,
Disciples of the drunken engineer
In Paris drinking absinthe, martinets
Of Marx or Machiavelli, the reports
Of adjutants, ambition and intrigue
Demand a closed community of fear.

"The cities are at war. The cities hide
In peace all outlaws. But in war our heads
Are price to either side, Chungking, Madrid,
Berlin or Moscow, London. We can choose
Trisecting angles by approximation
But will not find a corner. We're a tribe
Among the polygons on polygons
To find the square of circles, but we'll squeeze
Within the decimals by luck, not justice.

The states, the parties, move by polygons,
Dislike to calculate complexities."

We talked those nights till curfew and beyond
While others died. But all of us, he said,
Lived our sonata. First the man alone,
And then, the man in cities. At the last
The man alone. Those nights I saw him stand
Looking at Federico. Knew he'd sworn
His heart to square a circle and preserve
That outlaw from all armies. I have learned
Tahl fought beside our loyal partisans
And did not fail them. But he first fulfilled
His private fealties as man alone.

Those nights with Federico I believed
We still could trust one tribe and hate another,
But all I learn, a prisoner in Spain,
Will prove as well America or China,
Russia, Britain or your chosen nation.
We can not cut the world like cards, by colors.
And men with honest hearts are often outlaws.
Federico held the mask of death
And Tahl, the mask of life. Their Janus answer
Demanded love more personal than juntas
And loyalties more valiant than their fears.

Federico talked of death that hugs
The ground and gapes like laughter, towers of silence
Holding flesh to vultures and the sun;
The figures of Christ in all our country churches,
The human hair, the painted, dripping wounds;
The death of children and the jaws of Baal
With fanfare, cymbals and the beat of drums
That once in Carthage fed with living food
The horned, bull-headed image. And the jaws
In every flaming city feed — though drums
And cymbals cease — *delenda est Carthago.*

And Tahl repeating after him, "*Delenda*
Est Carthago." Gravely smiled, the eyes
As black as olives and the sea I've seen
Off Finisterre in winter. All I heard
That night seemed two men singing. I have wondered
If they had ears for future fires and thunders.
Federico scanned all dance as death.
And Tahl said wars would burn beyond our seasons
So long as hate and cities lived together.
"If we live close enough to love each other,
We make a choice," he said, "for life or death."

"How can we choose?" I asked. "Did Attila
For all his butchery ride brother-blood
And slay his closest kin?" "The men we kill,
Playing racatac from roofs and chimneys
Are also brother-blood," said Federico,
"For all their treacheries." "We choose to kill,"
I said, "or choose to die and still the choice
Is death, the bull fight." "Or choose death with honor,"
Added Federico. I snapped off
The lights for curfew. Through the night Tahl's voice,
"The corporate lie which no one must betray."

Prisoners' nights are always dark. I think
At night of their two voices. I believe
That if I die, I die for love of Spain.
But Tahl will come to die because he loved
Felipe, Federico, Alison
And others that I cannot give a name.
He was a curious kind of citizen
Whose tribe has always been, whose victories
Are not recorded, whose defeats are hidden,
Whose tribe perhaps increases, being borne
On music and more swift communication.

His race is rare like instruments he chooses,
The last *alboka* and the lute he made,
He said, in Antioch for orchestrating
The sound that voices make in many cities,

Voyage by Land

The vertigo of horror and the drum
Of fire. "But I must find," he said, "a music
To build once more such walls as Palestrina
Built against a world-destroying fear.
I go through cities listening, and going
The way of cities, sure as oxygen
And gravitation have expected war."

His race is common; "the electric cells
Of our potential whom," he said, "a war
Disturbs but as the wind disturbs, who live
Our possible births and unpredicted deaths,
Immediate friends most real and every claim
Of major crisis sold by paper vendors
Believed immune from feuds with backstairs neighbors.
The flotsam of the chromosomes submerging
Equal love and danger, they will cast
With tide an average of peace and terror.
Their heroes are the accidents of weather."

He was as rare as tarpans and as common
As men who talk of death and draw their fingers
Sharp across the throat to say summation
Which is the end of life. And he would joke
With Federico, saying time and weather
Would teach him less respect for death's gangrene.
"We are less quick than navvies, train conductors,"
Said Tahl, "to learn what pageants, banderillas
Would disguise, that death is sudden." Once
Looking down at me half-wryly said:
"Miguel, our friend hates death because he loves."

They left one bitter day in January.
"And will you come again with victory?"
I asked. "Miguel," he answered, "crime
Is colder than this morning. We have talked
Of Walther. Have you seen a praying mantis,
The delicate wings, the claws like invocation,
Ogre in ambush? Or the fire ants climbing?
The fulcrum flight of hawks? I think that powers

Have interests here that pulse without a heart
And where the heart stops is the place of death."

And last he said, "Miguel, I've heard in Egypt,
To send the body safe upon its journey
The scribes and the embalmers were entrusted
To place the great papyrus on the breast,
The Coming Forth by Day, the guide and chart
Toward peace and resurrection. I am told
The documents were falsified and many
Scribes grew rich who buried spurious papers.
I think defeat defers to time and weather
Which may defer to ants and hawks and ogres,
Who fear us only when we conquer death."

I felt the callouses along his fingers
That meant both strings and triggers. I looked up
At Federico and he spoke. He said
"We've seen the dead who die by repercussion,
The body quite unscarred. I think the air
Explodes, as Tahl has said. And life departs
More terribly that shows no burn nor bloodstain.
We learned of death too simply who have prayed
To Christ with dripping wounds. He dies again
Without the mark of thorns. In some new year
Perhaps we may expect new resurrection."

I walked Madrid alone. The days were cold
That January. Saw the marks of flame
Above the traffic. Held against my mind
A line of Heraclitus: "The soul of man
Is a celestial fire." I have not seen
El Tahl campeador nor Federico
And I may hang or rot in this foul den
For asking death with honor. I shall hang
Without remarks. I have seen fire, heard thunder.
I asked him once at Alcalá de Henares,
"Where do you go?" "Where all men go," he answered,
"With the sea's turn, the voyage of a planet."

TAHL: BOOK TWO

CANTO V

THE TWICE-BORN

The Dead God

ALISON:
Near Jerusalem he said
He had found the grave of God.
You and I remember when
Athens and Whitsunday's moon
Led him to the grave of man.
Now to last denials come
The fourteen days of halcyon
Never less of peace than here;
Wherever sea-blue birds may fare
To tranquil waves, a sea is loud
Upon this land. And in Madrid
We sang no mass this winter day
For man or God. If here we die
As well we may — this afternoon
Like ritual we counted bomb
And bomb till twelve; last night we ate
In ritual two Spaniards taught
Twelve grapes. Then shall we lay us down
Like Persians north? Or toward the sun
At morning like Phoenicians? Last
With Athens or some Christian ghost
Turn us toward the dying west
In this our death? Or quetzal-dressed
To ash and Aztec sacrifice?

The Dead God

Scant ritual may grace a death
In this new war. And every birth
Comes casual, catastrophe
More sad than watching old years die
Like gods' Decembers earthward bound
Or flung to sea till spring shall come.
Here in Spain they say the wine
Spoiled last spring of too much rain.
Here all symbols stand reversed.
Rain is sorrow, birth is death,
And hope envisioned in a cross
The Indians' swastika debased
To hell's intent. Here "Christ the king"
Is warcry with a churchbell clang
To murder all who come unarmed
In Christian peace. Here Calvary
Comes out of season and the cry
Of thorns assaults the Christmas star.
December's guns make August thunder.
Now the dead alone may bear
The upper air; the grave has turned
To refuge and the death-bells sound
To save the living under ground.
The solstice with all signs may change:
A god at Christmas leave his tomb;
And man grown tall be born again.

IRIS:
Not every letter come from Alison
So latticed in with riddles. I have saved
This page most dearly. Facts a mind can hold;
But must make study of the shape of words.
Yet facts themselves may build uneasy lessons.
Like the doctor that she was she sent
A primer first. In June from Paris gone
To join her southern gentleman; of Jim,
Bayonne with spires, the gorse, the bracken downs,
The shores of Biscay and the Basques at home,
Of limestone peaks, low sea-walls, fishermen,

Their boats, their two-wheeled wagons, and their women
Mending nets. Her purpose too. Had walked
The quais Magellan left to see the world
And traced his navigator named El Cano.
I walked the present. She had walked the past.
Nevertheless the diary that burned,
Columbus' own that she had hoped to read,
Lost with a ducal palace in Madrid
Came news as new as famine in Bilbao,
Newer than renaissance amenities
Of suave mid-month July in Lequeitio
Where she'd met, she wrote, two friends of Tahl,
Two Austrians. But in these days we've seen
The past make present enemies of friends.

Early summer's primer that we scanned,
George and I in London, followed fast
With harsher grammars. We with autumn come
Four thousand miles by water and by land
Seemed further still across a gulf in time.
"Irún," she wrote, "has fallen. Very soon
I think San Sebastián. Tahl tries to learn
His flying lessons over. He's become
A connoisseur of guns. Though Jim has joined
The foreign volunteers, I'm not alone."
Shells in hot red flashes, night explosions,
Haycocks burning, pigs and poultry driven
Down the boulevards and bank vaults piled
On trucks. And spies. And rebel ships at anchor.
The land's defense unguarded from the skies.
"A battleship, its single smokestack smeared
On this calm August, shelled the Calle Ronda,
Killed a man, a woman, and two girls.
A two-stack warship and a cruiser shelled
Nine days. Water is scarce. We hold the forts."
Bilbao, late September: "Tahl has gone
On errands south against the German fliers.
Felipe says the old Breguets are useless
And hopes for Russian biplanes." Michigan
Guarded us with yachts. Each night, the mail-planes.

"Iris," said George, "persuade her to come home."
Her November stamps were French. But hope
Burst with the broken seal. "This year I've earned.
And if I die, I've met with history
True as Columbus or a Mayan town."
She was often far from me. We'd played
In parks together, shared a desk, had taught
In the same school. But Indians to me
Were childhood games. To her a culture lost
Who would lose nothing of the crumbled past.
She would not swim a middle depth. I think
Of her in earlier summers at the cove
Wading for starfish and as sudden dived
Beyond my dare and depth along the reef,
My frantic eyes half-blind with glare and sun.
And now I groped her mist of calm detail,
Guncotton, mortars, small arms, *bacalao*,
Who'd talked of pictographs, hieroglyphs
And manuscripts in ancient tongues — now bound
On missions after food for trapped Vizcaya.
"Stephanie and I go free in this
Imperiled world," she wrote. "For Walther's gone
Annoyed about some business in Shanghai.
He dragged us out of Spain, but we'll return."
George swore at Tahl for leaving her alone.

"Tell George," she said, "El Greco's *Count Orgaz*
Was lost in the siege of Toledo." Then we quarreled
For he would shout that only common men
Could trample it or let it burn. He scorned
Her faith and mine who led more honest soldiers.
Her winter letter late. In March we talked
Less of Madrid than of a plane that crashed
In San Francisco bay with all on board,
Though not one name we knew. And rising floods
Along Ohio and the hundreds homeless.
Capronis, Junkers, Fiats and Savoias
Or Hotchkiss, Maxim, Lewis might be names
As strange as Mexican wars or Baghdad's wonders,
And nitroglycerin and kieselguhr

Less dynamite than steel strikes or the Windsors.
General Mola's boasts and heavy glasses
No clearer than December in Nanking
And China's warlord kidnapped in Sian.
George raised a wall on China and on Spain
And teased me for concern about the steel mills.
But Basque berets and fired *esparto* grass
Ran tangling through my dreams. That rioting
In the Piraeus, Alfred walking lame,
Converged along mesetas toward Madrid.
"The war has come." "Of course," was George's answer.

"And who gets killed," said George, "are the devil's martyrs.
That's a Spanish proverb. And let Tahl
Tend his *alboka* if he likes. Or come
Like Alfred home, get sons and mind his business.
With Alison here to help you in September."
That she did come, you know. And Juliana,
If children could remember, would recall
She turned her eyes toward Alison the day
That she first knew one face from any other.
But all my anxious months I had bad dreams.
Churches turned to fortresses and plains
Rose to a bloody moon. And Alison
And I seemed wanderers in dripping mines
Shaken with bombs. In Paris, Athens, George
Shouting: *"Rien ne vaut ça! La guerre! La guerre!"*
And I read much that year. I sewed and thought
Of landlords safe in Biarritz, of serfs
In these our years upon seigneurial farms,
Reviewed Asturias, studied the last elections,
And almost prayed for the child within my womb.
But, clearer than Mosca or Marx, Michels, Pareto,
My grandmother's prayers, or George's love and teasing,
My dreams and Alison's world ahead in time
Like the nameless growing child who kicked at darkness
And Tahl, the chaser of planes, the flying questions.

And this last bulky package when it came
Speaking Madrid but wearing postmarks: England,

Though full of bombardiers, escapes, and censors
And violence normal as a talking picture,
Brought other news than calendars will measure.
Her letters I sent always on to Alfred
But took them once more with me to the lake
Where only grackles and the first spring swallows
Moved the air. The water chopped the pier
In sunlight paler than Madrid on fire.
But other fire and other light she mentioned
Stirred me also. Seldom those scant weeks
At Christmas she'd seen Tahl alone. But once
They spoke of Dante. He'd most often stayed
Some way through hell to watch Odysseus drowning.
But what might follow I could prophesy
Surer than May and June. Together first
We'd found it: 'And I saw light flowing
Like a river, living sparks turned flowers.'
He'd answered her with stories of November
In Madrid, that night of fire: "I saw
Infernos deeper than the waters lie
Below the land. And shall we hope to find
Illumination fit for paradise?"
I thought of the boat the night we crossed toward Athens.

Yes, this is her own script. She always had
From childhood this same legible, firm hand:

ALISON:
And Iris, if you'd thought that Tahl had changed
In Paris more than a scar on his face could change him,
You'd have more wonder now. His drifting toward
A name for God and angry cynicism
Have met within him in some dire explosion.
All of us move toward crisis. Federico
With eyes like Malaga grapes, this Lazarus
Saved from Granada, like a walking ghost
Fights the life we give him. And Miguel
Exchanges scholar's wits for soldier's silence.
Our insides jump at every crash. Each car

A zoom of planes. *Salud!* The women armed.
The children wild as foxes. Cordite stench.
Houses like cadavers, entrails showing,
Dissected flesh and bone. The heart hangs naked.
Some eat gruel, chickpease. Others dine
At the Chicote and the Molinero.
And Stephanie who says she's never seen
The backstairs of Vienna suffers most,
Encountering this world's face, the skin torn off.
I sometimes think she's braver than Jan, the girl
Who knew Tahl as a child, with her convictions
We who grew without much pomp or money
Hold more easily, that human beings
Owe each other love and common living.

I may be traitor too, defending minds
Enduring crisis as a wound's gangrene.
Miguel has warned me that a man like Tahl
Walks target for the shadowing suspicions
Of those he serves, for just such hesitations.
The anarchists who hold that natural goodness
Spontaneous unites in natural chaos
And turns to natural order as the atoms
Or the social insects; or the Marxist
Exalting loyalty and class obedience
Are nitroglycerin and kieselguhr
To blow a path through hell. And I believe
The smothering precedence of landlords, magnates,
Priests — not all, but those whose power is temporal —
Are present hell with all roads blocked to heaven;
And far more dangerous for crying Christ
Than those whose myth cries natural salvation.
The blood that made the Spaniards vomit, seeing
The temples of Montezuma, was more honest.
Mole-heaps must erupt. But peasant wars
These ten years past in China and the blood
Of just and unjust shed from Finisterre
To Almería will not be enough.
That minds must bleed and heal the Marxists know,
But, worldly priests, they judge who shall be saved.

We too are willful. Tahl who will divide
His strength. He saves Federico. Plays with time
To reach Felipe, fight on his own terms
For the surrounded Basques where hope's least likely.
I in my own willfulness to wait
With Stephanie whose heart's a pendulum
Between a Hapsburg haughtiness and faith
In a theoretical truth of human freedom.
Alone, I'd join with Jan. But Walther's name
Opens doors red stars still frighten fast
And these fast doors must open to this war
If it's to be a path of liberation
And not exchange of tyrants. You might say
We're liaison department. We may save
A few from gunfire's indiscrimination.
Madrid has arrows pointing to *refugios*
And few will check the politics of those
The morgue receives. But we alive to run
To cellars cannot amputate our past,
Can only hope to mend until we're buried.
I think that Tahl at last may disappear
Anonymous, a decimal with others,
And not come home unless he's forced, alive
Or dead. Or home? He lives upon the globe.
Though I'll admit I have a heart could hold him.

We are the funeral wakemen, unheroic.
The Concha nor the sloping avenues
Of this city drain our blood. We help
The seasick children safe to France. We watch
The spate of bullets, but fight no great battles.
We watch thin faces war with desperate eyes.
Treacheries on both sides. This plateau
Of sand and clay endures like every nation
Scum on the troubled stream. I am afraid
As often of the officers who reason
As of blunt arrogance and superstition.
The talkative revolutionary poisons
Our strength sometimes as fatally as typhus
Left by heedless armies. I have hope

Sooner of one convinced miliciano
Than of the quibbling necktie politicians.
This Christmas under the shelling Tahl and I
Remembered hearing Händel sung in Boston
On Christmas Sunday; speculated why
We met in Greece who both were born New England.
Händel's solid harmony that turns
'Good will towards men' to counterpoint and comes
'Glory to God' in harmony again
May also bear its part with posters, slogans
We serve in our dark tunnels toward salvation.

If I reach home, I'm bringing in my baggage
Some scores of Tahl's to peddle them. I wish
That I had heard his concert those two years
Before I knew of anyone alive
Much like him. Jim, of course, with his big plan
To split the universe. But now he's gone
To nearer risk. And if he should return
With a whole skin I think that Jan will have him.
Tahl says these scores have firmer bass, and less
Flamboyant orchestration. And he tried
With a guitar to show me. I could hear
Invention wonderful enough but still,
As on that night I met him, something mad
That dazzled but allowed no resolution.
He says if he should write a mass at last
He will address Felipe's God we met
Last summer when we heard the congregation
Sing in Guernica. And Federico
Has a faith eludes the priests but sounds
Like valid music. Only Stephanie
Insists the mass embalmed with Palestrina
And right humility is imitation.
She's like sherry, light and pungent; still
A tartness hidden. Worries him, I think
And gives him fevers. Even so, I love her.

IRIS:
At these words you've stopped. And so did I
Each time, and even on the day in spring
I sat by the lake and read them, though they came
By then without surprise. And George looked up
When he first read them, shook the page with laughing:
"Alison has her yellow hair," he said.
"Eyes with more of music than his masses.
But being loyal to his concubines
Isn't the quickest way to get him married.
If she'd met Margot, maybe she'd have kissed her?"
My long devotion fought the acid dash
Of his last sentence. And George turned his mood
Like litmus when he saw my face. I think
That only Tahl and not in that first year
Knew her frightening heart, too wise for rancor.
We're more afraid of justice than of guns
And tremble at forgiveness. George has feared
The peace within himself and so he fights
All that beyond our quarrels makes me love him.
But I'll not interrupt. She wrote:

ALISON: "In war
The act encumbers talk, but meditation
Overtakes us, soldier or civilian
Waiting barrage, standing in line for papers.
Being too weary for thought, we often think
More actively in action's ebb for thinking.

To such an ebb we came on Christmas evening.
Jim was not with us. The Americans
With winter filtered in and the brigades
Increased. And Jim was shifted east. He's fighting
Along the Tajuña. Paddy came on leave.
With Jim we missed Felipe, youngster only
As I've mentioned, but a solid man,
Square as his shoulders. Makes me think of Alfred.
Felipe flies a Russian Chato now
Over the northern valleys. Tahl has joined him.

The Twice-Born

We left Madrid in January, ordered . . .
Thirty of us cast out like Judas' pence
For legal neutrals. But our potter's field
Sprouts to wheat in England. We're at work
With British plans to rescue Spanish children.
If I come home, I'm fighting too. Here's warning.
In these two months I have set down for you,
As I set down last spring our shipboard journal,
One single night of talk in months of running
And only chance it came on Christmas evening.
Don't picture us in mudholes. Wars on cities
As yet leave oases in parching fire
And though we die in minutes, somehow chairs
And ceilings seem secure. We were as safe
Perhaps as on a boat across an ocean:

TAHL:
Midnight. We're alive. They've hit the tower
Again. They've gauged that Garabitas line
More predictable than lightning. Phones
Won't ring tonight. Felipe told me once
If the bell of the hour and the bell for the lifted Host
Ring together, you're forewarned of death.
And so it's midnight. And there's not a mass
In all Madrid. By now they've sent the bell-girls
Even from the wires. The self-made exiles,
Denied the comfort of a superstition,
Can learn to guess a gun's trajectory.
But who shall tell us why we hope to live
Who make so great a science of our dying?

PADDY:
I been places. Dying's not so lovely.
Whether you're socked with sunstroke on the brain
Like on the Tanezrouft. Or boiled in fire
Like them in Martinique. You ever see
That hill called Mont Pelée? That ugly hump
Blew off when I was ten. Don't think it don't
Do something to a kid to see a town

Shoved under in red-hot mud like old St. Pierre.
I've bummed from Fort de France to Panama,
From Sandy Hook to Singapore and Kobe,
And we never get used to the dying that God thinks up
And can't go laying blame. It's all a war.

FEDERICO:
Sorrow-torn as living flesh is torn
Ripping the nails from undefended hands,
What remains for symbol? Only simple
Pity and the hospital that looms
Above the century of Napoleon
Inherited by Baudelaire, Verlaine,
The surgeon's pincers on defenseless cities.
We revert to understanding dimmer
Than Punic ports dragged down when Paddy's God
Drowned those red hills of Dido in the sea,
Who understood the spirit as a dove,
Appeased the bull of power. We are more lost
Than they. Now Christ, his birth and crucifixion,
Two thousand years Barabbas' jubilation.

STEPHANIE:
The Nuremberg decrees this past September
May be Barabbas' triumph. Do you say
Perhaps Teutonic knights or Hohenzollerns,
Richelieu or any British statesman
With a monocle, or to be timely,
Señor March with sugar funds and petrol
More culpable than Mont Pelée's volcano?
They all intend toward good as they define it.
Perhaps the papers signed by Maginot —
Have you heard? do damage here in Spain
More than Bonaparte. But we keep Christmas.

JAN:
Someone's wrong. Perhaps it's God. I think
Of Jim. His father writes him angrily

For fighting here in Spain. But there's no answer.
His great-uncle Will with his brigade
Fell in Kentucky fighting for the North
And his great-uncle Jim with his brigade
Fell in Virginia fighting for the South.
After that Civil War they were brought home,
Those brothers and above their single grave
Their father's words, the sum of his bereavement:
'God alone knows which of them was right'
On the single headstone. Electrons strike
On atoms, ionize, make paths of light.

MIGUEL:
The answers change. Copernicus was blessed
To die before the Pope had time to read
The earth had been misplaced. And when the knights
Marched on the Moslems in Jerusalem
Perhaps the courtiers of Arabia
Dreaded that horde as our lost friends have feared
Red stars and hammers. Call this revolution
Roman *jus civile* and *jus gentium*
Bound toward greater justice. But the cause
Is cloudier with dreams than Palmerin
Or Amadis the Gaul. We grope in signs
More dire than Farinacci or Laval.

TAHL:
Our histories are histories of crime.
But we shall not solve questions by reversing
Numbers here and there in older answers.
The masses sung in the Invalides each May
For Bonaparte recall persisting praise
Of tyranny as heroism. Lines
Between the merciful and cruel slide
Toward a red which gives a longer wave
Of light and sound. But still the prism shines
And the first source of that first light unanswered.
The Russians' legal witch-hunts or the rope

That hangs America with martyred Negroes,
The honest heads still thrust on pikes in China
Weigh our hearts to the Egyptian feather.

ALISON:
Each answer at the last reads in a sign
And we grown bold to make ourselves the priests
Of our own understanding must be rcad
In many symbols. For the knot implied
In ancient dances with the sword, the bull,
The gelded horse, the beating heart torn out
From man alive on sacrificial stones
Read crime and expiation. We have gaped
On truth as Indians now stand and stare
At pillars in the jungles of Quiriguá
And turn our backs on death which is one answer.

PADDY:
Dying's not lovely, I'm saying. But no use yelping,
Wringing your brains. The holy fathers pray
And they got brains, the good ones. Ten Hail Marys
Save my skin. And then you join a union
To keep your neck on and your fists from idling.
It ain't so hard as you make out, this living.

STEPHANIE:
This is indeed the truth, if you insist
Our Christmas must be solemn. Where indeed
But in the Church we find the sum of wisdom
Greater than your hated priests' defections?
A Fra Angelico I understand
Sooner than prisms or the rules of unions.
The Church remains, the rock of civilization.

MIGUEL:
Perhaps you will defend the Inquisition?
Explain why mercy needs a fleet of galleons?

Or why our Christian kings were so unkind?
I think the orders setting up the guns
Shelling the tower tonight were signed by Christians.
A most precipitous rock, this civilization.

JAN:
I think the people die for lead and zinc,
For coal and salt and copper. As for light,
Perhaps some faith, some God, like X-rays can
Cure the flesh or burn it. And to use
Such rays takes training. Our reflexes tuned
For flying planes must lack such education.

TAHL:
Spain, like lost Atlantis flung again
Above the sea, throws every ancient question
Dripping blood and salt. The bull rites died
On pompous matadors. But here the Church
Bred saints and torturers and Jesuits.
The cartel-gold of Mexico, Peru,
Squeaks copper ghosts in shafts on Rio Tinto.
Here music still remembers that the dance
Reports the fundamental act of love,
Of flesh before the spirit. Spaniards know
The wit, the art, the sleight of violence,
The prism from Don Juan to Don Quixote,
Señor Death and the scream of true *flamenco.*

STEPHANIE:
Is it this season makes you delicate?
What of *flamenco,* pizzicato, swirling,
Pausing, the clattered guitars, and that harsh shout,
The twirl and shriek of frantic lecheries,
The pulse of castanets. Come. Say it then.
That love is violence intent on death.
Where the passion's angrier, I think
The power to quell it must be angry too

Who even dance at mass, as in Seville.
It is no chance that fire and rape are more
Than merest rhetoric for men at war
And hate, a curse on the sex of those who bore us.

PADDY:
It ain't just Tahl. You're speaking fancy, too.
But you got something, lady. Like they say,
Nobody loves you maybe but your mother,
May God rest her. I seen ships and war.
It's dirty like you mean. And how you clean
The stinking mess except you say some prayers?
I ain't out to save the world. But Christ,
I'd pray for them poor Chinese guys that's got
To look at their own bosses selling girls
Like hog feed. Sure. And then the Japs come down
And split the rest like little grapes. You know.
It happens here. And that ain't lovely neither.
But I know something. Signs don't make no difference,
Yellow or black or white or sacred hearts
Or kissing the cross. You got to love, not hate.
If you got love, you don't go playing ugly.

FEDERICO:
Is there no other hatred? Other death?
The men who tried to kill me kissed the cross
And burned my books. I had not thought they burned
My books because I had not written down
Quintillas to the glory of the Church
But only spoke of Christ and love and death.
Their ignorance? For I am like Quevedo
Lost in signs and ambiguities
And see with Goya truth a laughing monster.

ALISON:
The dance which serves for war and love compels
The dancer toward a deeper mystery

Which has no name but love. Our ignorance
In every power of sex and trade and war
Trusts the mind but not the will that moves
All power to its last transfiguration.

TAHL:
But how shall we achieve the figure turned
From joy in violence to joy in peace
Beyond destruction? Is not wisdom lost
Like Spain's wild horses? Neither word nor tone
In any rarest balance can design
Answers till the heart itself is ground
In anguish angrier than signs and visions.

MIGUEL:
Does the antiquity of error prove
It must be truth? Else then the Pope should play
At toss with emperors. Or should we stop
With Leibnitz or Spinoza? Or revert
To Dante and his two most sacred cities?
I think our planes must strafe with sharper engines.

PADDY:
In Sicily it was, in Taormina,
I says to a Father, "All them peasants
Pulping lemons going to sometime turn
And eat them. See?" And he says, "Patience, son,
God don't pay on Saturday." I says
He pays out slow. But I don't mean no harm.

TAHL:
Once God paid on Wednesday. You remember,
Alison, the ship there off the Concha
And that old man. I saw the shell that burst
And struck him down, the head still whole. The face
Came like a face I'd seen, a haggard woman

In a woolen cap who turned on me
For staring once, two years ago that seem
Two thousand years ago in a New York
Unreal as death. And she was death out walking
And so I went to Egypt. That old man
Looks at me. You've said that God likes music.
Albokas and guitars I'd immolate
For one good chance to push that ship to hell
With an enharmonic shift of dynamite.

STEPHANIE:
You are much changed. I do not think I like you.
I'm almost serious. But tell me, would
You make an end of all the ships? For that
Perhaps you're called a hero. But they shoot
Murderers. You follow? Should you kill
Walther? You will find him in Shanghai.
Or strafe the wealthy gentlemen of Hamburg?

JAN:
I am more angry that the children die.
You will not save them, Tahl, with fantasies
Of sinking navies. There is more to do
Than your boy's voyage to unlikely Chinas.

TAHL:
Yet the unlikely Chinas and all vision
May serve to guide the act. Miguel takes hope
In his denials. But his affirmation
In some community of citizens
Is not more real or less than sinking navies.

FEDERICO:
But you will not escape in your denial
Unless you die of it. You burn your music
To a god will take revenge against you

And what you see and hear will scald you more
Than oil from ships in seven burning oceans.

MIGUEL:
And what of you, my friend? You go now with him.

FEDERICO:
I have cheated death. I shall pay interest.

MIGUEL:
I cannot judge who cheats. And who has lost
All answers must survive in taking orders.

FEDERICO:
By man came death. And I participate
In an atonement, first and last of answers.

JAN:
Have you ever been in a spin? The plane gone twist
And bound for death as if it meant to kill you?
Pull back the stick. You're dead. But push it up
To dive like dying and the ship recovers
Level. You're in charge. And yet it goes
Against the blood to shove it so. We learn
Without believing till the spin comes on.

STEPHANIE:
But all belief survives in courtesies
That bow to all and keep their own opinions.

TAHL:
Yes, Stephanie. At peace we best survive
Disdaining every gaucherie you'd call

Bad manners and at last fanaticism
To keep the decent courtesies of freedom.
But as no nihilist, though you may bend
In wind, you will not also love the axe
Prepared to slash the treetrunk and to ash
Consign the stump of freedom. I have seen
A man, Thanasie, newest Spartan chieftain;
Walther, most lamentably your husband.
Each in his own way discovers one
Of two old kinds of truth. Their faith receives
The glory from passivity in herds,
The tribe's abstract entirety preserved,
The perfect *one* with cyphers following.
Our war is the more desperate that moves
Against a cloud of cyphers and no telling
By star or swastika or any emblem
Nor name by nation which of all the faces
Loves his helotry before his freedom.
If there are heroes they must be such men
As love and doubt their flatterers as they
Can love and doubt their enemies. I think
At last a man's account is to all men
With numbers positive and no man nothing.

ALISON:
Your secret cry, the whistle of the bat,
Has more of meaning than a common joke.
I've heard that their wide wing-flight in the dark
Brings them unerringly with dawn to sleep
In their first home. And even from migrations
By signs we cannot read to north and south
On all the continents and every ocean.
And now you come by anniversary
Upon a birth foreshadowed. I'll not say
By book a saga for a man of sorrows,
Call him Attis, Osiris, Prometheus, even
The tall, white, bearded man whose mighty helmet
Swung the bright-green quetzal feather, all
The avatars of one persisting sign

Of such a man as you desire, the one
Buried in birth with winter and recovered
Alive in death at springtime. Only cyphers
Look upon this sign without a question
And none of us are cyphers. And no man
Is cypher who has loved or seen one vision.

TAHL:
And do all truths succumb to death? The pride
Of tribal glory is the death of rebels.
And the proud glory of indifference
Is death to love, the death determinate.
We are afraid of music for it hurts
To break the tomb we build with our own hands.
In my whole flesh this night I take a wound.

ALISON:
Iris, he was smiling then. I saw
Miguel look at him nervouslv and frown,
His short, dark body restless. Stephanie
Turned her cool eyes away as if she'd looked
Politely at indecency and shuddered.
Only her lower lip one shade disturbed
From her impeccable amusements showed
Some deeply held complexity alive
That she mistrusted. Like a well-bred child
Cheerful at weddings, awed at funerals,
Jan sat silent. Paddy sound asleep
With wine and his first leave in three months' fighting
Bulked like Mont Pelée itself, erupted
In sudden snorts and snores, his peaceful conscience
Over us all, a mighty, tamed volcano.
Only Federico moved . . . an image
From El Greco, less than carnal thin,
The skin a curious gold like leaves in spring,
His dark head bent above me and his mouth

On mine as if he'd never hold again
Man or woman. Windows shook with cold
December wind and gunfire. Federico
Turned and knelt by Stephanie. He laid
His head upon her knees. And there was terror
In us, even Miguel. The sirens sounded.
The planes came. The breaking glass. The cries.
But Paddy slept. And we were not afraid
Of death. Miguel had slid his fingers in
Below his collar as if something choked him
And Jan had bent her head. But Tahl and I,
His hand in mine, were watching Federico.
Saw Stephanie, as mothers hold their sons,
Lift him up; a Salome transfigured
She held him with his head thrust back against her
Only a moment. Then the knocking came.
The hospital. A call for Jan. Miguel
Left also. Paddy heaved and growled in sleep.
We four were not together once again
Until we left for the coast, the boat toward England.
They jumped the ship at Vigo. We were off
St. Vincent when Tahl walked the deck and said:
"Alison, if through the road to war,
I should come back to music, you will know
Why guitars and horn cry like *flamenco*
In a human voice will cross the phrase
Descending to the tomb of one laid down
Upon the knees of one who weeps." He'll go
Alone, I think, for Federico walks
As if he looks for death. But we have come,
Two of us, to lands which unlike maps
But like the earth unmarked to azimuth
Still indicates a crossing with the stars,
And if we live, we shall go on together.

TAHL : BOOK TWO

CANTO V

THE TWICE-BORN

The Risen God

TAHL:
The swallows now above the roofs of Paris
Rise to quiet air. If I might say:
Expertus vacuum Daedalus aera.
But I cannot, my dear. And that old Roman
Speaking man's temerity on wings
Might have foreseen a folly sadder far
Than Icarus. But folly is too fine
A word for my foolhardiness. I am
At most a murderer who still walks free.
I see, now running on events, the world
Slip beside me backward as the landscape
Slides the running train. And on this slide
I now myself return as landscape only,
Incompetent to be the engineer
Transcending time. Yes, Federico's dead,
Embracing death he looked for, but his death
Remains my guilt though no one ever find
His unaccusing corpse. I'll soon go down
As nameless and with men I do not know
To cross the Pyrenees again, assigned
As others may determine to battalions,
A poor replacement for the men now fallen.
And how shall I be four at once? They're gone,
Felipe, Federico, Paddy, Jim.
The four known dead of many great men dying.

The Risen God

Here I wrench myself on this last morning
Of my sick memory. The flight too easy,
Alison, too easy. My five wits,
If I had had them, should have warned me, knowing
God so prepares the nemesis of those
Too brash. But when Felipe fell, that last
Of the great yeomen tumbling from the sky,
Decision seemed appointed. We had hidden
That old crate so long there in his orchard,
Salvaging parts to make it fly again,
The flimsy moth that used to spin along
The coast to spill advertisements, the one
We practised in. And when the boats came back
Laying the mines again and that same stack
Puffing its smoke on Puenta de Galea
As last year arrogant against the Concha
And not to shell a city now but starve
In May those children who had starved already
More than they could forget in January,
The moth, no match for vultures, could go up
On other missions. We had laid away
The oil tin packed with dynamite, the other
Filled with oil. We'd cut the belly out
To make a door. That smugglers' country knows
All smugglers' arts. The plot moved easily.

Durango, Guernica gone. And Mola's troops
Swung forward like a scythe. At last we rose
Crazily over the hedges, staggered up
The straining engine never made to pull
Two men, let alone our bulky freight.
Federico in the fuselage sprawled
Had said he'd pose for Jonah in a whale
And laughter'd jarred the figures in my head.
And it was cold. Below us crawling mists.
Here and there a fire. And flashlights sharp
On mountains like blue beacons. Then the bay.
The surf along the estuary curled
As white as maps. But questions in my head.
Suppose they come? We had no guns. My mind

Kicking the rudder, hauling the stick. This moth
To shredded butterfly in one chandelle.
But everything too easily. The sky
Clear above the bay and the machine
Perhaps too small to trouble listening ears.
They tossed below us, drifting like two sticks.
One floated lazily. The other steamed.
Danger asleep. My hand for sign. Let down.
My sweat-soaked shirt felt upward draft. I heard
Nothing. We pitched. We leveled. Then a sun
Came out of the bay at midnight. Smoked. And burned.

We had done it. Yes. The ruddy flame
Flashing in smoke like an ascending star
Toward quiet night. With luck. I dipped the wing,
Swung for the headlands. But the hissing air
Went soft. The trusses bent like sinking dreams.
The wind up dropped us backward, horizons sagged,
The sloppy stick spun back a rubber band
Snapped and dangled. My stomach in my teeth.
Sweat in my eyes. We'd done it right. We had.
The best tradition. Surprise. A navy now
A few tons lighter. We were lighter too.
As if the cotter pins, the whole damned shear
Flew off. As if each antique spar took off
On its own screws and left us wallowing.
I tried it toward the wind and coaxed to freeze
That mushy stick. Stay back. The engine up
Full boost and howling. Aileron turn. Most over.
Back and to center. Nose down now. A spin
Diagonal. Ready to jump. Dead motor. Slide
Slushed and filled like a rowboat. Felt it going.
Bailed to the drench. And swam. And dived. And shouted.
Fought the drag. But he wasn't there. I wake
At night and work it over. The cut for bombs?
Sucked under when we hit? I dived and fought
At salty cold. Found nothing. The night. The sea.

I wake up at night and work it over.
He was there, smiling, a little grim. His hand

The Risen God

Palm up, face dim, eyes coal-bright, lying there
Back of my feet, his left arm strained to guard
The clumsy bomb-door. After that the slip
And holding control. I did not look again.
He might have dropped? He could have gone so, doubled.
He might have jumped? And yet I felt his hand,
I swear, against my leg when I went up
And over the side. I do not know. The words,
Alison, four notes, four notes that drove
Schumann mad, the Beethoven phrase, it goes:
I do not know. I do not know. I know
There's gossip how the battleship went down.
Some say she struck a mine. But my eyes saw
Our first tin lumpy fish go through her stack.
Saw her blow. I don't know those who died
That night. And all my life I've walked with those
Four tones. But now they hurt my ears. I knew
When Julian died. I saw Felipe's plane,
The fire-burst and the Germans turn the V
And leave him falling in an April sky.
I thanked the fisherman who hauled me in
And dumped me from the trawler into France
As I'd thank Charon, wondering why I lived.

The earth has taken Julian. And the air,
Felipe. And in not quite what you name
My metaphors together they submerge
With Federico in that bay among
The granite islands, as a sea I sought for
Having recalled it dimly from a day
My father died whose face I cannot see.
I could dare to say perhaps I live
Because your spirit has demand and power
Not my possessing as the petrel flying
Above the drifting mariner. But dare
No such conclusion. I have been beholden
To so many and have served so few.
Though out of gunfire, out of that May night
Alone and searching in the firelit sea
I come toward some great core of sorrow Julian

Knew who had respect for death. What toll
Shall I pay Alfred that my wits must needs
Cross bridges on his wound? Or George who winds
His decencies more inward out of fear
I might reform too strangely, but will fight
To send me money that he understands,
Like one more lifebelt. I have thrown Federico
To war's Moloch. And impersonal
Or personal, I willed. And somehow failed him.

No sand and lime of death, no alkali
Of life can I compound to make a glass
Even so clear as Egypt's ancient skill
To see a way through death, its three dimensions
Of time, the sea, and personal interventions,
And with them all some complex variable
No glass nor wit can compass. Who can say,
I ask myself at night, why Dante died
After the *Paradiso*? The Venetians
Killing Ravenna's captain, wounding the crew,
Compounding for war with Ordelaffi's florins
More than mosquitoes flourishing in swamps
To give a poet fevers coming home
To funeral in Ravenna? So by day
Waiting the call in this odd ruse we play
Of catching volunteers to fight a war
The whole world ought to rise to as one man —
We go like criminals, take picnic bags,
And cross the line on foot. And so by night
I see Madrid again, your head lain still
Against my shoulder on that Christmas evening
And Federico running twice from death
And even I not knowing how he died
In those scant minutes toward eternity
We could not miss by checked ignition wires.

Remember Jim, his patience to expound
The electron's energy of ionization
Ripping the proton free? The lonely proton
Meeting its wandering opposite and then

New radiation? Seems as though he held
The nucleus of the sun within his hand,
Shooting it out with formulas. But now
That head lies somewhere on a hill in Spain
Called Pingarron. Where the radiation
As he fell? The anger in Miguel
That Paddy died, those mighty guts blown out,
Before Brihuega, never lived to hear
The shout in glacial March at Guadalajara
Over the snow and mud that blocked the wheels
And gave us chance and clearance. Could we sight
Our wing-tips, we might know if vertical
Agrees with lateral, horizon keeled.
Jim said to know the first state of the atom
And its demise was to report it; but
We know the first or last or know the course
But cannot capture all three states together.
The only constant is the fact of death.
I've the clothes I walk in. You've the music
In your cases. I to General Mola
Bequeath all rare all *albokas* and guitars.

Now Bilbao and the mist-green hills
Echo like lost stories, like the Goths
Fighting Huns and trapped in quagmires, crying
Women and children. All a thousand years
The northern farmers heard them when the moon
Was misted, crying in the bogs. I hear
Behind the Three Crown hill and pinchbacked mountain,
The whitewashed hermitage, San Marcial, voices
Crying a thousand years for murder done
By man's own will, Durango after Easter,
Guernica more than a week before Ascension
And fewer to rejoice that Christ had risen
Finally to take the chair of judgment.
In that country we first heard the lark
And triple-engined planes. For iron tilts,
The steep brown peaks of mine slack they will take
The country of larks and orchards. Shutters are rusted
Since you left Bilbao, shops have locked

Their shelves with fractured dust, the dark sour bread
Is sourer now, the airfields still too small
Under the granite mountains and no prisoners
Are exchanged. "If God is possible,"
Felipe said, "He lives. We think of Him,
And He must be." Do you still hear him there
Beside the oak, that day at Guernica?

Hear him along the docks? And how he sang,
The seawind spanking his hair. In the old tongue
The words: "The waters of the sea are vast,"
The mellow Aeolian tune. And now no more
His stubborn, earnest face, the blue-gray eyes,
His boy's voice stern: "Why should one be surprised
That ancient faith contains both false and true?
My fathers held to freedom and to God
Who punishes the proud. And these are truths."
Bending his knee against the marble bench
Behind the oval council hall and shredding
Roseleaves, telling you the seamen's stories,
Ships compact as Guernica and sailed
To nameless landfalls on America.
The oak's untouched behind the council hall,
The leaves uncut by bullets. But the oxen
Died in the blazing square, the wooden wheels
Burned, the houses fell upon their cellars
Burying their dead. The tubular clusters
Fell precisely. Bombs, torpedoes, planes
In fifties came. The hospital gutted. Sector
Bombing, great precision sharp machine-gunned
All who fled beneath the April trees.
Fallen five days before on Mt. Arraig,
Felipe. Has he heard of Guernica?

Like thorny gorse on the massif of Sollube
The Basques to hold their land against the sea.
But we've seen fire; we've seen the foreign armies
Riding against republics. Three weeks past
Federico climbed with me the hills
South of Bermeo. There we saw the fires

In Guernica. He said: "Felipe lives.
He was too strong for death." I understood.
Just one full month before, Good Friday night,
The two of us in those now flaming streets
Had watched retreat of men once more betrayed
By careless men and malice. But to church,
Felipe, with his blue cap in his hand.
"Why do you pray?" I asked. He answered me:
"The Navarrese pray also. We are brothers."
"And whom will Christ forgive?" asked Federico.
"Whoever wills to meet the will of God."
"How do you know his will? " Felipe's eyes
Drew Mondragon blades: "Perhaps you mock
At me? Or at yourself? I have not lived
Your years, but I shall need no priest to teach
Such answers. All who love, who love my people,
Fight." "And if you die?" asked Federico.
"The word," Felipe gravely, "sacrifice,
Is a very big word to use upon Good Friday."

And if the tongue of the Basques is lost at last
And none can sing the song Felipe sang,
"The waters of the sea are vast"; and gone
The quiet yeoman's towns and none survive
More than the codes of just Atlantean kings
That Plato dreamed or heard of? There live none
Sons of Felipe and of Federico,
Begetter of words, I heard no word of sons.
I walk the parks of Paris, soon the time
To tie the new-formed fruits against the wind.
Easter two months past may cancel out
In counting death. March was a hungry month.
We watched for British boats. Isaiahs none
To turn the armies from Jerusalem
In the prayers of brothers though they sang
In one republic till the galleries shook
With Christian hymns. The Duke of Alva once
Struck the dikes. But these French gutters ran
With massacre in most unSpanish names.
If bloody lands beyond the Caribbean

Bled to the Pacific for a crime
Called faith in God, Felipe's, Federico's . . .
And long ago in Alexandria
Hypatia stripped by monks and slain with tiles . . .
Who met Felipe's Boeing in the clouds,
The fireball falling, west of the mourning town?

Yes, I go back, go back to Spain, go back
In time, came back to Paris, ever look
For you and you not there, not where you walked
Those months without me in Bilbao, where
You sat with Stephanie come back to Paris;
Am I to be forever running after,
Chasing you around the world and mostly
Seeing you in riots and in wars
Or on a boat and mostly in the dark?
I would have liked to live among the Basques,
To play pelota, own a bright blue trawler,
And find you hillsides full of columbines;
Grown old and wise, elected to the junta
In peaceful years with trumpets blown for honor
And fires upon five peaks. I'd even pray
With my peers before the eastward altar
In the oval council house. We'd row
The inlet, look for Jaizquibel, and towers
Shading with the sunset. I can be
Very sentimental, very lonely
In the Luxembourg with evening drums.
But I go back to rifles, substitute
In the late quarter of the game for one
Kicked in below the belt and one face down
With the three hundred dead upon Pingarron.

Sixty-nine thousand, Alison, is not
So many. There is China. There is Russia.
Sixty-nine thousand dead now in Euskadi,
Slain in the name of God and Christ the King
For mines the Germans and Italians covet
And pay out Christ to gain. Exfoliate
The ugly past into the ugly present,

The Risen God

A stripped tree carked and twisted in the wind.
Under dove-silver Fiats, fish-fin Heinkels
And the holy ghost trinitrotoluene.
When I was coming down the Guadarrama
Last October, stalking through the pines,
They gave the odor of death, embalmer's balsam,
Fragrance of death from bullet-shattered stems.
I looked once at a leaf. And always come
Despite the dogmas and despite Miguel,
That Stoic, and despite irrelevance
Of saints, Hail Mary's or the casuistries
And incense and the crimes of churches thrust
On Russia, Italy and Spain like stakes
For murderers impaling innocents,
I always come upon the ancient sign
Of death and life, the tree. And though librettos
Falter, hear a music like redemption.

The buds have burst on maple, poplar, willow.
And I shall tell you what I've told to no one,
Holding it close, my only memory
Except the sea the day he died. My father
Took me into the woods and held me high
On a December afternoon and showed me
How the winter tree branch holds each bud
One trace of color in the common gray.
And once he broke a winter bud and showed me
The flower, like feathered dust, within the leaves.
What he said to me I do not know.
I might have been just three that year. His face
I don't recall. But still those winter trees.
A burning tree? Felipe? Federico,
The May-tree cut and lost within the bay
Like gods you know and talk of, flung to sea
With prayers? I always hear that blue-capped boy:
"Whoever wills —." And all of them made choice
And all their will was love. And once I learned:
'Affinities of beings of the same class
Are sometimes represented as a tree.'
Perhaps it is the great ash, Yggdrasil,

Which, nourished by the Norns, preserves the world;
But is a twisted tree and bullet-riddled.

These are the years when only dead men dance,
When cans and gaspipe grow ingenious, when
The cartridge feeds on sugar, and the lovers
Invite the contraceptive shallow trench.
Below the loom of buildings, from the plane
Humanity's processional bacilli
Parade in air too deep for any voice.
And still the murder amplifies. The planet
Shrieks. And music cedes to noise. We slam
The final catacombs with sounding engines
Until we're deaf with thunder. Julian's father,
Who was my mother's brother, used to say,
"Listen," when thunder came. "God reads his book."
Felipe's father taught him that he ought
In time of death of neighbors rightly lift
A tile from the dead man's house to free his soul.
And now the roofs fly off and air must shake
With souls in every latitude who meet
Perhaps in that lost day of measured time
Where air meets air to make the planet's round.
What do they say in that lost day, escaped
The *Schrecklichkeit,* the classic Clausewitz
Astrologies of war? Too simple far,
Dismissing Federico to the ocean,
Felipe to his ashes on the mountain.

The solitary man as lens refracts
The light, his image always indistinct.
He holds a static power to be condensed
Through many mighty surfaces adjoined
To operating waves of light and sound.
You know from such conclusions I go down
To be one rifle in the thinned brigades.
But I have not forgotten surfaces,
Condensing with obedience to power,
Take insulation also, plate with plate,
The mica laid against the metal foil.

The Risen God

Our fathers learned perspective, how to shape
The mass in light, the single sounding line
To massive sound. But I cannot reduce
My faith to the bacillus or to motes
In energetic motion. Though we read
Our fate no longer in the flight of birds,
Nor pray and fast for a returning sun,
Nor beat off wolves who might consume the moon,
Though hid in Tarncloaks stranger than the legends,
The greed of Nibelungs, the dwarfish men
Hugging iron, still consumes the world;
And love that taught our fathers in their visions
A name for God resists the dwarf abstractions
To rise again, an infinite contradiction.

If I would play the gallant, I could say
Because your life is mine, because I watch
For news of London and for news of ships
To take you safe across a space of sea,
Because I have persuaded you, against
Your own desire, to other strategy
Than simple battle, that our hopes survive
To bear your presence in a span of peace
Before the fires rise up on winds to bend
Disaster's tip beyond this sea-wall, say
Because you live and are so separable
From every other life, I can persuade
My doubts to trust the soul's reality.
And so I am persuaded. But the proof
Could stand exception if I had not seen
The cities burn. We lay on parapets.
Took aim by street-lamps. Fought in attics. Shot
At men. Not knowing other names I called them
Each, 'Thanasie,' Europe's whole revenge
Of Greek on Greek. And Federico called them
Each one, 'Judas,' for a Christian crime.
But each one had a name and in his eyes
A soul, a finger's print unlike all others.
And had we not God's hand against a tree,
We'd still the labor left to see and name him.

The Twice-Born

Our words these years are crumbling words. This page,
Failing your address, will wither sooner
Than the Sphinx called Akar, sooner gone
Than that lost manuscript you hoped to find
Still bright with Mayan inks. It's common fact
The tunes that Lope heard and Calderón
No more to be recovered than the script
The flute boys knew who played for Aeschylus.
In what shall we survive? We hope for sons.
Whose children saw the blazing plane go down
On Mt. Arraig? And where the dark-haired daughter
To set out fair the words of Federico?
I have walked the bookstalls by the Seine,
Looking at the words and at the waters,
Walking by day one cold, recurring night,
Shouting his name, the sea against my ears,
The salt against my eyeballs, groping and diving.
I take the heft of Jim, a giant child
I carried down the corridor the day
The Riffs broke through the schools. And Paddy's hand
Yanking my hair, his roaring voice. I've said
I will trust nothing, say it's Walther's world,
The slithering, cold ninth circle, treason's home;
Or warm wind met with cold, like Stephanie
Between two worlds, a paradox for angels.

In what shall we survive? By no poetics
We could make, as if to say, my music,
Should I live to write the *magnum opus,*
Might cut a ragged symbol into time.
Easy and as treacherous as planes
Botched with scraps and wreckage, to believe
An art survives, and hardest for musicians.
And all the wreckage I could cull from Cairo,
Antioch, anticipates Vienna;
And Mozart, Beethoven may not survive
Ten thousand years ahead if all be lost
Like cities in the sands that blow toward China.
The simple tunes the people most remember
Are only gay among the younger nations

And old songs dignify their strength with sorrows
Changing less than new-made words can change them
In the recurring themes of death and love.
The sharpened fourth, the flattened seventh bend
The brashest major mode in every tune
Brought nearer truth in long remembering.
In any cadre I am only one.
My chances sank a ship. And every one
Who died that night in burning oil or drowned
Was one with Federico. And they died
A death as sudden and as unexplained.

In what do they survive? And how explain
What has no exposition? If I live,
I'll see your eyes again, but they'll explain
No more than any music. What we ask
At last is mightier than exposition
To break the nucleus of suffering.
I do not know who wins the war in Spain,
The land of widows, and if we are driven
Back to the sea's edge or to the mountains,
I'll only know it's not the end of time
And that we shall not have deliverance
While anyone believes that any man
May blow a ship and take impunity
Or praise. I go. To fight. To kill again.
The war did not begin in Spain. And not
At Concord Bridge nor here in St. Antoine
Nor Russia's kremlins. And the end's not soon.
However much Felipe may have known
When he said, "sacrifice," I heard a sound
As on a Friday in Jerusalem,
Another word and a command: "Atone."
We expiate offense. And we are judged.
Forgive me. I am solemn. I went down
Self-willed, in a spinning plane. I was alone.
I could not find him though I called his name.
We foundered in the night and in the sea.

TAHL : BOOK THREE

CANTO I

THE FOURTH WORLD

New England

ALISON:
The fourth world, as he says, still separate
In many minds I meet, as India
Lay in wait three thousand years apart
From land their poets named, when Africa
And Europe known, here Asia's alternate
By other names; America, partition
Bounded least, all boundaries' transition.

Tonight they heard his music, fact as strange
As to imagine where this night he lies
With rifle, boots, and blanket, to avenge
Ancestral crime, forgotten treacheries
Even within this city where on graves
Two hundred years the battered slates discern
A massacre and ghosts of revolution.

In this half year of my return, myself
As unfamiliar as the nine young quetzals
Brought this year from Guatemala north
To turn their emerald heads in iron zoos.
Unheard the gun-sore, blistered hands expressed
The month of wars, July, toward Lukouchiao,
And iron doors upon surrounded Basques

That harmonies, ascending, cut more harsh
And hurt the unprepared, quiescent ear,
His audience makes note; but in the hush
Of student heads have any heard him where,
Among the Spanish spruce and brambles, breath
Cuts visible life upon the frosted air,
Or felt the cold bolt slip October death?

Do not misunderstand me, Iris. When
Juliana squawled in her first gulp
Of separate life — and now this month she suns
As amiable as if old wisdom taught,
And not her untaught fortune; when I look
At sprawling adolescence stretch and squirm
Anxiously toward answers, I'm abashed.

For by such accidents I also came
To birth, to books and journeys. Did he walk,
I asked myself this summer, on the calm
Of lanes and pastures, make a lazy joke
About the clematis called virgin's vine
Or nightshade berries currant-red and green;
No burning stake save hardy dahlia's flame?

Thinking is too easy. These young men
Each day before me and the clear-faced girls
Are Tahl and George and you and I. Coercion,
Arbitration, and decision all
In operation, subterranean
And astral truth essayed. But will they come
From thought to act in ultimate decision?

And will they come by signs? As I once heard
In these same dusty rooms a voice expound
The legends of the Navajos and made
Out of the "woman who changes," wife of the sun
Upon her western island, my own meaning;
And you were the wife of the moon, the white-shell woman.
And the stories were wanderers' stories, a long migration.

Now my own voice expounds. Like fifty targets
The heads above the notebooks. Which is shot
By the arrow among the hogans that had slain
The terrible god, "The Gambler," him who bound
The wagerers to stake at last their freedom?
And dead, since no god dies, took life again
And played his gambler's game with other nations.

I've asked myself what unmarked roads converged
To meet with Tahl. Those summers by the ocean
You used to scold me that I often dived
To look at snarling seaweed near the rocks.
He'd understand. But would he also take
My telling how the gilded letters stood
Against the reredos on Easter mornings?

Do you yourself remember? How the words
Shone, half-hidden: 'The resurrection and — '
The high-banked flowers hid the rest. They blurred
That day of two closed coffins when I held
Your hand until it ached; for years afraid
Of cars. Though longer since Tahl's father died,
For fourteen years I've seen those two closed coffins.

His mother died the night that he was born.
He did not run beside her or stand still
Watching her knit blue mittens; never found
Her sleeping, the spaniel's nose against her arm;
Not waited her waking smile. He did not sail,
As we did, trusting to our fathers' hands
Managing rudder and sheet to an off-shore wind.

He had a cousin also; but recalls
No grandfather like ours who brought our clothes
Warmed from the kitchen. But that scar he has
From God knows whom who shot him on Parnassus
Is like grandfather's — or did you not notice?
After he fell that year on the rotted wharf.
And he'd no grandmother like ours to raise us.

New England

You knew her holidays; but she's become,
As I see now, for me a daily road
That sent me straight toward Tahl. From her I learned
A goodness not an easy godliness,
A harmony which was not innocence,
Her slyboots chuckle ready to dispose
Of every pompous truth to further question.

She said a conscience never should rest easy;
That God was there because we could not think
Of God unless He was and is. She held me
When my long legs were much too long for dandling.
Samoset's words or Massasoit's treaty,
And never mind the ironing, she'd repeat,
And Great Queen Sachem's death at Mettapoiset.

She'd let me shiver though she held me close.
"They killed her braves. She fled into the river.
She drowned. And on the shore the white men found her,
Struck off her head and set it on a pole.
The Indian prisoners wept." Or of King Charles
Rebuked by William Penn: "'If their canoes
Should find the Thames, will you vacate or sell?'"

To kinder death than the Queen Sachem gone.
And Jim's gone too who took his dearer head
From Allegheny hills to Spain's Pingarron.
At home he liked the colored women nodding
Among the coleus and geranium
On window sills. "They watch the streets," he said,
"For years. For hope or death or what's a-coming."

Without his urging I had never seen
Ajusco's craters, the cyclopean mounds
Below the lava, Teotihuacán,
My first acropolis, nor ever plumbed
The compound characters of Yucatan.
"Chemistry's my bible. Yours," said Jim,
"May be their stone astronomy of time."

Jim's gone. But still there's Minna. Lost one son,
She still will call me "daughter." As I've been.
She's still my Spider Woman of the legends,
Never niggardly of ready answers,
Having love enough. Have so belonged,
Like Tahl, to those who love. And still apart,
Like Jim. Like Tahl, the too-inquiring heart.

So three, most curious three and strangely bound
By what seems least the heart, the counting out
Of atoms and of histories and sounds,
And all to make a world. As Jim would find
Its substance; I, the painted manuscript,
The legend of creation, lost; that orchid
Tahl has looked for, trinity compounded.

So lost the heart by count. And then you asked
Not star-read mathematics of A.D.
Beyond the calendar of Gregory,
From Tikal, lost Itzá, when I came back
From searching tumbled drums in fever swamps —
You asked me of the henequen plantations,
The living, the chicle hunters, nearer questions.

So you and I together to an Egypt
Where fellahin competed with the tombs.
And I have not forgotten Paddy's quip
About an Athens that we had not seen.
The roads converged on Sunion. Yet I've known
This Tahl with his odd name but days by count
One year that brought us separately to Spain.

The night off Cyprus when we heard him play,
The unkeyed fingering of his guitar,
Like music on a new periphery,
A Russian music as the edges stir,
And Chinese, Spanish, even to the Maya;
Even the Aymará on Titicaca;
An India of new discovery.

New England

The musician and the engineer
Were not perhaps by accident so met
When Tahl came looking for me on the Concha
A year ago July. And his approach,
Jim said, for him was photographed in color
That takes a shift toward blue; his light depressed
Made him capitulation in a jest.

But the musician and the engineer,
Both art and technics one necessity
Toward common preservation, drew more near,
Entrenched and camouflaged humility
With brothel jibes and oaths like stevedores,
To common peace through chosen agony
Than closer-bred tall gentlemen might dare.

The dogs ran wild with winter in Madrid.
And men like Walther judged the rabid crowd
One more canaille in kennels full of dogs
Fit for whistles and by orders cowed
Or out of hand shot down, a martial tread
That missed the off-beat in the rushing herd,
The sharp guerrilla on the well-paid guard.

That off-beat's in Tahl's music. When we danced
To radio one night in Lequeitio,
Though Stephanie demurred, the true askance
At novelty, we tried to show her how
The rhythms break to hold a power against
The measure's tyranny. You'd understand —
The too-neat jazz of the Parisian band.

The young ones caught his beat tonight. The others
Complained of the percussion; curses, screams
On an excess of trumpets, the deceptive
Cadence ending, ending and unended
Might trouble more than nerves if they suspected
That he means what he says, the tonal rub
More politics than dowagers observe.

The trinity of timbre, pitch and rhythm,
The *pace* of the flute and pace of horns,
The mass of lower strings among bassoons,
The snares and tambourines, to me, make one
Inevitable and confident assertion
I trust won't be his last and he'll come home
To more than overtures and indignations.

Now he writes, I'd say, a kind of *Egmont*,
But he would take such judgment as offense
In giving him so much against the master,
Knowing himself he starts upon his shoulders.
That I love Tahl is much because his praise
Never runs scant to pay his debt of grace
To every friend and past inheritance.

Two sounds within his music, interval
In time I heard the evening in Madrid
He tried to force six strings to teach me all
His orchestration; said it was the bell
That sounds for fog. Tonight it has recalled
Our summers by the cove. The marked unknown,
The word across the mist on fishing-grounds.

And much I do not know. The August days
With Alfred and with Elsa contradict
With their too much applause what George decries
With too much deprecation. A defect
In Jan with our brief meeting seemed nostalgia
For Tahl who was and not the man I met
Transformed in Greece and suffering from Vienna.

And George and Elsa both, it seems, conspire
To train me toward a jealousy or care
Of Margot whom you've seen and I have not.
The maniac that's half of him I caught
With dawn among the Cyclades. The night
On Sunion showed me none lived more aware
Than he himself of all that I might fear.

New England

Felipe's death and Federico drowning
Have slain in him more boldness than could die
In fifty years of cold philosophy.
I've not forgotten he went back to Paris
And George implies: to Margot. I confess
I'm not so curious to question him
To past occasions as a present comfort.

It's snow and winter coming, ice along
The gunsights, lice and mud and ready dying
In war too few of those I live among
Give alms of half a thought. Shanghai has fallen.
I wonder if the Doctor's on a gunboat.
I'm surer of his health than I'm prepared
For Tahl alive with four already dead.

In winter the Pawnees thought the gods withdrew
But came again with thunder in the spring,
The clouds like tipis from the west to show
The sacred messenger's descent with lightning.
I wish I knew nine songs of sacrifice,
A door to the promise, the Mother-Sunset-Yellow.
But Federico's lost, his death untraced.

The shags from seaweed snarl among the islands,
The canny divers may alone discover
Where Federico lies. The partisan,
In war so much misnamed, may disappear
Misnamed or nameless. And can I rest sure
That Tahl is right? That some may better bear
A part in peace with medicine of learning?

In this fourth world still bathed in *fiat* peace
I may be mad as he, in my precautions
Of pride in peace that's like a white man's boast
The red men dead were merely wildcats slaughtered.
And what's a wildcat ghost? And least at peace
Remembering that 'resurrection and — '
Comes last. And first, a crash and the closed coffins.

TAHL : BOOK THREE

CANTO I

THE FOURTH WORLD

The Midlands

IRIS:
The middle class in the midst of the middle west;
Do you see us, Alison? The in-laws,
The baby, the lighted tree, and everyone pleased;
Four grandparents doting. And the pause
To hear the broadcast news, a rite; the deaths,
Nanking or Teruel, like bells that pass
On ambulances rushing unknown victims.
Whoever's dead, he's none of our relations.

Or none of theirs. Of ours? The news looks good
From Spain, the big push going, victory.
I talk of painter's whims and infant's moods,
But haven't forgotten riflemen can die
In winning battles; and that Paddy died
Though standing at Brihuega. And I see
The trudge in the bitter snow, a Valley Forge
With colder quarters and a bloody siege.

And yet they hold the salient; and the brag
Of cutting Spain from Spain demolished where
They hold against the braggarts. Little thugs,
Says Mother, in her boys' clubs, always waver
And retreat from honesty; they thrive
Only on others' fear. Yes, though she's here

Ostensibly to comfort me, she's found
The settlement house already, native ground.

She helped the holiday. And Dad was braced
As usual with enterprises. Boasts
He'll pipeline oil from Tulsa to the east.
Cars in Greenland! China! Combines! Trucks!
Pointing his exclamations with cigars.
"You know!" he says, "they flail by hand! in baskets!"
He still repeats the tale of his first garage.
And George admires his bluff and Mother's verve.

Though her committees and her projects give
George his favorite sport, he doesn't know
Himself, I think, what makes him want to tease
All simple effort. In him gone askew
Perfection disillusioned. Families
Should all be clever, cities like gardens. So!
Not quickly? No? And that's his kind of rage
Against the relativities of love.

George played respectable sire. But the good old grocer
Overlooks his whelp like a missent order;
And George's mother fears her changeling son
In silence, knowing tolerance no honor.
Yes, gone with kit and contracts. Arizona.
I miss him. And if Julie learns to steer
Her cereal spoon between her nose and chin,
It won't be soon by George's ministrations.

Mother thinks Julie looks like you. I stopped
George by taking the cue in high to pull
Your mother's pictures out. And Julie shows,
I must say, dignity. Though how to tell
That, at just four months, must be false hope
That she won't catch our restlessness, but keep
Whatever family trait gives moderation
To my red hair and George's divagations.

I have enough of his impatience, though,
For patience with him. I still want to drive

Fast and get there soon; and not your still
Appraisal, like your mother's. She could move
Like breath in silence and the ginger spaniel
The liveliest air around. Except you'd dance
Unpredictably and let me tear
After the sunlit wheel of your flying hair.

And yet we balance. Tahl? I can't be sure.
His engine runs too quietly. Explosions
Periodic always damage more
Than the shafts they blow in. He's like Jim,
A well of thought blown off in act, a roar
To blast the tackle and derrick. You'll forgive me.
Jim's gone. I know. My parallels imply
No earnest of Tahl's separate destiny.

This spring the Russians flew across the pole.
On porches in the dustbowl women rock,
Splint-thin, each face eroded like the soil,
But they're in motion. All machines at work
And all deft hands. While good old grocers stall
In market spins that drag centrifugal,
We're gathered in and all of us in motion,
Colliding or bowing in a transfixed ocean.

Tahl knows the ocean's shifted. You and he,
By going back in time, have found a route
Neglected like the icecaps that now fly
The future's flags. And I surrendered doubt
Of your time-past when I saw Brittany;
At Kériaval, on a cabbage patch, the dark
Shade of dolmens; and the five-mile march
At Carnac of three thousand megaliths.

When we saw New York again; and when,
And daily northward up the lake, the towers,
The menhirs of this time — six thousand pounds
At auction, you told me once, that Stonehenge sold for;
I thought the British paid too much for stones —
But then you told me megaliths are found

The Midlands

From Spain to Palestine and in Japan,
A nameless marching, as in Morbihan.

The men with cigars like Dad, and listless stiffs
Who sleep in movies, men on clanking girders,
My favorite Negro cobbler, make a tough
And steel alloy; though not from metals newer
Than stone dolmens. Tungsten, chromium,
Molybdenum, manganese, just new-old names,
Like Julie's, since George knew a man called Julian
Who died too young for time to disappoint him.

In the shifted sea Roumanian oil,
Mercury from Spain or Java rubber
Grabbed or paid for run together, all
The unexpected neighbors who discover,
Like us, our near relations. Alfred's son
A boy he wouldn't be if Tahl in Spain
Weren't Alfred's friend. From all time-past we build
Toward bridgeheads in a fast contracted world.

I am too confident, you say. Because
No bamboo gouged by bulldozers to roads,
Nor rubber tires on rickshas can evolve
Fast dikes on China's sorrows. None can save
In April constitutions those who starve
In India while words, by sabotage
Of those beyond sabots, grow versatile
To break alignment with the active will.

But that you give the active will your word,
Nor ask, like George, for absolutes of sun;
That Tahl should call our bridge and tunneling
No simple contract filled and free on board,
Make these no accidents you are my cousin,
That Julie's name recalls a man named Julian.
Though lost our unimportant names, they bind
Some knot in history to final tension.

You must have heard this morning's broadcast saying
One of our planes has flown new airlines joining,

The Fourth World

By Kingman Reef, Hawaii to New Zealand.
But where is Kingman Reef? The infant burbling
There in her crib — she doesn't know. Nor I,
Though I should read the map. But Dad's been saying,
"Nonsense!" to Spain and the riot we saw in Athens.
That's Kingman Reef to him. It has a name,
But it's just not there. Too far. In an unknown ocean.

TAHL : BOOK THREE

CANTO II

THE TREE IN THE FOREST

Barcelona

JAN:
"No matter where you strike, a rod will fall
The line of one parabola, the fixed
Down-curving center to the drag of earth."
This Jim said. And he is dead. And Tahl,
Healing three wounds, from Segura de los Baños,
Lay on a bed in mid-March Barcelona.

"No matter where you strike, the stroke will fell
Trees in earliest bud. The sawmill sound
Of flying engines loud, no one perturbed
That Peter Strauss or van der Lubbe died,
Poor lackwits. No reprieve." And this Tahl said
Healing a bullet-grazed lung in Barcelona.

In Barcelona ten o'clock and still.
At ten, eight minutes past, the air aloud.
"On Berchtesgaden's rock," asked Tahl, "who heard
The axe on Austria falling? " There are sounds
Of fire, of falling no one hears. Who heard
The glide of planes from Palma de Mallorca?

"From Friday to this Friday March," Tahl said,
"A charcoal sun from Austria to Spain,
Death without heat, unnatural season, air

Crashing the unseen branches." And I said,
"Tahl, be still. You must not talk." None heard
From noon to noon the planes on Barcelona.

"Breath from the house. Breath from the sagging lung.
What forest holds against this wind? A death
With thunder after death sucks strangling earth."
Tahl — he'd crawled a road in crossfire, dragging
A wounded man, a man anonymous
Like three days' death in mid-March Barcelona.

Who in the sea hears bridges falling down?
"Though that dry creek, the Manzanares, hold
Madrid, the Marco Polo's out and stunned
Great China, and across the Moldau tremors
Of grid and truss from Palma de Mallorca,
The air-swung span from Palma de Mallorca."

Because we could not hear, we were afraid.
Carmelo, Tibidabo spitting, spitting
Guns at nothing. None grew brave on drinks.
We fled the broken arch of waiting, waiting.
The subway cars ran through our sweat, the pouring
Waters of fear in the tunnels of Barcelona.

Three days we bore. The balconies hung down
Raveled with silence. Searchlight, range scale none
Saw. None heard. And no one wept among
The airdromes. No one wept. No, not the child,
The socks torn off, the head beneath a coat
Against the curbstone on the Cataluña.

Nobody slept. And everyone ran. Or stopped.
Or whirled. An aimless turning. Shrank away
Into the choke of floating dust, the scream
From ten o'clock by moonlight and to ten
Clocked with sunlight, clocked to three and three
And three again, the bombs on Barcelona.

Barcelona

We rose like paralytics. And we walked.
Traumatic women strolled like tourists gazing.
Not Rachel in Madrid, nor toward Córdoba
Miguel more near than Jim a year in death
To the broken arch of fear we crossed to end
The fear of air that burst in Barcelona.

And was he there the more, by white walls trapped,
Tahl who did not walk the three days' streets,
The rat-run while he lay or talked or slept
Under the sputtering guns at nothing shot
While fifteen hundred thousand vomited fright
In thirteen raids on mid-March Barcelona.

It was the fear. Not death. The fear. As few
Have understood. Not even those who crept
The long retreats through vine and rock to come
Out of the rout of Aragon. They watched
Jut and shadow alert. But fear was not
Sudden as Spanish dusk on Barcelona.

Tahl was mostly silent, lying still,
The stertorous audible breath alone betraying
The bound wounds. I'd find him reading, laying
The papers, the pamphlets, heap on heap beside him.
And then they shipped him north. I did not see him
Again till their last parade in Barcelona.

I tell you quietly. Two years of war
And more years since have taught me war is most
Its silences. The silent pictures lit
By Metro flares in eyes of children stifling,
Fighting for air in fetid crowds, the child
Who looked at the child face down on the Cataluña.

Tahl said the tracks of skiers at Saint Moritz,
The Café de l'Europe in Stephansplatz,
Heil Hitler! Perish Juda! and *Sieg Heil!*
Were stored as baggage in a tourist bureau

The Fourth World

That he had passed one summer in Vienna
To fuel death that rode on Barcelona.

Tahl said: "Out of silence, fear." Who heard
The sound of skiis, the vanity grown drunk
On syllables? Tahl spoke of Stephanie
Who had not heard the wheels toward Liebknecht Hof
But few years past, the ambulance that hid
The arrned men gunning hope in new Vienna.

I looked at the child who looked at the child who lay
Under the coat on the curb in the Cataluña
And neither would sail a boat on a stream that led
To a peach blossom China. And we knew
Too late who briefed the pilots on Mallorca,
Screwing the air with lies for Barcelona.

You've seen the photographs. The captions said
The "reds" had done this crime in Salamanca,
But black, white, brown the light recorded plain
The socks torn off, the head beneath a coat,
Lamp posts, dying trees in Barcelona,
A ronda no one named in Salamanca.

The silent glide, the camouflage of planes,
A forest cover, governed altimeter
For "all clear" over silence. And I think
Miguel, a prisoner in Seville, and Jim
A year in death, know silence like the lies
Flying unseen to Munich and Geneva.

Barcelona was a patient pricked
By panic hypodermics. That we ran
Like fatuous rats in caging streets a proof.
The heartless needle probes. But what it proves
Is a corrupted truth. And silences
Unprobed sink deep the lies in Barcelona.

"The absolute equality of death,
Even this," said Tahl, "is powerless

To save us while the majesty of lies
Masters silence. We are tricked by air."
I thought of the bridge, never by bomb destroyed,
That fell by repercussion at Culera.

There's no sierra now, no path beyond
To hide the children in a fruit tree grove.
I have seen pain and see no end of pain,
Nor poison of noise nor drug of silent dread,
The fear of the windless sky. To put out fire
They ran the hose from the sea in Barcelona.

Jim at Pingarron, Paddy at Guadalajara,
And the nameless man who lives because his voice
Caught at the ear of Tahl in crossfire. Men
On ladders toward the sky, the blazing attics.
And not all traitors tourists in Mallorca
And not all traitors trapped in Barcelona.

Under a quick last glare of blood-red sun,
The end of the three days' raids on Barcelona,
Below a bulging window-frame a bed
And an ownerless cap that hung from a white splinter.
In what do we survive? I have known fear
Of silence more than death in Barcelona.

TAHL : BOOK THREE

CANTO II

THE TREE IN THE FOREST

East and West

THE DOCTOR:
East and west converge and in convergence
Convert philosophies, as I'd been saying
Two years ago July when last I saw him.
But you have seen him since. You had not known
Other Americans in Bilbao? Saw him?
Saw him again? And earlier, the women?
I thought I'd seen him too. Beyond the path
There near the wall, the bookshelves now in sunlight.
March it was then. And cold. My nose in my collar.
But there he stood, bareheaded. With snow in his hair.

If that were he or this were he? Like saying
This Kitai Gorod is not the Chinese Wall.
A matter of object and shadow. No, not Tahl,
This Muscovite I saw among the bookstalls.
Somewhat about the eyes, the stance, the born
For sacrifice, but not like those despising
Life who are more readily assassins.
Shanghai, the Hall of Confucius, the Old City,
Like this. The benches, the sun, the heavy trees.
A year ago there. Now here. Identical treasons.

Identity? Itinerant we see
Friend and enemy in repetition

East and West

Suddenly on corners. In Nanking
On Chung Shan road, the false fronts and the awnings,
A boy in blue cottons shot down. He too was like him
On Hsing Ying road. On the corner of Foukien highway.
Flaming Shanghai, looted Nanking, and death
By sweat and lice and the knout in various nations.
Among these states more likely you'll mistake him,
West in Kazakh or south in Azerbaijan.

A fault, displacement, law of motion turning
The mountains on end, the forests headfirst in water
And this time's population shuttled, spilling
New passengers at unexpected stations
By similar architects. The Hankow Bund,
The Wuchang Yards, still Brooklyn and Manhattan.
Identical boulevards in parallel cities
Like these concentric with the Kremlin, turbines,
The black maria, the traceless disappearance;
But the face on the corner familiar; eternal recurrence.

Disaster's not decision. No. And fact
With person set in motion? All since Athens
Operates on sophists and musicians.
In Shanghai, the funeral of Lu Hsün,
The scholar banned and hunted for his courage
Lay in honors of state. And you will see
The Komsomol nostalgic for the Czars.
Convergence which engenders revolution
Culminates most oddly in conversion;
Soldiers contemplative; artists, men of action.

Mitsui, quarreling with Iwazaki
Over the mercury was once the Manchus',
Miscalculate, perhaps, as Hadrian,
Fearing the Baltic, loitered on the Danube.
Mass orgy to mass grave, last executions.
Nevertheless, one man's exempt from motion,
One intricate mind, like stairways in Peking,
One face false clear as a reflecting pool,

The Tree in the Forest

The eyes like shadowless water. His name? Walther.
Occidental? Oriental? Walther.

In Shanghai the bomb for the *Idumo*
Missing the Emperor's fleet. But he's still living,
Walther, two minutes south of a smashed hotel.
Shanghai, true habitat. But in Nanking,
The raids in yellow autumn, still conspiring
For hematite, arsenic, tungsten and galena.
Unquestioning that man was born to suffer,
Lamenting the avenue marbles, Noah's Ark marching
In crude green camouflage, the road of the Mings,
Mourning agreeable death in the beautiful tombs.

I once saw Walther bow to Itagaki
Whose teeth most neat and gnawing were less subtle
Than Walther's fingers, stroking a greyhound's back.
First Bilbao; now Vienna fails him;
Retires: Hongkong; soon Lisbon, Buenos Aires.
The gambler on the gambit of destruction
Laying his bets on both sides, never loses,
Numbers predictable. And never suffers?
The polychrome beams of Shanghai and the evening races;
The greyhound stolen perhaps. But the master's living.

You remember Tannenberg? That year,
A quarter century gone, and you a child.
Walther, the enemy-at-large, in Paris.
The Russians routed east. In flight. And yet
Lost Tannenberg in that debated August
Withdrew the guns from Paris. Now in Moscow
We're paving the tortuous streets beyond St. Basil.
But he knows philosophers' gauges catch no evil
And such men, well advised, will never kill him.
The spy in the courtyard does not recognize him.

Would you recognize him? Kharkov's tower
Of skyward offices? He'd come to Russia
Paying respects to the domes of the Redeemer.
The Buddhist rich in opium, the monk

In Mediterranean orange groves, compeer;
Stern with singsong girls, knows Greek, is graceful
In murders, no amplifiers, talking films;
To grandmother's peasants once the "little master"
North of the Alps; the world's his present gamble,
Canonical Proteus of Grand Hotels.

You think that I admire him? I have seen
In the Casanova in Berlin,
In London pubs and here along the Arbat
Other men who live anonymous,
Knowing confession's signatures are false
To falser matter not alone in Moscow
And wrung from blood by other arts than music.
Yet this one lives unique, more permanent
Than a Chinese landlord buttressed by his gown.
A most rare find for antiquarians.

Yes. Yes. Vorovsky square. But you'll learn more
Outside the embassies. The city's changed?
No, not unique. For though the planes came on,
In Hankow, the Negroid tunes, the cocktails.
Geneva? The Quai du Mont Blanc, in those lost years,
Not there. But try in the Yablonoi mountains,
In Taimyr. You don't know where? Kamchatka.
Not Shensi? Yes. You'll see the same convergence
In chapters new-appraised when murder's over
And reprints edit altered roles for villains.

Once here. Now there. The twice-surrounded armies,
No oil, no shoes, the bare feet black with cold.
From the balustrade on the river's edge, their cousins
Along the creeks, Whangpoo, Soochow, their poles
Bv day; by night, the huts. The wounded fell.
They thatched the trucks like hovels. And the blast
That lost Chapei again. Five years before,
The flaming bombs. No novelty. Not Spain.
Behind the walls where sun sets in Shanghai
We dined, expecting the cruisers steaming in.

The Tree in the Forest

The new hegemonies, the pincers close
On pincer points and some will break upon
Imposing circles. Austria displaced
Breaks France. You'll see. Perhaps not accident
The West Gate of Shanghai looks much like London.
Those who mumbled sunflower seeds in Russia
And watermelon seed in older China
Assent to tobacco and chicle. East and west
In new miscegenation. And the pillars
At Changsha are Greek by Jefferson.

Perfection uncongenial's still perfection.
A transcendental dreamer, now. I like him.
No compromise. I knew one once. A youngster.
And if you have seen Tahl, that one his cousin.
Object. Shade. Which shadow of the other?
I thought I knew. You like this chance guerrilla,
Amateur *brave,* musician imperfect. Chimera.
You came up, as I did, from the south,
Watched on the steppe, in the stubble and fog, the figures,
Horses or men. They shift. No telling the colors.

In Oro del Rhin, I hear, the cups were spilled
On raided Catalans. D'Annunzio's dead.
I saw him in Trieste admiring roses.
I understand the permanence of brigands.
The Ringstrasse I hear a week still strewn
With flowers in honor of bandits. Tyrolean spring.
The busses still run to Changsha; like crossing Kansas.
You can see the Kremlin clock. Not noon.
Is your watch so anxious? You'll like sunlight
More when you've survived this town in winter.
They dig canals and make the climate damper,
Their plans omit both famine and bronchitis.
Whether it's Pushkin, Lermontov in duels;
By one ukase, a million dead; they're thorough.
If their Cromwellian righteousness perhaps
Finds pocket Zaharoffs in every barroom;
Ekaterinburg; they manage. A kind of perfection.
But Walther knows Lucretius is hermetic

Beyond the testaments of Marx, Lenin,
The mastering object mastered. You'd not like him.
You'd not like me if you had learned more Russian,
The sooner to escape me. Don't be anxious.
The posters lamenting Madrid in Chu Teh's mountains,
I assure you, I didn't destroy them. My introduction
Will serve you, and not to prison. We'll be going.

"The cartel against good will is the fear of 'will be'?"
Well said. But mind. False spring is spring too early.

You do not like injustice. Wreckers' trials,
Downing Street doubtful, Ethiopians slaughtered,
Gandhi's Ahmedabad, by spindles, smokestacks,
And frontier law unlawful, good men murdered,
And criminal whips from Mukden to Berlin.
Must I be obvious? These evils none
More full of lies and all incomprehensions
But this — the numbers quicken. Domination
Now sudden come makes sudden overturning
In conscious crime and conscious opposition.
Sun Yat Sen upon the Purple Mountain,
And sanctified Mount Vernon. Not forgetting
The treacheries at Canton? The Continentals
Starving while purse with congress fought? The shot
In the innocent theater not the major hurt
But blood in trade behind tall Lincoln's back.
The potash cartel now, the bloody weekends,
Mere detail in the universal pogrom.
Sink steamers, junks, below the French Concession;
But the Emperor's cruisers come. The ports have fallen.

Mere history. We have no newer villain.
You and I and Walther, several others,
Corporals, lieutenants, cast, the actors.
And your musician too if he'd content
His proper talent. Let him here recover
Their southern tunes called "noises," "little thoughts."
And we can all be pleased with crowds and singing.
Laying the foundations here for the tallest building.

Let him run scales for that. Not this corrupting
Wits and music both with indignations.

He'd learn again *Hospodi Polmilui.*
Oh yes. They've not forgotten: Lord have mercy.
Not among furnaces; not at Dneprostroy.
He likes such curious matters. As in Shensi
The younger devils march all day still humming
A classic tune they call *Unending Sorrow*
For Lady Yang long dead. You've met his lady,
Tall and thoroughly woman and I liked her;
But not her friend who called him Dionysus.

A metaphysical disease, to find
Eccentricities portentous. Music
Apt for Euripides and Bacchic women;
Purpose, a God and not quite Aristotelian.
A copper for tea by the gates in the narrow lanes
Once in Nanking, an old man telling stories;
When heroes thought of the universe, he sang.
But heroes seldom commit the crime of thinking.
Grant you, Tahl won't kill with ease. No strut.
But lynching his skills on the tree of his good intentions.

Found him, a student, knowing the *San Kuo*
As if he'd spent his nights on a heated k'ang.
He'd choose Ts'ao Ts'ao to play archprince of villains
Before a Borgia or the current gunman;
Count Emperor Yu to ultimate Ming and Manchu;
Ever the vagrant dilettante of visions,
In India the acolyte of Vishnu,
Wearing God's monogram between his eyebrows.
If you should meet him here or there, remind him
That Dionysus' death was from the people.

You say he thinks the forest and the sea
Have meanings. Musical, of course. I think
All meaning's last determinant, the cities.
The assassinate Czars, the shots at the Winter Palace,
Ball-bearings, automobiles, and cutting tools,

East and West

The case of the Shanghai airdrome. That there moves
Old magic in this world, no doubt. I've seen
Conjuring tricks with snakes and trees. And powers
Are powerful unobvious. We hide
In motion faster than the eye can move.
Yes. Noon. We'll go. The droshky's obsolescent
Like junk and ricksha soon. I used to count them
Along with obelisks across the bridge
To the office in Shanghai. Soon no more letters,
Cancelled in half the world, through Yangtze gorges
Running the white water. Soon we'll cross
The gap from Peshawar to Alma-Ata
Quicker than post, Danzig on toward Bucharest.
Rivers dynamic, lightning made and measured,
We change. By flight from here to the Golden Gate.
Muddy loess and steppe cannot impede us.

But Levanevsky crashed, was never found?
And how can I make sure of constant factors?
Glaciers again on Baltic shores? Perhaps.
When Breslau's dammed, and Flanders in eruption
To turn the paths of usual battle, when
The Elbrus and the Matterhorn sink down?
But a starboard-lurched *Panay*, her white decks pummeled
By Pittsburgh steel from alien planes? He's puzzled.
He's not, you say? Nor you? And I misjudge you?
Myopic old man in parks. And too impartial.

I think that war's to him impersonal.
And that's like Walther. As for Federico,
I have not heard of him, but that's no matter.
Here in the soviets I'll tell you more
Of Timbuktu and the dyepits of Nigeria,
More matter than Spain when you're a man grown older.
Political jackpots lie in probable futures.
Spain and the treaty ports for the major gambler
Already a past event. He's not like Walther
Whom you resent? Be sure he'll die much sooner.

Yes. Chung Shan road. Much like him. Below the awnings
A boy in blue cottons shot down. The first mass grave

The Tree in the Forest

I'd seen, a young man walking on Culloden,
The burial place of clans. We all die sooner
Perhaps. We may like Nashi disappear
In Yunnan's peaks with flint and edelweiss
Lighting a waning fire and, throned on peach trees,
Our nearly forgotten devils. The embassy. Here.
Grimy? Yes. Like the twinned beasts of Nanking.
New paint, poor camouflage for obsolescence.

If, where, when, you may see Tahl again,
Tell him that orchestras still use directors
And that's his classic calling. This world's end?
In high Sinkiang, in Gobi, last men slain?
There might be two, you say. And one survivor.
The one killed first, be sure, will not be Walther.
You'll watch for him? A wire or two you'll tap
But will not turn his wound wires all together.

In embassies take thought for the states of Georgia.
No necessitous fact they both lie south
By compass on America and Russia;
Identically both secessive, both recovered.
Separate in space, inconsequent in time,
Accidental all identity.
I don't know Federico. What of Tahl?
Guerrilla? Unarmed composer I left in Vienna?
Remember I said: chimera. You'd prefer
The unicorn? Yes, once in China. Bronze.
The moon upon its back. In clouds. *Ch'i lin.*
Head of a horse, beard of a goat, the tooth
Of a captured whale. Amoebas are more solid.
You listen for trees. In the cities? This he taught you?
Tell him his business is music. The gourds of the Negro
With noble bassoons. And that he might hear in Honan
"Arise, ye prisoners" on a bamboo flute.
When you see him, tell him if he fells
Old trees with weapons hidden, better parks
Like that near Kitai Gorod; then bars; then bagnios.
But simpler and far more subtle, needing directors,
The orchestras gather still in the best hotels.

TAHL : BOOK THREE

CANTO III

THE TREE IN THE GARDEN

New York

ELSA:
Not all, as Alison heard; a few, hard pages
Permitted entrance to this public praise
Accepting music all grandfathers hated,
Rejecting all the hard, new grandsons raise
Late oracles. And I had hesitated,
Even I. But listened. Heard
First drums. The low strings stirred;
From alto horns the reeds to branches sprouting
Flute and flageolet. Repeated. Sound
To glockenspiel, to clustered fruit; leaves rustling.

What others heard, the hundreds in their rows,
Who knows? Shaped sound, to me, no craft of measure,
Physics of sound nor dialectics. Move
To images within, unwilled, a pleasure
Like love, beyond debate, which can approve
Nor disapprove; remember
Only the after-dream; engender
Image or child. The flute. And quietly:
Alison. The rowan tree, September
Six months past. Red clusters. Leaves. The sea.

Courante and saraband? How dance these sounds
Like fire and crash of pouring slag, like steam;

Catwalks, stacks and girders, pulleys strained.
Eclogue? What Maecenas here lie calm
With called-for music, soothing sleepless minds?
But soon as dreams, as soon
Treble trumpet, bass trombone,
Some vast, high line of sky, some city seen
Filtering haze through violins. Then gong.
Then wind-machine. Flute, flageolet, return.

Return, familiar sound. Two hours remained.
Immortal patterns fixed, the signatures
Familiar, reassuring. I discerned
Relaxed, indifferent neighbors. But recurred
To nights before toward dock and river, forms
Of pipe, of stack, of chute, to me no name
Black beyond the windows, and a drain,
With man-hole black, uncovered, red flares blazing
Bright and guarded. Suite? Partita? Dancing?
Flare in a city, shouts, and sudden warning.

In the violins the stressed harmonics
Slightly out of tune? The clarinets
Sforzando in A, in F most delicate
Like some uncertain contradiction struck
With gourd and bamboo pipe, some noisy rebec.
Those months lost in Egypt?
Margot's eyes, exotic
Topaz, warning? Threat and prowl, a jeering
Taunt like children taunting, Buck's gang vexing
Helpless scapegoats. Taunt. Repeat. Repeating.

We are at peace. And we are not disturbed
By all we do not know. A blazing cone?
It might be. Not a tree at all. The Serb,
The Bulgar, Cantonese in films. Berlin.
No picture. Not Vienna? Not Madrid?
We clapped the waltz. Applause.
The clever composer, applause;
Symphonic purée, digestible, well-cooled.
I know why I was angry, then annoyed;
Like not remembering, quite forgetting, a word.

Three springs ago. And once had Alfred said
The tunes in Viennese cafés were old?
Three seasons old, old jazz, American jazz,
Old and long ago. But Tahl, he'd held
A gun. I've never held a gun. George heard
That films in Madrid were old,
Old, American, old,
Three seasons old. Tahl trying the third of a tone,
An Arab, ancient interval. Who heard
A third of a tone? Who cares? Scales fixed. Like doom.

Perhaps the crash not slag, not shrieking steam.
Perhaps a plane gone down. But Alison
Had letters from France. He lived. But what might come
Out of Aragon? Not then. But Jan
Later from Barcelona. The unknown.
Just restless. Slightly ill.
Just — something not quite well,
Like letters from Cairo, from Athens. Washington,
I'm told, sets pitch for orchestras. They tell,
By radio-tracked balloons, the coming winds.

He drove on iron stake and sharp, steel prong
In hidden hills of Aragon and dust
Red in the wind. And tunnels. Heights too strong.
Summer, no water; winter, the ruthless frost.
Hotel called Florida in Madrid. The gong
At that third turn. And Jim,
A man I'd never known.
"Old soldiers never die." No tune. The words
Written from lands unseen. I ran the crowd
Colliding toward dinner, racing the theater hordes.

Coin in the slot and served. Who plowed? Who plowed?
In Aragon the dust, the fingers numb.
Vienna the week before. And still unknown
Except the picture; Stephanie, her name.
Alison said: London.
Said she'd gone to London.
Audubon. Lewis and Clark. American.

The Tree in the Garden

Buck. The tree in Maine. That orgiastic
Slag, fall, tree, through all familiar music
Annoyed by the flare, the flute, by the warning chromatic.

But I as they, still face and restless hands.
And from the balcony, the still heads ranged,
The curls, the hats, the few, the gray-haired men.
I thought that I'd take Buck to Washington.
Show him museums soon. And we'd go west
To see Dad's farm again.
All the roads miles long.
And thought: That's it. Habitual migration.
Blue flags. Marsh. The farm. It would not come
Chromatic. Just sea. Just sun. Just sound. Just: sound.

TAHL : BOOK THREE

CANTO III

THE TREE IN THE GARDEN

London

STEPHANIE:
Once on a time, once in Spain, with the flagstones, the tiles, the majolica, indigo, scarlet,
Cedars and clematis. Austria. Once in Vienna the Prater, the candles at night and the lindens.
Now from a plane unreturning, in passage to nowhere, the woman secure in her prison
Dining with friends. While a chancellor speaks his farewell to the air, she has smiled upon figures in dreams
In a dusk as of curtains like purdah, a mind safe asleep, or, if sun, in a warm, pleached arbor.

Trusting you, *Dudelsack.* Tahl, I am lost. And not for a flirt or a paradox, saying
My gestures for causes, the children, the wounded, a sleep-walking now in my prison called England
More ghostly when fogs of this March swirl upon us who cross with the horns and with lights through the mist
Every night after hock very cold and the dancers, the chattering tables, beside me the exiles
Called Basil, called Igor, called friends, and the three of us less than bouquet on a wine long-opened.

Never go back to Vienna? Could Igor go back to "St. Petersburg," he who in London

Remembers, before we were born, Her Majesty lying with palm
leaf and pall, the great crown above her,
The two grenadiers on their guard, at her death, in the chapel at
Windsor? Before we were born.
And before, and before, the slain czars, the Narodniks. On Basil,
most cordial to princes in Asia,
Something comes down very silently, still as a parachute falling
on last maharajas.

The ghosts of the air fly between us. Though seemly unveiled,
Biarritz and the languors of sunburn,
Were captive and childless by custom, at Salzburg, the coffee
house after the shopping, the supper
Too idle for anger. With Bismarck grown quaint and Napoleon,
one with the stern-whiskered emperor,
Tired Franz Joseph who trusted my father. You, the composer of
armies. But I,
Mistress, no minister; stripped, merely nautch girl amusing with
love songs the masculine durbar.

Once near Hendaye we watched burning Irún, that black sunset.
And once on our faces together
Because of a bomb. And you said, "Ten yards off." But we live.
Or you lived. I have fallen toward somewhere
Still as the lilac tree once and a murmur of images, Basil come
back from an India
Never more real in his telling than all I have known, more than
Walther, his banks and his mines
As closed as his heart. For the woman I am, find my analogues east.
The seraglio's broken.

And to the Casino each night there come several in saris and moving
like does on the dance-floor.
And I, maharani retired to the country house, dining in London,
another among them,
A recent distortion, like watching the can-can most pseudo-
Parisian in London decorum.
Basil says hunting cats, cheetahs, aren't set upon does, only bucks.
And I said to him, "Hunters

Take prey without courtesies now." But he's old; his love out of
heat, to a wit's dry fever.

And yet in his bondage to code and his age can remember the waste
of the Punjab gives water
And trees grow again from the man that he was and the price of an
Indian bullock can alter
His lyrical idols and parrots' green glint in the labyrinth temples
he's seen in Benares,
His dream of the Moslem device and the manuscript-delicate faces.
And Igor, twice captive,
Serene among test tubes, partitioning life in control. You might
like him, dissector of seeds.

But I, the once gently apart from the Austrian toughs in gray uniforms, even with Walther
Years in Berlin, I knew Hindenburg, Hugenberg, faces untroubled
by taxes, in bonds
To a name passing guards to the theater, the club. And again in
this land to the iron-gate hall
In the shire, like the tow-headed cousins abroad in the lane, little
thralls to the nurse and the pram.
And once there was war. But not acorns; not hungry; the wheat
smuggled in from Moravian farms.

I have seen them, the Billingsgate porters, the buskers who play
for the queues; in the doorways of Wapping
The girls, like the wenches who in Barcelona hung on the red-
belted stevedores. Bound
By the veils of a mind which is memory, I am your servant, subdued,
but enraged
At the shame. I have hated you, *Dudelsack.* Clung to last friends
on this island to which I have come.

Am born the new sister to Peter Schlemihl, am a woman unreal,
cast no shadow. Recall
How those in purgation and half-way to heaven knew Dante because of the shade from his fingers?
And now in this London, or down in the fields and the meadows,
your hand moves before me, upon me,

The Tree in the Garden

And I am afraid. As afraid of the *jota* of Aragon, jaunting cascade
in the strings,
The hand-beat, hard stamp, and the howl of the Moor in the
scream of Valencia, long and appalling.

And cling to my Basil and Igor, my shadowless partners, reality
past. They are old;
But shadow, no shrivel of age. For if Paddy I saw in Madrid had
grown old, he'd throw shadow
Like hills in the sun — Mont Pelée. But why have I so loved the sun
on the lawns, in the Alps
Between glacier and gentian? Basil, his Indian continent; Igor
retreated from Russia.
How might I ask or propose to encounter America? — Alps and
its valleys too vast.

We are Versailles, Taj Mahal, or three pyramids, anything solid
and dead and whatever
Took thousands of hands and the decades of years to put up for a
wonder. And Basil's content.
But annoyed that I doubt any virtue of empire. Your shadow of
hands, not my words be reproached
By the jut of his beautiful beard fresh from Delhi and Whitehall.
Though Igor can tell
Of a miracle clover from Egypt to sow on the waste lands, re-
deeming the desert and fallow.

And though in the midst of the dancing, applause for performance
and jaded with watching the wrists
And the ankles and thighs in a gloss of whirled light and the dia-
mond belts, all the peacock of feathers,
I think of your dancing that last afternoon in the patio — Alison,
Jim — and more strange
In your ease and your fire than an evening of titivate palates in
pleasures irrelevant — lifting
No curtain; am swathed more than women who thresh out their
millet in sun near the Indus.

No Lloyd's of this London assures me, a dubious cargo, to send
me a further adventure.

London

You being far from me now in some Aragon thaw and the news
very bad and the raids
On the ports and Madrid, should I now to your country, as alien
an India ever
As any Columbus your Alison knows of? Speaking six languages,
still never come
To Dravidian tongues nor Bengali. Amusing? But truly afraid of
your hand there before me.

What tongue should I speak in your land? In Igor's? To women
in scarves? — they wear orange I'm told.
In China? Wherever I'd go? Yes, I know. You say Elsa and Alfred
would have me. My words
Sounding rightly and British, but where shall I find for my memories warehouse? In worlds rising walls
Like that building just four years ago in Vienna, no sign but the
lone armored car and the Heimwehr,
And only knew afterwards — murder. "Dieu et mon droit" dé-
mode with the codes of Victoria.

I have tried to ask Igor, who's never returned. But only for answer
my question returned
With our child's tale of Untersberg where in the limestone the
peasants say knights lie in sleepy enchantment
Around Barbarossa. "And who has returned from that cavern?"
says Igor, all humor in hiding.
"You've heard who came down from a crag on the lake, Berchtesgaden, one year with the pear-trees new-blossomed."
Angry and cold in retreat, and his answer a taunt, like his teasing
of clovers with hormones.

Retreat by his choice. As for Basil, Moravian blood he's forgotten
in one generation
Of British behavior — gray top hat at Ascot, Hyde Park and his
tea cup, Guy Fawkes and the boat race,
Mild sky, modest rivers. I think of the women in Spain, the dark
skin, the strong bones, the black shawls,
And in flight from the village; of girls from Bombay, from Calcutta, in London. Of you who have known
Every road unreturning. But Walther rejected, for me now remain
merely alternate demons.

The Tree in the Garden

Your little Jan, like the dama-del-noche, a fragrance that opens in
darkness. And Alison,
Princess of Indies though met in the west by reversal of compasses.
Margot you speak of
Most kin to me in her profession to decorate truth with an attitude.
Every one, alien.
If I cease with the fortress and castle, they live, as you live, on a
road never ending. I knew
Federico must die in this end of his world. And yours never the
guilt. For this time would not save him.

And Igor says, "No." He says, "Nothing." And Basil will never
say "No," — being bred to evasions,
Staggering panic, rebellion, debacle by majestic detachments. But
I who am sent,
By a fortune of accidents, ever the absent from perils and never
to drown in that bay
Though our crossing twice over in gunfire. Tomorrow I go down
from London and far from Vienna.
Your hand searching cartridges south toward the Ebro? But no.
Shall I see it again when in sun
In the warm, pleached arbor, the pear trees have bloomed, and,
secure in that green, I am stripped and alone?

TAHL : BOOK THREE

CANTO IV

THE BULL AND THE UNICORN

Arizona

GEORGE:
No work. Just busy, Alf. This artisan's trick,
Plaster with paint. And the burghers, they like it. To place
The Indian torso, the bull with the bison, the horse
Unnatural violet, vigorous, ramping the mountains,
Mountains like Greece, land erupted and drowned. Odder fact,
The sketches of Moab and Jordan, our trek in the desert,
The drawings in Greece, to beget this too-easy commission.
I'd like to see Buck in the boots. See him rocking the heels.
You're welcome. But send him out here where the wrangling is
  real.
If I get six sons, they'll be freighted out here for their breaking.
Cattlemen thrive. And the puncher takes purse in rodeos;
Clip of the ponies, the dust, and the rope clean-thrown,
The steer by the horn, guard down, and out on the bronco;
Fair fight. But fake? Take the raddle-face female
In Stetson and levis, the hot dogs, the cokes. But the weight
And the wit of the men with the rope is still right. Which is fake?
What is not? In the glare of this garden perhaps you would match
Imported décor of the cypress to challenge the cactus?
Volutes in red tile. Hardly Indian, more than sombreros
Which, you'd admit, in this sun, make an adequate headdress.

Planes in the sky. Do they fly here? Come on. Make a dash,
Bit of business and out to the coast. But the mustang and wolf

Still among us. Just sport. Like the Brahma bull, humped and antique,
Set out at the gate with the one-hand rider rearing.
More decent than bullfights, the pikes and the swords and the ribbons
Dripping. Like Tahl. Maybe not. All the same, being doused
In the Biscay and still to go back. And the guy there who paced him,
Calling him "unicorn," drowned, and our cash sunk with him.
But must have been right. Not a bull, not a two-horned, bony-rump
Wheeler, charging at front. Just a unicorn, flitting
The hills for a virgin. Outgrowing that bull's head in Athens,
Old silver, the golden rosettes in the forehead. The better
He'd move to South Meyer Street, here where they're quick with guitars
And the whole world lives. Oh, sure. Crossing Africa, China
And Papago hair with a white man's britches. Where
He's native, mestizo. Annoyed? On the prod? Hell, yes,
He's a hero. And I am the dauber of murals. Don't tell me.
Uncritical. Out of my time. Even leave here too soon
For the desert in bloom. Condolence omitted. I know:
Taking the cushiony contract; selling my saddle.

Landscape's inadequate. Done with abstraction. The nude,
Problem in space and in light. And performance is cheap
For the club and the courthouse, a dash of research and technique
Like my young in Chicago, their not-quite-Gauguin in the lunch-room
And chawing on apples and painting the well-trained model
Adept to the pose without squirming. Now latest assignment,
Run mountains to moving cartoons for the screen and the canyons
With reptiles, the story of earth and the land in eruption.
It's art. Education. What for? But I can't be a Mexican
Poking the ramrods of industry, mounting great hands
With predellas of pistons alarming Detroit and New York.
Not for me. My machine shop as false as Manet on the grass
With his flesh and berets. And not satire; cafés, not with tails
And the bulb-breasted chits. Not spectacular; bridges and stations
With engines and arches. And not bilious death on the racetrack.

Arizona

Something sharp as mesquite or the spines of the prickly pear
matted.
Iris is hurt. Damn it, Alf. If she'd join me, perhaps.
Have I told you? The woman of Hano, Nampeyo; I met her.
The true potter's fingers. Went back to the old ones, the makers.
Strong hair, gray and thick, brown feet broad and bare. There's a
portrait.

Also these months have been north in the mountains and found
Like finding the murals I've heard of, Ceylon and Ajanta,
Something soon lost in the sandstones. Just God and the camera
Shoot you those pinnacles, buttes, the raw gold bloodied crimson.
Just gibbering. Sunsets in stone and all that. But beyond,
There is stuff here. A Navajo painting like genius. And color.
Make black, from mesquite; make red, ocotilla; the blue
From the pulp of saguaros. Inventor in fresco, and draftsman
Or not, solid genius in craft. Then a month ago north
Through the snow and the mud to the mesas, Oraibi, beyond
To the dances, the doings. And after the ride in the wind,
The devil's own heat underground and jammed in among Hopis
Happy as kids. But it got me. The one fire burning,
Old man squatting there, tending the pit. And the mudhead
For funnyman stunt. And the drums. And then climbing down,
The masks, the hoo-oo and the rhythm. The gourds and the
glow.
The ritual color. The shadows in fire. The motion.
The hair. And the feathers. And fringes. The pound of the
planking.
The rattles. It's something, I tell you, this dancing in *kivas.*
And afterwards talk. And the rite of the bath. In the snow.

What does it make? Out of Earps fighting Clantons at Tombstone,
Kit Carson, and camels run wild, and the chiefs in our jails,
The monte, the poker, the faro. The ash-pink wall
With Romanesque, Spanish Colonial, now in a row
With the olives and palms on the boulevards. Die by Comanche,
Apache, or very best cavalry, greaser or gringo,
And roll it all down to a crumbled adobe, the cinders
Of men and their shards in the baskets. Like Greece. And what's
gone

And what's come? Just no matter. Like Greece. Dancing drama.
The chanters
With chorus. The masks. And the symbols, six colors. All gone
Like the paintings in Hellas. The axes and war clubs, the arrows
With flint, and the war cries, the glyphs without meaning, the
cities,
Cibola tempting us always and lost — like Dutch Annie,
The prostitute. Nobody knows where she's buried. Too bad.
What's it make? The brass-eagle saloons and the murderers
Slipped to Sonora. Your hero won't see it, God curse him.
"You see it white. I see it green." Remember?
I do. And it's been like the itch in me since. To die fat
Like the Chamber of Commerce with shares in the ores and the
railroads?
But he can't win his war. And you can't. And I can't, either.

He'd better be jack with his jennies, a long-eared rambler.
He's got his bonanza already in music, but shores it
And loses the map like a sourdough drunk. In Spain?
Spain's here. So's China. All Africa. As for the father
Who laid out their mission here, nearer to Stephanie, Walther,
Than Spain is. Was Austrian once. Does it matter? Much simpler
For Julie perhaps to pull weeds and feed turkeys and maul
With a puppy coyote, grind corn, and kiss dolls out of
cottonwood
Tied with a rag, and wear silver. She won't. As for Buck,
Strutting his boots like a peeler. They change. But the boots
Could make him a rancher. And Stephanie now. You have seen her.
And if she's the woman you say, will she breathe in America?
Like Julie transplanted to pueblos? The nearest ward-heeler,
I warn you, may run her from town; or his wife will exploit her.
Transplanted, distorted, this country's uncertain of truth
As a Japanese compliment. But we belong here. And Tahl,
Let him jump with a smuggle of cargo the next British steamer.
Vienna gone. Japs toward Shanghai. And there's Moscow indicting
The last opposition. And "Goering Has Rattled His Saber."
And Adolf, in power six years, now assaults Barcelona.

I know. You read papers. "Buried. An Unknown Number.
Ruins of the Blood-Soaked Capital. Barcelona."

Unquote. But Mangas Coloradas dead,
Mangas Coloradas, chief of Apaches.
Ever heard of him? He was a hero.
Fought for his people. Death. Or the calaboose, fouler.
I've heard that the Spanish, like Germans, make violent warders.
"Our Fleet Plays at War in Pacific." Zoologists hear
A lecture: "The Adaptation of Desert Fauna."
Better than "War in Shantung" or "Defeat at Tortosa"?
Choose your valley or mesa. Don't hurry to die there.
In this country uncertain of truth, neither British nor Roman
Like the venerable priest that you left at Fiesole, praising
The Trinity. Not even Paddy, who knew, I've no doubt,
What he died for. Somewhere he belonged and we don't. Not in
    London,
Parading and snarling at Chamberlain. Feel no concussion
Of shells. Or we fly to the coast. Or fly kites every spring
With a headline for prizes. Just read. Says that up on the plains
One ewe dropped five lambs. Most uncommon. Your colleagues,
    the farmers,
Say "That's too many. Means war." In the tribes of Mojave
They put up a Cry House for mourning. And should we move in
    there?

One dead lion; fifty deer living. Folksay.
Simple fact in canyons north. Leave space
Around lions. And unicorns. Space: And we'll live. All the lions,
The bulls and the unicorns. Space. Like the sand and the buckskin
Of Indian painting. An art. When you render landscape
To blue and to yellow and black and to white for the east
Which was once the safe quarter. The circles for mountains, the
    sacred
Protectors. The triangle clouds. And the seeds. And the footsteps.
The rainbow around. And it's safe in that space. And it heals.
This painting in pollen, the crumbs of the larkspur and corn.
This painting in turquoise and malachite. Pontiff of line
With the forefinger, thumb and the palm in control. And the mind
Full of images set in their orders, all space, no perspective,
The circle and square. And tie up your hair for a sign
You have seen and destroyed. But the power resides. And the art
Of the drill and the loom and the brush all here. Can't take it.

The Bull and Unicorn

Can't take it in. Like the man from the desert brought back,
The body bathed slowly for hours, the slow moisture given.
And if he recovers, a swallow of water. The theme
Around centers. Old stuff. Like this "deserts and water." But fact.

They say beneath the universe a place
That's dark, no sun, no moon, no light. We've come
Up. Who came? And talking with men on the diggings.
They found once, they say, under cedar bark, one in his moccasins,
One with a sash from his thighs to his shoulders, and there
On his breast found a flageolet made of wood, the white beads
Set in pitch and still whole. But the man, he was dead. He was
dried
Like the bark he was bound in. Great travellers, gods and *kachinas,*
Old spirits. And I've seen the afternoon sunlines, the streaming
Called sun-rafts, divine transportation. But never came down
The gods' coral earrings, the gods, the blue bodies descending,
Never the gods coming down on the sun-rafts, kneeling.
Tricked. Could make a renaissance as false
As Venus by Italians; Tahl by Jordan
Fetching Israel. Four worlds below us.
If we dig, we come on further darkness.
That fool of ours, mudhead in Spain. Tell Alison
That he'll come back. But in Aragon, thousands. And rotting.
If he doesn't come back? And in thousands of years we don't find
him?
God damn him. No flageolet. And not likely a coffin.

You Indian, Alf, with your squash and your corn. I'll distort
The still earth to motion, go down through the shale and the quartz
To the granite, on dinosaur tracks to the trilobites, framing
The tilts with erosion to action, the teeth of the shark,
The algae and terrible monsters. The water has leached
And the drain and the curve make a subject, volcanic.
And seascape. Good stuff. But I'll still "see it white," if he means
It's mirage, what is true by distortion in distance. He thinks
Something grows. And that talk in the snows by the *kivas.* A row
Of their spirits with horns, the moon's color, just one near the
forehead

Arizona

Through hair, the false dyes, and the feathers. One horn. "Any
more?"
I said. "Any more unicorns?" Damn it, they had.
One of the clans. And strong medicine. Guarding the dead.
Headdress: one horn. Guard the north and the west. And a guard
For the south and the east; two horns; headdress. And Lord, they
were harmless.
But jar you a bit with their eyes in the dark. The grim ladder.
The snow on the rocks. What's it make? I'll come back. Learned
a knack
With gouache. And it's saleable stuff. If a bull, I'm antique
Like the Brahma. For speed and a trick. You know, Alf. Chuck
the lot.
For the gripes. I'll come back. Give a show. And get Julie a brother.

TAHL BOOK THREE

CANTO IV

THE BULL AND THE UNICORN

Maine

ALFRED:
Buck is growing faster than the weeds
He grubs at in the kitchen patch. But, George,
Don't bother yourself. No farmer. Amateur,
He can't learn much from me but trowel, rake,
And hoeing turnips. Mornings trots beside me.
Knows the beets from carrots. Supervising
Dahlia bulbs for winter. Then, the Twelfth,
When Alison drove down with Dad, hauled out
The boots to please them. But outgrown. Too tight.
He's quick. "Big box, Dad. Send them. By the postman."

I've told him Julie's much too small to wear them.
But fixed idea. In summer other children,
Dozens in the cottages. But now,
Alone too much, he talks to "Julie." Charming,
Elsa thinks. I don't. If you can bring her
East next summer, do. Some leprechaun
That he calls "Julie." Takes her up in planes,
Makes noises. Jabbers at her on the beach.
We'll have to cure him. And a mimic, learning
Every word he hears. Forever talking.

The Twelfth, for instance. Buck astride the railing,
The east door steps, the ones that face the ocean.

Maine

He ties the newel post with ropes and jogs
And roars to bring me running from the garden.
"Hahá! Hahá!" Slapping the reins and shredding
His shorts at gallop. "Big horse, Dad!" he whoops.
"Hahá!" Play dumb, "I thought you were an airplane."
Ignores me. Rocks the post and slaps his bottom.
"Hahá!" Then really dumb, to hear him shouting,
"He sayeth! He sayeth! He sayeth! Hahá! Hahá!"
That high-pitched chirrup: "Hahá! Hahá! Hahá!"

Began with the boots, of course. And Dad, old pedant.
No "ride a cockhorse to Banbury Cross." But give him
Mighty Job in good old-fashioned ranting.
Emeritus of arthritis. And his Alfred
Still no man of God, but peddling land
And truck, fights mildew, aphids, minor evils
When the world needs saving. Elsa heard
The reading. As he used to, from the pulpit.
Pound each phrase: "The glittering spear. The shield."
Old warhorse, preaching the Lord to his only grandson.

We're well, yes. Canned the corn and dug potatoes.
Boarded the cottages up. Three frosts already.
The hurricane just missed us. Tides ran high.
The backlot full of brush. The wind veered west
North of Boston. Missed. A cablegram
From Stephanie in London. Saw a headline;
Thought we'd all blown out to sea, I guess.
When I think of it, we're mostly missed.
Out of character, that slug I caught
In Greece. Just knocked enough to die in peace.

In the tropics weeds grow while you watch.
Then earthquakes. Then three hundred million cash
This hurricane has cost. Six hundred dead.
Shot to air and the Atlantic. If
The Doctor's missed his shooting, where's he at?
A year now since Shanghai. The Czechs. And Munich.
We're not caught. The boy not even sick.
Grow rich on auctioned bargains in old barns.

Kidding. But parasites, crawlers and borers enough
On trees, in blood, in brains, for us to catch.

That Dad's so wretched now, I guess. And Mother,
Her memory slips with age. They keep a nurse.
Hope Buck takes after Elsa. Seems to. Lively,
Seldom sober. But you can't keep track
Like butcher's scales and pumping gas, no gauge
For what may happen next. And I can't mulch
This pup of mine with straw nor use the pliers.
Can teach him to mend faucets, plugs and sockets,
Swing a hammer straight. To catch and pitch.
"Teach me to fly," he says. Again. Just missed.

From me can learn to drive the car. To ride
More than rail and post. And yarns to tell
Of Cairo and Jerusalem and Athens
When he's old enough. But come to think,
Our world's enclosed and never hard enough
For what he'll want. If I broke loose from texts
And Sunday service, he'll as soon reject
Our three acres, jump the easy fence
Of village artifice. If you can get
Six sons, big guy, all right. I can't raise one.

Alison's quite cheerful. She had read
News of the speech at Geneva, of course. Negrin
Will send them home. No word from Tahl. Not time.
You know that he went back again in August.
Into the lines. And then in late September
I heard a few of them recrossed the river.
Like us. Writes books-full. Then, for months, no word.
Maples and birches stripped now, color gone.
You'd know, no doubt, an ash tree's blue in autumn.
But all my life not noticed. Till Buck says, "Look!"

I'm wondering how Tahl would raise a son.
With Alison here, of course talked much of him
That evening. Cold. We kept the fireplace lit.
But Elsa too, we yawn at night — turn in.

Just humored Dad. We let him read. Returned
To his same chapter, charging out the horse
To battle. Didn't listen. Alison,
Dad's new favorite, his scholar, did.
I started broad awake, aware of talk.
Some term not right, translated 'unicorn.'

Think I told you, George, when Tahl was shot
In Greece, and fever-crazy. Howled about
Horses, unicorns. And so that night
After Dad had read, I thought I'd look.
For horses. Look yourself sometime. It clicks
With Tahl near Moab. In Apocalypse.
And after that, the usual glance at Buck.
Dad in his room. Asleep. The old house creaks.
But neither woke. We're growing old, I guess.
Hadn't occurred. I mean, so much. About death.

Went out. To walk the porch. I've heard no horse,
No bull, no dog, sits brooding over death.
Just us. But, words. They stick. "The day of wrath."
"Sun black." "The sea of blood." Like that. At night
Once summer's over, silence here like death,
Except the sea. No cars across the bridge.
No sound. Not even in the bay, the sputter
And chug of motors. Utter silence like
That space of half an hour before the end,
Before last trumpets and the thunder-smash.

Like that. Just still. Then suddenly a voice.
Another then. Ears strained. No more. Then saw them
Against the dark below me on the lawn,
Elsa, Alison. I stood apart
In darkness. Shadowed heads unmoving, turned
Toward the sea. I called. "Hello! Night watch?"
The shadows shifted. Elsa easily:
"Watching stars. Too early for the moon."

TAHL : BOOK THREE

CANTO V

THE SEED

Blood

TAHL:
What man I am returning?
                                        Alison,
Less sure and surer still than had I drawn
Through our unsure communication, note
By note, transition. Now this train —
When we left Spain they'd wreathed the engine, sign
Of life or death, with flowers and evergreens —
Goes up by parallels a France I'd seen
Some twenty months like twenty years before
And now near-winter had been spring and where
A summer's earlier diagonal
Had crossed this land before. Before. And so
In Spain had crossed, recrossed familiar roads,
Familiar rivers met, with each return,
Some unfamiliarity of time.

And so I am and am not whom you know,
Like sons who are but are not in their bearing
Those who bore them. And a birth the more,
This moving from Ripoll before the dawn,
Rain and icy tunnels, certainties
Only pointers marked, as Bourg-Madame,
Toulouse, some northern port and probably
Inquisitions. New professionals

Blood

Like doctors holding infants to the light,
Listening to the heart, at last decide
Whether new-born citizens may live.
And premature, if rumor's right. We hear
Whoever pushed our schedule those two hours
Knew that birth is perilous. The tracks
Bombed when we were due. We'd passed. Escaped
One risk of death in tunnels toward this life.

And bastards born, most grudgingly reclaimed
To name in law. And most of us are dead.
And some have said our number made no matter
In death's stratagem, so few alive
Or dead. In their statistics difference
So near to zero we may calculate
For nothing. Waiting orders, stringing wires,
Growling "soap" and "cigarettes" and stuffing
Caps with leaves in August, strafed and sweating,
The February cough, the penny cognacs,
Bully beef. Perhaps it hasn't mattered.
Like Addis Ababa, the black men barefoot
Bucking cotton sheets and leather shields,
Embroidered togas to a zinging steel.
The difference is zero. Where the rocks
And brambles crunch and fall and leave the man
Half a leg, the inefficient hand?
The difference is zero? Like the helmet
Useless as sombreros, when the bullet
Comes through hard enough.
You asked for this.
And now I'm out of it, I'll give it to you.
The guns are locked in France. As yet. We'll steam
Safe as babes well-born to Paris. But
Only young ones think this war's to win,
Go back to jobs and schoolrooms to recall
Like mist-smudge on the campfires, how the damp
Crept before the sun and being hungry,
Sick on unripe almonds. Surly, curt
In filth, and lazy, pingpong, singing, crouching
After dark with candles in the dugouts,

Itch and retch and spit and brave and whacky.
Like the earthquake underwave that passes
Shaking hills but still uncracked. A few
Loose rocks slip down. Like that. And some of us
Displaced. But if there's none reports the crack,
Then what's the earthquake? And no one to hear it.

The chalk at Teruel. It crumbled, glanced at.
Last winter in the snow, the time I caught
The three slugs in my chest. The sound comes thick
And grumbling in the snow, though sharp in cold.
I almost didn't hear that boy I dug
Out of the heap. And still don't know his name.
The difference is zero? And we knew
Less than the Thaelmann crowd or Garibaldis,
Less than the Greeks, the dockhands, than the French,
Good as their 75's. And all of us,
The more than fifty nations come to fight
Through fifty provinces, moved never more
Than merest thousands. In a war's equations
Who fubs the sliding scale of uselessness
For useless variation? What's it worth?

George said once in Paris . . . that a German
Painter of horses, youngster, thought we died
These years in wars to make an offering,
Some blood communion in a civil strife.
And then George said: "He's dead. Fell in '16,
Dragging a gun to war." And horses dead
Swell and rot. You saw them in Madrid.
And coffee tastes like rubber and the soup
Gets full of flies. My girl, if I know why
I pick you up so in these words to make
Some distant plunge for you in sticky fact
And still, as lord and master-like, had sent you
Over the sea to shove you out of this,
The reason is your asking, saying if
The answer is not zero, we must treat

Together of what is, as we shall treat
Of other matters and perhaps as strong
Contrarities as warfare called communion.

Should I be on this train? Or stayed defying
Law? Are we, called lawless in our coming,
Not to the end defiant? Engine running.
Running away? We sleep, play cards, or merely
Stare at frozen fields, or some like me
Hugging our knees, hunched in corners, scrawling
The changeless past to meet some future hoped for
Over oceans. Where does axis lie
Between assertion and submission, where
The center that controls the curve? Remember,
Girl, you are a scholar. I could see
An eyebrow feathering for double meanings.
Not forgotten Sunion? Nor the moonlight
On the Concha? Not Madrid, nor rounding
Cape St. Vincent? Blankets heavier
Since with mud and rain than moonlight. But,
My scholar, were we right who made our gesture
Versus law for right, but now assenting
To retreat from lawful lawlessness
In promises an enemy won't keep
Back to where's no shooting? Too much waiting,
Reviewed, paraded, fed, and thanks that hurt
More than shooting — like a heart that beat
Loud till my ears ached. And still I heard
Like mortar-fire you don't hear coming, something
Aimed to reach that heart. And we were leaving.
Austria gone, the Czechs divided, China
Running and turning, running, turning. Saying:
"Wonderful people." The football field at Marsa,
The Spanish marching toward our vacant places.
The flanking lines of cavalry, the puny
Mounts and restless; in the air above us
Ships above us, fighting still, the diving
Racket of the guns. And we were leaving.
Modesto, Lister, and the people's army,

The Seed

Wonderful people, ground two hundred miles
Of broken hands beneath the mounted guns,
Lost and losing. Ordered. And we've left them.

It's not the compromise or not. But which.
And no one everywhere at once. And I
Missing more than once who cannot talk
Of early Albacete nor Gandesa,
Nor dodging bonfires westward of Corbera,
Nor Caspe. Not even Barcelona;
Sleeping alive in bed while others died.
The Spanish six to one of us by summer.
Count brigades and generals. But which
Will add to what? And if the war runs wider,
How many heroes to how many villains?
What's the calculus will give the answer?

Which is law, what not? Our side still chasing
Hot heads pillaging and every city
Fighting little wars and every farm
Fighting its own against two angry armies,
And add it all to men of every color
Of face and politics with rapid pulse,
Muscles tense, their insides out and queasy,
Frightened of torture, of sound, of dust, of the moon,
A blue sky ugly as smell in July and water
Scarce and still the papers, reading scores
On football, bullfights, and the ticket sellers
Blind and hawking lotteries in plazas.
What law says, "Guns don't win. It is the heart"?
Recall Jan said in Barcelona saw
Women cross themselves and faint. We think
They will not solve; but figure in the answer.

Call names: as Lincoln, John Brown, Washington.
Call names: the Huns; the run-mad Roman empire.
Run up in clay like running figures painted
On pottery-bake that's hard to slit in August
Even to hide in, snaking your way in brush,
Pants to rags like fig leaves toward release

In pleasant Barcelona. Killing, scramming
To wooden planks that echo on a river.
"There'll be fiesta. Victory. Battles of flowers."
There were. That clear October day, the sky
Raining with words: "Goodbye. Brothers, goodbye."
We were tired with summer. We were tired
With autumn waiting. No attack. Parades,
Singing, banquets, marching through the endless
Sunlit cubes, the shaded parkways, youngsters
Riding on our shoulders. And above us
Squadrons on patrol and in our honor
Air and benches, balconies and trees
Shouting, "Brothers, goodbye." The prancing horses,
Anachronism of a glory gone
Like that brass band in hooded ponchos tooting
Valiantly just yesterday in Spain,
Playing on in rain and in the dark,
Simple, gay, like those in balconies
In sea-salt Barcelona in the fall
Waving goodbye. And standing last retreat
Before the gaudy platform. And the bugle
Playing taps for those, the dead, the notes
Simple and sad and clear in sea-salt air.
The sacred love of what? We know. And yet
It's not so simple; and much sadder than
The sound of Spanish bugles, sounding taps.

Clear as bugles. And more muddle than
Directions international to mend
A Maxim or latrines. One doesn't prove
The fact of fire by theories. I've heard
No one dug Troy to look for Chinese jade
And still they made it evidence in finding.
Not numbers only, orders of the day,
What idiot child or sparrow, dim-eyed woman,
Dying man, enforced determination
For me. And seeing worlds in broken crackers,
Moldy bread. And other sound I heard
In Greece. And then woke up in Athens raving.
And lived to see an afterglow on mountains

The Seed

Jim never saw, not on Pingarron, nor
Paddy in snow and rain, nor Mt. Arraig,
After Felipe's plane, the fireball falling.

Possessed or dispossessed and in possessing
Distraught with every plot and paroxysm
Planned for a dynamic hate in serving
Lords and puppets since the wireless winds
Like puppet string from Rome and from Berlin
To act in Spain. What distant tactic binds
The Yellow River dikes? Invasion drowned
In June, the river in October rising
Did its own disservice; Hankow doomed.
By what proportion suffering retains
The disproportioned price of right; and wrong
Fortunate in rivers, planes, and guns?
Make up factors left and right and names
Of parties commutating A to Z
With German air and British sea and land
And French and Russian land, to Tientsin
From Tokyo, distributing with names
Of those who died or haven't yet. How find
The differentials? What's the integration?

Smoluchowski. Robert Brown. The names.
Do they make difference who merely saw
That particles in liquid always move
And never stop? How many names to find
The average displacement? Not a one
To tell the path of one, one particle
Like airman, sergeant, runner, corporal,
Unless it's God, a term to use with caution.
We rig the atoms to the galaxies,
Ultimate metric light and gravitation;
And still report the nuisance: contradiction.
Searching equilibrium in power
Still lost the light of light or God I saw
Or thought I'd seen near Delphi on a mountain.

Blood

And here like France I cross familiar land
And still unknown and make accumulation
Of item and item and item, still to find
No answer until finding first the question.
Make it simple. Make it now: Miguel
Whom Jan says Rachel thinks somewhere in prison;
Makes the first uncertainty. Can't find
The present let alone his precedent
That put him in so luckless a position.
There tend, let's say, to be more prisoners.
The larger genera enlarge, let's say.
There tend to be more airplanes. Fallacy,
Of course. They are not birds who constantly
Destroy the insect and the seed and die
In dropping seed, by birds and cats and dogs
And men out gunning? But the fortress equals
Prison. But in Spain a church became
A fortress on occasion. But the same
Represents or does not represent.
Terms mount, descend, eliminate. Remain
The particles. The liquid: blood or sea.
And if he's drowned? Drowned? Damn it, Alison,
When Friar Roger talked of submarines
And flying machines and lenses and he spent
Some time in prison, and old Bruno bound
To stakes and burned — I'm tired probably.
No room to stretch. This seat looks wood; it's iron.
We've been hours in motion now. And cold.
Put ignorance for piety and put
Sacrilege for inquiry. I'd say
I'm tired and I'm obvious. Of course
The prison nor the burning's not the end.
And is it not? Not Federico drowning?
And if it's not, although it's obvious,
Perhaps should figure in, in figuring?

What is it in me always makes me listen
For smaller intervals than law allows,
The quarter more chromatic than the third,
The less than semitones? Should I not now

The Seed

Search out infinitesimals to find
That what's called zero's not so, modifies
The average displacement; prison roll
Claiming it's no matter which goes free,
The answer just how many; no concern
Of which man died, how many still to stand,
To take a plane, to run compressors down
To scout the ocean.
                    What for constant? George.
Miguel. The constant is inconstant mind
That knows the tug and pull of right with wrong,
Knows the French can make a Spanish tune
And Czech compose a new-world symphony
And that the *personnage à longues oreilles*
Is not a constant but through centuries
Takes various names by nations, can define
The general term by knowing it's most wrong,
Knows myth alone subsumes the general name;
There is no "Germany"; there is no "Spain."
Miguel and George. They know. Their constant is
Their knowing and unwilling. So make noise
Most often, least cohering, and the sound
Seldom music. The uncertain will,
The constant of the undetermined man
Coming on to prison or to fame
By oscillation of adjacent strings.
Artillery or radios, a march,
The clink of glass or coin. And they respond
Inconstant and rejecting all they've known
For what goes currently as act performed.

What integer, what instrument with strings
Plays one string only, positive, like those
The blind in hoods in Cairo or the woman
Playing on a camel's hair? They know.
Make sure the possible. Like Rachel, Jan,
Austin, Margot, variants but all
A school-boy algebra which can transpose
Only within the limits of the string.
As: fact of poverty; the simple fact

Of suffering and simple medication;
The fact of soul; the fact of flesh. And each
Where you will find them always integral.

What integers? What instruments impel
A longer wave than strings? The deeper drum?
Or moving in quadratics limit still
To something by a formula and found:
Felipe, Alfred, Paddy, Elsa. Drums.
Or simultaneous equations taken,
Worked together to omit unknowns.
Rhythms definite and countable.
Aiming darts or billiard cues or guns
Or whiskey to the jigger, Paddy, sure
Within his formulas. Felipe bound
By ancestors and air who knew a plane
At angle or in vertical, quite sure.
Though both of them come seldom, forest tomtoms
Slotted, drilled for news that travels miles;
While Alfred, Elsa, matched, a tympani
In quite predictable adjustment, knowing
What you strike will answer firm and surely.

But what of integers? With signs before them.
Always plus? Not minus, not to mean
For nothing, but to cross the line's direction
South from north? For is not my *alboka,*
Last abandoned in Felipe's orchard,
Still an instrument though negative
Perhaps in the expected orchestration?
Its possible remains in transformation
To the world of clarinets and oboes.
Suppose the drums alone be made to sound
Until the ear is deafened? Or the string
Repeat its range until you sleep from boredom?
Let's try a sum of wind. A reed that's silent
Still remains *alboka* left in orchards:
Federico — one we may not find.
Stephanie — she might survive the weather.
Walther — also silence, for the tone

Moves wind too high or low for ears to gather
In a dozen octaves. There's Thanasie
Long as a lama's trumpet, long and loud
And lacking stops or reeds, indelicate.
We reject him, say he's minus, pulls
Against the positive — but starts a current.

All the integers will make equations;
Instruments will make an orchestration.
Even Jim who's silent. Even Julian.
Somewhere they come in again. And Iris,
Buck and Juliana; what's he think,
That boy of Alfred's learning words and gardens?
Say he's four. Rebellious. How'll he learn?
There's a term, now. Take the term "rebellion."
Plus or minus? Some four thousand years.
At least, all rebels wrong and *minus.* They
Won, were good. We called it *plus.* But then
There was General Gordon in Khartoum.
He put down the rebels. Tribes were *minus.*
Grandfathers who mourned for General Gordon
Had grandfathers against a king; rebellious.
As for Jim, his grandfather a rebel
Others said was wrong and *minus.* How
A boy's to know what's meant by such rebellion?
While all our days the rebel's been in fashion
Until we won on ballots and the *plus*
Was rebel. But these very years in Spain
The rebel-*minus* turns against the ballot
And calls us rebel-*plus.* But *plus* with *minus*
Being thus confused, parenthesis
Shifting, signs then changing, — check for chaos.

Some score's been written. There's an orchestration
Never played. But it's not lost. It waits.
Or pick it up. Uncertain intervals.
Or sound like Walther's or like Federico's
Out of range but somehow more than zero,
Plus or minus. And perhaps unfinished;
Pages waiting somewhere in an ocean,

Blood

In an orchard, somewhere in the air
Coming down, but slow, the gravitation
Dragging what's too far, too small; or loud,
Too loud, and never heard. And we have known
Some. We call them integral. And others
Coming constant through the variations,
Adding powers and wills and suffering.
Or the music's plain and found; but missing
Signatures for time, the key; and giving
No one rule for right interpretation.
Still I'm figuring. And Julian laughed
And went on, light to color, color, light
And never hurt and said I'd split my head
And miss the music with much figuring.
And if I make the boat, then who'll I meet
And will that make a difference? Who I am
Within infinitesimals while you wait?
Am I the function of your curve? Oh hell,
Yours, girl — to double, double plus, my meanings.

Sure it's random motion, turbulence —
This chaotic scribble. It is shame,
Of course, because we are not quick to find
How to save a brother while he's murdered.
If you fly too high, and that's not high,
Some twenty thousand feet, you cannot judge
Speed or angle, crash upon illusions
Or must have maps, dit-dash, and instruments
Made of signs and numbers. And we go,
Each of us in this compartment jammed
And freezing, riding someone's wheels, and gambling
On a boat at last. But each a pilot
Up in the air alone. We grope around
In air for sound and on a board for signs
That we don't tip and crash, no longer bound
By crowd and corps and weight in simple frictions.

In an open cockpit sound will crack
Your ears in when the screw turns in the slipstream.
We look calm or sleepy, jogging, twisting,

The Seed

Watching for stations, but I think there's hearing
More than mine of voices in the slipstream
Shouting out to splitting decibels
All we've left, the living and the dead.
We must think fast and flip the maps, catch signals,
Check the stars, or we'll be down and done for.

TAHL: BOOK THREE

CANTO V

THE SEED

Water

TAHL:
And will this always be? Come out of death
And moving on the sea, the clocks turned back
And screws revolving forward of the sun
And the inconstant gypsy constantly
Of Indias and Chinas, every Spain
Evasive, unabiding? Boundary
Bound only in velocity of light
In vast uncertain space, no bound beholding.

A mere nine days of winter running come
Seems certain in despite of storm. The spray
Last night, upheaving second's space of grinding
Screws in air and dipped once more to salt.
But I, the kabbalist of sound, defending
Unsure thought with signs in air, acceding
Now to you and journals for your keeping,
Wonder if the gypsying be ended.
Knowing now your shadow here beside me
From seas that ran toward Athens.

Soon the dark
And, as last night before the storm, the sun
Again through westward clouds benign and streaming
Sudden brightness on the level waters,

The Seed

Image of a light you told me of
Among the thunders roaring on Madrid.
And now toward you forever. Shall we go
In truth together and upon an ocean?
Perhaps toward that Pacific you have seen
And I have not? And where the hurricane,
I've heard, in so much vastness sooner lost
In larger calm, all charts of weather failing
On that Pacific whose recurrent peace
Disposes storm to moment soon forgotten.

Now separate in this uncordial space
I set first subject first, as stars and sea,
The tide of light run out to sound and binding
Some immutable correctness finding
Signs of three or sum of classic *li*
Forgotten since the elephants in state
Brought tribute north to shrines in lost Peking.

Far from slaughtered gods and shattering,
Primal and impeccant matter found
From old *Yih King* of knowingness, apart;
First and major action, voyage timed
Even in December toward the spring
Nights of gold Arcturus, April's Virgin.
Need only triangles for declination;
Need only chords in three, the local hour
Of simplest Western sound. Tonight I'll see,
If fog hold off, clear Perseus in the zenith,
Unperturbed near midnight and to Mars;
On the ecliptic, Jupiter; and far
Southwestward Cetus from November's glower
Of monsters paling in the turning year.
And surely shall see Venus in the morning.

So simply by location to determine
Immediate navigation, we shall know
Ten thousand nights and mornings. We can bear
The future's pole toward Vega and endure
The tilt and drag a hundred thousand years.

Water

But we have said: forever; latitude
Governed by what's now invisible.

In the eastern Guadarrama once,
Facing my watch and setting toward Polaris,
The hour-hand toward the pointers, I read off
Vega on the minutes. Long ago
When I knew Elsa first and Margot, then
Came by chance on news of shifting poles
And learned to look for Vega in the Lyre.

So by a leaf and by a star before
I knew I lived in cities, but in air
And separate; and all that I have seen
Returning me to points within the air,
Toward sound that turns to last illuminations.
Nevertheless when most alone I came,
Stalking between the lines that brought me down
By measuring the Dipper on my fingers,
Upon Felipe's mission to Madrid,
Did not expect an Alcalá de Henares,
Federico nor Miguel; I came,
Therefore, toward a city, not alone.

But still the madman of the upper sea,
Watching, west and north of Perseus, cloud
And haze of light nine hundred thousand years
Before us, or beyond, the spiraling
Of further galaxies; or running down
The river Eridanus that flows on
South to the Phoenix from Orion's knee;
Jumping nearest Sirius, a leap
Beyond the five-starred Unicorn to depth
Unnamed by constellations; spurning these
Chords of ship with star, to navigation
Beyond the cloud's refraction, frontal storm
Scudding its crystal tracks in warning skies,
Beyond the years of present galaxies
Toward what we swear: forever; and to where
Within irrationals last music lies.

The Seed

Singing his last aria, the bass
Over and over: "And we shall be changed."
Rousing me within a mountain town,
And thought too young to notice. And they sang
Badly. But the bass: "And we shall be —
Changed." And later years the Christmas weeks
With Julian in that city on that harbor,
The aggressive voice. And you were there,
And Federico lived in Spain — unknown.
And Julian? I repeat myself, obsessed
By earth that shifts toward Vega; and would find
What sound can never analyze, but sounds
Forever and forever in the mind.

Here my first subject, in this upper sea
Walled with light. And if the moon looked down,
I've heard, there'd show upon our planet one
Line — the rampart west from Shanhaikwan
Running on wide China, wall and line;
But not its twenty thousand towers discerned,
Their crumbling since the forethought of the Ch'in
To afterthought, now air transgresses land.
Shall we not look upon the wall of light
And write it down? And from Jerusalem
Eastward stand the heights and there once burned
A beacon in the time of each new moon.
And on that minor mountain gods who died
And rose; and ever from the moon unseen.

That I know what I write in writing down
By symbols what's by instruments transformed,
Is music, seems most obvious. And yet
What is it that I write which listening ears
Will hear and what they hear not equal to
My knowing signals given? Shall not then
We read the proton, neutron, star, whatever
Ray's still far too hard for our perception
And still shall not disprove what may be read
Beyond the wall of light that binds us in?
What alien force it is that presses on

Water

Against a wall to break it we may find
Not alien save by fallacy in signs.
The Mongol herdsmen, barbarous and feared
By merchant-farmers, in their time arrived;
And now, time passed, are also counted men

All ships in sea, in air, now carry sound.
And when all hear? We stand a harder judgment.
Kayaks, run by outboard motors, turn
A variant picture in the paddle hand.
Setting sunbeams moving by a sound,
By sleight of skins and mirrors, every sound
Slips off its secret wire and alters meaning.
But necklace of blue beads on camels draped,
On oxen over Jordan, and now hung
On grinding motortrucks may still prevent
Some evil fought by faith not yet disproved
And is a music to the engine's gasp.

In wonders all his wonders he excelled,
Aladdin Kaikobad the Seljuk, when
He spaced his roads by huts and traveler's khans
In mercy on the wanderer. But roads
Ever end on that which is not said.
As the electron turns its path in light
Which would report it, every fact transforms,
The sought-for truth escapes pursuant sound.

Then? Correlation of distorted maps,
The photographs of hot blue stars misread,
Inaudible and long equations set
By lamps in studies formally to give
The long-formed ratio of the most minute,
One and one in any universe,
The asymptote to infinitely far
Toward which we move. If we must navigate,
You and I together toward forever,
Music of passage mostly mistranslated,
We must correct by motors in a kayak,
Blue beads on camels, or the airport closed

The Seed

To us beyond the Llobregat, by birds,
Two orioles you saw, the apple tree
You wrote me of last May in Alfred's garden,
And I, being hospital-sallow and south of Marseilles,
Remembered. That Cortez brought sixteen horses,
Politics of the league of Mayapan,
Make correction. So by sea to learn
No measure rests infallible, but leans
To matter lying near the system gauged;
And in such measure nothing isolate
But is found bound in closer measuring.

A further measure in the measured tune
Makes its tortuous return. We've plucked
Fruit of Newton's great simplicities
And left him in his inn upon the road
Like Eridanus toward the Phoenix, weightless
And imagined. But we grow more shy
And weary of all multiples, in awe
Of waves and clouds and every moving thing
Which will not rest. What mode but music gives
The least solidity to fact in passage?
Juice and blood and sea to waxing moons,
The radiate atom and all revolution
Still Pythagorean. We deduce
The sun and planets from a vibrant string.

Seamen knew before philosophers
That space is curved and the continuum
Of place is time. And now the nomad tern
From pole to pole outflown. But also dream
Of a Scythian lake where wild white horses grazed;
And he who dreamed beheld its bitter spring
And named it, calling it: the Sacred Ways —
The dream of distance hard and far and strange.
But could not dream that lake without the one
And one and one, the wild white horses grazing,
The leaf, the grass, the one by one assembled.

Water

Who brought out of China compasses
Pleased Prince Henry reading maps at Sagres;
Who ignored eclipses of the moon
For satellites of Jupiter had guided
Your El Cano who the first to wear
Circumdedisti me upon his crest
For mastering a globe. Once more we stand
Columbus-like against San Salvadors
Imagining again a wax-light rising,
Falling, though too far for any light;
And always here beside us stands our Sanchez —
Doctor? George? Or Walther? — who will swear,
Seeing nothing, nothing there. And still
Pursue like gazers from the moon a line
And do not know its name.

Wise men at war
Plug their ears to shut the major noise
And still hear nearer voices. When on seas,
In mountains lost, set track to objects near,
Holding watches to the sun to find
South and checking angles, even trees
In known prevailing winds. Or use a cloud
For ambush, knowing clouds are relative;
You may escape within, above, below them.
And nearest of all words you've ever spoken,
Rounding Cape St. Vincent, looking out
Saying westward lay the isles. And then,
"From those Azores one Benedict, now dead
More than three hundred years, went out to China
And there died. The holy brothers said . . ."
— There were stars. Your face against my coat.
I bent my head to hear you. And your words
Again against me moving on the sea —
"'Seeking for Cathay, he has found heaven.'"

Gypsies have three callings: metals; music;
Trading in horses. Their women are good dancers.
They heap at crossroads leaves to guide their stragglers.
They anger kings and are consigned to exile,

Catching bread and pennies by their music.
They do not stand on heights to calculate
By long sea-curve a global radius.
They are no Hakluyts in this universe
Collating histories of voyage. Never
Faithful Jesuits with maps of China.
But their women are good dancers — like
One who danced with me in Lequeitio,
In Madrid. Her name is Alison.

If you should read this ever, if I come,
My pockets full of papers, to your room,
You'll likely smile at me obliquely, raising
Your palm to your lips, that distant kiss you toss
Never like other women from your fingers.
And all my meditations gone antique
As astrolabes in our new navigation.
Disorder of *a priori* I have dated
From Greece and curving steps on which you stood
Demonstrating falsehoods in straight lines
To me the paltry reasoner, the rogue
Brash with magic words and javelins,
Harps and zithers, x and π and δ
And a times b; and then, the night on Sunion.

Once the ocean and the stars enough
And trees and horses. But the latitude
Shifts and up the wall of light there rise
New and unnamed constellations. You
Beside the car in Athens. And I saw,
Not Iris and not George and not your face,
But that one gesture, lips against your palm,
And tossing outward what's invisible
And was farewell and was a greeting given
Open, manifest, and something hidden.

I count days. Three more. And then the land
If no more storms on this Atlantic torn
By winter. Coming from incautious war
Ashamed at this, my new and excess caution.
Suppose it's just escaping was too easy.

Water

The flight above the Biscay and the bombing;
Now this leaving France — it's been too easy.
George again. I'm in his debt most oddly.
And then the Doctor plodding into Paris,
Glasses straight upon his nose and shining,
Too shrewd for sycophant, and still the flunky
Clever with ambassadors; and sent me,
Straight-tip agents harried to dispatch me,
Like a criminal. These nights recur
Those dreams in Athens. Ushers of the dead,
The ibis head, the jackal, always promptly
Marshaling me on. But never judgment.
Whatever kraken hides within this sea,
Not his, I think, to feed on. Did not die
Nor lose my eyes or ears or hands; my scars
Not even ragged; not the flesh exploded.
Threats at most. For taking you beside me
I wish that I were younger than I am.
Among escapes cannot escape, forever,
Some more impregnable disaster than
The death of friends — and wounds which are not mortal.

I'm grateful. But I'm angry. Had to leave
The gang there walking Paris till they find
The friends or find the money. They'll reach home
Too. Not quite so soon. But somehow bound
To passports, careful friends, in my return
To independence, more dependent, feel
Close-mouthed, recalcitrant. I have not spoken
Except in casual to any here.
The decks are full of chairs. Like years between
Julian's death and my first concert when
Seldom even Alfred, George, and never
Composer, performer, professor, other, taken
More than name, address; so, once again,
But awkward now and not too much at ease
In obdurate privacy. Perhaps it's not
Leaving the gang. They'll all come home. Perhaps
Since the old man came in and rubbed his glasses,
Appraising me, but amiably, and talked

Of some young chap who'd known us in Bilbso,
Some scribbling lad he'd come upon in Moscow.
And made me jog my mind. But I can't see
A face to match him. See a cloud of gulls,
The endless drizzle and the granite pillars,
The tall, brown, narrow houses on the river,
Endless windows; but cannot recover,
Through rising, loud, red-yellow flames that closed
Night in redness when the ship blew up
And threw its rising redness on the dark,
Any face or name. In these two weeks
Detail already slipped. And wonder if
It is the will rejects remembering.

Did I talk much in Spain? To whom? Perhaps
Should mount the podium the Doctor says
My true commission, merely beat out time
As I did once four years ago before
The smell of sulphur meant more harm than caught,
Wringing the nose, in college chemistry,
And not the Dead Sea stench; and fog was not
Cold mornings down the Nile nor April wind
Heavy, red and sultry; had not seen
The sandstones yellow as the caliphs' tombs,
Nor the dead kings in purple pyramids
Darkening through the marshes and the palms;
Nor crossed the Jordan. Long ago I'd read
Cement, the wall of Ch'in Shih-huang, the blood
And flesh of those who built his tyrant bulwark;
But, discontent, he burned the mighty books,
The scholars buried — breathing. Over Jordan,
Southeast, the wall of Tamerlane composed
Of bones, his slaughtered prisoners. Why not
Among green fezzes of Mohammed's sons,
Nor red tarboosh, ask why the exiles flee
Still to the desert out of Damascus, shunning
Its valley, its laughing market arched in steel?
But all I'd asked the smokers of nargilehs,
Gossiping, those over chess in the coffee shops, only
Questions of God and their music; and never of exiles.

Pursuing stars, stand free from pathos, think
Completion and correction adequate
Till come on second subject which has been
Since my father died, somewhere beside me.
Dying, exile, prisoners interred,
Enough on every continent. And then,
The will determines toward forgetfulness.

The old man now insists the gangplank's out
To Soviet Yakutsk, Johannesburg,
São Paulo, Fairbanks even, or Calcutta
Bossing jute, or some Pacific atoll.
Where've I been? The new canal in Moscow?
Shanghai? Nanking? Jim spoke of Hampton Roads,
The great, hellsnorting docks and wharves. And not
Seen. Though I've seen docks and wharves. But not
The ports that died with Paddy. What was saved
By Moorish men who bore their exodus
Not party to Columbus? What was saved
By Jews in Babylon? The Scythian
Lake where wild white horses graze is found
To give the Dnieper trafficking in Russia.
Nothing, the old man says, like Russian laughter
Gay at night in theaters. What lives obscured
Like Friar Roger's unacknowledged scheme
For shipping off toward India from Spain
You say Columbus read and never knew
The plagiarist nor who foresaw his plan?
No pilots now in jerky biplanes shooting
Duels from cockpits. None aim bombs by hand
But fools like Tahl and Federico since
Passchendaele and Ypres crumpled, when
We were too young to learn to spell the names.

When the world is small enough, believe
A Jim, a Paddy, a Felipe count
More than guns and dying. Erikson
Taking Bjorni's ship revisiting
The ports I know. But where've I been? And if
The Tajuña had not held and lost

The Seed

Under the raking bursts and withered vines
Those sharp hills last year, no more Madrid
Which is our hope. But somewhere in the rain
Jim on those sharp hills above Morata.
We say a road holds clear because he died;
As also Bjorni and Leif Erikson.
What did I want to save in Federico?

You know the music I had hoped to write,
A kind of elegy for fishermen.
I should have stayed there by that harbor, never
Strained my ears in Egypt, Greece, or Spain,
If all I learn's no more than this: whoever
Owns Vienna owns the Danube; whoever
Owns the mines can buy both ships and pilots,
Air or water. And who has ideas
Is dangerous. And that Pascal could think
Of adding machines and also think on God.
India has three sides. And Indus means
Merely: river. And the place called China
Is not a place where Jan and Julian played,
And not a bookish dream of hexagrams
And gentle meditation by white streams.
And that I've never been there. And have not
Seen even half the world. There's also Russia,
And two continents I had not thought of
Also in the sun. And when that sets
Tonight it will be still your afternoon;
And I shall never see your afternoon.
Not this one. You'll as likely not remember
When I come so much as whom you talked to
On this afternoon. As I've forgotten
Whoever it was the Doctor met in Moscow.

I am not in America. I wonder
If I ever was or ever will be.
Although American as saying mostly
Generic name for what by chance and oddly
Comes of mingled blood and taught to be
Companion of all men in every country.

But narrowly? Delimit citizen
To minding scores and ballots? When the Doctor
Says I should consider the Baron Tanaka
As well as Walther? If I take the floor
And say the Yangtze river guards or this
New road from Burma; and that women dug
And carried when the men lay sick of fever
And that we should consider . . . I'll be fired,
My name crossed out on all committee rosters
For the local alley. And mistaking
An idiot child for an adding machine or God,
Raise questions thought irrelevant. As add:
King plus people; people, priest plus king;
People plus king plus priest plus barons; people
Plus generals, bosses, priests, plus rich and poor;
And set them in rotation. Then I'll say:
They all need salt and air. And what's that prove
But I'll be fired? Or hired to play the fool?

The fishermen. You say they are descended,
Tugging in fog and depth, from partisans
Loyal to Sam Adams. And you said
The only hope you had, those months in Spain,
Remembering the addled mob who burned
The house and books of one named Hutchinson
Were still the heroes; and the mob that went
Marauding on Long Island we reject
As traitors. Had we lived between two mobs,
Would we have known so well whom we defend
In this late time? Would we have backed Will Dawes
Or Major Pitcairn? And I had forgotten
There were German mercenaries hired;
And volunteers against them like de Kalb,
Steuben; then Pulaski; Kosciusko;
The Chevalier du Portail and all the Frenchmen.
And I recall that all analogy
Is dangerous — like ideas; like thinking those
Who marched across Tibet in strangling snow
Two years ago had something less to do
With Marx, Lenin; and more with Thomas Paine,

Shattering class and caste to merely man.
I think we'd choose, in Pitcairn versus Dawes,
And not for sentiment; but for a sound
More like a heart than less effective drums,
Our motives mixed perhaps, and still compelled
By sea and stars perhaps . . .

And here I stopped
Last night. And now two days. In dusk we passed
Three schooners with the sun already gone
But light in the false day of last reflection
Lighting their bare spars. And thought again
Of men who died in the Biscay; and the long
Backs, the old green turbans rolling; and
Sniping at shadows; feeling the thick suck
Of flesh to knives; and the smell of oil and iron
And more. And thought I had forgotten. Merely
Hapsburgs, Bourbons again, a British umpire
For savage pun? Or Pontiac again
Taking the forts but just as surely doomed?
Now to the corporate state. And the odd function,
Technical, cancelled out, like Pontiac
"In a decent respect for the opinion of mankind,"
Irrelevant to Jefferson, Adams, James?

Someone in an ancient Roman province?
In a garden near Jerusalem?
And does he comprehend the men who walked
From Verkhoyansk to Fairbanks on dry land
Before this time of foggy seas rolled in?

Gypsies also work in metals. When
The Mongol Hittites, Aryan Phrygians bent
Before the spears of dire Cimmerians,
Did they know one man could hope to win
All magnesium in all seas? But when
That's gone? No copper ores in failing mines,
Poor pyrites in Himalayan foothills? And
No more planes. Suppose the bauxite's gone?
And we the people now like iron warmed

Water

To heat and heat, magnetic, powerful
Iron to iron drawing, but will come
To critical degree where power snaps;
And shall we fly apart as we had come
Together, like the valiant Spanish posters
For sake of saving one, to others bound?

Cleomenes in Egypt made his books
With false receipts to profiteer in famine;
Once Roman bulls all imports held in bond;
Once, lies on the Piraeus, growing fat
On panic from the news of wrecks. I think
We are mistaken. And may safely search
Here in music also, though we make
Now, within the space of one and three,
Numbers infinite in aggregation;
Within the wall of light the wall of one,
Disordered from its path by lost magnesium,
Failing copper, planes, and goods in bond,
But of itself unaltered. Power obtains
In Walther that he's quick at numbering,
Like copying the score of music given,
And he more quick than others. But will not
Create. He watches on a clock a time
Binding the world, but thinks it does not move
Beyond the orbit of his calculations.
The "if's" which bound the magnitude of wars
Very large in calculating minds;
But missing, somewhere forward, the mutation
Unexpected, ignorant there moves
The one in altered paths, the one evading,
By its first mystery, last alterations.

We are mistaken; are not iron. And
Some magnet does not break, unless it's broken
By the one who made it. And its power,
Like music, makes a trespass on all nations.
We make a wonder fifty nations meet
Inadequate among Iberians.
Inadequate perhaps as partisans

The Seed

Bleeding Missouri while the war was won
Mostly in other states by other means.
Vicksburg, Gettysburg make false account
Against the crowd along the Avenue
Before the White House after he was shot,
The gentle moan of dark-faced women weeping;
And every war still one and going on.

There in the cancer laboratories Jim,
The day before he caught his leg and fingers,
Fooling and solemn and watching the roof for breaking,
Talking of atoms exploding. And I said: "Salt."
(Being most chary of bugles, of women weeping.)
"Salt in the wit; in the blood. And Stephanie's husband,"
I said, "lacks salt; he splits it to gas and poisons."
And Jim said, "Yes. Just missing one electron.
So he's not solid. Not a stable compound."

None of us solid. All of us missing something.
Remember we thought the old songs had their strength
From sorrow — scale not adequate. And not
The blood enough for all the gracious saying.
You are not all my world. Nor am I yours.
And if we lie together even years,
Not completed though as toward completion.
And, if we say this to each other, safer;
And that I'll say it to you and you'll answer,
Yet more bound in saying, being surer
In love as a most Gordian synonym —

Which sometimes is called God. And here goes reason
Like Maillard, the dancer, once enthroned
And drunk as "Liberty" in Notre Dame
In the dizziness of revolution
Ousting the stone Virgin. We lie trapped
Between two kinds of gammon, "absolutes,"
Holy reason, holy church. And still
The tale of slaughtered gods and shattering.

Water

Those who find my music incoherent
Claim they cannot find intrinsic reason
Why the woodwinds there or bell or gong
At just this moment and not other; ask;
But mean to teach the author his creation.

Anubis, son of Osiris, now my jackal,
Usher of the dead. But also Horus,
Son of Osiris, lord of the day's horizon.
In Esdralon, the young, the scapegoat slain.
And Dionysus rent. And lechers, harlots,
Walking on water, women at wells, repeating
Far from Athens and Jerusalem.
And Jan has asked me; Elsa also, saying:
You believe strange stories? I could say
Nothing. But to you can say I'd read
Kant of Königsberg. And then I saw
Death and barracks. And the Arabs say
The camel knows the hundredth name for God.
Stupid, the camel, and frantic at falling. Should he
Know music? And lamas when they pray
Hold bell and thunderbolt and move their hands.
For us the crucifix more usual,
Though not our habit. Every year have seen
Death. And every age like music make
The tragic entrance. But I have not seen
Other departure but one, last opus when
The overtures were many, all preparing
Major action. I have heard we're born
To infinite behavior though so sprung
From countable, probable genes. And I have looked
For that which, being whole, need not return,
Having made its full return, and so,
Like music, is, the sound existing; never
Passing the bound of being. And is made
Under the mask of metals, woods and skins,
Not of the air but of one person making.
Looked at dying gods and there have seen
More than a game with trees and spring's returning.
Because the music's more than tricks for dancing.

The Seed

Shall we dance Paddy and Jim or Andreas mourning
His treacherous godson? How then shall dress out
Walther? But a mask, a snarl? And how
Felipe in fire, Federico in salt weeds rising?

Their common factor is no fact of bearing
Less than fifty chromosomes; not riding
A less-than-nothing planet; and not dying.

But is not all, to fix as in a sound.
But toward the sound. And there are many signs,
Tree and star and thunderbolt and warning
Metallic crash of gongs. But I have asked:
What is air? And space beyond the air?
And who are these about me who have come
Out of the sea and suffer in their coming?
But I shall come by one more night and day
One more passage of the westward riding
Toward a question I'd not asked, but taken
Of your asking still unanswered, asking:
What man I am, returning?

TAHL : BOOK FOUR

CANTO I

OUT OF TIME

Consummation

In the country of that which is making and has been making and is west or east only from where you are looking, a land called desert not deserted; and in it, trees.

In which are date palms, tall palms, land like Egypt, sand like sand toward Red Sea cliffs; saffron rocks, the hills of Greece; and myrtle like the myrtle of old countries, also oleanders; also silver water towers; roads on which the cactus flowers May and June and ironwoods will purple May and June; but they, in June, had left them.

In which red land below the red-blue mountains many wanderers; like Spanish priests were beaten, hanged, but still the people changed; for now the sheep and burros came and peach-bloom orchards, the divided not divided; no one knows who brought the corn and squash and beans, but had not always been.

In which red land below the red-blue mountains had been waters and great seas and stillness came like stillness on the sea and left the crusted sea-flight and the wind-demolished dune still drifting; and is found here much a man might not expect to find but, as in Palestine an earring made by Celts of Irish gold, much here is found.

In which sea-departed land were many who had been but are not now, who left the red-black cards abandoned on the crates and engines rusting from the flooded mine; in pueblos who did not remember Toltecs nor beyond the Mississippi builders of forgotten mounds, not more than people here who dug the great canals, the people who are gone; and of themselves have gone, the many none knows why before the Spanish, and were not by Spaniards slain.

In which now lawful land the law was made and it was good but here as everywhere the will not good; not always far from here, or here, the jacks among the broomweeds, here the crags, mesquite and soda lakes, adobe shacks; here also these twelve villages made Hotevilla from Oraibi by dissension and Bakavi, but together learn, if slowly, now the letters and the engines; memory dies; and from the women of the mesa rolling clay, to the women of the mesa rolling reeds, to the women of the mesa weaving wicker, once the words were marked for difference, even mesa to next mesa; now the law has changed for good or bad; none will fear a famine now; and so abandon hard-to-grind, the saved-for-famine, hard, flint corn.

In that suspended time before time broke to palpable division timed by war; and in the month of March which may be called The Little Thunder, is the name of this spring moon among the mesas; to the villages a day or two, both here and there came Tahl and Alison; but mostly southward in a town where George, the painter, also stranger, in a year ago that spring and winter, now they came and to a house; but neither chief nor chieftain's woman; one more face across the lawns and in the classrooms; one more face, though some who turned to look at her, the grocer loading parcels Saturday to stack the car, the Mexican to clip the grass and spade the garden.

In that suspended time when none remembered war except as something once; and if an Indian were mentioned, someone might remember telling them: you know the first man native to this state to die in France, he was a Pima boy; his name was Matthew. Never asking much. With chalk on boards Tahl scratched the notes and taught the rules of harmony as they were taught and paid his bills and hoped to pay his debts and no one asked him. Only looked because he had a scar; and said his wife was tall as he was; but they lived so far from town, we seldom saw them.

In that year the Indian caves repaired by engineers preserving by our orders; in that year across the River Llobregat the German shells and further bombs upon the harbor, up the piers, and then the nine Italian tanks in falling Barcelona in a January wind that scoured against the last boiled lentils, broken wheels, the scraps of paper, useless tarpaulins had hidden mobile batteries; in that year Pacelli, Holy Father, prayed for peace; in February in Hupeh the soldiers trained against the men from islands; in Rajkot the hunger strike and then they granted him, we read, this Gandhi far away but chronicled; and Prague; and death; and then:

In that month of March it rained one day as it rains here but seldom and then sudden and all day. The water rose around the hubs of cars and in the papers other headlines also: that Madrid had fall-en after war in war and fires; and north in Oregon the Chinese children marched against the iron bribes prepared for Kobe, Yokohama; and the Navajo and Hopi up at Winslow sat together in a council for preserving sheep and cattle, sun-ray-wrinkled hawk and eagle eyes below the head bands binding strong black hair against the desert and deceiving winds and distance.

Long ago the first mistake; and long ago the old correction made: that if the gods have blood then let us kill a horse, a bull, a sheep, and not a man. And now, like altars, bridges strung with clean new boxes, clean new cords, the fuse before and since the cycle of drought and moisture; now the trees are split to read the monumental rings, the pine, the juniper, the old sequoia younger then the first mistake, the old correction, young as Navajo, as Papago, as Hopi, younger than the rite of Cybele, the sign for mother, and her statue in cement protected well by Madrilenos to escape the spite of war; but did not also block the subway mouths and by the tunnels came the troops who took Madrid and papers said: the city — fallen.

Long ago the Papago remembers bringing from the east the white charm of forgetting, from the north the red charm of forgetting, from the west the black charm of forgetting, out of the ocean painful charms, forgetting under the palo verde, tamarisk, Spain and China, that the warrior, on his return, has mighty power, therefore he must suffer, four times four of days apart, for his purgation, sixteen days in cold and from the fire, before the charms are sung below the lava rock, the low and easy voices, firelight warming broad, brown faces, war and power by charms forgotten.

Long ago the painful charm forgetting; many signs forgotten as the womb and phallus counted one to three in secret sign which is a mystery condemning who betrays to suffer death by drowning. Who told Martin Luther, Robespierre what would happen? As to propose a route from Spain by way of China or America, but never come by way of Faraday or Einstein further than a light beyond the span of red and blue, and who escapes escapes a moment only in a death by drowning; until the trumpets in their sounding further red and farther blue shall break magnetic number, last disposing erg and Ångström, less diffractive blue, refractive red to stillness after mighty oscillation; out of thundering northern dams, the red charm of forgetting; out of eastern icy caves, the white charm of forgetting; in suspended time of minor mystery, the stranger men and stranger women to themselves and others not more strange than any first or last which never is, but may be called, the year of consummation.

In the country of that which is making and has been making,
In that red land below the red-blue mountains,
The sea-departed land, the lawful land;
In that suspended time and in that year,
In that month of March when Prague, Madrid,
After other cities, before the other cities — fallen.

Their house far out, a new site toward the mountains; not their house; they weren't here long; one term. And though our colored houseman went there every Monday, Philip said she kept the house so well he hadn't much to clean except for parties. Once in March, an evening drive, we stopped and there found Philip and his wife I'd never seen before and several Mexicans as well; and Philip's wife was singing and the gardener, Vicente, banging a guitar. And when they went to mix the drinks, my husband said to Tahl, above the songs and stamping: "What is this? Your private league of nations?" After that we never went except when we were asked. The music noisy. And I saw her dancing though my husband says she is a scholar. Tahl grew very tan, and then I wondered how he looked like Philip; but my husband said, more like our Chinese grocer, when he saw him walk alone and thinking; or could pass, if he would wear a silver belt, for someone off the reservations. She was blonde and very tall. I was surprised to see her dancing.

Their house far out. He used to come for me and take me every Monday in the car. I told him that my wife could sing. And after that they came for us on Sundays. My brother said, "Look out. It is a trick." Then I was mad and thought I would not go. I said, "Is this a trick?" He didn't answer straight. Said, "Philip, you will like this story." Then three Mondays in the car about the men, our people, who were in that war in Spain; and one who looked like me. And, after that, we kept on going, Sundays.

Their house far out. He used to come for me and take me every Wednesday in the car. And said, "Vicente, can you play?" I said that I am good at the guitar. And then I brought my sisters too, on Sundays. They made *tacos,* taught his wife. We used to teach each other dances. Didn't know about this thing in Spain. But then was March and all of us were feeling sad together.

That's their house. I mean they lived there. It's my father's house. But she would wave to me and I could sit right there, could climb the wall and watch her. And she gave me violets. Vicente worked for us, so I could go and talk to him. He bows like this and puts his arm out. Like a dance. And Sunday nights I'd lie in bed and listen. But my father always said, "There goes that gang again," and shut his mouth up tight the way he does when something's wrong. And once I sneaked up on the roof and they were sitting right below me on the porch and I could hear them plain as you, and she told stories and I liked them. And he drove me down to school sometimes, and after that he'd tell the stories too and once he brought me home from school and sang. He said, "This place. It makes me feel like singing." And a song about coyotes. And I told him I had never seen one. Only heard them yell at night. And then he said, "I hope you never do." And then we made a yell like a coyote. And we laughed. And then I told my father he was nice. And then my father said, "He keeps the place as well as I could ask." And after school was out, they went away. But still I sometimes play the stories. They're about the bad coyote and the Spider Woman, and about the woman on the island and those brothers killing monsters.

In that house to see her dancing.
In that house on every Sunday.
In that house were sad together,
But the house was far away, the painful charms from far, across an ocean.
In that house the woman on an island;
Brother, son, or twin who once slew monsters.

In that house he watched her. They were ribald. They were easy. She wore blue and green. He held her often by the hips when she came suddenly and in an apron, speaking of the water heated for a bath, a shave, or speaking of his dinner; once because a rainbow — look — just after brief spring thunder. And he picked her up so by the hips, a long, strong toy with tall-corn hair and she would wing her eyes and say, "Don't let me interrupt you. Go on thinking," and he'd bend her then as if she'd break but would not break and suddenly as if, no, not so much as burn a finger, say: "And what will happen?"

In that house she told him stories for he asked her always: "What will happen? What will break? And what destroy?" The stories of destruction, stories saved like colored maize within adobe jugs and in a thousand years as fresh as in first harvest: how the people thought the water monster took revenge because Coyote stole his children; how the wicked men, the evil wives brought evil, and the flood that followed on the dance at Palotquopi. How the sun and moon were motionless until a man had died; the sun and moon were glad, for in that death they moved and liked to move. The man who died went down a world and lived beside the Two-Who-Go-About-Together who are called by their great name but hard to say, but so she said: *"Ethkáy-nah-áshi."* Still the monsters brought destruction, for the sun and moon were pleased with their destroying. Before this world was made, were also men and women, quarreling because the woman ran beneath the Water Horse and, after that, they lived apart, the men from women, having trouble. Then came wind and thunder, moon and stars, but not until the Monster Slayer left his twin called Born of Water watching on the burning, sacred reed, and went to kill the Rolling Rocks, the Staring Eyes, the Centipedes, the Crushing Rocks, the Cutting Reeds. And then a flood. And then this world was made. She a child who told the stories; he a child who heard the stories. All night long they leaned against each other, sleeping.

In that house he woke up in the night and thought: "The heart can stop. The lungs can close. To look upon the body naked, see the blood, the tessellated cell both thin and strong against the corpuscle, the active current of the nerve invisible. Here in darkness hiding more than hidden here beside me." Then beneath his eyelids came the ancient, eastern herd, one-horned, four-footed, chaste and wild and swift and kind and in procession toward the tree that holds the sun and all the planets; and they moved upon him as a wave will move when in the pool the stone is thrown, the mighty oscillation spreading. Said, "Persephone. Not Hecate who rises late before the dawn, who bred the furies, nourished death, the threeformed moon." And drowsed and stirred and woke her, broke her, savage ever; did not break, the yielding mouth compelling as compelled.

In that house on Monday morning at his desk again and Philip there but since he knew him, Tahl called out, "Just say it, Alison, the line again." And answered him within the doorway. Rapidly and gaily: "'Then said the spirit of darkness, in making the world, "Now that the world is so beautiful, let us now breathe on it, let us breathe into it — spirit."' That is the song of the Holy One, Spirit of Darkness." Philip said earnestly, "Shout it." They were half-gay and half-solemn, the three of them, shouting and singing and over and over, like children.

In that house they learned the world was made by singing, by the mocking bird, canary, hawk and swallow and the catbird and the chipmunk smoking, singing, so escaping from the evil and the darkness. When the spruce and fir and pine had failed, the tall bamboo grew upward, upward, bearing all the people upward through the worlds. In this world they met Masauwu, lord of earth. He wears a bloody mask. He walks at night and carries fire. In this world and on this world the white man left them. He went toward the east. And when the Spaniards came, they thought the white man had returned who had a book; but was not he. But when he comes, the book of wisdom will be underneath the rest. And when he comes, there will be peace.

In that house they learned the world was made of Mother-Water. Here the mountains. Then the fire. And after this, the men and women, lifeless till the wind and air. Then came motion. On the fingers wind and air set marks, the print upon the fingers none alike, the wind-trail on the finger; so came life. To a man or to a woman often homeless, often beggars, spirits of the other worlds teach much and useful.

In that house they learned the world was made by one called Love-A-Mother-Gives-Her-Child, the male god, maker, and his hair is bright. He is born of sunbeams and the light. He made mountains. They appear and disappear. He made ants and midges. He made one whose name is Wound-Within-A-Rainbow who is both a man and woman. But the world took fire and burned and still is burning. But the great bamboo within the bright red mountain upward to the second world and there the mountains and the bees were made and who? *Ethkáy-nah-áshi*, Two-Who-Go-About-Together.

Who? *Ethkáy-nah-áshi.* See. I'll draw it for you. Here the housefire east. Here the west, the footsteps coming up upon the rainbow, through the guarding arms of Two-Who-Go-About-Together, toward the cornstalk which is life between the rainbow and the lightning. And who sees this will be blessed and will be healed, who know the road of Two-Who-Go-About-Together.

Who? *Ethkáy-nah-áshi*, who were four and were made two. When they drew breath came rain. The flowers grew. They sing of gifts and they bestow them on the Young-Man-In-The-Darkness, on Young-Woman-In-The-Dusk. They were four and were destroyed and were made two, were burned in fire and from the ashes of their burning born each man and every woman. They were made of morning light and they were made of evening light and they were four and then were two and called: Two-Who-Go-About-Together.

Consummation

From that house they saw the star-ray bent to earth's refraction; saw the pathway of the stars, is called the roadway to the throne of thundering Zeus, is called celestial river, path of souls to last Valhalla, path of souls who go to villages that wait within the sun, silver street to fair Caer Groyden where to find the mighty king. Out of union and dividing how forgotten: how the cells from being two, made four, the chromosomes dividing; but among us, after worlds and worlds, of four make two, make one. Invisible, as rods and clocks in every thinker's dream of how the world is made. But always first was light. Always, while the worlds were made and after worlds were made, Coyote prowling, making mischief. When he saw the people happy, then he thought of making trouble.

Before that house was made, when Tahl was nine and Alison was eight, the men went out to Sobral in Brazil and to an island east called Princes Island. They came back to say that starlight curves within the sun's attraction. And while that house was made, the men, with glass and guess, to see how two make four or four make two, and two make one. They do not fear to meet a death by drowning.

In that house he watched.
What will happen?
In that house she told him many stories
And they leaned against each other, sleeping.
In that house he woke up in the night and thought:
The heart can stop.
Shout it over and over like children.

In that house they learned the world was made.
There will be peace.
After light and after first creation:
Two-Who-Go-About-Together.

Out of that house, out of the star-ray bent,
So by a leaf, by the cell of a leaf,
So by a star, the light of a star,
Four make two and two make one
And so make three and do not fear.

Do not fear. Do not fear. Do not fear
A death by drowning.

In this house creating and destroying, holding the curve of the shoulder in the curve of the hand, the head to the upraised knee, the tensing arms, the free-curved hair across the forehead heavy, falling, then: For creation is not in the instrument, not in the body, and not on the paper with lines. But sometimes in quietness leaning against him, he with his finger caught under the lobe of her ear and his thinking its delicate curve very fragile; then it would come.

In this house the need for creating was saying as sound alone says what is many; and therefore the harmony sometimes too strange for pianos for all complications availing in tempering scale. But must add to the sound here a resonant shell and the sound of the gourd ringing juniper seed, the sound of the gourd ringing pebbles, the pumpkin shell soft with the sound of the maize, the drum made of reeds with the drum of a log, also pear-shape and cone-shape, the rattle oblate like the shape of the earth, and the sound of the lightning in wood whirled and wound like the voice of a bull. For the action not all and the thought is not all, but the freeing of that which is locked in the light to the saying; so also the ready guitar which is old and in Egypt of earlier glyphs among symbols for sound.

In this house knowing music more simple in skies still Platonic, for those toward Nirvana, for there all is one, only one. But the world that is four and the world that is three, also two, also one in a syncopate motion, in moving extension and toward the horizon with sea-beat and heart-beat, the rise of the blood and its draining, the season of trees. Here also the bird and the frog and the toad in the simple essential of seeking creation, preserving, becoming in time in an agony seeking creation, so singing for threat and for union and guarding.

In this house to remember the answer of others to questions of sound in its shaping. The medicine man makes a song for its healing, for chasing of devils, for driving the evil. The song for the sick is the sick man reborn. The song against prowlers, Coyote abroad in the night and his thieving. The song for the marchers in cadence. The song to make growing. The song to strike enemies blind. The song of the thunder is: "*Thónah, Thónah,* below and above; *Aiéna, Aiéna,* within the black cloud," again and again and the land growing beautiful. Say it then, Alison, say it again as the Navajo singing: "'There in the mountain the Holy Young Man; and he lays down his child and his song. There among mountains the Holy Young Woman; she lays down her child and her song.'"

In this house it is not from the hawk nor the bird over oceans, nor from the red rain spider, red as a mountain. But is of this time and this place. You, not the Amazon, not the hetaera, not of madonnas, of songs from the past to a present of singing, make, in this music, a moment alive by a sign. Christ by the Yaquis restored from his grave with the rattle of gourds and the copper bells sounding, music for birth by a sign. Mystery first is the womb and the phallus; they are a power and where there is power, speak softly. Know other names, but the medicine men will advise you: toward power speak softly. The act to the rite is the first Dionysus. After the first is the coming again after justice and journeys and freeing the dead. The signs lie apart in their times; but together as that which has happened reports, out of time, in the mind, which recovers. The delicate lobe of the ear very fragile. The cup of the ear is destroyed. But far away coming, and never the trail on the finger the same, but ever recover the shape of the sound.

In this house apart, but as nothing apart, not the strangeness of stories from those who have died or are dying; for have they not said that we come from the light? Have we not said that we live in the light? Sound is a color, a shaping of light. The source of the rain is the lake and the ocean. The kernel of maize, by a sign, is a kernel of salt. If in this time was a little like dying, we died for the death of the ear to the shape of the sound.

In this house apart but as nothing apart, not the strangeness of stories, the soft words to say when the power is greatest, the sudden-shift mood from the laughter and teasing. What are the snake and the rainbow? Sounds for the signs which will hold in the world with their binding from spreading forever and ever in space like the stars from the glass and the travel of thunder. Take her, her arms full of linens and scattered, and so of a morning. Afterwards why do we ask of a story? Not of the Zuñi, the Ácoma, Hopi, the people of peace, but most often of Navajo, youngest of peoples? Because they are moving, forever are going. When there are bird songs and rain, out of darkness and dawn came a cry. She was born. And her name? Changing Woman.

In this house she told the story, old, revered, by old men told among the hogans; so she told him: "Born of Changing Woman, sons. The name of one is Slayer of Monsters; the name of his twin is Child Born of Water. Here the signs are inter-signed. Their father, the sun, is her father and husband. These are her sons and her brothers. Or he, Born of Water, the son of the moon; and by that they are cousins. She is the earth and the daughter of earth and now has departed. She lives on an island. But if you are taught, you will call Changing Woman, calling upon her, the Woman Who Changes; she guards you from dreams." He said to her: "So, by her mercy, now Cybele, Isis, Persephone, Maya, Maria, and mighty Kwan Yin, never more evil dreams."

In this house the story of brother and cousin, the Slayer of Monsters, the Child Born of Water. How over cactus and reeds to a river to visit their father. And first for their guiding and guarding the old one who showed them a path: she is called Spider Woman, is old and is wise and a helper of men on their journeys. So to the terrible house of the sun, utter blue of the turquoise, and there thrown on knives, for the test is the torture, the sweat house, the poisonous pipe and the bone-crushing stone. But by mercy of woman, the wife of the sun being child of the sun and their mother and sister, survive to the gift of the sun. They are given their arms and the rainbow and light, for the vigil by fire and the slaying of monsters.

In this house she said: The old men sing this song for soldiers going toward the enemy across the waters; also sung for those whose minds are sick; and good to hear the story of the mountain, like a flower with four petals, and the Spider Woman, old one, helpful, and the traveling on the clouds to reach the sun. The place of departure is marked by a cross, its color is blue, and its name is: the spirit. Child Born of Water watched over the reed how it burned till his brother and cousin should call him in need while he went on the earth and prevailed over monsters.

In this house a story ended. How Coyote made coyotes, more coyotes, mad coyotes, mad, wild dogs whose bite gives madness; while with guardian hail and thunder, wind and rain and water monster, Changing Woman travelled west. Over mountains, through the canyons, one by one the clans departed and increased against the warning: then would earthquakes come, and wars, and many troubles.

In this house a story ended. Changing Woman in her turquoise house upon the island in the western ocean. Love-A-Mother-Gives-Her-Child, he who made the clans, his bright hair shining, walked toward her upon the ocean, came and went. And the brother-cousins came and went upon the island, to the earth and from the earth, going to and coming from the people. While they came and went, came others, very young and very small, boy and girl, who learned her songs and taught them also to the people. And the traveling boy was called: End-Of-The-Created-Law; and the girl-child walking with him: White-Shell-Woman-Of-The-Future. Love-A-Mother-Gives-Her-Child, he who made the clans, departed. Said: Watch for fire or flood or cyclone. I will come again. Fear the day a rainbow stands and binds the sky from dawn till sunset. Fear a rainbow all day long. On that day a dreadful thing will happen.

In this house creating and destroying
Earlier glyphs among symbols for sound,
Singing for threat and for union and guarding,
The Holy Young Man and the Holy Young Woman
Lay down a child and a song.

Never the trail on the fingers the same,
But ever recover the shape of the sound
From the death of the ear to the shape of the sound.

In this house her name is Changing Woman.
Never more the evil dream.
In this house resides the brother-cousin.
Always the vigil by fire and the slaying of monsters.
In this house he asked her and she answered:
Earthquakes come and wars and many troubles.
In this house a story ended.
Fear the rainbow all day long.

Now in this room. Though once asleep in crawling straw, in vines, the rifle at the knee, the folded arms, the head in helmet gouged against the peeling mud or, in the slit trench like a grave, the twisted shoulder pillowing the head. "But that I sometimes turned," he said, "when I remembered, west, for you were there. Not often. But at times." And she is here, has been here month and month and month. "All right?" "Yes. Yes. All right."

Now in this room and common in common, rigid shot swollen and sharp. Hard word. Soft word. Quick.

Now in this room. Not quite. Now slow. Good woman. Gone breast, gone eye, gone tongue, gone flesh, come flash. Mouth in the mask, ask air. Air. Roar in the ear. Shuddering wire alert and adroit in the circuit and arc.

Now in this room in the tousle and damp and at dawn can see mountains. And then come the eyes again asking, and bald as the glans and the grape: "Who are you?" "Who are you?" Here in this room.

Who are you now, the eyes in the rain forest staring through millions of leaves? Who are you, hair like a Pawnee so stiffened with sweat and grown darkened and wet? You on the yawn, in the beard of the serpent? The crab will not look. The cat will not look. Look at me. Open your eyes.

Who are you now in this room and in dawn can see mountains? The stalk of mescál and intoxicate root of mescál, the firespindle, sacred and guarded, the right of the One-Horned priest; he brings it from far to the people of peace. Devil's claw also is spiny and long and the bringer of lightning and hid in the bundle. Shut the eyes hard. Open them. Yes. It is good. You are falling asleep.

Now in this room and awake in the light after dreaming. "I dreamed," said Alison. "I dreamed," said Tahl. The trail on the finger is never the same, the dream not the same, the flash not the same nor the flood on the wire. What will happen?

Here in this room I dreamed of the cactus, the cholla with spines. The bushes apart from me, fighting. The sun very low. The mountains to westward were black. The mountains to northward were red. The mountains to southward were blue. And I stood to the east. The horse, like my horse that I rode when we rode to the mesa, ran south and ran north through the cholla. I called to him. Then we stood east and looked west. The cholla made marks like a footstep and handprint in leaping and fighting. The sun very blue like a stone in the west. The sand very pale. The footsteps and handprints were red and were yellow. The chollas were crosses and wheels as they rolled. Then writhing among them the giant saguaro, holding a jug in his arms, bending and rolling and three times and four times and heaping a mountain of spines stripping off like a skin. I saw a blue larkspur far west; a fir tree stood north; a rose tree stood south. "What shall I give him?" I thought, "For now he is hungry." You answered and asked, "What is light? Truly?" We walked in the cholla. The sharp branches crumbled. The giant saguaro rolled down like a hoop and he poured from the jug and the water came over. Then I woke up and here you are leaning above me and looking at me in the sun. "That was a dream," he said. "Sleep again, darling."

Now in this room I dreamed of your eyes. I entered them, found on a shore many people and bending in steam moving rockweed and leaning on shovels and wiping their faces and waving their aprons. Then out of the ashes three logs and I knelt on the logs and I heard someone talking. We rose very high to a broken-back mountain and always my hands at my eyes and my ears, for the feathers came thick. I brushed them and brushed them. I saw that the sea cut the mountain in two. The mountain was here and the mountain was there like a mirror in mirror. My face in the glass and I shaved very hard all the feathers, the white ones and blue ones, the black ones and pale ones. They heaped on the glass like a cone and they glittered like sea-fern in water. Then the glass cracked and I started to run toward the ocean. I felt very thirsty, but thought, "Do not drink." My head hurt. I pulled at my hair for it ached. It grew dark and above me a comet that slit like a sword. I thought, "There it is." I came to the water and thrust down my head for it ached. And went under. And then I woke up and lay watching you. "That was a dream," she said. "Sleep again, darling."

This room is not here. It is anywhere. Let us go east again, back to the apples and dahlias, the sumac and alders, with Alfred and Elsa this summer. And live near the ocean.

This room is not here. It is anywhere. There near the ocean the work will go better. I'll help with the garden. You'll help with preserving. We'll help. And the sun there is milder.

This room is not here. It is anywhere. "We'll be missing Vicente who calls you *Señora Azul.*" "And Philip who says for a joke, 'Mucho hombre!' and grins when you thump the piano as if it's on purpose so stubborn." "And Philip's wife singing." "The little one over the wall, who hid on the porch and we found her." "And treasures the turquoise we hid for her there by her father's *ramada.*" We haven't seen jaguars or lions or even coyotes although they are here in this country. And whom shall we miss?

Out of this room and this house and this land
What will happen?
Here in the land of the red-blue mountains
They have been good to us,
The boys and the girls on the lawns, in the classrooms,

The generous lenders, the evening callers.
We are not lonely. But let us go back
To the apples and dahlias, the sumac and alders.

Consummation

The room is not here. It is anywhere.
Time was not here. Not for us. It is time to go back.
An ocean is west. An ocean is east.
But let us go back for a while
To the ocean.

TAHL : BOOK FOUR

CANTO I

OUT OF TIME

Contrition

From position and perception every season takes proportion.
These coincident in time with accident of all recorded voices
Count for quantum in the time, make the sum in consummation.

This was the threatening summer. You will remember that
    Warsaw
Fell in the fall of this year after murderous weeks in September.

Iris said: When we were youngsters, I wailed all the louder
If Alison wept. And Mother says seldom
Anyone found what it was that we cried for.

Margot said: Coming from Europe that summer, assembled
The troupe and I trained them, the girls. And than any in Paris
The band far more clever, demonic with drums and the brass;
These dark men — they bulge the piano until it's alive
As a woman and swaying. The bull fiddle shushing and slung.

George said: When Alison went very white
In the smoke and the noise, I ran up for a cab.
The night stuck as thick as a fever with heat.

Contrition

Before the storm broke, we got back to the house,
But lightning was forking the lake.

Iris said: Tahl had been snapping the muddlers
Out of the highballs and breaking them, splitting
The splintering wood with the nail of his thumb.
And I thought he was thinking. We knew in that summer
The big work begun.

Elsa said: August they came to us here
On the coast. He talked much of the Negroes who played
In Chicago. Some wonder upon the trombone.
And a trumpet that talked till the ceiling had split.

Alfred said: When they came up here in August
He said, why'd he go to the Greeks, to the strummers
In Egypt. The colored guys had it. They'd make
With a drum till it talked. A piano could walk.

Stephanie said: In this summer my coming
From Europe. Here, quiet at last. And the days
On the beach in the sun. And the six of us swimming
Together. With Buck, you know. Safe in the shallows.
We lay on the sand. I protested. Said, "Tahl,
But the masters still teach you. Not all syncopation
And drums." For I thought he'd forgotten. But then
He'd said, "No. When a new child is making, there's nothing
Forgotten." We lay very still in the sun.

George said: That July, if it wasn't the music, he talked
About war. For the months in the West hadn't cured him. He'd
growl
On the racket, the praying for planes, and he gave us enough
Of the fellows who fought. But a good deal too much of the
treacherous

Jerries, sad Wops, and the Church, and the fat bags conspiring.
I stopped him. Said, "Listen. We know you got hit. And so what
Were you up to? It's not eighteen months merely stinking in
holes."
And I put it out slow for he wasn't half listening. "What," I said.
"Listen. I'd just like to know. And exactly. Your job.
What in hell did you *do*?" Then as if it weren't news, he came out
With it. Said: "Well — reconnaissance." Short. "Be specific,"
I said. Then he ground it, "Well — hedge-crawling, ditch-sneaking,
counting,
And smelling the wind. And you heard what you heard and sent
back
To the big shots. Make plans, then. Deception. Surprise. And the
shape
For the jump. Then some sniping. Or wiping a guard." Then he'd
sit
And snap muddlers. Or beat it out back in the rests for a gab
With the leader to get some conceit of the devil came out
Of the trumpet, perhaps. And then he'd sit down again, saying,
"It's done with the lip." And then it was time. For the clap.
The dillies pranced out on the stretch. And she knows a few tricks,
Prima donna. Yes, Margot. And slow by the tables. Parade.

Iris said: She'd changed. More like her mother.
Alison. And as we all knew then
Carrying the child. But for deception
Or defense, that stillness, merest guess.
"Usual," I hoped. "And nothing wrong."

Alfred said: August, if it wasn't music, he talked
Of the West. And he'd tag with the boy through the bushes and
dunes,
Buck yipping after him, splitting the syllables, rolling
The "r's," "Younger Bro-*ther!*" hard after him. This topsy-turvy
Of games, something Indian. Taught him to fill up our pipes,
And to hold the match properly, say, "Younger Brother." And
Tahl,
Strictly to ritual, "Thanks, Elder Brother." He wrote it

On sand with a stick and he taught him the letters. And sometimes
Turning up pebbles for spiders and telling long yarns of the old
ones,
Some old Spider Woman. And filling the child with the nonsense
Until he goes wild if I kill one. The four of us mostly,
That's counting Stephanie, there on the beach. For they minded
The sun, that is, Elsa and Alison. I wasn't there
Every day. Had the office to keep and the property takes
Tending to — more in the summer.

Iris said: George, he may go,
But he comes again crawling, a good-natured hound,
And I whip and he yelps. But a horse
May not take to the whip. He may rear and run off,
Or the spirit may break.

Margot said: In July, in the hot, gusty nights
He'd swap yarns with the boys and we'd do all the dives
For the sessions. They all came to know him. They'd play
When they saw us come in. But I knew he'd go soon.
The mosquito that night in my room. When it stung him,
He said, "Have you heard? Where the parasite boards,
The female's the carrier." You might say I showed
Some annoyance. As meek as a monk if you crossed him
At once when you felt you were right. Not as neat
As a joke and mosquitoes. I said I would hate him.
He said, "That makes two." And he didn't mean Alison.

George said: I thought they had straightened it out. Watched him
work
That last week like a Polack, dug in at the desk that I'd rigged
There in the loft. Didn't talk. And I slogged at the paint.

Iris said: After the night we'd come back
On the quick, we stayed home. Though the men sometimes gone
Half the night, he and George. Or Tahl went down alone.

Then I knew. And George knew. And then one afternoon,
Taking out Julie for sun in the park,
Along by the rocks she helped Julie to walk,
Bending above her and guiding her. Wanted
To say. Then I couldn't. But Alison looked
As if she had heard. She said, "It's all right.
Don't be afraid." And Julie, red topknot
Bobbing, the animate sunbeam there, mimicking,
Carefully, "Don't be afraid."
And Alison catching her up.

George said: They left in a rush, making off to New York,
Meeting Stephanie's boat. She'd arrived. We were glad. And they wrote
About folks of the young engineer that was Alison's — Jim —
Who didn't get out of it — Spain. Who comes safe; and who won't?
Stephanie, safe and in quota. Before the war broke.

Stephanie said: Where the river comes in from the bay,
The men walk out backwards and thump with the heels. I asked why.
Buck said: "Don't you know? It's for clams. They jump up." And he marched
On the ooze, digging in his firm heels, and said, "Look,
Stephanie, look!" Then above us, a day on the beach,
The plum tree, the thread of the gossamer down from the branch,
Spinning and struggling. I said, "It's as if it were dying there,
Writhing." But Tahl said, "He does it to live." And then Alison
Looked at us both. And I was not amused. Was not cold.
Was not angry. But strange. For I'm mostly, or had been, amused.
She, so much still and at ease, saying suddenly, "Stephanie,
Run with me." I was afraid she would fall and I ran,
Plunging straight into the waves as I never had done,
For the sea is so cold there, but followed her out as she swam
Toward the rocks at the end of the cove. As we lay there, we watched him
Alone, far away, on the sand. And then she said, "Stephanie."

Contrition

She was not smiling nor angry. We were not amused.
I never had thought it could be. Not like this. It was late.
A full tide. When the sun's in the west, there's a glare on the
water.
We swam for the shore. "Mind the rocks," she said. "Sun's in the
eyes."

George said: In July though we didn't say much, we got nearest
A fight that we ever did, though we had sparred for a decade
Or more. Never reached for the belt. I was grousing about
On the bastardly brood of my colleagues, the charlatan stunts
To set canvas in motion and cut to a further dimension.
And said I was through with that kite-spin and Disney had caught
All the motion you'd ever put into a surface. I'd thought
I could say something once. I had quit. But the business is good
And my hand is well in. And Tahl gave out with question but
meant
Accusation, "So? Treason?" That put me in sweat and I strafed
him,
"Your big-gun ideas," I said, "frigging with God and His light.
You're just a damned parson. Like most of them, fake." He let out
And he jabbed my arm back till it creaked. But lost guard when I
shot
With my foot. He came down. The house jarred. And the women
were out
Or they'd heard. Then I jawed him. "O.K. So you puke. Have a
drink.
And take Margot," I said. "She's your kind. She won't mind if
you skip
Now and then. She's your style. And you're rotten as I am."
He'd got to his feet. But his eyebrows stood out and the nostrils,
Flaring. His scar had the twitch. But he swallowed the drink.
Felt good as glory. Could kill him. He's big as a horse.
Didn't. We don't. But I told her. She said, "Are you jealous?"
That's Iris. She knows all the answers. And so I stick with her.
"O.K. Then I'm jealous," I said. "That's all right. And he's good,
At his job. So am I. But he also sends solid. I can't.
And so what? Can she manage him — Alison — merely with
looking

That look of hers?" "If you're a painter . . ." — I didn't like
'if' —
"You do the looking," she said. "When they're dancing together."

Elsa said: Stephanie being here made us think more
Of the news. We got somehow to roads. And Tahl showed on
the map
Where it ran from the bay of Bengal and then up to Chungking.
And he said, "There's another, to Russia. And one from Yunnan
To the south. And dug mostly by hand." And then Alfred rang
in —
It's his favorite speech: "It comes down to the man, at the end.
The machine is the devil for fooling us, making us think
That there isn't a man at the plow and the shovel." But Tahl
Was quoting the Doctor, describing the barrows they rolled
Against floods, how the coolies crowd out on the mudbars with
stones
In a snag made of rope and of willow stakes hustled and thrown
For a stop-gap. "This struck me," said Tahl, "when he gave me
the name
For the flood in the spring: It's the 'Peach Blossom' flood." Then
he left it.
They talked of the torrents that run in the Alps, in the Tyrol,
In Switzerland. That was what started it. Tahl saying first,
"What about Basel?" Stephanie startled, it seemed.
She said, "Basil?" "No, Basel," Tahl said. "Not a person. A place."
But still she seemed troubled. "Oh, Basel," she said. "That's the
bank.
Walther would know. But I don't." And then Alfred said, "What?"
As blunt as he can be. But Tahl said, "I didn't mean that.
I meant it's the place that was picked for the Jews and their plot,
The lie of their running the world. And Doc says it was borrowed
From Russia, the Tsar's gang, Ochrana. It's now Gestapo.
Rosenberg plugs it to Hitler, a whopper, and now
It is German to kill. It's fantastic. The murder, the *putsch*
And the pogrom grown up from a yarn and a lie." Then I heard
Stephanie saying, "Vienna. It's madness." Felt sick
As I've often felt since, with the news and the photographs. Then
More than riots in Athens, or Alfred, his talk after Europe,

Knew something was wrong. But won't let a thing go when he wants it,
Not Alfred. "This Basel," he said. "Weren't there Hussites? And councils?"
And Tahl looked at Stephanie. "Your turn," he said. "That's your blood,
The Bohemian." "Yes," she said, "heretics always." And smiled
And as lightly, "His ashes were scattered and thrown on the Rhine."
"So the barons got paunches," said Tahl, "and the peasants who backed him
Chased from the barricades — wagons." But Alfred said, "No.
The cardinals out with their swords and they rushed the cathedral.
There were the prostitutes too, one apiece, for the churchmen,
And chased from the streets when the Hussites assembled. The junk
You remember from school. But I wrote that all down. That impressed me,
The Fathers at Basel, first hiding the drabs, and so curing
The Church." "There were also," put Stephanie quietly, "treaties
Which severed the Swiss from the Hapsburgs." "We'd say, so much good,"
Tahl concluded, "but look at the lies. Almost think hell let out
Northwest of the Alps, on the Rhine. A good city, no doubt,
And no fault of the voters. Bad luck in their visitors, handy
To river and rail, a misfortunate city." "This bank?"
Alfred insisted. "It's merely in Basel," Tahl answered,
"And highly respectable, coincidental. Like torrents
And mountains, both neutral to lies international
Hounding the twelve tribes of Israel. Also the councils
And treaties. If maybe the Vosges and the Jura conspired
With an Alp and the Rhine, so to smash and to drown,
It'd do only harm. Patient innocence crushed
While the lie has grown up and walked off."
                                        Then I thought to ask Alfred
Afterwards. "What were you getting at?" "Damned if I know,"
Alfred said. And he went off to sleep. But the one other word
Roared in my head. The lie — that walked off. That one evening.
Confusing. I couldn't recall anything Alison said.

Margot said: The man had moods. I knew
When things went well. For he'd talk nonsense then.
And call me 'slyboots.' Most ridiculous.
Odd, of course. How much we'll never know.
What names, perhaps, he made for Alison.
He was not often solemn. But more often
In that month, about the music. Hurt,
I knew, the night the boys closed up. He'd quote
The old plantation tunes. They'd turn him off.
I think they were ashamed. And afterwards,
"They don't know what they've lost," he said. "They've got,
Thank God, the others who know better. Want
And shame and bondage are no shame that make
Music which can shame the sham of masters."
"Very well," I said, and meant to nudge him
Out of that sententious stuff he'd take to
Out of something black he sometimes carried
Like a smoker needing shots. "This makes
Your being such a wretch so very useful."
I was often angry with him. "Look,"
I said, "at you, at me. We run with drums.
But you know that it's real. The fever in us
Makes the dance. You would not be those faces
At the tables. Slobbering. *Voyeurs.*
They never dare to break. Just peering always.
They can't. The bandman. Lord, he's furious.
They will not even clap when hell's let loose,
Till every nerve's alive and standing up.
But there they squat because they're dead. You're not.
Or are you? But I'm not a sinner. See?"
I don't know why I said it now. He'd never
Called me one. He's not that clumsy. But
He irked me, lying there and looking glum.
"You'd make a portrait of a suicide,"
I said. That got him. Ever notice things
Repeating? That's what makes it hard in dancing.
Not just belly writhe, the stance and kicking.
Need to be more subtle, wrist and ankle.
But like those years before, again he took me
As if he'd strangle me; and then let go.

But this was different too. Because he said,
"Not what you think. It's not the jitting gut,
The being hot. And you're all right." "Oh, quite,"
I said, to mock him. "You may spare yourself."
I missed him. He was good at everything.
He even drilled routines. You'll hear the band.
And they can send his stuff. They know it. But
This drummer never gets it right. It's not
The color of the skin that makes a drummer.
This one is too nice a boy, no doubt.
She must have had it. Something. Don't know quite.
"Margot, you're all right." And I suppose
He meant it. Like his saying that last night,
"It's just I love myself too goddamn much."

Alfred said: Much bosh about New England;
New England this, New England that. Like Elsa
Guying me, when we first met, because
My father was a preacher. And as if
All the preachers hadn't gone out West
To make her what she is. If they did that,
They had much better luck than Dad with me.
I say we're all the same. And yet there was
A way of Alison's, to me New England.
It's the smile. My mother had it. Just
As if they knew, in merely being born,
There was a joker somewhere in the pack
To cross the trick. Buck's got it too. Not like
Julie. Not the gurgle. And it's not
That he's a boy. And always had it. Just
A kind of wariness beneath the grin,
Some reserve you can't expect to take
Just to flash an ace. And Alison
Had it. As most women don't. I think
It gave her stamina. And Dad. He liked her.
Failed, those years he knew her, but his eyes
Were sharp. He knew a spirit. And I've thought
Alison alone knew what he wrote . . .
Tahl, I mean. I'd say to him sometimes,

"What is it you do when you write? And what makes it so hard?"
"Transitions," he'd say. Or, "The balance." And still none the wiser.
I didn't know more except what I had heard. And he said,
"I'm working with voices." "You mean a cantata," I said.
"Yes. But not quite," he would say. "See here. Take the muting,
The play on the bridge and the timbre. It all goes together."
And I'd try to read it. He'd say, "You see. Bass clarinet.
You write a ninth higher, a major. But it will sound low,
Rather sinister. This is the A, written up minor third
Of what you'll be hearing. And then there's the matter of speed.
You can't hurry brass and you can't hurry voices." I'd listen.
I didn't get much. But she knew. And then, Stephanie, too.
She could follow the score. And I know the two months they were here
There was trouble. But if you are looking, you'd better look straight.
And whatever he did, it was Alison. When we went up,
He and I, up to town — he was hunting a school, as you know,
To stay east — we had started. He jammed on the brake and he backed
To the drive where the women were standing and called to her, "Alison,
Promise you won't swim alone while I'm gone." And she said,
"Promise," and smiled. She'd a way with him, keeping the rein
Without pulling the bit. It depends, as you know, on the people.
Stephanie — just there's a dignity there and a wit
I don't get. So you stand at a distance and look. And the both of them,
Stephanie, Alison, handsome. And he could move in
On the two of them. Don't see it often. A *noblesse oblige*
Of some sort. If you can't make a mess of it just by yourself,
You can't by yourself just get out of it. That's as I see it.

Elsa said: That's when it happened. The night they were gone,
Alfred and Tahl, up to town. And there wasn't a light
In Stephanie's room. And then Buck was asleep. And I looked
Down through the garden for Alison. Finally found her
Walking alone on the road by the shore. And the water,

Contrition

As sometimes it is in the evening, dusky, still blue,
But the eddies are viscous and black, and a multiplex crystal
Out where the moon's coming up. And we watched from the point.
You can see it from here. At the edge of the bay. And we talked
First of the trips they had made in the West. Of two words
That George wrote to Alfred. The words were *kachina* and *kiva.*
I take it *kachinas* aren't gods but a kind of a spirit
That watches and helps. And that was all right. Then I asked
About *kivas.* She started to tell me — the way you go down
On a ladder and this going-down, a descent in the earth
To a time that's before and to where we come up from, or
  something
Like that. And a *kiva* is never for women except
They may go to look on at the dances; a kind of retreat
Where the men go to smoke and to think. And while she was
  talking,
I had been watching her face. And Tahl's coming again,
So many years gone, stirring much I'd forgotten, especially
Julian. The pictures he'd made. And the one Tahl had found
After the funeral. Sorting the paints and the canvases,
Found that last sketch on the drawing board, merely a sketch
On torn paper. I'd lost it long since and most likely to scrap
That we burned when we moved from the city down here before
  Buck
Came along. And I tried to remember it, watching her face
In the light that comes dim from the road. But recall I had thought
That sketch was more Julian than anyone else though the face
Was the face of a woman. But Alison leaning beside me
Suddenly shivered. I thought she was cold. And I said,
"We'd best go on up to the house." She said, "No." It came stifled
And hoarse and unlike her. My own heart constricting, I thought
"Stephanie." Groped for her arm and I held her against me.
And then it came out. But was not as I'd thought. And a wrenching
More savage and terrible out of that stillness and calm,
Choking and hard. And "Hush," I said. "Hush, now." Like talking
  to Buck
When he's angry because I have crossed him. But desperate, and
  not
Knowing just what I should do. Had she struck, been resentful,
Hating her, blaming him, I'd have agreed. There'd be something

To do. But I held her, this frightening child in my arms,
In the seawind and starlight, who punished herself. "And I don't
Understand." That was the most of it. And I tried saying
Soon he'd get over it. And I was right. But that
Wasn't it. "But why *am* I like this;" Just as simply. And asked
As if for a help none could give. The lips trembling. "I don't
Understand." Nor did I. And I wanted to. Never the more
Than back in the days when Tahl talked of his work and I never
Could follow him quite and I knew that he knew it and so
He would leave me. "But tell me," I said. And I felt her against me
Rigid, then easier, quietly now, and she said:
"It's not for possession. We've talked of that often. I'll never
Be him and he'll never be me. And you know it's like that.
But I want to be all that he needs. And he says so. And then . . .
And then I am angry. Furious." Since you've not seen her,
I don't know whether you can comprehend
That night, my helplessness. For she was never
Angry, never furious. If she'd been
Anyone but Alison, would not
Have thought she told the truth, that there could be
Behind that gentleness a fury hidden
That could hurt. "It's that I hate myself,"
She said. And then the mouth was still. I looked
And saw a smile like Tahl's sometimes, and like
That boy of mine as if he knew some joke
He never tells. "It's merely — " and she turned
And looked at me and in her eyes the tears
Like the moonpoints on the water wavered
But held back. And then that smile. She said,
"Being like the others. Womanish.
Vain." At that, I took her by the shoulders —
Preposterous, now I think of it — and felt
The strong bones there — a pygmy so, beside her,
Shaking her. "If ever anyone
Was not . . ." I sputtered. Then she took my hands,
Holding them in hers. And then she said,
"I'm glad you think so, though you're wrong." We walked
Along the shore again. But out of silence,
Just the drag along the beach, the sound
Of undertow on pebbles as it comes

Before September storms, her voice again,
Steady, heard her saying, "It was good
In the West. We were alone somehow.
Out of time. Though you're not right — just fond
Of me, as you are fond of him. But Elsa,
Don't be afraid. I think it's all right — now."

Stephanie said: It must have been nearly the end
Of September. And Tahl was already in town.
He came for her that very weekend. The term had begun
At the school and he'd found them a house and to save her the
strain
Had seen to the readying. Cold. And the dahlias had blackened.
Elsa, from the stairs, was calling Buck
For bedtime. Alison, collating, scanning
Passages, had put aside the books.
She helped Tahl much — the text. But now with Buck
She knelt there by the fireplace helping hunt
Pieces of the puzzle I had brought him.
Of these United States, a jigsaw cut,
But simple. Buck could manage it almost
By himself, but seemed much more content
If someone were beside him. Elsa called.
He came. He'd always take my hand most gravely,
Say goodnight. And then kiss Alison,
On the cheek. Perhaps it was that evening
Because he knew that she would soon be leaving.
He stood beside her as she knelt and said,
"Now I'm going to say goodnight." And then,
His child's brown paw, swift, grazing at her hair,
Hesitating, "Just like Brother does."
His serious face, the mouth as still as wisdom
Pressed against her ear. I saw the flush
Surging at her throat. He went off, padding
In his moccasins, but faster than
His usual for bedtime. What he'd seen
And when, who knows? And I had known that brief
Salute at the lobe of the ear, though never the gesture
Of hand. And I waited, alert. But she turned to the books.

Asked me a casual question. We sat by the fire,
Talking together, untangling a knot in the text.

Iris said: Whether a gift of seven meanings,
Whether a dream means anything or not,
She wrote, in early October, the house was pleasant,
An hour's drive for Tahl, and near the sea.
But having dreamed, in the equinoctial storm . . .
And as she wrote, "Mere nothing, Iris. Woke,
And just, the sea was roaring. I had thought
I had gone out and toward the beach alone
At night. But Tahl was there before me, walking
In the breakers. Then I saw him plunge.
Then nothing. Only darkness. Climbed along
The rocks and called him. Dived. And then I found him
Face down. Floating. And the drag was running.
Felt it catch and spin us. And I held him
One arm under, head against my breast.
And I was saying, 'It's like Federico.'
But then saw Federico near the rocks,
With Stephanie. And so I fought against
The tug and swirl and tried to reach them, heard
Their voices, calling. But I could not fight it.
The tide was running out. I could not fight it.
Going out and down, his head against me.
The way it was the night I took my courage
And told him how it hurt. And I had wept,
I must admit. And he had been as still
As this, and heavy. But he'd come alive,
Though stricken, just as I was. Very gentle.
But now he lay against me and the drag
Stronger than my fighting and I know
I prayed. 'Not now, please God. Because the child . . .'
And woke up sobbing. Tahl lay there beside me
Sound asleep. The storm was very high
And breakers all next day. We went to watch them
Before we left that evening. And that night
In our new house, I told him. He looked worried,
Dreadfully. I'd thought that he would tease me.

Contrition

Not a word. Just there, for minutes, held me.
Till I who said, 'What is it?' 'I don't like it
Much,' he said. 'That's all.' I don't suppose,
Iris, for a moment that it is
More than nonsense. And I'm not afraid.
But wish I could forget it." That is all
She ever said about it. But I've thought,
Since, it's like the rachet of a lock.
You know how, in the summer, doors don't fit
Sometimes. So you slam to make the catch.
The harder you push, the wider the door springs back
With every shove. And even Julie knows,
At her age, that you cannot fix a lock
By slamming it. But I'm impatient. Shove
Or slam before I think. The sunporch door —
Where Julie sleeps. And more than once have heard
Her chirp, straight out of sleep, "Don't, Mother. Don't
Do that. It won't do any, any good."

These coincident in time, a game
With folded papers, pass it to the next;
"He says." "She says." Every mind at work,
Waiting for the sequence. When the nonsense
Made, by accident, a pertinent
Conjunction, we were most amused. Or struck
And still, the private thinkers taking thought.

Summer threatened. Warsaw fell that fall.
In September, murder. Then no cars.
No trolleys. Lack of water. And the corpses
Long untended. Curfew. Pull the blind.
Do not look. The street was called "New World"
In Warsaw. Shambles. Broken wires. We lived
Through the siege. We butchered horses lying
At the curb. The coming tanks. The worst.
Buried soldiers where they fell. We placed
The helmets on each grave. We were contrite
Or we were not. The sound was: boasting; crying.

Both. Upon the air. And heard or not.
To the papers several pictures wired,
Of mounds in streets, the graves, and out of boards
Found in rubble made the crosses, nailed
Askew, set up in haste, and marked upon them
Names. This was in Warsaw. In Shanghai.
Nanking. Madrid. The cities. Shock troops riding
Lie and feint and ignorance, disguising
Love in all its orders, aeons old.
Counting now the quanta in the time,
The treacheries; and marking now the mounds
In every street. In rubble find the staves.
Hurry. Nail the crosses. Write the names.

TAHL : BOOK FOUR

CANTO II

OUT OF SPACE

Birth

Monday: the beginning of one week.
Less three hundred miles by land won't count
By space like half an ocean. Alison,
Space between us now irrelevant
And any week apart, new assignation
Within the indeterminates of time;
Like this child of ours who is, is not,
Will be a January wonder, still
Already is, another work to be.
And nothing wonderful in being born,
I suppose. It is most common. Home,
And Monday next, a mid-December wonder;
Old Darbys and old Joans will laugh to see us
Celebrating one short year together.
And yet as long as life, if only so,
In living it, have come on half an answer
To myself and you. Have been ashamed;
And known you more, in my shamefastness, strong
In all that's ours, none other understands,
As we not them. Is not the rented novel,
Morning-paper scandal. Vanity?
Is vanity than treason more the devil?

Like being here to sell the work unfinished.
Then surprised. Had watched the great man reading,

Tapping the score and nodding. Then his saying,
"Power. Yes. And yet the number's down.
Yes. An average orchestra. The chorus
Modest. No frenetic Mahler. Good.
But, yes. Magnificent. How old are you?"
As with relatives a boy again
At picnics, anniversaries, essaying:
"How old are you? And getting on in school?"
Watched them beaming, nodding, "Tall. For his age."
Hearing my uncle bragging, "Smart at books,
Yes sir, Tahl and Julian. They don't take
From my side, no sir." Feeling proud and somehow
Like apologizing. Do you know,
Alison? You must. And yet it's not
Easy, if the work is big. He says
It should go on the air. And that means more
Than if it's good or not. We'll have to beg
The time. Will pull no Crossley rate, but stop
The ears of housewives and the racing fans,
You understand. And then rehearsals. "Man,"
He says, "when Hanslick took three years to set
The Ninth! The price! The time! To these new men
No future's further than tomorrow's deadline."

And then he looked at me more sharply, took
My hand, as they did once, I've not forgotten,
When I was a child, my father lying
Motionless. A great commiseration:
"If you'd stayed here with us. Have placed your work
Now and then. But you need friends. It is,"
And then that thin-boned, old-world face before me,
Fine nose drawn, "it is the politics
Of fame you have neglected." If I have,
I say that I don't give a damn and spend
The afternoon with George and Jan. And still
Knowing he's right, apologizing most
Perhaps to you, in this as other matters.

Monday. Six days more. You've heard by now
From Iris, of her father's new commission.

Birth

George came raring through the train-gate, chortling:
"Think of him, that blessed blusterer.
Old Ed. In China. Won't he crash around
Like an accident in porcelains.
Ed!" George groans. "That's politics. But then
The old guy's got a heart. He'll get along
If it's just trucks and oil. But what's he know
Of what it's all about?" "Do we?" I said.
Then he went earnest on me. "You're the guy,"
Says George, "to send. Hell, corporal, there's your war."

Just taken Jan back home. Or so it seems.
Who'd ever think the world's so turned around.
Not you, but Jan up those same brownstone steps.
Jim's mother was, as usual, alert,
And George got on with her at once as I did
In those days this summer. Calling her
"Minna" in the first half hour, Town Hall
Full-house, between them — as she'd only made
The world this minute. Here! Remark the polish.
And that's not Dutch, I take it. George observes
"Like Bess" whom he now swears has taken vows
To save Detroit while Ed saves China. How
George laughs and loves her, "Battling Bess! *Belle-mère.*"

Minna praises you. Poor Jan, well-scolded,
Rejecting Will, disrupting Mother's plans.
But having earned her wings again, she's leaving,
Bound out West on Thursday, new-commissioned.
For all the genteel trouncing, Minna's proud,
Proud as if she'd raised her; irony,
Like her growing calmer over Jim.
Consoles herself he'd not betray patroons
Nor cavaliers. Though Will still chafes. You'd think
His brother died while bombing bank accounts.
Hoped to find Will Senior. Have not seen,
Since Julian, other thoroughbred. And true,
Hunters come from racing sires. That proud
Implacable head. But he'd like George. Be useful.
Politics? Mount box, a demagogue,

As you've said, for someone else. Or sweat
To save some kid from snagging with a rule.
I'm fed with that. This rote and note. Not Bach
Walking in from Arnstadt all the way
To Lübeck just to hear what Buxtehude
Managed on an organ. Meditation;
Two, the most it takes. Composers' tricks
Promiscuous in classrooms make no children.
Allowed of that this afternoon and George,
As you might guess, belayed me: "Psychopathic."
And yet he thinks so too and why he traipses
His portfolios as big as floors
To show; and goes commuting Hollywood
To save his soul from wilier damnations,
Taught too many highlights in red apples.

The world has turned around. As if we'd gone
Up in air on rockets, so displacing
Everyone at once. The idle tramp
I was, and look: as bothered as a father
Ought to be, no doubt. And Ed in China.
Jan, her wars and airplanes. If you'd known her,
Shy, in braids and bloomers. Here you say,
Stephanie, who thinks she'll go to work
"Like an American." I know. She'd blaze
If we as much as thought she's ornamental.
The world on skids. This business now with Russia
Shooting Finland, snow on every headline
Freezing blood, and every word from Poland
Turning Spain to faultiest rehearsal.

Even George in somersaults again.
You'll see next week. And these are something more
The sort of thing that Julian taught him, turned
Savage and with fangs. Like me, a run
From first geometry and back again
Through much that's seen and heard and is not said,
His chalkish black and ocher reptiles, glauming
Beasts with paddle feet, primeval jaws

Chawing dwarfish horses; and the worms
Strangling pterodactyls; and the sharks
Splitting hoary mastodons, up-riding
Seas of lava, live and dripping. Jan
Turned them over silently. He's found
A way of rendering the world, a gloss
Of worlds turned upside down, a chaos rolled
Upon itself, the doctor in his gown,
Tuxedo gentlemen with drinks, the farmhand
Slick and gangling, long-haired women wound
In saurian trees, and hoofs upon ball bearings
Wilder than wild iron. Intuition
Grimmer for its patient rendering
In a living texture. Not the airman
Who can reconnoiter bridge and river;
But the creeping private, like his fears,
Closing on the river bank to measure
Speed and depth of water, there discover
Quicksand bottom. Pound the key. And running
With a drying heart: "No way through here.
Send. Quick. Send. Tell them. Stop them. Tell them. Go
Higher. Lower. But no crossing here."
Like that. He's got it. And if Jan had said
Nothing. But came out with it. She said:
"They're like your music, Tahl. Before you went
To Egypt." And they're not, of course. Except
The seeing in embattled beasts the fable
Of another death. And George has sat
Two hours now without a word. Came back
And he's just sat. And I can't break it. Tried.
The most I got, his saying, "Go to China,"
Which was, agreed, restrained for him. Not dared
To mention yet my morning and the hope.
How, I can't see yet. But this is Monday.

George's beasts no stranger than motets,
My cantus firmus, polyphonic choirs
From all devoirs to Master Heinrich Schutz
Or Chladni via anxious, wise Rameau
With the marimbas and the pueblo gourds

For knowing what's to know. And if it is
Too much to pray the orchestra will guess
In what last act they may participate
Within the text for double choruses,
The ritornel upon guitars before
The voices for the rising of the dead,
Hold fast the hope that since my saying serves
Not of itself but in the men I need,
These fellows on the air who pyramid
The strings on horns for curtained sound before
A play's last lines, the craft of sock and segue,
Can seize the ears until the heart's alive.
They're not afraid of any rhythm heard
From Alabama to a Zuñi fair;
May manage what the schoolmen would distort
By dread of rule and rote, proliferate,
Not like the virus, cancerous, not like
The terrible, rigid crystals that can move
Only as the wilting leaf's diseased;
But of their self-catalysis, a grain
I cannot rouse alone, but must depend
On ears not limed, who know the form to be,
And so with me erect the living word.

The mutation of the virus is
The peril, good gone wrong, our knowing forrn
Within its form may not rest good forever;
And what is life prepares in changing forms
The time's surprise. More wonder that the fine
Old man this morning knew I'd not intend
Mere shock; and that together we're agreed
The physicians of this birth must be
Uncommon ready. If the virus is
The living gene gone wrong, then more's the care
Who controls, and how, without a pause,
Into a key remote the theme can move
And what it has to do with milk cans punched
And spilled and ten smashed eggs in Poland, when
The conquerors display almighty power.

Birth

The ceremonial emetic is
Not of far and strange, but simples made,
The larkspur and the cliff rose. Say to George:
See here, you've tried. But hard. As I did once,
Tearing ceilings down about their heads.
And that's one road. Beyond that finding is
A further secret, simple, clarities
In six parts moving. Let the wind declaim
In symbols made by fingers, at the last
Will purge the heart the fist can only smash.

And that is it, at last. Who knows except
A rare old-world baton, perhaps? Or you?
But sometime, somewhere, others to discover
It is the inward movement of the whole,
The shattered center first; then, affirmation,
Makes the nemesis of merely punching
Milk cans in a starving world's despite;
The tuba's boast inadequate to make
By himself sustainedly a tune
Except for wonder that will end in laughter
When the tuba player is disarmed.

It is the words and music make together
Final credo; for the substance is
Neither words in all the languages
Nor the sound in all device discovered;
These co-ordinates. Between them lie,
As in unfathomed light, uncertainties
And probables. As on that day we stood
With Alfred's father, grave; behind him rose
That cross; and knew behind us stood the few
Who cared and came. And all the words were old
And what was making common and predicted
As the child we'll have. And yet we knew
That what we made was something more than flesh
Only in that sign behind his head.

If I'd say that to George, you know he'd snort
And so consign me farther than to China.

And yet we've said it in these pages peddled,
Public, even for price. And if he hears?
If anyone at all? Or if I'll come
Next Monday home and finish it, of course,
No dial, filament, from microphones
Ever take it out? I think it is
His sitting there, apart, and lost. And how,
Except the sound, the color shaped in distance?
What road survives that we could reach each other
In our prides and silences? Suppose
That's why it's like apologizing, having
Made what cuts, invades, but must be said.

Tuesday: I am glad there's Buck. More glad
When there's our own to ask for simple answers,
The uninvestigated certainties
Trusted for one kind of truth. Remember?
"Why is Monday, Monday? Tuesday, Tuesday?"
And I was lost at Tuesday. But you knew.
A god of war. How near majority
The gods of war in any week of days
To seize majority in these, our years,
Beyond our private battle. George has gone
Bearing all his harness, and I'll meet him,
Minna and the rest, this noon. Who knows
What may come for him with Senior holding
Chairs among trustees, and Junior also,
Known here. I've been phoning for appointments.
Hopeless. "What's your name? Who? Spell it, please."
The more a most irrelevant adventure,
Cutting out like this to fight and sell
By poor intrigues a scratch upon stiff paper
While the world's more fiercely bought and sold.

And then, last night, while I heard George not sleeping,
Loud with silence, thought the past we've dug,
You and I, the least we've ever mentioned,
The years when you and I were merely sprouts
Like this one that we count for, nameless weight

Unrecognized on records. And I thought
George's beasts and my guitars have come
Not of ourselves, but of our moment born.

Yes, George spoke this morning. Silence made,
As Mozart knew, its own access to music.
Now till noon among the living here
Less a name than all the books they read,
The facts before me we could not acquire
By advent simultaneous among them.
Like the oyster and the crab dependent
And apart upon a common ground.
For Buck and for our own, their common feeding
Skills in scanning streaks upon the water,
Blowing smoke and currents in the grass,
Cattle tucking tails to coming winds,
All the art of reading land from planes.
"Teach me to fly," says Buck. And Jan will teach him —
With Buck and ours as readily surprised
To learn a woman once was unaccustomed
And derided for presuming. Strange,
Even reviewed. And far as Bardi, Fugger,
Our first world, the world of Rockefeller,
Harriman and Morgan. Who would know
At Martinique, young Paddy's first volcano,
That wave of earth, at Montonombo, settled
A canal cut through by doubtful dealing,
So by damage joining world with world.
A man at Sagamore then much debated
As the name our lad will sometime learn
To date his year of birth. As we have taken
Nothing new that China fears Japan.
The long essay of liberty with order
Now completing the Siberian wonder,
Flying taigra and tundra, he'll assume
As true and far as tales of giant bison
Found with darts in red and ancient sands.

Merely people, trusted and mistrusted.
Coyotes here as jackals once in Egypt.

Out of Space

We hope to meet a god or Spider Woman
Promptly. But coyotes here. No hope
They'd settle with a legend in a desert.
Or merely move to Asia or to Europe.
The pack is here all right; their demonstrations
Anti-everything except deception
Reported in small print on inside pages.

Shall we be moving like the thirty million
Under droning bombers toward Chungking
With two-foot toddlers younger than their eyes?
Age of corundum, far in scale of hardness
From the age of common salt to save us.

Once on France and Belgium. What will happen
In the summers he will not remember,
One and two and three? And what will happen
When he does remember? As for me,
The *Lusitania.* And nights and nights
Dreams of ships careening, death by drowning,
When I was five and hardly knew the name,
But was one year away from death and sea.
Years later, you, fourteen, mere months away
From that crash of cars, the day the sun
Blackened and the night across the snow
At past nine in the morning; and thereafter
Saw them coming toward you, man and woman,
Eclipsed by wheels of snow, the sun's corona
That you stumbled after. You will tell him
That. As true as causeways rediscovered
Out of months in Yucatan, as true
As long-nosed monuments, the limestone mouths
Wearing last dim stains of old vermilion;
True as sun's eclipse and ships gone down.

Shall we one night be running with him, fleeing
Sky and sea, the tragic sequence coming,
Possible in our ambiguous futures?
Fantastic. But you understand. That morning
In Chicago when the youngster scampered

Birth

Scuttling down the area and clutching
Bottles stolen from the door, we watched him
Go and never thought to shout — accepting
Loss as merely fatal — merely. Shall we
Always wind the clocks, expecting morning?

So asleep in daylight. You with Julie,
Two of you, and tumbled in the chair,
The picture book slid down, her noddle limp
Against your arm, and your dark lashes down
And hers upcurled; and both of you as calm
As if the world's forever kind to those
Asleep. And she'll remember. Who they were,
The three or four old harridans attending
On my bed or seen like kobolds looming
Above a kitchen stove till I was taken
Up from the sea and into mountains, never
Knew, the plant transplanted, never knowing
What life lost in roots ripped out to sun
Too early in the morning. For that reason
What you find absurd, my clumping in
To watch you merely cooking — merely. Smiling
That deprecating smile because I lounge
Over socks and neckties just to watch you
Brush your hair. And what has that to do
With China; western islands? Shall we find
A week less cumbered with the gods of war
To take this plant of ours up safely, going
After orchids and the Polynesians;
Teach him orders of the orchid's horn
Far as deer's horns of the Aurignacians
From an air raid warning? How'll he fare
On China's rivers thirteen years from here?

Tuesday later: Here's a day uncertain
As the likelihood of earth when only
Waters were divided from the waters.
As to say, I've spent the afternoon
With Minna; and she's wound about with schemes
As if she'd hung her web from every rafter

Money'd ever laid for power to swing on;
Her Southern gentleman and portly son
Both upon her errands. Comprehend
More than in Jim's tales, your explanations,
Jim — his radium, retreat to Richmond,
Last to Spain, escaping with his freedom.
We won't escape. Not simple as it seems.
Walther in Vienna, his allusions
Most adeptly chosen. Merely change
The method and the patron; very like
The corporation, is anonymous,
Compromising with the legal fiction
That the arts themselves are glorious.

Like Fray Antonio Soler my work
Take dust two hundred years unshaken; like
Ferranchere, since none now trust guitars
In formal dress. As well go back again
To a more recent calling, quickly find
A corporal's employment to offend
More notorious corporals; or assign
My ear to catch an Oriental tone
Reporting sounds as of peach blossoms gunned
From purring air. How many times I've said
"I do not know"? I have your letter here
And wish I might reply, your champion,
Taking the world in lists. But still no news.

I walk the studios tomorrow morning
With Young Will for mighty squire. Am sure
Only every morning that you're there,
My very "clerk of necromancy." Signed
Here asseveration — term, forever:
You are the best of officers in war
Best fought, the tactics of most strength engaged
With scantest damage, greatest power deployed
For thrust and capture. Now affirm belief
With Celts and Greeks a woman may indeed
Be warrior most shrewd. All enemies
Flattered in their free capitulation.

Birth

Our variable constructions still may fail
A present equilibrium. No hope
A Mozart, Beethoven; but not so much
As live three decades more to one *Messiah.*
Not die, as Paddy hoped, at least a colonel.
But — most dangerously am content
With loss — to know, save you, no loss is fatal.

Wednesday, now, Querida, and again,
As any day I ask too much of meanings.
Day of grass and trees. And why you think
Woden, god of wisdom, had one eye?
To see with two is to be compromising?

You say 'Gamaliel' would be too long?
They'd likely call him 'Al.' As Dad was 'Bart.'
Not this world's time to say 'Bartholomew.'
Since spring, not thought. With your dissenting vote
Against a dynasty of Alisons.
And Hannah, 'name of grace,' from favor since
My mother's time. No Julia, Julian? No.
Your father, Ethan? Federico, 'ruling
Worlds at peace.' Or Alfred, 'counselling.'
Patrick, 'noble.' Have three Williams. Odd,
The Doctor and these new attendant Wills
Supplanting Jim. There's Philip. Or Vicente.
Jan. To be her mother's daughter, surely
'Gift of God.' Good, hopeful Giovanni
Of Milan who swore he'd seen on Mars
A centered cross, a signal, and canals.
Now grant canals. And he is dead. The year
That I was born. So look too hard for signs.
Baffled most by these obstructive labels,
Yours and mine. This 'Tahl' — a name to die with.
It was, Aunt Julia said, my father's doing.
Doc said: Maybe Tamil, even Toltec,
Arabic. But thought it sounded Sanskrit.
Make solid citizen — an Edward, George.

And let this 'Tahl,' if it survive, endure
On pages that the studios won't have.

Or I don't think so. Talked with engineers,
Vice presidents, directors. See the hazards
Philanthropic, the sustaining program,
Rheostat against sustaining income,
Low return; as we have taught platoons,
Minor skirmishes for present valor
May obstruct the plan of major mission.

By that, be sure no incidence of war,
These newest murders, ravaging the ghettos,
New-dug graves in parliamentary gardens,
Taking time and ammunition, meaning
Armored thugs on major, ugly missions;
Somewhere live the ghosts to rise against them
Among one hundred thousand million stars.
Whether Simpson, Rowe or Dowland played
Violas, gambas, lutes in German bands?
Will they raze these graves; here ghosts are waiting;
In France and Italy, who controvert
With strings the Hessian habit of cornets?

But here, to slay Tchaikovsky tunes enough,
Stolen, dress a soapbox full of hearts;
And income flowers from patented cathartics.
That you've found in *Enoch* that the Christ
Is called a great-horned bull and white, no darker
Than this air's indifferent to meanings.

Let's go slack. For Julian's father taught me,
Making bows and arrows that we treasured
Till we shot too well, a bow that's strung
And kept will break. But run the thumbnail up
And let the cord hang off until you're ready.
For what? For something riddling and unseen,
One one thousandth smaller than a cell,
The smallest known and smaller still to build
A power of unpredicted combinations

Birth

In "square root of minus one," the "time."
"The waters fought with Tiamat" — and gave
In relativities of emphasis
Sapiens, weighs nothing, current market
Bargain, cheap, one dollar. Soon it's Christmas.
At Easter wives set flowering plants in windows.
Why? *Nocturna chorea elvarum*
Et spectarum, dancing on the grass
Till no grass grows, so deep the footprints burn.

No, not even angry. We've expected
Shooting, missing. What he may have meant,
My father, giving me this name, won't work
Like *Sesame.* But if a name to move
Tiamat, a minus-one, to keep me
Toward your heart returning, I'll defend it.

Thursday night: and Mjöllnir has come back,
It seems, from chance of casting. Or by Minna,
New avatar, her role as Spider Woman?
Struck this morning, jarring on my ear,
Thunderbolt command. When I'd arrived,
His greeting, thin mouth droll: "I see you are
More wily than I hoped." I let it go,
Matching pleasantries. "And here you see,"
He set it out, "I have it back again."
Snapped the pages over. Thought of you
And Stephanie, your faithful copying.
And is there any man more damnably
A pensioner than I am, these last years?
I don't know where Will took it when I left him,
But there it lay and lies, the master saying,
"We play a game. And they will send, annoyed.
I shall be difficult." Last Monday slipped
Away with that baton that once I held
In this same city for a colt's reward
And heard applause five years ago. Now heard
There'd been a conference. And still there's nothing
Sure. And if it's sure, I've not a chance.

Out of Space

Holding guns and blackboard chalk and only
Whipping time to adolescent ears,
Am not elect. It's his. Not mine. He'll turn
The rhythm where he pleases, cut the choirs
To his own drama. What will come is not
As we have made. A recapitulation
Through mitosis in prehensile mind;
Like our chick with notochord and gills
Repeating to what's ours but separate man
And may be unlike us in heart and head
As tapirs are to horses. Do you guess
That mighty day of aeon-hours the sun
And moon and stars first set upon their motions,
They were accommodating in their turnings
Or shifted from their arbiter's intention?

You'll understand me. Not to play young god
To this toybox creation. I suppose,
As shells throw off expected repercussion
No matter the trajectory and distance,
It will go off without me. His élan
Perhaps no more than mere discrepancy
Between pianos and the violins
In keeping key — or will at most contract
Slight poisons that my polygraph will read,
Knowing the heart's true state, but no one else
Will guess it's not quite well. The zygote makes
Only beginning of beginning. Darling,
Trying this I feel, I watch the words
Betraying other troubles. Not afraid,
The two of us, my black imaginings
Safe within your shining. Take it just
I'm talking of this work and nothing else,
A lancelet we have made of sound to see
If it evolves a meaning like a man.
If it become a man, it must proceed
By wills and alterations not its own;
And if the will be strong enough, survive
Its handling and endure in essence. Vain,
Believing, since there's no ideal sustained

Except by infinite approximations,
That here, where I'm most closely hit, I'm needed
More than anywhere in the arrangements,
Once the germinating seed is sent
Upon the world. Though that's assumption too.
For it may lie stillborn upon his desk;
His game of "being difficult" may work
Its favor, as he says, or it may not.
I like things simpler. Though I know they're not.

Three hours so with him, I could not go
Out to Queens with Jan — mid-morning flight.
She'll make the coast tomorrow. George not back,
He and both the Wills, new quidnuncs gadding.

I rode this afternoon. But don't much like
These tired nags and hacking in a park.
Have felt all day as if I'd like to break
Something. But it's no use getting drunk.
I'm growing old and sober. Now displaying
The world as I have heard it. And, good God,
I shave, and find the glass ridiculous.

Friday. No, it's Saturday. Near dawn
And still no news at all except I've spent
More wind than need be spilling out my lungs,
Having known so long that words convince
Less than orreries still meaningless
To those who'd not admit the planets move;
And since, for faith, no orrery's to build,
The least convincing. Seen the gang at last,
As I had promised; George along, agog
And Junior too, to meet the men we'd praised,
Jim and I. His curiosities
Outbidding doubts, Young Will most generous,
Messing all the tribe. Must say the club
Didn't seem to suffer from invasion
Of our "whacky bastards," settled mild
In mufti, with their spout of wives and offspring

In a year's return. And Junior's plan
To show off George, the drawings spread to look
Before we'd downed too much. Knew what he meant
By worlds turned upside down, remembering
Jim and all the others not among us.

As you'd guess, expected kind of rough-house,
Yip and guff, and nothing there to make
A solemner reunion than you'd meet
Of veteran boilermakers, barbers, bookies
Freed from heat and lathers and the chances
Losing much, but showing profit. Pleased
With being soused. And Spain so much displaced
By new reverberations as to seem
Gone as wars that Will's great-uncles fought.
And not portentous. Just the cords let slack,
Out of ambush. We won't need a draft
When we go in again. Expect we must.

But why we'll go, as various in colors
As the rout I brought upon my head
By neglect of my best habit, shutting
My large mouth. And George to boot me in,
I think to demonstrate repentance, dousing
Embarrassment with brotherly intentions.

You have observed a crowd run high and then
By some inverse proportion of the number
Of the bottles up, they settle down,
Any mob of men you pick, to quibbling,
Even snarling. I'd kept close. It was,
Suppose, my long impatience with this week
Running out and nothing gained and finding
Europe and the West have locked me off
Too much from such a guild as may exist
For private way of practising profession.

And so tonight I shot. And they don't give
A damn, not most of them. Why should they? Not
Their business, as they'd say. But I let off.

Birth

And first, all right. The music's safe enough
On one keyboard. They, the fed and drowsed,
Talking through what's not too strange and distant.
But then I have to give a lecture, showing
What it's all about, with diagrams.

George says, "Just lit up like a city." Wrong.
Though every word I uttered, shape in light,
Round as Junior's graying head. Absurd,
This "Young Will," "Junior." Curse it, he and George
And I, antiques, as Jim would be among
These cheerful ganders. Never thought about it
Over there. The others, Greeks and Czechs,
And Thaelmanns, Garibaldis, much like Paddy,
So our seniors; but the crew that tumbled
From these shores and now but one year older —
Perhaps my playing pedagogue because
They're young men still. Then so much more the fool,
Knowing myself in any dawn no elder
In this world's affairs. Now George asleep
Under the grin he dropped with, looking at me,
Babbling to himself, and repetitious:
"Lit just like a city." But the words
They didn't want to hear still march around me.

I'll not sleep until I've laid them. Like
That dream I had in Judah, would not rest
Until I'd said it plainly. Nothing here
That you've not heard. But now it's seized upon.
And saying it, perhaps a night quite soon
I'll find last resolutions, seeing how
The chorus from the 'cellos and the drums
To *finale* rising make an end
Adequate to all I have begun.

Because they said: "That's hot." "That's Spanish." "Negro."
"Sure, Tahl. Sure you'll sell it. That Chinese-ish
Indian, or what. Get used to that."
"Sure, Tahl. Sure. You'll sell it." "Give a prayerful
Earful. Sure. For that, old ladies like it."

Out of Space

As you'd guess, not many. Five or six
Who hung around. And liked it when it sounded
Just a kind of yarn. The crosses found
In Etruscan dust, old water lines
On farms among the Alps with bones of sheep
And goats and dogs among the muddy piers,
The urns beneath Italian fields, the mouths
Westward, sealed, the circle and the sign
As those in Troy, Mycenae and in bronze
Beneath the British downs. And those who moved
With incense toward great Isis in communion
Sharing honeyed disks, the consecrating
Wafer for the bull and serpent given
To the people in the holy times,
Cross and circle. And beneath the sands
Of Khorsabad and Nineveh on stone,
On ivory, the ornament of kings.
The temple out of solid rock once hewn
On that island off Bombay; the caves
Of Elephanta; and the massive rune,
The one you saw in living stone, Mitzlá,
City of the Moon. The marble found
At Knossus, earlier than Moses. And
The massacred two thousand once at Tyre,
The massive crucifixions so designed
By learnèd, clever Alexander, fouling
Bleeding Phoenicians on their sacred sign.

Cool and far away. And then Peru,
The neophytes in sunlit robes and on
The breasts the scarlet like a cross to frighten
Spanish friars, fearing Satan laughing.
As in Yucatan, the old salvation,
Itzamná, displaying symbol none
Surpassed, to mark the God, no other image.
Palenque once, and Mayapan, and once
In walls so jungle-lost, no name surviving.

And while Itzá and Tancah still had flourished,
The prophecies fulfilled, the streamers coming

Birth

Like the sun, the Lord of the Sky appearing,
Sign before the bearded Spanish doom.
From India to Egypt ever sign
Of god of gods, the Amerindian emblem,
Fathering sun, the sign of life, of wisdom,
Fructifying, sign of land beyond,
Land of life to come. Generation's
Search as in Chaldea, from the long
Sepulchers, from monolith and cave
The *Tau* and key of sacred Nile, mutation,
Flesh to spirit. Serapis preserved
Older than the Ptolemy who called
Its ancient emerald wonder out of Europe
And locked it in the labyrinth to guard it.
There two wonders bound together: man,
The engineer, to dredge that lake and maze;
Man, the priest and king, to mark its center,
Sign of life forever; till time's turn,
And Theodosius' spearmen to destroy,
Breaking the emerald wonder. Long forgotten,
Also, order of the day, two thousand,
By Alexander, Golgothas at Tyre.

The repetitious sign surviving stain,
Emblem, flesh and spirit, and conjoined
With streams and vegetation and become
Hieroglyph of life, the wheel of sun.
The sign is not of those who bear the sign.
The *chilan* saw the white and bearded men
From bright *likin.* He said: "Let this be known.
It is 'the green tree of the world.' It is
'The first tree of the land.'" Let this be known:
The sign is not of those who bear the sign,
The saving signal in the slaying hand.

The thunderbolt in Jötunheim. And Thor
Valiant to retrieve it. This be known:
The thunderbolt now lost in Jötunheim
Turns about until its arm breaks flame

On blackness of the thieves who raise it, roaring
On Vienna, Warsaw, from Berlin.

Once at Palenque, Teotihuacán.
The cross, Tlaloc, the sign of rain. And find
Among plantations dark-faced women knowing
A cross, the sign of storm. In the austral islands
Cross and circle. Emblem of the Zulu.
Emblem on the knives of Danes. A sign,
The mark of once good fortune to a gibbet
With the turn of time. The cross-wire burst
In flame. The cause of death. The cancel-death.
History athwart the stars. Forget
Once two thousand Golgothas at Tyre.
Theodosius' men who sacked the maze
Below Lake Moeris. "Soldiers, leave us this,
The emblem of the life to come." "Destroy it."

Merest fungus, moldy; morbid growth
Now abated? Think no meaning, noting
Signs of suns or swastikas abused.
Wise ones dead who knew. As those we saw
Among the western deserts, old and dying;
No young brave appointed to their learning.
Death of ear and eye, and deaf and blind,
Warring, whoring, never more to know
Upon the breasts of mummied death preserved,
As well the Norseman's mark and sign for heaven,
The ancient sign above the lake Tung T'ing
Among the spear-sharp orchids, bright pavilion,
The number and mimetic meaning: union.
Hieroglyph of sempiternal fortune,
That to-be-recovered promised land.

From stone to bronze to iron, to the year
Of the crossed wire, forgetfulness or fear
Of sign in spirit, the four-petaled flower
Of Troy — and in Chaldea — and in Egypt.
Sign conjunctive with the moon, the sons
Of moon, the suffering gods, the time repeating

Sempiternally. The sign of light,
Of cardinal points, the sign of space in bounds,
Of all the world, the old gammadion
Now to thief, assassin, discontent
With only loot and blood. Lock music. Burn
The books. And steal, defile the first of emblems.
Killers by castration wearing in
Bold lapels the lying, fertile sign.

And symbol of the thunder. Who has gone
To visit thunder has foreshortened time.
Sky and water, plumed and horned, the serpent,
Gods on rafts, the whirling crosses, cross
Of these four sacred streams — and always watch
Téoltsóldi, water monster — known
The long, transforming, ancient testament
Out of cave and lake in transformation
Death and birth, and power with wisdom joined,
The two trees felled and crossed in last of signs,
The 'game of Troy' forever circling in,
By walls and streams, the labyrinthine road
Toward peace, the dream of last Jerusalem.

Consider Samsi-Romanu who stood
Eight hundred years before old Pilate's time
At Nineveh and carven on the breast
The sign of life, the cross for resurrection.
Of gypsum, marble, jasper, emerald,
Chipped on granite, run in bronze, the sign.
Quetzalcoatl, rude, in wood, the source,
The life and promise of the life to come.

Too many dreams of heaven? Have there been
Too many acts on Calvary to swear
An eternal city toward which man
Participates unjudged, since none may judge him?
In the time the peer of every man
In everlasting jury coming on
To endlessly recovered Bethlehems
Through death to endless lost Jerusalems

Out of Space

By a thousand, untranslated names
Of the sounds by endless time transformed,
Until remains but particles of sounds,
The undenoting music most unheard.
Veneration damned for being old
As puns on venery, the chase for love
In all the paradox of suffering
Disdained in all its signs. Our agitation
Aimless in a rout of blood and clocks,
The crust and crack and clack of battle lost.

Not for the weapon lost but weapon held
Forgotten or untaught, without a meaning
Or manipulation. Never learn
Easily; and easily forgetting
Fatherhood and brotherhood, the sign.
The spirals coiling and the galaxies
Beyond the million, million years till now
More closely turned, rotation toward what time
The avatar of Vishnu shall descend
The tenth and final time, his horse come down
With blazing wings; when Shiloh come, the people
Gathering, the stem of Jesse, branch,
Spirit of wisdom, knowledge, counsel, might,
And this Lord's fear, the ensign of the people
Last upgathered from all islands toward
The place of tabernacle from all lands.
To that last term of life the golden thread
Bound in moon's first hall, the sky, and bound
East and west, the lasting web of Norns
Broken, Dionysus and Osiris,
Vishnu or Bahana, Itzamná,
Promised, come again. The conflict ends
Of the divided spirit, *mana* broken
And restored with the Malay's lost empires,
With the far-fabled cities lost beyond
A broken Montezuma and this world,
America, of names forgotten, land
Of rivers, red-red land beneath the sun
And moon, the measurers. We have forgotten.

Birth

We, the sons of the son of Joseph, named
Manasseh, named 'forgetfulness,' forgetting
All our toil and all our father's house
To reach this land of Egypt we must leave,
Inheritors of Bashan, giants' land.
We, the sons of the son of Hezekiah,
Named Manasseh, named 'forgetfulness,'
Itching after alien shrines and bound
In thousand fetters, whipped to Babylon;
We pray not nor repent; are not returned
Like him to purge a people. We remain
Manasseh, fattening on the flesh and shedding
Blood of innocents. Jerusalem
In every land most learnèd in the flesh,
The first created cross; but untransformed,
Forgetting the mutation in the garden.

His father was Norwegian. And he asked:
"On what day were you born?" And then I said,
"I have been told, on Sunday." And he said,
"I thought so. It's a thing my father told me.
'Children born on Sunday see the elves.'
You, it seems, have been collecting trolls."

The challengers. The several. Names no matter —

"For Maryskirts. The first day of the week . . .
And if He was, He was not God. So. Spare us."

"This time? We'll make it good. We'll fight for that.
But not your bloody Phoenicians, broken statues
In lost Egyptian lakes. 'Spare us, good Lord.'
Blame it on Him. That's easy. Let Him fix it."

"Humility! Come! Come to yourself, old preachka."

The silent murderer and soundlessly
Swims and wades and fears the sound betraying
Broken branch or tinking knife on helmet,
Lies immobile. Said, "There's Federico.

None of you had seen him. That was when
I fought among the Basques."

"Sure. Sure, we get it.
Lost friends. And so did we. And won't rise up
For all your oak and ash and thorn whatever."

The sign, creation's tree, Samsâra-Vriksha;
Sign: first of trees and sometime Yggdrasil.
The ash by Urdar's spring, the fountain's heart
Heat and light, the circle holding in
The universe, the farthest ring of light.
A city of that light and from it coming
Time and term of life upon the rainbow,
Spectrum by its name in all the nations;
Trail of Nayénezgani, monster slayer.

"Splendid collection! Trolls!"

"The thunder-stone
Never failed to hit a troll." On Friday
The son of Frigga died. December once
The festival of Balder, son of light,
The tree his sign, the mistletoe his bane.
Only the blind one hurled, so slaying. Still
Unransomed god among the withered trees.
Let George report. The worm will rise upon
The wingèd world — in colors. Compass, once
High secret of the priests, demeaned to gadget
In boyscout pockets. Can we so deflect
The inclination of the earth toward Vega?
Kindergarten. But a child can hear
A higher pitch of sound. Can you restore
So sharp an ear? Or having learned to broil
A fish, choose birch or maple, does this solve
The living cell?

"Your dish, not ours."

"Sure, gaze
Upon your belly. Some of us fill faster."

And more of that, of monks and cods, but spare
Your ears the billingsgate. I opened up
That gate myself. And wide. So let it go.

But one who said: "The napkin. What's the doodle?
I get the cross, the squares and points. What then?"

But then, against my shoulder, Will, and drawling
More like Jim, and mellowing the air:
"Easily. Two shavers, Jim and I,
We'd worked it out. We called it, 'Walls of Troy.'"

"We started left, not right," the Norseman said.
"*Det meka ingen difrens.* Got more meanings?"

The Pima's road to climb the upper world.
Or Spanish fathers brought it to the pueblos.
Or you had seen it on a Cretan coin.
Stephanie, at Chartres. A way to heaven,
A maze that goes one way and no retreat
From this one labyrinth except returning
Endlessly to where we start from; "Troy"
Or way from underworlds, or run-around
"Going to Jerusalem," a game,
Ambiguous diagram. May choose your meaning.

Then one: "This shandygaff. But you could fight.
We saw you. Whence this *padre*, Holy Joe?"

"Shut up, shamrock. What Tahl means, the books
Burned. All that."

For part. Said Alison
Could tell you. Once they burned the books she wants
And long ago. A bishop, power afraid
Of power, time for measure. Said: Ximenes;
Granada purged in damning manuscripts
Of Islam to the burning. Aztec, when
From all Anahuac the mountain heaped
Blazing on Tezcuco's market like

A fumigated pestilence; his name,
Zumárraga. We cannot think so much
Destroyed in just one market square.

"You think
House-paint will succeed? He can't."

Recall
Ch'in Shih-huang, the powerful, afraid
Of power, of words' artillery, "destroyed"
The long-dead Mencius naming sovereigns third,
The people first in orders. Chinese elders,
Every book "destroyed." But found in walls,
In beds of rivers, fragments late recovered
By one wise girl discovered in Honan;
And from a blind man's memory repeated;
But was not all; some part; and age-long labor,
Venire facias, haltingly and lame.

"You're O.K. *Allrightnick.* We don't mean
That you can't have your show. But listen, Tahl.
Add Mithra, born from rock, and shepherds, midwife.
But now I mean for serious. You think
A 'kingdom come' can happen? Here, I mean."

Take you "for serious"? Then answer: No.

"Then why exhume the graveyard?"

George put in,
"Don't take him hard. Plays Grandpa now and then.
Golden boughs. Me too. Celestials parking
Evergreens on graves to save the soul.
I guess you told me that. It doesn't add
To more than comfortable if you believe it."

"Buy it dime a dozen out of Asia.
And whether we come back and do it over,
As Hindus say — or once-through, like your puzzle —

The world's plain dirt. We have to kill the brutes.
Then kids can live. That's all. Don't need this squirm
And clinch, to prove with bloody crucifixions."

Never need. What is the need? In knowing
Apache's "vision" is a sign of life;
Zuñi's "vision" is a sign of death?
Device and rod, my way of seeing, hearing
Circumference of tree with sea. In knowing
You. And Julian. Losing Federico.
Somewhat more than merest incidentals
By what I cannot prove in knowing love.
Where's wit enough to keep it for a word
Which won't define in other ears? No coin
Weighed the same on correlated scales.
More wisdom or more cowardice, to hide
The legend in a chorus? Let them raise
City of the sea, Jerusalem
More real than any city with a name;
Let sing the dead are living in a sign.
Manasseh will forget. I make it hard.
Not simple. As to say, defying prides
And silences, what's in the music said:
Affirming flesh, the spirit not denied;
Affirming good, the evil not denied;
And history athwart the stars, despair
Except we have been taught and taught again
By repetition, to this final sign
I had most feared, but could not keep me blind
And deaf forever, having seen the cities
Falling, having seen your eyes, and searching
All one night a burning sea to find
What mercy lies beyond the wrath and judgment;
To say, whatever courses, trees, or waters,
Roads or crosses glimpse and echo, never
Glimpse nor echo utterly destroyed,
Called bud of lotus, heart transformed, or orchid
Of life's complexity — *He is.*

And so is said or is not said, remains
A music still unfinished in the mind.
I have not finished . . .

Here I fell asleep
And woke, my head upon my arms, my back
Stiff as it's not been since Spain, the nights
In that infernal damp. We stumbled up.
The pounding. Bellboy breezy as they come.
"For you, sir." And it lies here now beside me.
Still thick with last night's smoke and talk, I know
Enough to know its meaning. It's 'no go.'
Magister will not risk it. And the stations
Won't risk me. And so I shall be home
On Monday. And have still to finish, bound
Upon the further hope. I thought to take
The next train out. But George slept well. He's clearer,
Loaning me his wits. So wait tomorrow.
Tomorrow wait — the Frenchman, the Brazilian,
Mexican, Italian, once again
My "Buxtehudes." Maybe learn. It's not
To be a Saturnalia this year,
That's sure. Except the usual in crimes
Here and over waters. As you heard
On Wednesday, or have read, the scrap they had
Off Uruguay, the *Ajax,* the *Achilles,*
Exeter, to send the pirate down.
Now up the Plate and trapped. But nearer now.

I have promised. I will finish. Promise,
If the world permit. But nearer. "Waters
Fought with Tiamat." That's true enough.
But there's no hope while Tiamat's abroad,
We'll come to any Sunday God can set
In "minus-one" and see that "it is good."

The best I'll manage, Monday to next Monday
Any week, to swear that I go home
To one who's not so much a saint I'd fear

Birth

I must compete with archangels; and still
She's somewhat of their orders. If this be
Idolatry, just grant I have two eyes
And so must make my compromise with God.
The best of snares, at least. Yes, I'll be home.

TAHL : BOOK FOUR

CANTO II

OUT OF SPACE

Death

We were strangers. That is, he up there
And we back here in chairs. Except I came
From the town they lived in. Sitting there
In my chair. And he'd come back. Been gone
Once before, that winter. But this time
For weeks. And I was thinking. No one there
Knew. But I did. How the neighbors said . . .

He asked a question. Just about a triad.
I was thinking. And it hurt. For there
He was. And with the scar above his ear.
We always wondered. Harmony is hard.
But that was easy. Could have answered. There
I sat and started crying. We were strangers.
Because his wife was sick. His child was dead.

Afterwards his hand upon my shoulder:
"Want to tell me?" Said that I was sorry
That I had cried in class. I said, "I'm sorry."
I couldn't tell him why I cried. Besides,
Perhaps that wasn't why I cried, for sure.

Cold. Yes. Even for a January
In this country. No, I've not been here

But once before. Ten years. The snow's deep there,
Sir. Not much farther. Ground's too hard? Well, then,
In the tomb. Until your men can turn
The earth. Won't take much room. Yes. Here. The names:
Hannah. Yes. *Bartholomew.* Yes, here.
Julian. David, then, and *Julia.* Never
Knew them, so to speak, sir. Only here
Once. No kin. I knew the father's cousin,
Julian. No trouble. Over the line, in Maine
And home by nightfall. Name? I'll leave the order
Since you think it should be done. There's room,
As you say, upon the stone.

The woodchuck saw his shadow yesterday
And so the winter's long. But, Elsa, how
To tell you. Not pretend. I'm hardly gay
And cannot go to see the sun myself.
I'm not to be let free this week. But bless you,
Coming as you did, and Alfred. Why
This? To Tahl? For me, I'm half-alive
Once more. Though troubling him. With asking why.

Why? Why not? Why not? Are born to die
For all the labor. Can endure it. Down
The ships each day. The tireless air reporting
Ships gone down. And there was death in Spain,
And we endured it. There is death. And why.

In the woods the buds are closed and waiting
And some will die of ice or wind. Not easy,
Knowing what is not to be determined
Till the moment. Once a knot of workmen
At an orange crane. With ropes and poles
Straining at a boulder in the snow.
And something slipped. The iron shovel dropped
And one man fell. The children crowded up.
They shoved us back. And then the whisper, "Oh —
He's killed." Like that. Which man among the backs

Workman-blue in snow? We say no scheme
Determines. So it might, by chance. And has.
But hold myself. I thought that Tahl might break —
With that much-torn and asking heart of his —
Might go a little mad. Perhaps he does,
But will not show me. Most that he'll admit,
His fear that I might go. Because his mother —

But I am here. And why? And troubled most,
Not knowing who he was. What can you say
About a boy alive three days? Afraid
To think and not to think. When does the child
Become a child? The one Greek manikin,
The dead soul borne on wings. I know it is
Common. And will be. How many lie
'Died, three days.' 'Died, five days.' How many?
That we should think it does not happen. Only
In grandmother's time. "Did not know how," we said.
"We know." Do not. The will is not enough
For this. But is. Am lost. But not. But most —
Not knowing who he was.

The only name I'd ever heard them say.
Whether to be done or not, I did.
Someone had to give it to the records.
You know that, Elsa. Couldn't ask him then.
And she too weary. And it will not matter.
Sometime I shall tell them. Later.

Iris, if your calendar agrees
With mine, it's spring. And what is done, is done.
And sometime . . . Sometime, yes. So Alison,
Your unpredictable, too much indulged,
Has come alive again. I have. I'll stand
As firm as Khufu's pyramid beyond
A Nile of tears. Remark, I've not forgotten
Your worst of all comparisons to dare,

Death

That year in Egypt, saying when you saw it
Jutting there above the muddy plain,
That it reminded you of me. And how
I teased you till you wept with laughing, saying,
"'That was not what I meant, at all.'" Not this.
Not that. Indeed. That I should be old stones
Five thousand years in weather! Your protesting.

I don't know who I have been. Something gone.
But Tahl is always here. You'd not believe
How gentle, how he's patient while I am
Too long a patient till it's spring again.
And it will not be right. Not ever. And —
Other things are far more wrong — the bombs;
Grandees returned to land in Spain; or wars
Beginning, ending; and beginning. No,
It doesn't make it easier, my saying
Really earthquakes, suddenly eruptions
Long before Voltaire and near as Paddy
At the age of ten — or if the oceans
Operied as they have and many towns
As sudden gone how many times — what one
Child, the more or less, that it was ours?

The going down, the dark red pain, the haze
Of wondering why the silence. Could have been
More dreadful now, I know, have been most wrong
And monstrous. It was right to see him. Calmer.
Tahl knew that — and insisted. See him always
Whole, with that strong head, the perfect arms
That fought, the perfect hands. The terrible hope.
One in four will live so and recover,
The infirm heart contract and hold. They promised.

But knew no way to know. And nothing known
Except to wait. And waited so. And lost.
The heart at term would not, the ligament
Would not. I tell myself it's not more strange
Than death of sea birds, white and raucous, flying
Above a low-tide sea. And there are two

Serene now, there, upon the last of ice-break
Undulating in the mist. I watch
A lone man with his collar up who walks
Bent-shouldered over pebbles and wet sand
Every afternoon. And why his heart
And yours and mine and Tahl's and all we know
Could make the last transition and the lungs
Not fail and why the blood should serve us well
Within the given changes; not for him.

But was he anyone? A person? Living
Those three days of struggle. Can't go on
This way. You used to say, if I had been
Among the old divines, you'd see me ride
Valiant to the Indians, and pin
Upon my dress a learnèd argument
While tomahawks were sharpened. Truth, no doubt.
Preposterous. If any woman bound
Upon the tree of life so, ever, been
Insistent to know more than can be known,
She is most perfectly rebuked. And please,
It's not to tear myself again. To find
That I cannot endure forgetting. Rather
Say: it's sorrow. Look. And hold it. Know
The steep, dark silence, not pretend I like it.

It fell upon Eurydice in meadows;
The venom drying that bright heart.
Late Orpheus to this Taenarian gate.
Behold him. Hear again the living voice:
"My wife is the cause of my coming."
Never turn back,
Up steep, dark silence climbing.

Iris, we went out today. As far
As to the line of pebbles by the shore.
Remember how George told you the arroyos

Filled? And late. Sometimes a whole day after
The mountain rain. Then sudden torrent. So,
Within late March, the spring comes back. We talked.
The news of Ed and these new wells sent down,
The gushers up the drill beyond the Shan,
Beyond the seven bridges. When I brought
Again to asking, how the one and world
Come into being. If he was. And how
Once from the bay off Marathon the men
Brought up the round, bronze head, the young boy's head
In ancient bronze. Tahl knew. He would not listen,
But held me there beside the sea and told me
How in Yunnan among the crowding mountains
Towns in endless summer. In Szechwan
The nation in retreat and struggling. Saying
We'd go from the south of rice to the north of millet.
And many die. But we could go there. How?
Now western war runs nearer. And our choice
Is not our choice, as once. But he has told me,
As he had not before, of much he'd done
In Spain. Could try again. Or only fight
Among the others. Much that I had learned
With Spanish children terrified of planes —
And there — of use. And we could try again.
Going there, among the crowded mountains.
Northward, find your father. Would not mind
The caves, the shell-torn hills. We might get through.
The Doctor. We could write to London. Basil.
And have I told you Stephanie's with Minna?
I'm stronger. Knew she'd like to go. I urged her.
Not that. I've known them both too long to doubt
Or wonder, now. These months have been much longer
Than merely months since May and since September.
So much, not all quite real. That he should be
Three days. And then just Tahl was there. But always.

The leaden spell is broken on a stone.
Mother of the fields in sorrow searching.

Out of Space

And she was not Eurydice. Was called
Persephone who holds the deadly keys,
The poppy seed of quietness. The seed
Of pomegranates is divided. Who
Are these reported risen from the dead?
Not lonely Orpheus among the stones.
The sibling ones go down and come again,
The children of the grain who come again,
Who were together first in Hellas known.
And he was Dionysus and returns;
And Persephone with spring has come.

Minna, since you ask, I'll try. He'd say
It does not matter now. Although he works
Harder. But the air's too loud. He hears
The Norsemen now go under and the Danes
In April terror. And each night we walk
The shore — as if he watched, as if he'd turn
In one hard glance the threatening armada
Out of sea and air. But I am stronger.

So the sea returns and he comes home
And works. Because he must forget. And I.
And we do not. Are not oblivious yet.
Wondering why. But sometime. Yes, again.
We're still ourselves. And others have lost sons.

But nothing's to be done until it's finished.
The year goes on to this sharp washen blue
Of April sea and under red rocks darkens
Sundown after sundown. And the salt,
Whether life or death in this sea's fragrance,
Blows within us. And we cannot die
For all we ask of death. And though he write
"Apocalypse," for us not yet the moment
Apocalyptic — months of genesis
And hope departed, once; but not forever.

You say Tahl's visions and his private language
Shut you out, as Jim once closed a door
Against you with his symbols and his numbers,
His murdered atoms, and his politics
To culminate in last incomprehensions
Of his way gone beyond the doors he closed
As fast as ever door upon us fastened,
Wondering how this boy of ours would grow,
If he had grown. And if the heart had closed.
It would not. And no chemistry or art
This day knows how. And Jim would understand,
Knowing how much was not to know. And Tahl,
This chemist of old dreams transmuted, also
Has his own way of acting manifesto,
A politics. If you and I would know
What he is up to, we cannot neglect
That John's Apocalypse was manifesto
Also, in his time, against a Nero,
Name of Caesars who would count again
In hidden numbers of a Rome returned.
If in oppressive years the good go down
Under the steel and acid, will not drown,
But will transform, and all its words be fables
In living code decoded underground.

And when the words themselves corrode, return
In music resurrected. For we think
Even sound, the seventh and the triad,
Sinister, augmented, not apart,
Not isolate or neutral, moves inbound,
Will not escape the cosmic turn; the chasm
From cave to surface, when the bridge is blown,
Still to cross on viewless sound. If Jim
Shut you out by Helmholz and Dirac,
And Tahl by scales we do not understand,
If they reject the solid Brahmsian sound
For universes pierced, too wide in space
Among the points secured, they will come back
As in Tahl's way, old way of the quartets,

The phrase completed not in *tutti* but
Completed in its parts from instrument
To instrument until melodic line
Stand free in air and time assembled, till
We tolerate the unknown scale against
The new-recovered diatonic, firm,
The once-unknown against the known already,
Comprehended in transfiguration.

Will not be formula already known
Or Jim would never need to find it; not
Of matter never known or never worked
Or neither Jim nor Tahl could ever use it
More than I could draw conclusions on
A world whose history had never been,
Nor we could make the substance of a son
Beyond the uterus and semen. May
I not offend you, knowing we have come
So hard against first matters, cannot fend
For honesty, beneath the euphemism
This late time. And if in truth you mean,
As you have said, you would not live much longer,
Having understood our Senior with the years,
Yourself, your other son, unless you come
To us and Jim and Stephanie. We are
Not indeed such strangers; but much moved
In your demand. I've known you, that you stood,
For Jim, his balance, as he said we stood,
You and I, against him in the spin
To hold him in the circuit. And amused
To hear Tahl say I am his anchor tone
Insuring scale's return. So now trombone
Or trumpet, tympani, no more flung in
To trample the cadenza out of anger;
To make the hearer chuckle, rather. How
They are alike in that, both he and Jim,
To chase the universe like furious children
In good earnest; and as quickly tumble
Worlds upon their heads to make you laugh.

And even loving to expound the laughter
Like this sage of mine. I say he's bound
By his obsessions in C minor. Then
He'll come to me mock-rueful, say can't help it,
Done it. Have his punishment. And promptly
Prove there's no tonality to have
So perfect — like his smile that is a smile
Chromatic — three points down. Perverse as Jim
Making games about uranium.
Tahl, for favorite vice, the tones they called
Bhairava, is a Hindu *râga* played
Once at dawn, the seven-tone veneration;
And then he'll rag it, three-four, six-eight time,
Shuttlecock for jest. But is no jesting,
More than Jim's, to take apart the world
And rearrange its terms. Tahl's first intention —
Beyond those years when only Alfred knew him,
Elsa, George, and Jan, and when he made,
Like the Russian, that great talker, come
To be good king among us here, the measure
Cold as a piano and discovered
Unity most tenuous, the drums,
Percussion, world at base, by thinnest strands
Held to mind's invention of inventions
And worth a stop to listen; but remember
Only wonder — as Tahl says, "No hawser
Tying bitt and bollard" — but beyond
The wit's *meccano,* nuts and bolts of sound —
His first intention was — to be the voice
Of fishermen and children. Write a mass
Without a church in orders, to be sung
In summers on this coast with flowers given
To going tide, to write *memoriam*
Men who've gone upon the waters dragging
For a feast and drowned. He says he'll never
Write it now because he'll never know
Enough to match the master's *Benedictus,*
The man of Bonn who sent the violin
Out alone to render mercy's errand,
Harbinger of peace; and none, Tahl says,

Will ever find a better for that mission.
For the children? We have said no more
This year, as you will understand. Last spring
He had a chorus ready, from the songs
I found among the pueblos and the chants
The wondering Navajo remembers. Coming
Often to the house, the young men, evenings.
He has a way, as Jim had, going on
Months alone; and then as soon come in
With trouping voluntaries. Have been none
This year, of course. We have been much alone.
And, now that you have Stephanie — again.
What would you understand? Six languages?
May we thank you all since she's determined
Now to bind herself to these assignments,
Changing words for wages. But she speaks,
In any language, as you have discovered,
As Tahl can hear, to pitch that's absolute,
In hearing perfectly the way the world runs.
In figure she may swear to you she's deaf
Or had been deaf, her years of growing; blind,
The years with Walther. Eyes and ears were there.
And very handsome. Do you think, or not —
Your being so our "mother" — we become
What was, within our making, always given?
My knowing that we choose, and sure of that —
Here, on my least philosophy, confounded.

You ask, if Jim loved metals and machines
And atmospheres and colors, what could make him
Turn so aside, the road run up Pingarron
To his so soon an end. I'd say because
He knew the metals and machines inclined
To rule or to be ruled; and choice alone,
Who would be their masters. And you ask
Who were Tahl's instructors. Give you names
Of dry and thorough martinets he claims
He never loved but would not be without them.
Give you instruments — deranged piano
George cartooned, the berserker; the strings

Of his guitars and other nameless fashions;
The horn he ran with, years among the bands
In years that George knows better. But will answer
Nothing to discover how he learned
Except his every day of life in asking
Any face or book to his own sea
In its own tides take threshold from his mind.
He says he cannot play a flute; and yet
He writes one like its maker. And could run
His lost *alboka* out of heavy *aulos*
To a susurrus and bell, a shepherd
On farthest hill. But now I wander further
Than farthest hill from answer why he is
A red guitar and still a bell for Sunday.
You will indulge our having not grown older.
And you have known me. And I love you. Tell me
Who he is. Or Jim. Should I tell you?

They, the soldiers. No academy
But leaves them uncommissioned. They, the askers.
Somewhere few remember in his papers
Numbers Jim wrote down. But won't salute him
Often in convention. As he'd written
Those days before we knew him, name on records,
Tahl, his prize-takes — now no name to mention
For more than, "Oh," and not, "Of course." And even
If never more citation he remains
With Jim and Federico, I believe,
With men the world would lack, were they not born —
If ever unacknowledged. More to say
Than formula or symphony or poem
Last will say of them. And that not finished,
Symphony, or what they'll call it when
The cataloguing pencils must assail it;
Opera of which the act ensued
Before the sun was made; and last event
In oratorio of prophecies
Too hard for easy ears, perhaps, too hard
In hope which holds no easy promises.

He will finish. That I think, though born
Ever doubtful, never sure. No hope
He would come back from Spain. Not after Jim
And Federico. But he came. And then
Too sure that in this year there'd be a son —
Who is not. And for nothing we could do.
The circle turns. And having lived so long
With my lost empires, knowing that the lost
Appears true loss — forever — am not sure.

Except that I believe. For surely something
Must, beyond the death; for, being sure
No history survives but in its change,
Something still escapes. And that endures.

Was not the dark boy, image made, to stand
With armlets, gilded staff and sandals,
Eyeballs crystal and obsidian
Before his sepulcher. Will not be found
Under five times five of weathered dunes.

Was not the dark boy, image made, to stand
Transmarginal, subliminal
Within the time contingent? But the hand
Opened there to find him. He was gone.
And none now know him though he bear a name.

After your long silence, Jan, concerned,
But now are not surprised. In this year's change
Having your own war to fight; and won,
We take it; though not calmly. Risk enough
Up there with your wild fledglings, taking air
Within their unsure hands. But now to be,
If we can understand you, dive and burst
And test until the engine split from strain
Or not; and now within your hands your life

More thrown on chances. Being so the mistress
Of yourself, there's none of us commands
You should not do so. As you say, a plane
Must have its test. And that's your choice. God keep you.

And so you may have long as yet to live
As any, with the world across the waters
Coming down so fast we had not dreamed
A history could slip, a house of cards
Upon the jury as in Wonderland
Screaming, "Off with the head" — and Holland gone,
Belgium, Luxembourg. And having heard
This morning that Peru's been shaken, wonder
If somewhere Solon's watching, sure of worlds
In one last gulfing fire and water gone.
The day they broke Sedan, when Tahl came home,
You'd think he'd no profession but a gun,
If he could find a matchlock! But no joke,
His being restless. For it's nearly finished.

Yes. Not copying. But nearly done
Since May came in with so much blood again.
Late spring of dragons half-track, and the air,
Rooted in falling petals, spills machines
Shooting, swinging down. Tahl meant to write,
As once his master when he signed his *Credo*,
"God above all." But question hovers. Not
Escape, as you suggest — "he had his music."
Far more than mine, his health, our house to keep,
His days and nights, encountering with death.
Creation, sound or son, a death's defiance
He still must make, each day a justifying
Of that he cannot answer more than I.
Not "mine" but ours, the fortune we most hoped
This time, this year. And not. As if we stood
Secure in harness, venturing toward "nothing"
Which still is "air." We've met the earth again.
But there were three who made the leap. And one
We looked to find. Not there. We keep on living.
If he now hesitates to sign — one line —

Out of Space

It's not alone the child, the question — also
This rout of maps. But nearly finished. Few
In his first hundred years may read, discern,
Detect his stratagem and ascertain
The equilibrium accomplished, how
The sequence follows sequence and it mounts
And falls by purpose and his will. What coils
Or crystals, willing tubes will ever have it,
He is determined that the air shall take it.
Puts on old rogue — says audience may leave
And we'll not see them leave. But he'll admit
He wants a probability of hearing
Uncommon. Tease him. Say he's vain. Too close.
Can play a game on 'vain.' And there we leave it.
It's no safe word for us this year. Too much
Has been in vain. Though I have come so far
As half a day without remembering.
Not waking up to ask myself again:
Why? To us. Perhaps because we've asked
Too much in these last weeks, as once in Spain,
Why? To anyone. And can there be
Those who will and plan that others die,
And so compel us to our deaths against them,
When death's enough already? Let it be
Simple as that. As I can say to you
Or Stephanie, as even not to Iris
Who has not watched the children dying. Why
Tahl is more impatient, even as you,
With watching war come in across two seas.

The world has blown a post, as Jim would say.
The acrid fumes that wrung us once in Spain
Blow across two oceans. Few I talk to
Know the world's a blown-out battery
And nothing runs again until it's mended.
Not having chosen, now must choose perforce.
As you could see when trainers' fields were closed,
There's still a life to live. And in the chances,
Still the choice. If not this time a son,
Then time remains. And I still hear you say

As on that last long evening in Madrid:
"I am more angry that the children die."

The theme in various keys, the rounded phrase,
Classic first announcement, modulated,
A mighty music, once a known salvation.
Now, by grace or choice, by instrument
To instrument accumulate the phrase
Finally discovered and the theme
By graduals to the assembled form,
Is music also in the groping time —
As I am Tahl and you are Alison,
Apocalypse of genesis recovered
In final judgment. Once I had believed
The world of one repeats the multitude;
But is not so. The telescope has given
Answers false to microscopes. I've seen
No mob assume the analogue of one
Or two in meditation. Have beheld
The atom never analogue of stars,
Although we hoped the easy answer there.

Came down from house of winter, house of frost,
The great Himalaya and the yielding nullahs,
Passage down the rivers. And will rise
Above the cones on passages in air
And find we know and do not know, between
That unthought and all that's unconditioned.
"By whom willed and directed goes the mind
Toward its object? And by whose command
The life, the first cause, move?" And when the Brahman
Chose his form to answer Indra, came
As woman, daughter, hue of lightning, answered:
"Whom you saw was he. Without him nothing
Moves." And that same he who disappears
Sooner than flick of eyelids. Find no atom
Analogue of stars though they abide
Together in the thunder. Never finding

Any perished quantum repetition
Of any other; each its own momentum,
Spectrum, wind-trail on the finger. Find
In action, mutilation; and contrive
Least mutilation when the one is made
Perfect in the breath of life. Perceive
Aggression first of crimes against the one,
The trusting heart assaulted. And perceive
That power has two faces, therefore choice;
That sorrow is enough without the will
To strike the stricken down. I have debated,
Cried against, withheld; but I have written —
In this year in which we lost our son,
In this year in which the sons are slain
And others risk the slaying, so the daughters
Have no more sorrow save what's not to cure
And saved from sorrow sown in willful power.
Sorrow enough and death and wounds enough
Without our will. And that we choose, can write
On this last page and in this Maymonth given
As will not end our years while man on man,
Woman on woman, man on woman, raise
The treacherous cry and drive the nail, have written
Beyond the day the lines broke at Sedan
And since you stood beside me on the shore
And strong again. It is enough. Have known
From "*alle wymmen*" "*hevene it is me sent*"
And so my "*love is lent*" "*for thinë sake*"
"*Levedi.*" And her name is "Alysoun."
And who he was and now anonymous,
Five hundred years have gone and trouble none
Who he was or who his Alison —
One madrigal of recompense to fend
The armored ships. And who he was, our own,
And is and is not ours we called our son;
And that I've held your anguish and my own —
The flesh is made and broken to what purpose?
To days so brief as hardly take a name,
Three winter days, and gone. As if a hand
Came out of air to thrust us from our questions.

Given. Taken. 'Love — nor comprehend.'
I shall not comprehend. Not this. But given,
Your hand — in mine. If God indeed lie dead
In reasoned shroud, within that shroud, alive,
Attested blood in living flesh. The deaths,
Seven across the heart. And then, our son.
A heart we could not mend. Have ended. Strung
On ultimates, presumptions and rejections,
I know your love a reason more than reason,
Being, the possession of the dead
And of the living who remember death
In love's regenerate and mercy. Signed
In my own fashion from one master learned
As he upon his *Credo.* Genesis,
Apocalypse, accomplished and transformed
Only in its shaping of the sound
Which was and is. As his, upon the *Credo.*

And it is ended, Stephanie. But is
No end, to see it lying on his desk
And our ears best to hear but have not heard
As he has heard it. And is not the end
Of living. As that heart which would not hold
Was not the end of sons, though never known
Who he might have been, with that strong head,
The perfect arms that fought, the perfect hands.

It's not the end of wars, the frantic ships
Crowding bloody channels from Dunkirk,
Entr'acte only in our long retreats
And long attacks, the millimicron death
Terrible, particulate, and not
An end. Not yet. And Tahl and I alone
On our near shore where fine-grained sand once bore
Volcanic heats and there the pebbles lying
Old as life, five hundred million years
Of molten rock congealed and are not first
In genesis which has no end in Paris,

New-lost Verdun nor at the anxious boats
Fleeing the guns' eruption. We have kept
And lost. And, listening, sooner should have known,
As Tahl, Felipe, Federico, Jim,
The cable hacked, the cross-ties burned, the mined
Defile, broken axle, gun-frame sprung,
May still keep liaison within destruction
Of known communication, one patrol
Against irreverence of false selection,
The arrogance and ignorance outdone
Never by the ear gone deaf to claim
We do not hear and there's no trouble; where
They fear the music or the book or climb
The mouths of undefended schools to cut
The tongue out. Never cease because we say
We had not seen it with our eyes. Have learned,
You and I, by fortune and misfortune,
By every woman's benison of signs
Quieter perhaps and so like music
In history's aggressions and disdains,
Subsisting magma of our hearts to move
The sharp, primeval seas of Adam's scorn,
The first of wars and also lost and won
Though most by camouflage and indirection
Toward the temporary arbitrations
Between the nourishing cell and flagellate sperm,
The drench and bleeding. Come to double term
First in every recapitulation
Versus slave and master to assent
Capitulation mutual — as we've learned.
And if the woman's merciful in legend,
Then, shall we say, for having longer known
What brothers learn in armies, as he says,
"To hurry better, waiting," or the rash
Hero have small profit in his death.
The songs I found last spring; the mountain chants
Which are to sing in winter after frost —
The sign of the man on the rock and the sign of woman,
One and same plumed arrow, spirit feather.
Are not apart in faith nor in contritions

Death

Born beyond the clashing rocks, the path
Of all the paths we go upon together.
If this he knows within his own creating,
And you've known this in anguish of desiring,
And I have known in my new-lost creation,
As Federico knew and why we loved him —
As Walther does not know and we have loved you,
Your tolerant mask will not rip off, your saying
"Will judge no man a villain" — what we've known
Is our mad kind of reverence for breath,
The soul, by name you choose, maligned, mistrusted,
Remain a willing congregate of fools,
Agreeable, preferring foolishness.

We have been seen before, I think. Are not
Bacilli new-exposed in able lenses
New-discovered. Though perhaps more wary.
Rifles locked, but loaded, I believe,
Is order on reconnaissance. Perceive
We've spoken less of music, more of battles
This harried spring. And you've been one among,
Dislike to be alone. And I have been
Seldom for others anxious till he came.
But he has been among, apart, has been
Impatient in whatever alternation
Marked the day's location. Why he seems
For all his recollections and his reasons
Never cool philosopher, whatever
Hours he takes for all his meditations;
And why together we may comprehend him,
Knowing him neither still nor moving, mine
And yours, *Tondichter* for us both. I know —
Though have no hope, intention to convince
Even Iris. Most incredulous,
Incredible, except our crediting
Among us, all since Spain, against our angers
And our possessions. Shall not waste ourselves
Protesting you to me or I to you
Or he to both of us. We've known the heart
Unreliable as life and also

Only heart to trust. We've made our worlds
And seen them break and mend, contrarities
Of knowing, daring, wanting, being still
Active, passive, neutral in our times,
Ally and enemy within ourselves
Till we can know the route ourselves have taken
And road we've found, a zone we can survive in.

We are not separate nor ever can be,
Neither from ourselves nor Federico.
We know ourselves within each other. Only
Do not know, reach never absolute,
However far the walls push back, and yet
More sure of what has been. Can count the wounds,
Parnassus and Segura de los Baños;
Alfred walking lame; and yours and mine,
More private in our scars. But most believe
That evening in Madrid we heard Tahl saying,
And three of us who knew him, how he'd gone
Reverse in time and come again to say,
And unafraid before our eyes, he'd taken,
Lifelong, a harder wound. I have not known,
As he in many years before we knew him,
Those first white roads that he went back upon,
The words of the master of death to Nachiketas:
"No mortal lives by the incoming breath
Nor by the breath outgoing, but he lives
By other breath on which these two depend."
If that be true, have we then lost a son?

He's not so far away as in my words.
But is less hard to hold so in the times
Neither awake, asleep, nor dreaming, when
No eye beholds the light, but light comes in,
No ear attend the sound, but that sound deepens
Beyond the threshold, faith, a final sanction
Mightier in what's lost, most lost, the sign
Against a torture, steel against the knife
No knife will scar or bend. If that were in him,
Is — though gone so soon we had not named him,

His three days' time; and none beyond ourselves
Will hear he ever was, from spring to winter —
Recover faith, a fashion of believing.

Mistress of six lexicons, you'll smile —
My present occupation — in Tahl's legends,
Finding out his China. For him found
Diversion in new questions. I will tell you
I've learned a word: "to hear." A character
Saying "to hear" says also "to perceive,"
To see and hear at once as thunder comes
Immediate on lightning. Long ago,
Then most by Jim's persuading, ran among
The Mayan pictures; make new game of finding
New-old picture book with Chinese brushes.
And I have learned today two symbols drawn —
May say, "to love"; and painting them — that, strangely —
The sign for "mother" with the sign for "son,"
The love a mother gives a child. From spring
To spring again, the finding. In the desert
Found and told him, of the god creating —
How Indian singers read the ancient name:
"Love-A-Mother-Gives-A-Child" — he came
From out first light upon our insufficience
Making man and woman, first of legends.

I've loved you more that you have asked me least
After anxious fevers, drag and calm
Which are, for fact, irrelevant in knowing
How birth comes on, the common way of mothers
Toward recompense in hope. I'd dare suppose
Even my mother's spaniel, bitch with eyes
And cheerful tail and doleful ears no wiser
Than we for clinics, classic syllables,
Of how it comes and which will live. But only
Ask me now, so late. Yes, found a name
Tahl loved. And was most dangerous to think of,
Now, it seems. He'd never have a name
Without a meaning; meaning "recompense,"
"Recompense of God." A silence wiser

Than any saying, that we've never said
The name since this hard winter, cannot judge
The recompense we'd choose, nor make it surer,
Angry that the dream has been denied.

It's not the end of life, with many ending.
Sea narrows on two lands, the crowding ships
Under the flailing planes. Is not the end.
And most we have already said, remembered:
In sua voluntade; is not easy;
Nostra pace, moment's peace recovered,
Never kept for sure. We cannot say,
Untroubled, while we live. No saints nor martyrs,
We are too curious and far too restless
For their assurance. But may let it stand,
The Tuscan's word, survive in older seeing,
In sua voluntade; live the time
To where we're going next. I cannot say
So soon, with war come nearer; and the laws
Coming which will call him. But will manage
As always, as we have, the choices, knowing
The sea is in our blood and that the sea
Is full of nightmare kelps and vines, maintains
In its cold light menageries unknown
Within the twilight depths, electric corals,
Sponges in unrotting ooze, and ice
Below and sun above; and that the moon
Has not run out its time. And once I said
This Tahl of ours was very like a fugue.
But he insists the composition's changed
In these last years and I am counter-subject.
And if a fugue be nothing, save it grow,
I am indeed but part myself without him.

But I must stop. I'm here on our own rocks.
The sun and wind both strong. The ink is drying.
There's no more news, no more than ever is
Within a world. Some matters are accomplished
In time. His music. Some are not. For us,
I am alone till nightfall when he comes.

Death

There is no other sound except the sea.
The boy would be four months this week. Is not.
The best we manage on this map, to know
Terrain, which way is west, to judge location
By littered stubs, debris, at most accepting
Rough validity for our believing.

We may not analyse too far. Assume
In sua voluntade, formulated.
And if it were not said, would have to say it —
If not between nine hells and maps of heaven —
Among necessities of bed and kitchen
And readying the table, waiting sundown.

Haven't hurried, Mister. No one told me
There's a rush. The dead will keep. You think
Old men like me take fancy for a winter,
Freezing my old fingers in the snow?
And spring and summer have my place to keep.
If you're a farmer, as you say, you know.
The crops won't wait. And if it is September,
Well, the stone will keep. I'll cut it now.
Done before it sets to dark. Come back.

You like to watch? Don't mind. You knew them, did you?
Hannah. Restless. Sailing-man, a wild one,
Likely. Never saw him. Mind the dust.
Your lungs ain't used to it. This iron rings
Loud, a bit. So. There. We got the measures.
Good granite. Mind the dust. I cut them all,
Every single name, young man. So now.

Mind the dust. We're done before it's dark.
There he lies. I guess he warn't so long
As his name. There now. I'm getting old.
There's not a young one here has learned the trade.
Who will put my name on stone, I says?
Never you mind. Won't matter. There now. See.

Out of Space

That sun. Not even gone beyond the mountain.
Glad to oblige you. Young man, let me tell you,
All things done in time, you see. There. There now.
Nigh to fill the stone now. So it be.
God rest them all. There now:
Gamaliel

TAHL : BOOK FOUR

CANTO III

INTO THE SEA

The Boundary of Truth

The boundary of truth forever trenched
By river's fall and pendulum of sea,
By light within the light, the source of light,
The one unbroken circuit still to be;
To each what may suffice still insufficient.

By moon and hand's electric lantern marked
Each route to each acropolis; and tracked
The caves beneath the citadels; assault
By excavation, deposition; rake
The posthumous crater's sediment and remnant.

Among uncounted multiples report
One unexplored acropolis, the search,
Recovered and forgotten, still dispatch,
The one unbroken circuit still to be;
To each what may suffice, still insufficient.

Within the bounds of probables you'll swear you've never heard my voice. And yet the voice is heard among the frequencies, dispatches most, and most unsigned, but still a voice, if soon a voice forgotten. For the record: met the Doctor first in Moscow; met Felipe, Federico, also Tahl in a Bilbao now forgotten. So I meet you now in London. And your Christian name is

Basil and I've heard the name before, for we, most nameless, check an ear at least at Whitehall, know the world contracts, as you yourself discover; and I may, by chance, with being, as you say, professional, a traveler, come up in time with Walther — as I've come, by this you tell me, on a wire that leads to one you've never met and still, you say, have given word for.

Within the bounds of probables we'd swear to many voices never heard again, as I'll, for certain, never hear Felipe, yet you'll hear his name, I swear, if, in the turn of time, you find the climate gentle in Euskadi. As for Tahl or Federico, have not seen them since Bermeo in a last defeating April, now a nearly four raw years away from London. I did not expect the more our ancient friend met once upon a bench beyond the Kremlin in a cold and humid March, that I should hear his dry and omnipresent voice this year in London in a rather warmer winter. "Out of bounds again, young man," he says. "The boundaries are closing inconveniently from lunch to cocktails. Have you eyes to check the signatures of Constantines converted and donated, Charlemagnes in collar, tie, and epaulettes and diesel boots upholding *civitas terrena*? Here's dispatch will need more Cicero than lawyers and more Homer than homerics, night's reporter best in fine detail of wounds with the precision of physicians." But you know him. His remarks perhaps need not survive the burning of the Guildhall which we watched to keep the new year warm; nor all the books within the Temple blazing. It was Sunday night. The tower off Fleet Street burst its clock face in a most unnatural dawn.

Within the bounds of probables not likely we shall live to watch the world burn up. And some run toward and some run from when sound of fire's a tocsin on the eardrum. And that springal that you both have sworn for, that he be admitted with the thousands, I have heard, who now across the wide Pacific still go west, while by a consular suggestion, other thousands still run east, tall springal going west, we shall suppose, since you have vouched for him he will not harm Hongkong and since the Doctor's filled the pouches full of affidavits that, except this one young man, for some American ancestral reason, was most oddly present once in Spain, is moderately clever and can be relied upon to serve a country whose announced, perfected, and amazing art remains the art of transportation — so the papers sealed — is that young man of whom the Doctor said and, I've no doubt, to you, that, if the army will not have him for the slugs I understand he caught most oddly once in Spain, and, if you ever see him, you will also recognize him by a scar above his ear — and for his known susceptibility to fevers — then he might remain at home, a gentleman, with honor. And I had not known until the Doctor told me that the fellow's music is indeed a first vocation and you say your very charming cousin tells you that the music is to be performed in this new year. My first vocation's also talking, and, these years I've found most unexpected stages for extended conversations — as to listen to the Doctor speak of palm canoes upon the Niger while the smoke blows hiding-screens around St. Paul's, a tropic mist of thermite and magnesium with a new year coming in.

Within the bounds of probables not likely that the learnèd gentleman departs for Africa because he has acquired a learnèd curiosity about the men who still inhabit caves in Sangha. "If your much admired acquaintance," so the Doctor says, "would like a tour by air, I'd recommend the Wakham at Dakar or choose the splendid field at Gao. If he wants music," so the Doctor says, "then let him come with me to hear the Malinké who are the more efficient in performance since they tie their harps upon their drums and so can march to battle with a minimum encumbrance. Let him come with me this winter. We will be the last of swallows. When they're starting south, they take the upper air. Their flight is indiscernible." And then his owlface never blinks but, always, as you know, the noncommittal, bulging eyebrows. "If he likes," the Doctor says, "I'll help him to his place among the players of marimbas, for, although upon the records they are known official beggars, they are masters of the Niger and the chieftains live in most respectful terror of their singing. There's a place of all the world where men will tremble now before a traveling musician." If the swallow be not of itself a flying pun enough, I think our friend is, at the least, of weaverbirds he says in the acacias of the French plantations live at Gao because it is an oasis with many trees. In Moscow, where I met him first, this weaverbird said war, to Tahl, was an event impersonal. He would not listen to me when I mentioned a Felipe, Federico. I might say I think the tree which issues passports to the one is not acacia and the weaverbird is misinformed. And yet I'll say, if you can understand me, sir, that by whatever wings we fly, we are impelled by smell of fire, a signal sense of something wrong.

Within the bounds of probables you would not say that one who was by legal sanction for some years to you a kind of in-law should compel me more than you, and I the stranger, that by chance I found in Russia I had missed him though I'd seen him in Euskadi where he summered with the columbines and swallows near Bilbao and has not, we think, resided with the cowslips and the nightingales of Kharkov, let us say. Walther. I go after him and you are not disturbed because I find it useful that you say I'll come upon him, if I like, this year in Lisbon.

Within the bounds of probables the more improbable that in your sorrow and dismay you should these hours sit quietly beside a table here with me, so nearly stranger, and the smell of smoke still sour in our clothes because I tried to save him and you tried to save him, but we watched him die, your friend, the aging Russian who you say was British of the British, having lived for fifty years in London. And you sent him home your monograph upon the rose-red city of Jaipur, the floral manuscript adornment of the second arch of some great prince's residence; he sent to you in India his latest formulas for clever poisons that, by paradox, bring life, not death, to clovers. And there is, you say, a fair pavilion out of marble, pearl, and emerald was built upon a man-commanded island in a lake at Udaipur, and, if you chose, you'd like to die there very far from my reporting damage done to docks at Hull, and here old Grub Street gone down flatter than sometime the walls of Romans. I will tell you — once a question asked of Tahl by Federico in the trench-scratched fields below Bermeo: "Why do lamas off in Lhasa fear Jerusalem and Mecca?" And Tahl answered, "They would fear the Jains who walk Ahmedabad if once they scented likelihood a present Jain disputed them in present powers and possessions." Then I noticed them. But Walther's no affair of yours, you say. And may I give you now a question? Tell me why an Eton tie is badge of honor as it had been made in Mecca for the friends of Mr. Jinnah? Prove I am the first of first barbarians. I do not understand as much as your best Hindus who pay honor to Ganesha who, you say, is god of common sense and shrewdness and no nonsense.

Within the bounds of probables you'd like me muzzled, drugged, or caged. Unfortunate that it was he; and it was I who came along and tried to save him, this sad, bearded man who knew the ways of plants. And hugged to jet for draught, the fighters made us channel through the smoke — too late. His head was broken by — let's say — neutrality? Legality's most curious. You may be prosecuted for permitting lodging to known criminals and traitors. Who permits that Germans die on German wire by British purchase or that British ships go down by German submarines well-built with French aluminum? Weigh sunburnt rocks at Malta to the islands off the coast of South America. How relate to this misfortunate occasion, that your agèd, cherished Russian was this night sent off to a more distant Petersburg, by fall of bricks and blaze most undeserved? You find me rude, avoiding codes permitting question only by most circumspect of indirections. But sodality of international nobility has made an error that you'll not admit; your guards with guns these days exhibit most atrocious manners. I embarrass you. I've had no sleep a week. This morning I reported, too, a fact of transportation. There, within the City, came on Addle Street and through the bombs and fires the sign still hangs and says, "ONE WAY"; but in the morning smolder no one walked or drove through Addle Street because the smoking bricks were higher than the sandbags and were very warm for winter. No one very quick to find Chungking. Nor very quick to say what day Lord Privy Seal Saito murdered, either. Who will know by finger on a map, Durango? But I would indeed have saved him. And I'm sorry that a friend of yours lies dead tonight in London.

Within the bounds of probables avoiding Addle Street and other, wider thoroughfares, the busses changing routes — in China, trains don't always run and there's some transportation difficulty in the seven largest cities — but we know your friend, at least, that he is dead — upon a world of very many persons missing and most unexpected meetings with a large proportion of us in the air and on the sea. And once Felipe said that Tahl had joined the Basques because his habit was to chase the sea and having started long ago too often coming up too late. If he is now, as you have said, to go on this routine and civil mission in assistance of west China's transportation, he's perhaps a man who wants too much, to walk a sea before a road's been built, will come too soon. But he won't hesitate to lay his fist where it can be most use. Felipe was the only one I knew could spar with him and touch him.

Within the bounds of probables he'll find some use for ears in digging roads, no doubt because he may have heard last year the sound of oars that dug across to Dover and has heard the humming covey, birds, their eggs now laid on fire alive and shrieking over Kent and Dorset, flat, enduring Essex. Do you know the Great Controller, he who reads the table of the squadrons and balloons and guns that nuzzle air by night and day? As August — birds escorted; gone the convoys off the Thames; birds escorted, larger escort, gone the airdromes and the houses. As September — at some fifteen thousand feet against the sun, the Prussian Cross and Crooked Cross; and in the mild September air the long white feathers on the canny kindly chosen Sunday evenings after blaze-up all the drowsy afternoons along the wharves, and, dusk to dawn, the motorcycle screech along the craters in the carols burning four days after Christmas. Early twilight now new sun pulls tidal waves of fire to seal the streets of this acropolis and heart, the new aurora borealis showers sparklers in an out-of-season thunder, heath and forest, house and ship, crescendo, now fortissimo with smoke along the Surrey hills beyond November's baleful moon. November, Saturday, report, on Athens fell Italian bombs, and Friday next, report, on Coventry, the German bombs. December, thirty miles away, watch London burn, the embers flying, drenched wood drying, sickly sweet aroma of the burning tea in bundles and the scorching poisoned air and steaming hawsers from the baleful moon on Coventry to then recite the list of cities.

Within the bounds of probables might say that everyone came back next morning through the new triumphal arch of twisted steel and always knew the voice along the wire reporting also matter crucial in department transportation as the bleeding boy reporting to the warden: ". . . but I've lost his bicycle. Blown off it. I got up, sir. Nothing left but just this bloody single wheel." Upon him tip and run in baleful moons. The roof curves slowly and the floor splits inward like a V or wing of planes, and down, a pudding spilled; and rubber burns to choke and rum will burn to sear and pepper burn to sneeze and burning summer autumn winter spring in burning England.

Within the bounds of probables you wonder why, if all my other purpose is to ask you news of Tahl by unpredicted frequencies I have discovered will transmit from time to time some news of him, I keep you here where any moment sees the floor attack the ceiling. It would not become you, sir, in age and dignity which I respect, although you doubt it, that you sit conspicuous, alone, and shedding tears because the friend you've loved for fifty years is dead. And so I talk. I'll tell you what I heard Tahl say to Federico in a room as much like this as once Bilbao was another little London, and we too, four years ago this very January, thinking any moment that the floor would meet the ceiling. "Whoever says, 'not fellow' will atone. And nothing expiates till final expiation, till forgetful, deaf, and blind attend what cause is first of causes, that the broad head say to long head or the long head say to broad head 'no' and 'no' and 'no' from fear and pride and dizziness. For every blaze that fires the tree, this 'no,' its name."

Within the bounds of probables Tahl's gone or soon will go toward this Hongkong which, as you may recall, regards this year centennial in British claim; and there, I understand, the tunnels are dug in as you report they are on Malta, and the island is beleaguered, though the planes come in and leave, as he, no doubt, will come and leave; and if a woman's with him, is, no doubt, of those I saw and took the names of once for boats across the Biscay guarding glancing anxious-over-shoulder children with their crowding heads not looking just to find a star to wish on. You will say he's not in England and you'll say you've never seen him. But, believe me, I am sorry that your friend is dead — was killed tonight by falling bricks, by fire and crashing beams.

TAHL : BOOK FOUR

CANTO III

INTO THE SEA

In Air Alone

In air alone who will survive attend
The whispered counsel, Níltche, called the wind,
To guide Nayénezgani, monster slayer.
From air come down who will survive may learn
Which landing's safe again and may depend
On whispers in hotels, the barfly's rumor.
In air alone the barrier may turn
To air, the rotted moats forever spanned.
Make one by one the choice of final danger.

In air alone who will survive attend
Both that which is and him who is and neither
Will escape the air without the other.
From air come down who will survive may learn
An Aesculapian intricate, the motor
Ganglion of living engine's fiber.
In air alone the barrier may turn
To air by imbecile derangement sooner.
The neuron slit, the slowest to recover.

In air alone who will survive attend
To malleable air as man the finder
Quick to wind and engine, dialed whisper.
From air come down who will survive may learn
No one alone of who went up, went down

To send each tone, vibration's calibrator.
In air alone the barrier may turn
To air from fire below, the dive to fend
The gulf of smoke, to thrust the quaking ladder.

In air alone who will survive attend
What objects past the wing and prop go down,
The tailspin blazing tank, the slipstream tumbler.
To air gone up who will survive may learn
What fellow slipped the chock and wheeled the plane
Against inglorious battle's last dimension.
In air alone the barrier may turn
To air, climb up the clock the friendly stranger.
Collision never was the final danger.

Into the air together saw them go.
The gray sky's clipper from the icy bay
To weather west and nothing to remark
In, "Jan, goodbye," except their coming back
In some next year. Then clearance, distant wing.
And so by days and islands toward Hongkong.

Here a city, dock and field, and here
The parks, as once in Barcelona, towers
Against an ocean. Here *paseo, plaza*
Steepest tilt in February glare.
The shriek of brakes. Not yet the slivered bomb
Among the days and islands toward Hongkong.

They will survive so sure a flight. As sure
As that they have not fled. Make no retreat.
Make next attack by flight. Of that more sure
Than any surety of where they've gone
To silk, to clay, to cotton coats, to mountains
Unknown as coral islands toward Hongkong.

They will survive so sure a flight. As sure
As pilots swing on four-strong engined power
Inclined on seven thousand miles of wind.

In Air Alone

Watch sharp for sparks in oil. Of that more sure
Than willow-tinder huts and caves in mountains
Beyond lagoons and islands toward Hongkong.

More sure, I think, than Spain, decrees by famine,
Than Rachel learning mercy's retribution;
Miguel — his neck was broken in Seville.
He lives, she says, to hold his skull. But prowling,
Those with truncheons ready, France or Poland,
Or draw him jeering nets around Hongkong.

Among the living dead the dead live well
When half the world's become a Devil's Island
With hunger not enough nor daily whipping,
The mocking idiot's delirium
Of niceties, inventions. As for Jim,
Let him rest. He need not fear Hongkong.

We may survive or not. We are dispersed
In world's uncivil wars. The armed civilian
Turns oil to rubber, wings to dynamite.
Or burns the bodies faster. Hell grown clever.
May you not see the children die nor run
To nightmare futures further than Hongkong.

I saw them go. Heard, "Jan, goodbye." And gone.
Should best stay home, you say. I have not gone.
No, I have come. I gamble nerves with planes.
You say no woman's business. Alison,
Her books and gardens. Tahl may add a sum
Of tools or tunes. Let them beware Hongkong.

But watch the engine's torque and warp the wing,
Set trimming tab and rudder. Thrust and drag
Is every law of voyage. Some stay home
And some do not. And we were once in Spain.
And Jim is dead. And we shall die in time,
If not on Devil's Island or Hongkong.

I'm calmer than you think. I fly each day
And sleep at night. And am no neuter. Calm.

And neither cursed nor sad. But I have heard
The grown men shriek, the young men sob. You think
The wager's less in risking Alison
Toward any airport nearer than Hongkong?

A hypo will not cure a dumdum bullet.
Hot water bottles soothe no perforations
In punctured kidneys. Shall we overcome
Inertia? Use the throttle. Moderation.
Do not choke too hard. A punctured body
Crashes hyacinths and almond blooms,
Pressure's variance with turbulence
At minimum. The fires, Madrid and London,
Spired to blaze that sears a pilot's cockpit.
They say I may not go. Or would you care
To battle sixteen thousand feet of flame?
The most important airfoil is the thrust
Of the torpedo prow. To Honolulu.
To Midway, Wake, and Guam, the unknown islands.
In this year there were one hundred thousand
Qualified civilians at controls,
And some that I have trained. Five years ago
Uncounted thousands whom I watched. They died;
Or lived again, like Tahl. And long before,
A man named Julian. Later, one called Jim.
And when they said goodbye, I did not know
That I'd not say hello. The crankshaft turn.
Please check the gauge for oil. And check corrosion.
The course of flight's affected by the steel
Magnetized within the plane. And Jim,
Smiling — said I'd stop in China. Wrong.
I have come west enough, enough remains
Along this earthquake edge. I'll wait again
This spring and springs to come the purple lupine,
The exaggerate glare of poppies, sea to mountains,
Fly minutes to the desert and recall
As if by echo Spain I might have seen
Except I chose such wrong July to go there.
Enough that's here and wrong in February,
The long estancia's echo and the wharves

Echoing. Some stay. Some go. They came,
Tahl and Alison toward this Pacific
And then went back again. It was not time.
And they have come again and overpassed.
With these steep streets a glare of ice they left.
"Jan, goodbye." Made clearance. Circle. West.

"The tone survives the flute," Tahl said. "The tone
Unchanged, the common pitch, the planet's air
Shaped and sounded past the forts of language."
Makes voyage once again for his own reasons
Now with hers. Engage the starter. Gone
With several strangers, also toward Hongkong.

Most likely to survive, I think. Though not
Because of simple flutes he said they'd learned
For calibrating stars and days and tones;
Gauge gravitation on a bamboo pipe
Once cut upon the mountains called K'unlun
Beyond the islands, far beyond Hongkong.

TAHL : BOOK FOUR

CANTO III

INTO THE SEA

In All Time's Change

In all time's change
Let the vine turn from the arrogant instrument.
Wounds by the practical pruning knife often grow
Cankerous.

In all time's change
Arrogant husbandmen careless of nourishment
Clipping to symmetry trim till the vine suffer
Barrenness.

In all time's change
The practical conscience may estimate consciousness
At the periphery vagrant, the twig
Insufficient.

In all time's change
Deviation, a function can not be removed from the
Instant
Except as the season fall thereby a vine into
Barrenness.
Dionysus to Bacchus will seed, by mutation efficient,
Again Dionysus.

Do I think he's changed? Unfortunate
That you have come too late and missed them. Left

In All Time's Change

A month ago this week. You've never seen
Alison, of course. And as for Tahl,
Change enough since those ten years ago.
Five years ago, my limp-foot. Brawl. In Athens.
And am I still "old prophet"? I suppose so.
Won't change for a broken heel. Or do we? Never
In those old nights of mighty talk concerned
With war, that's sure. And though I don't look here
For Caesars or Garibaldis, foggy nights,
Sometimes I think my spading, forking, feeding
Subsoil as I can in this stiff earth
Until the final frost, I trench and harrow
Geography of battle. Minor bastions.
Perhaps I've grown more sober. Maybe so.
Shall citizens all stand at the gun's point?
I thought that once in Athens, or, exactly,
In Piraeus which lieutenants read,
I understand, with an Italian legend
On current maps for quickest route to Athens.
Well, let it go. Come in. The air's still sharp
Here, in March. Come in. Today you've missed
Elsa, too. In town. With Dad. He's failing.
The boy's at school this time of day. Sit down.
That's his picture. Yes, he looks like Elsa.
She keeps the camera busy. Here they are,
Tahl and Alison in January,
Out there in the orchard, west. Good shot.
He hasn't shrunk, you see, the lanky racer.

Ten years seems little time. You've not much changed.
Though plenty to tell, no doubt, as I have. Tahl?
In Spain. Out West. They lost the child. A year
This January. Very day. This picture.
We'd just come back. Had driven up. In snow.
A year. To the day. They'd never seen the grave.
I took that business over. And there's no one
He knows now, in the town. They melt away,
These hill towns, as you know, with every storm.
Through drifts. No paths, of course. But found the stone
Clear — to the base. They'd said, "The child." "The boy."

Into the Sea

I christened him myself. The only name
They'd mentioned. "Gamaliel." Came up and stopped.
And she said, "Oh." And he said nothing. Looked
At her. And we stayed back. And that was all.

Elsa caught them afterward, here in the orchard —
Covered with snow from pelting each other. They'd left us.
Run off, running wild through the snow, like two young horses.
We've changed. They haven't. Something doesn't age
In him. Or rather say that he's grown younger.
Sometimes I think the oldest we have seen him,
Those nights ten years ago, and first old age
When Julian went. Though keen he was and quick,
And much in these last years to scar and break him —
And he is broken — yet there's lark and larrup,
Some power or pulse, since days he crawled through Egypt,
Our catching him strayed like a saddle-galled monk on Jordan.
And now he's gone to China. But what's happened
Since up those flinty slopes along the Nile
Chasing the "slayers of cave dwellers," "hackers of cities,"
Discussing Tutankhamen, turn-coat, prospered
Like Luxor's yellow walls with bougainvillea
While Akhnaton by his neighbors hustled,
Thrust to a borrowed tomb, his name defaced —
There was Alison. And there was Spain.
Neighbors! Confound them. The talk. And the boy dying.

Here. Sit down. You'd like a drink. It's cold.
I tell you, fellow, I am glad to see you. Someone
Who knows him as he was and is. Confound it,
Except for George and me and our own crowd,
You'll run against the damnedest strange opinions
About our best precentor. Just December,
When he was in the city at rehearsals,
I went about with him a bit — to listen.
His colleagues saying now the greatest years,
Europe's best, this new world's first adulthood,
Here great art, great audience, so why
He'd choose this year departure? You know how
He shuts his mouth and smiles and calls it answer.

In All Time's Change

He's not changed. Perhaps he's right. And then
The week we closed their house, trucked stuff down here,
Sent some to George. The questions down the street.
You'd think high treason, going off to China.
Perhaps he's right. Perhaps there is no answer.

Listen. You're good for a walk. Here. Take this muffler.
We'll sprint to the cove and feed ourselves. What's that?
What's she like? That's hard to say. You know
He's always a demon for finding you out. I asked him
Why it was he sometimes called her "Deirdre."
Good Lord, you *do* remember. I'd forgotten.
This time he said, "Because she has three lovers,
Naoise, Ainnle, and Ardan." And then that grin.
And George will be as tongue-tied if you ask him.
It doesn't serve us any use, you know.
No doubt she's the girl monogamy was made for.
But in their scramble, learning, making ready
For all they'll need to know in this new venture,
He'd call her *"Hsiao hsin."* He says it means
"Little heart." She says it means, "Beware."
What's she like? What she'd have to be, for him.

She sounds unlikely? But I warned you. Elsa?
She's my kind. Fellow, I am glad to see you.
I've lost ten years already. We may yet,
All of us, like Tahl, join the immortals
Off in the peach-tree paradise he talks of.
He'll see the real ones this same spring, no doubt.
And they'll be back. A year or two. A contract.
Now you mention it, I do recall —
George told me. But you wouldn't think, to look
Along that river hung with icicles,
Peach trees now, in China and Arizona.
We'll catch the seasons, flying continents.
And better for the crossing. As tomatoes.
Crossing them now with currants from Peru.
These new ones seldom wilt. But who'll explain
His going, by tomatoes, to his neighbors?
What's he up to? Technically, observer.

Uncle of Alison's there, needs adjutant,
I take it, with the new roads going in
Opening the west to India and Russia.
And a touch of political trouble he can't fathom;
And Tahl's to be his diver, eyes and ears.
No more detail. Except that Tahl once spoke
Of someone called Miguel, mistaken, thought
This Yankee took Madrid for sport. In Spain,
Similar mission. He went north. Went back.
But I've learned this, in Athens and Vienna:
Observer's often camouflage for actor.

Yes, you may hear his music, come this autumn.
He's set it in rehearsal and he's left it
With several of his apprentices among them
To nurse or murder. That's a kind of scandal.
But I believe the young ones know him better
Than some of his peers on index. I could tell you,
Hear him talk, you'd think there's nothing sadder
Than playing pedagogue; and then discover
He prays and sweats for them all, like sons and daughters.
He's got his chance, to go. And so he's left it.
But if you're near the city, you will hear it.
A local station. Friends of Alison's,
Who backed him, shook or threatened, bought the time.

His friends. God keep him. That last evening here,
He said he'd never write a note except
From Julian down to our young Buck, we'd made it.
I say it is the young ones, and perhaps,
Now I think of it, the old ones — Dad —
Who know him best. However much he swears,
There's something simple, easy in his soul.
And yet you'll find who'll tell you: hard, or proud,
Aloof, fantastic. Even, Lord, ambitious.
They see him leave the work. Go off. They search
Their souls to find his dire and dreadful purpose . . .
Won't have it just what's most his restless hoof,
His liking the world and hating treason and murder —
And maybe something pulling the whole world west.

Maybe it is a peach tree in the wind . . .
Too many guns. Whatever it is he looks for,
He never thinks that he's heard all the answer.
Maybe it's so that he stays young forever.
He keeps on thinking. And we've changed. We don't —
Except when he's around, or, like today,
Your coming unannounced and time to spend,
Sit the day out, wear the night down talking
Of what we're thinking, as we used to. True,
He's a fighter. Those days in the desert
When we'd left the Jordan — that was sport,
Of course, vacation soldiers. Now recalling
Canter, yelling, wonder often how
I managed. George, of course. He likes a fight —
The ruddy glory of being noisy. Tahl,
I guess you've always known, could always make me
What I never was. And I suppose
That's why I took this heel-split in that tavern.

What's he fighting for? well — God. It's odd.
Just spilling it out like that, straight into chowder.
Over to Greece. Then got his head clipped. Named
Thanasie. Drove a Mercedes. Now, I wonder.
No doubt the latest thing with armored turrets.
And sure, he still has theories. He'll trot
From perfect One to just no "one" at all,
To right side up — excuse it — a Christian cantor.
Precarious futures. I suppose we're chasing,
Even you and I, some kind of being
We could take a look at. Yes, you're right.
I'll follow him as far as that, to say
It's not in hard-crammed facts we'll save our souls . . .
The grab in the spirit, big "I" — and how to ride it.
And then met Alison. This Federico.
A young Basque named Felipe. And again
His usual woman trouble. And it adds
To something hardly orthodox, but still,
I guess, a kind of Christian. More of John,
Dad says, than Peter, Paul — if you can get it.
Suppose he'd say again, as in his music,

Something we did, and nothing to his credit.
He'd turn perhaps a physicist, you thought.
He might turn almost anything. May yet,
With all that he'll be up against in China.
It's maybe what he meant in saying that
You don't dispense with "why" in knowing "what"
And all he knows of "what" won't be his answer.

If you don't mind, we'll take the other road
And go back through the orchard. Take a look.
I'll show you my new grafts. Come through the winter.
At such things I've a hand in recent years.
Julian? That last night when they were here —
Seeing the grave again — I'd often wondered
How to make connections. We were sitting,
Five of us, there in the kitchen where it's warmest
Here in winter. Dad there. In a doze,
Nodding by the stove. And first, for answer,
As you'd expect, a story. Some Po Ya
He told of, played his fiddle or lute, whatever
He played, alone, on an island under the moon.
A young woodcutter listened, understood him.
Po Ya went off on journeys and came back
To find that his young friend was dead and buried.
And there he broke his instrument. But then
Alison said, "You wretch. He wants to know."
So we went into it. Can't give you all,
But here's the gist — that Julian's kind of thinking
Might not, Tahl thinks, have lasted him. You, too.
We'd rather a habit of thinking Julian knew
What there was; mere dullards so beside him.
And that'd still be true. And yet because
We've not caught up with him is not to prove
He might not go beyond himself with time,
Except he was cut down too soon. Tahl says
That Julian was — well — Greek — or an Egyptian.
He held, we felt, some mystery of knowing.
Tahl thinks we all are partly right. And Julian
Maybe saw how the mysteries composed
A signature of something real. Tahl said:

"Saw 'something' indescribable and dim
Which by the world renounced is come upon,
'Something' dimly beautiful, the first
Orpheus, Dionysus. 'Something' failing,"
And then he looked straight at me, "in Piraeus,
And on Parnassus, in Vienna, Paris,
And, last, in Spain." But here we are. You see
How this old stock has taken? Bark's as firm
As if it had been born there. What he means?
That war, I think, and burning, all that's come
Needs something more than dimly beautiful
Or myths of Dionysus to believe in.
Elsa asked him then about the priest.
We'd met one in Fiesole. Called Austin.
"Though I'm not sure," Tahl said, "if I had asked him,
Julian might have thought all politics
Indifferent to the city he could live in.
If I had asked him, I believe that Austin
Would demonstrate that politics remained
Inalienable in time. And I believe
An Austin nearer right. But I've my doubts
Of his devices for assimilation.
The freedom of saying 'no,'" Tahl said, "will break;
But not to myths of simple dragons fled
By waking up to a cold, unfleshly morning
Confident you have transcended reason.
The freedom of saying 'believe' will break," Tahl said,
"With paying many landlords for permission."
This music that we'll hear, come autumn, given
All his conscience and her patience, makes
Toward more than 'something' — balance. What they've been
And are. I don't expect that China'll change him.

Man, I'm glad to see you. It's as strange
Walking here with you in my own orchard
As it was here, that night, and natural,
That evening in the kitchen by the stove.
Dad, in his whiskers, muttering. But, come in.
Ever try shoving your feet in the oven? Works.
Here, have an apple. Nearly dug the barrels.

They'll last out April, though. Dad? Well, I'd blundered,
"Since Julian's dead and you think he'd have changed
If he had lived . . ." — that sort of thing. I heard
Tahl stepping on my brake. He can. He said,
"But in that he lives, he lives in God."
Quietly. And simply. But not Dad,
Old ranter, roaring out, "My chosen vine . . .",
Roused up, till the kettle rattled with his shouting:
"That thou shouldst crucify me!" You'll imagine.
If we'd had lightning bolts in January,
We couldn't have jumped much faster. Thought he'd drop.
Due for a shock. But no. He looked at Tahl
That way of older men — this priest I mentioned —
Old Doc, across his book when Tahl drove in
To bury Plato. Old Greek, Andreas.
Can't say just what it's like. The way perhaps
Those yearlings Tahl has left to train his chorus
Look — at Alison. What Elsa means
Perhaps, to nick me, saying I watch the road
When Alison is coming, as if I hoped
For sunrise from the south — and got my wish.

Yes, we've heard. They wired. The ocean over
Week ago. They're in Hongkong. And soon
Or maybe now, much farther west — or east —
Depending how you look. It's safe? Lord, no.
Of course it isn't safe. What is? With now
Jettisoned bombs on Europe . . . Asia, longer.
Who's ordering the drinks in La Rotonde?
At least they won't pull down Napoleon,
His cannon column. Melt Chopin for casings
Shipped from Poland. Hear the cannon trust
Does service. Table and cue. The score's unsettled.
Tahl doesn't expect they'll like him where he's going.
He said as much. Sure, there'll be those who like him.
There always are. Not states nor boundaries
Determine who likes whom. Asked Alison
Would they come back if trouble really broke.
That smile of hers. "Do you know Yun Chung-tse?"
Trick mirrors, so she says, for chasing foxes.

Then, lashes up. And straight. "But all devices
Inadequate to save Wu Wang, his friend.
Chung-tse went into the battle himself." For her?
They still keep school. And she spent months in Spain.
And if she finds an hour between the raids,
She's after what's to learn among the tribes
In those re-opened mountains. Chasing moons,
You think. As he's been moonstruck, too. No doubt
You'd say it to his face. He wouldn't blench.
George tried it. Answers, only that left eyebrow
Slightly askew to show he's not dead-solemn,
"Sure, George. Your friend, Wu Kang, at the yellow moon-tree,
Condemned through all eternity to strike
The stalk and try to cut it down. He can't.
With every blow each new incision closes."

You know, of course, our men, the Flying Tigers.
That's all this Buck of mine will hear about
And damned determined no one goes to China
For any other reason. Anyhow,
With Tahl explaining to my sprout how guns,
Four at once, can fire through one propeller,
How to distinguish bombers from pursuit,
I heard him also teaching fliers' rules,
The boy reciting them back like catechism.
Your guess, as mine, if he'll survive in China.

Are you still superstitious? Queer. Remember,
"Won't own a set of books in a full edition."
Still think you'll die when you do? I've grown more wary
And think sometimes — for instance, something in it,
Not planting trees in waning moons. And lately,
Tagging me, field and office, that a death
"Never comes once, but soon come three." Discover
I'm saying; That boy of Tahl's. And, by the way,
There's answer for you. Who'd anticipate . . .
That trim young mare; and rugged as he is . . .
If ever there were two who love each other
And ought to have. . . . Well, let it go. I tell you,
I'll never understand them. Since last summer

Into the Sea

They've been the calmest people you could find.
Some unconcern that's not indifference.
Perhaps they'll chance it over. It's quite likely.
Me? We'll have another. Damn it. Money.

"Periphrastic." Old Doc. Haven't heard
A word. Five years ago. Vienna. Thinks
This world's a great periphrasis of something
Simple. Not here finished. And Tahl knows it,
And Alison. And I do, mostly. Still
I think of Alison weeping those three days
We sat it out until we knew for sure
That infant, though he fought, could not fight out
Against a leaking heart. And heard her sobbing,
"Is he someone? A person?" How's to answer.

Dad's next. Absurd, of course. We're not of blood,
Tahl and I. Not table, cue, to make
Carom in single game. And likelier
Mother, lost in worlds where nothing matters.
Gnawing in the brain. Best spray myself
Tomorrow when I go to spray the apples.

Won't answer, here, or India or China.
Down shore some miles from here the tide threw up
A dozen crates. Among the planks and lifebelts.
Bombay. To *Canada.* Packed in Bombay. We notice.
Living on the coast, we see the wreckage.

Don't hurry. You'll see Buck. He's full of war.
Halt! He'll come in. And count-step. Halt! Present arms!
Maybe she's right. ". . . need only fear destruction
When it attacks within the soul's dimension."
Maybe he's right. "When man is man destroying,
There's no escaping from the soul's dimension."

I bud cuttings. Stock nor scion, neither
Dominant. Just wish his neighbors were
Good listeners. You always were, old man.
He buds cuttings. Land engrafts with land.
Nowhere too far to feed from stock to scion.

TAHL : BOOK FOUR

CANTO III

INTO THE SEA

When Transforming is Transfiguration

When transforming is transfiguration,
Pillars stand between a wide lagoon and quiet river.
Marble man with hollow cheeks and wide and gentle mouth.
Memory remains.
Marble man with eyes both wise and merciful
There enshrined forever
for whom he saved the union.

When transforming is transfiguration,
Pillars stand between the sea and sea-eroded land.
Memory remains.
And one there flung himself upon the cliffs for having seen
A black sail riding doom upon horizons.
Upon that ship the careless son who came a savior
Bringing liberation.
Lord and father, death on Sunion fallen.

When transforming is transfiguration,
He transformed was lord of seas,
He transformed possessed the great white bull;
He transfigured was a lord of seas,
He transfigured last will own
A heard and viewless horn.
All their pillars stand. All their pillars fallen.
Only sound. Only sound remains.

Into the Sea

On the dulcimers prepare
The tune of long-haired girls.
Honey's the color of true-love's hair.
Dulce melos.
The tune of sea-run creeks, of lonesome valleys,
Of stalwart men upon the seas and valleys.
His Virgin Mother did the Child chastise
With the bitter, bitter willow wand.

On the strings prepare
The words in warm July.
In candlelight of night confirm,
By thirteen signs, a Jonathan
Went wounded home from Lexington,
His bullet from the scarlet men.

On the strings and horns prepare
The compass running of a river.
Here Columbia between the rocks
Falls to the Pacific.
Later, the beautiful orchards.
We saw the sea from the cape called Disappointment.

To the lyre and aulos tell the legend:
He had been to countries dark with mist;
With Jason ventured for the golden fleece;
Had slain the torturers, the robber Skiron.
To free his people from the silver belts,
The false sea's lord, the white bull's domination,
He left his lord and father, promised, waiting,
On that cape and sea-lord's cliff at Sunion.

On the strings and horns and flutes prepare
The bayoneted madman with the beard.
And not enough, beside his dying sons.
We hanged him.
But his soul goes marching to the strings and flutes and horns.

On the strings and horns and flutes and drums
With blue and gray and black and white and blood,

When Transforming is Transfiguration

To the gentleman whose sash was red —
Red is blood —
The gentleman whose tunic crumpled blue —
Blue is air to breathe —
Said, "Let them take, take each his horse to plow."
These men, hand in hand, at Appomattox
When the peach trees bloomed.

To the lyre and aulos tell the legend:
Daedalus with Icarus designed
The labyrinthine house, the double axe,
And, our December, rose from chains and sprockets,
Rose in air — a bay off Carolina.

Against the twelve-tone pipe the sound repeating:
If the father die, the son may live;
The bull of Crete, the bull of Marathon
Also slain and offered on the altar.
Despised, sent out, and fled from Attica,
Theseus far from Sunion, exiled, dying,
He who brought our freedom was transformed.

If the father die, the son may die.
In December valleys barefoot men
Who followed Jonathan that he was shot
By a bullet from the man in scarlet.
Father, lead us from December cold.

On an April fallen now is risen
From the pillared altar by the river,
Hollow cheeks and wide and gentle mouth.
Father, lead us from the noise of battle.

Never boast too soon.
The patient fathers father careless heroes.

If white-skinned bulls, such power be slain,
The people freed of tribute,
The young man in his triumph coming home
Lost Ariadne who was merciful,

Into the Sea

Let ride the death-black sail of funeral.
And those dim eyes on Sunion's cape have burst
The bonds of light and broken sound to crying.
Gather the broken lord from surf and spray
Under the cliffs of Sunion.

If white-skinned bulls, such power be slain,
The people freed of tribute,
The young man from the woman has accepted
The cross-hilt, willow-leaf, bronze blade, and leapt
And slain the mighty-shouldered, two-horned power.
And power is transformed,
The labyrinthine galleries transformed,
The power broken and the pillars fallen.
Gather the broken lord from surf and spray
Under the cliffs of Sunion.

If white-skinned bulls, such power be slain,
Who are these to sacrifice still coming?
The redly dark as alder bark and once
Among the bison on the plain. Were once
Bison known in Spain, in Altamira,
In the grottoes, red and black and brown.

If white-skinned bulls, such power be slain,
Who are these to sacrifice still coming?
The richly dark as ebony is dark
And durable and highly prized. Were once,
Beyond the Nile and over mighty rivers,
Lords. The pillars fallen, only fallen.

If white-skinned bulls, such power be slain,
Who are these to sacrifice still coming?
The honey-bright, the peach-bloom, skin of almond.
But if to give, then honey, fruit, and tree branch.
Lord, the pillars fallen, only fallen.

If white-skinned bulls, such power be slain,
Who calls the surgeon to the sacrifice?
Attend this serious bleeding. Wrap them warm.

When Transforming is Transfiguration

Here naphtha, alcohol, and turpentine.
To see their injuries will make them sick.
Bind their eyes and do not let them look.

If white-skinned bulls, such power be slain,
Who calls the woman to the sacrifice?
To wash the dark red blood from lagging veins,
From jetting arteries the bright blood streaming.
The fire was red. Their nails are blue. Make warm
The shuddering eucharist. Lay gently down.

Of transforming and transfiguration
First transforming is the bull called god.
The young man who will slay him ends the tribute.
First extension.

Of transforming and transfiguration,
First transforming: Riding Scyths. And riders
By archipelagoes. The soil and blood
To other brotherhood. Transforming. Nor
To Indies nor to India alone
First extension.

Of transforming and transfiguration,
First transforming: On the Peking pike
The ballasting of stone the way to Chosen.
The yak with crescent horns, the plodding zos
Among the middle mountains. Trails by cattle.
Trails by hunters. Skins of cattle, raft
Across the rivers toward the lands of cattle,
The cattle humped and horned and polled, the zebu,
Kaffir's bull, and ox, the long-neglected,
Toward lord of bulls and one-time Crete,
The bull transformed, the lord of bulls and islands.

Never boast. For not in us salvation.
Were never first not last, the sons of Theseus
Who slew the bulls of Crete and Marathon;
And, by forgetfulness, his lord on Sunion.
Know the good. The good was in the freeing.

Know the evil. Often, in forgetting.
None shall judge atonement, retribution.
The woman merciful, one night forgotten,
Still attended, found upon an island,
Gone with Dionysus to the east,
Gone with Dionysus to the west,
Departed and returned through many seasons.

When transforming is transfiguration,
All assist and all beware
The work without, the work within;
And know transforming is the first,
Transfiguration is the last.
The sum is liberation.

On the dulcimers prepare
The tune of long-haired girls.
Honey's the color of true-love's hair;
The grape where blue's most black, her hair;
As ruddy rowan shines her hair —
Dulce melos.
The tune of sea-run creeks, of lonesome valleys,
And up, swing up, swing up, swing up in the air.
The virgin Mother did the Child chastise.
The bitter withy, bitter willow wand.

Because these years so much has been transformed,
We thought Buck ought to know when he grows up
What's happening; to make a book and bound,
A record of his time. And so I clip
The pictures and the headlines. But I've found
Never time to bind them.
How Tahl laughed to find them
Stuffed among my recipes. Said, "Elsa,
Take care you don't serve spiced 'pursuits' for breakfast."
Months ago. Before they left for China.

Now they've left Hongkong. Planes still on schedule.
Gone northwest — Chungking; or west, Yunnan —

Kunming — depend on space and time. We know
Only what we hear. These raids on London.
Germans now in Athens. Radio.
Whatever Buck's doing, he listens.
"Chungking." "Athens." "London."
He's seven now. What does he think? He'd not
A sob or start when Alfred's father died.
Kept on whistling, "bombing" the east porch.

I wonder what Buck sees when he hears "Chungking"?
"Athens"? "London"? I see porcelain,
Jade and willows in the prints, still knowing
That's not China. Tahl and Alison
Talked of botany, law, and books by thousands
Brought from China. Now
In Washington. And how
We've learned from Chinese farmers. Then that song.
Buck knows it now. They taught him. *Feng Ch'iu Huang.*
What can he know of "lovers ever-living"?

Excited now that George's child is coming.
They're moving east. New York. A trial to Iris,
The new child due, just three months off. We're hoping
A girl around may be right antidote
For shrieking planes; we're keeping Julie. Waiting
For news, of Tahl. More cause
Than "seeing the world." The laws
For men his age to travel. As for that,
We know them. And those two have never gone
"To see the world," to point it on a map.

I miss them. I miss Alison. Last summer
Walking near the marsh, the monarch's flare
Of wings on purple weeds. Her eyes much keener
Than my own. The light, that under-glare
Of thunder coming, sumac leaves turned over.
Shrill of birds. She saw him,
That one frightened fledgling.
I thought . . . Gamaliel . . . the Spanish children.
I think of her. She's like an orchid. Strange,
Complex, both strong and delicate, enduring.

No letters. Just in brief. "Arrived." and "Leaving."
The last she wrote, she told about their crossing
Great Salt Lake. Because I'd told her once
My grandfather had seen them drive the spike
That joined the rails. She wrote about the arch,
The San Francisco bridge,
The ferry through the fog.
Of course old Granddad's gone. And I've not seen
My father eight years now. First Buck. The trip
For Alfred. But we write. Don't seem apart.

We'd Alfred's father here with us, the last.
Already here when Tahl and Alison
Came the final Sunday. When they'd left,
He turned his old keen eyes on Alfred, "Gone,"
He said. "The young man's gone. They're going home."
"They're coming back," Alf said.
They're going to China, Dad,"
I said. He would not be put off. "Gone home,
His failing voice, "to show that girl of his
To those his fathers came from. Going home."

"He's sick and old and wandering," I thought.
But listened, both of us. Along this coast
In his young days, he said, the skippers brought
Among their crews new men from western islands.
We strained. The words came hoarse,
"And your grandfather's eyes
Saw their great stone temples on the headlands
Far in that Pacific. Mind you, Alfred,
That young man had a granddad. Going home."

He slept, then, in his chair. We thought we'd look.
'Were navigators by the stars.' 'They built
Decked ships, both caulked and pitched.' 'They were much sought
For crews by Yankee captains.' 'Eyes are black,
Sometimes oblique.' 'Skin, olive.' 'Mouth well-shaped.'
'After the chief, the wife ranks first,
And then his brother.' 'Formerly worshipped
In groves of trees with pyramid and altar.'

'The men are notably tall.' And, 'orchids grow.'
'On various islands nutmeg found and ginger.'

Of course they've gone to China. Had their word.
And there's not one of us has ever heard
From Tahl of those Pacific islands. Rather
I'd call it spice to dash a thought with. Ginger
Comes from China also. From Malaya
Nutmeg, also. And these old coasts gather,
Sweet as nutmeg, spice of recollection,
Sharp as ginger. Condiment. And whether
It's true or mad, it's like. And I have loved him.

And I can't quite forget. But Alfred thinks
His father only wandering. Now he's gone.
And Buck's great-grandfather, we know, went out
With others. And no doubt he saw those islands.
Marquesas to Moluccas. Cloud of islands.
Red rock. Black sand. Green water.
Mountains. Volcanic. Picture.
Temples with images. Some are called "Dangerous Islands."
Overgrown gardens. Nutmeg. American. Dust
On eggnog. Whether it's true or mad, it's like him.

TAHL : BOOK FOUR

CANTO III

INTO THE SEA

In Complexities of Variation

Try the tune with variation;
Complexity of complication:

The children at the tree. The children at the tree.
No one turns a Maypole now.
The cordite sours the Christmas bough.
The children's hammocks swing between
The rails that run beneath the Thames.
Swing. Swing up in the air.

The children at the fire. The children at the fire.
No bonfire's built for games well won.
No summer campfires in the sun.
Asturian miners teach for trade
The game of well-thrown hand grenades.
Swing. Swing up in the air.

The children off to school. The children off to school.
The concrete bombproof's near the yard.
The iron doors will open wide.
Four by four, well-drilled, march down.
To soundless skies march up again.
Or swing. Swing up in the air.

The freeman's child grows thin. The tyrant's child grows vain.
The tyrant's soldier floats face down

Where five Dutch children pushed him in.
The Danish children study guns
Because a Czechish boy was slain.
Swing. Swing up in the air.

The Belgian and the Polish Jew.
Allons, enfants! Where shall you go?
The Welshman's child beneath the stairs
Lies and sings and says his prayers.
Dig in. He's trapped. Watch there. The timbers.
Something fell out of the air.

What does the Chinese child remember,
Come September, four years old?
Tunnels and sounds and a weeping mother.
Four long years of fear and hunger.
Who will find her now a father?
Something fell out of the air.

What does the English child remember?
He is seven just this May.
Lights at night. And burning houses.
Was it just this last September
All his cousins drowned together?
Something came up from the sea.

Count out. Count out. By fire and tree,
By soft torpedoes through the sea.
Count out. Count out. By name and nation
Bonfires built for celebrations.
Try the tune with variations.
Swing. Swing out of the air.

"Julie, now's your turn. You tell a story."

"I came on a train and it goes and goes.
What I like best is lakes and lakes.
I came on a train to here."

Into the Sea

"That's the ocean, Julie. Say, 'The ocean.'"

"Ocean. Ocean. Ocean. Ocean.
Anyhow, it goes and goes."

"Your white bracelet, Julie. I won't hurt it.
It's a game. I'll show you how to play it.
First we'll put your little white bracelet here.
This is east."

"What's east?"

"It's east. It's where
There is a war. Now, Julie, please sit there
Because your overalls are blue. That's south."

"What's south?"

"It's south. It's where the deserts are.
I'll put my pencil here because it's black
And black is north."

"What's north?"

"It's north. It's where
There is a star. But yellow color's hard.
And now I've no St. Johnswort. That's in summer.
It's only May."

"What's that?"

"It's yellow flowers.
Say it, Julie. Say 'St. Johnswort.'"

"No."

"Please. He says I have to say it. How's
To ever know except? Please say it."

"No."

"Please!"

"Violets!"

"That's *other* flowers."

"No."

"Well, Julie, anyhow we have to find it.
I know. I'll just sit here myself. It's west.
And Dad says I'm a towhead. And I said,
'Why do you call me that for?' And he said,
'Because you got yellow hair.' Now. There. Pretend
There's now a spider."

"What's a spider?"

"Julie!
Spiders are bugs. They're good. And in the summer
I'll find you one down there. We'll maybe look
Even today as soon as tide goes out.
I like when tide is out, except it's queer.
You die when tide is out, he said. But they
Always say, 'No, never when it's high.
You might forget and catch a wave. You wait
Till tide is out.'"

"What's *die*?"

"It's what they do
When they get old with whiskers. Maybe why
I don't die when tide is out down there.
But now, *there's* Spider Woman."

"Where?"

"Why, *there*.
In the middle. See? I'll take my pencil
And make a little tunnel. Now she's coming."

"Where?"

"*Please,* Julie. Now she'll tell a story.
Only you mustn't tell. Not ever, ever.
She says no one believes the spider's stories."

"I'm afraid."

"We're safe as safe in here
Because your overalls are blue. Don't cry.
We won't play Spiders. There. *I'll* tell the story."

"*Lakes!* I know about lakes."

"I know about lakes.
They come all nights when Indians make singing.
They come from Dawn Lake. Once a boy went with them.
He said to Younger Brother, 'I will see you.'
But Younger Brother's gone, so we can't play."

"I have a brother."

"Have you? Does he wear
Blue overalls, like you?"

"Yes . . . . I don't know . . . ."

"My Brother's a biggest horse. And he can fly.
Look, Julie, past the tree. The rocks. The tide.
It's lying still and shivering. It's turning.
I can go alone when tide is out."

"I want about *lakes.* And horses. I *know* about horses.
They go in the park. And boats. I want about boats."

"You want to climb the tree? Don't have to stay
Now we'll not play Spiders. Come, now. Up!
There. I'll put my arm around you. Look!
The waves are off the rocks. I like it here.
Up here . . . in the leaves. It's like . . . to fly.

Julie, do you like to fly? Quick. Look!
That's the oriole. Now, honey-girl,
Would you like to fly? Like orioles?"

"What's 'honey-girl?'"

"Why, what he says to her."

"Who's her?"

"*You* know."

"I know! We go for lakes!"

"And did you swim? She taught me how to swim."

"I want to swim."

"I'll teach you how to swim."

"I like him. That one."

"That's a robin, Julie.
His front is red."

"My hair is red."

"I know.
But this is feathers red. But I like best
The oriole. You want to climb down now?
Be careful, then. Here, I'll go first and help you.
I know! Come on. In the box. We'll play a war.
Here. Make a great big trench. Now, see. Oh, Julie,
No! Not just dig anywhere. Like this.
You make it big, to crawl through. Where's your bracelet?
I know. The tree. I didn't mean to leave it.
We'll use it for a look-through. Handkerchief!
Sand won't hurt it. Camouflage. Say that.
I like it. *Camouflage.* Two . . . Three . . . Four . . . Five . . .
Now, when you shoot, you catch them. Bing! I know.

We'll use your bracelet for a bomb. There. Wham!
Be careful, Julie. Sand might hurt your eyes.
But first we have to have the planes. Zoom! Zoom!
Then, wham! Now here they come. Zip, zip! Now, there.
They're dead."

"I said it, Buck! I said it! *Zoom!*"

"You really say it loud. I like you, Julie."

"Then tell about the *lakes.*"

"I told you, Julie.
We can't play Dawn Lake. But I know Wu Ling
And that's a kind of lake."

"Well . . . Wu Ling lake."

"There's your bracelet. We don't want to lose it.
Now this will be the village. By the tree.
You have to have a river. But the brook,
It's there across the road and near the marsh.
We have to stay right here. So just pretend.
First an eagle comes. A magic eagle.
And then I kill him."

"Why?"

"So I can fly.
You say, 'Goodbye, Wu Ling.' "

"No! No!"

"But, Julie,
If I'm Wu Ling, I have to reach the stream.
And then I'll find a boat and that goes down.
It's dark, a cave. And then a lovely place.
You say, 'Goodbye, Wu Ling.' "

"I want to come!"

"But, Julie, that's not in the game."

"Yes! Yes!"

"Just say, 'Goodbye, Wu Ling.' I won't go off.
I just pretend. I'll tell you all the things.
The river, in the cave, and where I come."

"I want to come!"

"Well, then, you be Wu Ling.
I'll be the village. But I'll kill the eagle."

"But I don't *know* the story!"

"Well then, just
We just can't play Wu Ling about the lake
That's in the cave."

"I *want* about the lake."

"I know. Don't cry. I know. *We'll* just be *both!*
The tree will have to say, 'Goodbye, Wu Ling.'
We'll, you and me, we'll just both be Wu Ling
And fly and find the boat and find the cave.
The tree will have to say, 'Goodbye, Wu Ling.'
And then we'll fly on eagle's feathers. See?
The eagle feather's magic. See? Oh, look,
The tide is really going. We can play
Wu Ling down there. Much better in the cove
With really rivers, really caves and lakes
When tide is low where you can't ever go
Except it's run way out."

"And we won't fall?"

"No, Julie. I'll take care of you. I'm strong.
Besides, it's only really little rivers.
Remember? Where we're going?"

"Ocean. Ocean."

"It's maybe, 'sea.' But I like better 'ocean.'
It sounds like . . . Zoom. Like waves. Like zoom, zoom, ZOOM!"

TAHL : BOOK FOUR

CANTO III

INTO THE SEA

All Judgment Fallible Except the Last

All judgment fallible except the last.
No Delphic word, no pilgrim from T'ai Shan,
Quincunx of sacred mountains, here attest
The serpent dead, first python, oldest dragon.

Within this quiet room. But have you heard
Of Europe? Thousands competently done
Neatly to bath and ashes? Who will dread
The clever massacre, the quickest poison?

Within this quiet room. But have you heard
Of thousands driven cleverly through Asia?
The genitals crushed, the rape, the severed head,
The fine aesthetic of the art of torture.

Within this quiet room. But time, remaining
Past each barrier reef and shallow sea,
Abides Australian fauna still sustaining
The mesozoic reptile company.

Within this quiet room. But night commands:
"Mark green." And swing the handles, train the muzzle
Through the sight, the cross within the circle.
Heavy caliber focus. Mark red. Mark green.

All Judgment Fallible Except the Last

Naga, winged caduceus, long plumed serpent,
Jewel of Delphi, Thebes, and Babylon,
Poseidon-sea, earth-shaker, cosmic water,
Procreator, spouter, long-tailed dragon.

Devourer, pitiless dragon, foulest dragon,
Dragon of earth's periphery and spectrum.
The blood runs cold. The heart devoured. Resume
The serpent's coil. Surround this quiet room.

Within this quiet room. When overpast
The last imagination, mounted skulls,
This dragon mound of Time, the stopped throat pulls
Against the ineffectual strangled scream.

Mark green. Mark red. Mark upper, lower target.
Periphery. The serpent. The heart's apple.
Do not forget our anger. Do not forget
Through the sight, the cross within the circle.

Do not forget the fine aesthetic. Would you
Have your son the delicate crusher of genitals?
Have your daughter determine by exquisite slaughter
Who may survive for her pleasure? Say it so. Softly.

There's no use screaming. In this time. Has happened.
We thought we had killed the python, the elegant dragon.
Some who will die. Who wished to slay. Remember.
Do not forget. Do not forget their anger.

Uncertainly, faultily, check with the heart, the skulls.
All must judge, upon this mound, this treasure.
And, overpassed, find measure of their measure.
All judgment fallible except the last.

It is too soon to judge there is no hope.
I keep, as when they left, no further doubt
Than we still have that Dad himself survives
In spite of winter shooting on the Yangtze,

Into the Sea

In spite of January's civil wars,
In spite of much we cannot understand
From captured cities to the western mountains.
Where there's no wire or wireless, where the word
Come out from where they've overpassed Kunming
Takes months, we still may hear. And, Mother, no one
More than Tahl I'd trust to find a way.
That country's not more strange than any country.
Men and women live among the mountains.
Have you never thought our country strange?
I have. The time Dad took us West. We saw
The derricks standing out to sea, the mission
There above the bay. I'd never thought
Of derricks in the ocean; and, above them,
Earnest monks in cassocks. When we think:
"America" — the laboratories, schools —
As Stephanie says, "The 'thank you' and the smile
That's really meant." Then, thugs. And noise. And shoddy.
That time, the mills — the tips and furnaces —
The one thick-muscled man outside. He turned . . .
And on his hip the holstered gun. Who is
American? Or which Chinese? We talk
About the Russians. Austrians. This week
With Stephanie. And she's no stranger more
Than Minna. Almost think she's far less strange
Than either of the Wills, the father, son,
Their world of landed eminence recalling
No first garage to grow from. Yet we talk
One language and it's not by dictionary
Of Richmond or Detroit or this New York.
We sat about at dinner. Heard the broadcast.
Russia, newest victim. Will and George
Discussing prize fights and Joe Louis winning.
Leningrad. Toward Moscow. And I thought,
They also sit at dinner. Argentina
Through Brazil? That dream I had. With Julie.
George shouting, "*La guerre! La guerre!*" I'm very well.
No dreams so far, with this one. Will New York
Remain unstrafed, unburnt, for this one's coming?
The Huns will have too much to do, this summer,

Gorging Russia. Perhaps it's Alison
With her intelligence of dying empires
Makes me fearful, confident at once.
It's Tahl. Or you. Some commonwealth surviving.
No sounds but clicking icebox doors, no sounds
But elevators in the shafts. You said,
The first time you saw Tahl, you felt the room
Shake when he came in. And George remarked
About the suffering Chippendale. We knew
What it was you meant. George knew. He said:
"From any high hill a man can take a landscape
Between his thumb and index." George has changed.
Again? Of course. I don't mean pendulum.
He's only nearer George I've always known.

Monday evening. Fire with fire in Russia.
Senior speaking of fires, Virginia woodlands
This dry spring, the speculation whether
The fires were set. The library. And Minna,
Looking about at the prints, the books, the lamps —
You know they've George's painting of the dragons —
"And must this burn? Tell me? Why were we born?"
Upon that trim insouciance I have mentioned,
Junior's ash snapped off from his cigar
Down his tie and crumbled. Stephanie
Seemed to avoid his eyes. But it was George . . .
He'd behaved his usual self for hours,
Turning prize fights, race tracks into game
Semi-unprintable, feinting for Stephanie, gamer,
Except for Alison, than any woman
Flirting, to outflirt him . . . Stephanie calling him
"Papageno" . . . pleased him, and annoyed him —
This Harlequin of mine who said, "We're born,
Minna, for exactly what we own
When we've lost what's ours." And Junior brushed
His ashes — his expression worth a portrait
Between his connoisseur's appreciation
And wish, I much suspect, that he had said it.
And I'd remembered Yankees in Virginia.
And Stephanie met Will's eyes. And Minna said,

"Coffee, Papageno?" I wanted to hug them,
All of them. Senior asked, as if he knew
What else I'd been thinking, "There's no news?
Iris, there's no news?" What Dad has written,
No word from them nor from the crew or plane,
No news of crash. Perhaps beside the lakes.
Investigating. Hoping. Stephanie said,
"Tahl came through the mountains there in Spain
Alone and by the stars." And Minna said,
"Alison never was afraid of country."
Of Jim and Alison in Christmas weather
Ten years ago, nine years ago, out hunting
Beside the James, below the Blue Ridge mountains,
Ranging high ground, low ground, through the brambles,
Grass and foxgrape. "Partridge?" I asked. "Quail,"
Senior answered, "but we call them partridge."
"She could handle a twelve-gauge gun," he said.
Desultory. Commonplace. "Jim's hill."
"Junior's woods." And Junior saying, "Once
I set the ace of hearts into the fence post
And Alison drilled it, first shot and quick draw,
And with Jim's 45." I'd never felt
So far from Alison. How do we know?
In Yucatan a year. Then, Christmas weeks.
Incidental. Jim, although he'd talked
Always of Alison's "gyahdens" (I have her plants
With me, here, you know. They're flourishing) . . .
But now, here, with his people. . . . Not as strange
As we have felt with George's people. Still,
Something we've not known. That evening, debating
Our dismay at official assassination.
And arguing over Spain. Then Junior said,
"I've thought about Jim's talk of gravitation.
How Newton's laws would work where force was weak,
But needed further formulas to cover
Stronger forces. And that may explain
Jim, his going." Minna saying, "Will!
Why, Will!" Like that. And Senior, thin and grave,
The true old mandarin, his long hands arched
Over his cup, "Yes, Minna. We forget

This heir of ours, once on a time, could not
Appreciate coloratura. He develops,
As we do, with age, an ear." He'd turned
To me, "George knows. I've told him. My opinion
Of common men as we're all common men,
Worth the saving and may save ourselves.
But I most feared, for Jim, he might be caught
By those who make the fetish, saying prayers
To Man, the fetish. I shall always say
My younger son fell martyr to a cause
That's to his credit. But the while he lived,
I hoped to show him Thomas Jefferson
Did not displace the Deity by saying
There is virtue also in the people."
Gravely. Just that moment. Minna asked me
If I had been admitted to rehearsals.
I've not gone, though I shall. Most capable,
The orchestra, they say; the chorus, learning.
The young conductor Tahl preferred, in charge.
The singers "mixed," they said. And I protested.
They meant the Negroes. And perhaps, was clumsy,
Protesting. Stephanie was with me, saying
Tahl said, if they were "mixed," then so was he.
And Minna's forthright. Likes us so. We left it.
It's definite. September. Over the water
Terrible deaths and ruthless. Mother, no,
I do not worry, never fear. Because
Julie is all right. And Alison
Herself, almost the day she left, and feeling,
As you have felt, that I might have bad dreams?
Assured me that it's most unlikely. No.
He'll be born. Or she. And live. I wish . . .
But they're alive. I meant to say, we went
From Papageno, sopranos and rehearsals
Off to Senior saying that he thought
Whoever writes Tahl's notices should not
Neglect the Mozart clarinet quintet.
And Minna said, "The *Lacrymosa.* But
Tahl has lived to finish. And . . . the *Flute.*"
And George said, "Might include a Salieri.

Himself. To plague him." Stephanie was quoting
Tamino's song about the night to vanish.
"And when will there be light . . ." I try to tell you
Because there were just six of us and still
Were always eight of us. No matter how
Minna steered us, Senior would come back
Or George or Will. And even Stephanie . . .
Though often easiest in raillery
The while they talked it out, tonalities,
Contrasts, themes, not text to music, music
Turning text to state of mind. She said,
"G major, Papageno. That's your key."
And George at loss. He doesn't know the *Flute*
Enough to catch so deft a point. Though Minna
Screened him with observing Alison
Had told her Tahl insisted on C minor.
Senior, looking up at George's painting,
"Yes. C minor. The dragon. And darkness." And left
Poor Harlequin more lost. Young Will remarked,
"I think it's rather Handel more than Mozart."
And Stephanie said, "You mean a source in common."
And Minna, "Yes. In that he's gone beyond
Wagnerian dissolution and come back."
"But that is still 'beyond,' I said. And this
Sent us into meaning, saying 'beyond.'
The *Flute,* as Stephanie says, was nothing new
In fugue and arioso. "But the structure,"
Junior said. "And when I first read Tahl's,
The first time, when he came, we tried it over.
The architecture . . ." Whether the palace baroque,
The skyline of New York? To say 'beyond'?
And we agreed they both achieve and build
Within their times. And if there's more C minor
Attacking E flat major, shall we judge
That, for the last, it's one beyond the other?
I thought of Alison loving the *Alleluia*
Every Easter. Wished I hadn't seen her
Suddenly there. And where, this April past?
Three months now since they left Hongkong. We turned
Around and around, the six of us, attacking

Theories of property, debating
Aristotle and what's Christian "common";
How to judge. What Tahl thinks. What Jim thought.
If man is free and still not man to trust?
Trying to remember. Whether love,
Perfect or imperfect, can survive
In how much common goods for good. You know —
How who's to say who says what's right, what's wrong.
And how such talk moves on around the world.
Magellan. And El Cano. Junior saying,
"Yes. On his face in surf and pierced with lances,
Magellan, at Mactan." I said, "El Cano.
He came back." And Junior said, "Serrano
Married a woman from Java and never came back.
The blood of that crew is still flowing the veins of the gentry
In the Moluccas." "Alison said," then Minna,
"'The once unknown against the known already.'"
Mother, all that evening. Coming back.
They told of someone . . . Minna's family . . . going,
When the Pacific was a Spanish ocean,
To study its winds and weathers. Then I thought
Of just three years ago, Tahl still in Spain,
We read of a tribe discovered, unknown thousands . . .
East Indies, an island valley. Said so. Then
George, suddenly, so loud the Chinese cups
Shuddered . . . , "Damn!" It came, as once in Paris,
Shattering; but this time much less anger,
More like anguish. He stood up and walked
Straight toward Minna. There beside her wheeled
And faced us. "Look," he said. "If we must talk,
Let's have it out. They're gone. And it's my fault.
I dragged him out of Egypt. Why? I sent him
What he'd need to keep him there in Spain.
I put it in his head to go to China.
Why? Because it's what I'd do myself
If I'd the honesty and nerve. I haven't.
What did I do in Greece? And Iris knows.
I sat there shoving them in. And it was Alfred.
He got slugged. And it was Tahl who grabbed
That damned lieutenant's gun. I'd like to tell you.

Sure. I'm Papageno. I've no manners."
"George," Minna said, "sit down." He sat. Or crumpled,
There on the floor beside her chair. Like shame.
Like that which should not happen. Blurting out.
And he kept looking somewhere toward the windows.
My throat clamped fast, like nightmare. Must say something.
My voice came hollow, "Weren't they always going?"
And Minna, echoing, ". . . were always going."
Then Old Will, sternly, "George, get up!
Come here." And George unwound himself and came
And took the cigarette he offered, sat
On the divan beside me. Watched the windows.
Stephanie, then, "But, Iris, do you think
Something in us moves us where we're going?"
I heard more questions there than this she asked,
But struggling in the silence, could not take them.
"Tahl," I said, "before we knew him, knew
About Huang Ti, the wheels, the boats, the flutes,
The phoenix and the unicorn appearing
Within his garden when he came to die.
And that *San Kuo* and those who fought Ts'ao Ts'ao,
Chang, Liu, and Kuan, the league in the peach tree garden . . .
And Ts'ao Ts'ao's navy sunk with firebrand arrows."
George spoke, at last. "The painter, Ts'ao Fu-hsing
To me like Polygnotus lost at Delphi,
Rendering the sack of Troy and, counter,
Odysseus down to underworlds for answers."
I saw us then like shadow play, our figures
Rigid in their gestures. Minna there
Substantial, her firm hands dropped in her lap
Motionless. And Senior's cigarette,
The pale long holder, motionless, in air,
Waiting. Stephanie half-leaned across
The edge of the table with books, one slender palm
Out-fanned, and fingers poised, as if she'd speak,
But did not speak. And Young Will in his chair
Clutching its arms, his pudgy knuckles blanched
And stronger than I'd thought. And I myself
Somehow there chief actor and my voice
Distant, through a shadow screen. I said,

"Alison. Indians. Their sacred mountains.
And Tahl had told her of T'ai Shan, the others,
The mountains at the quarters, in the center.
Dragons. Serpents flying. In the jungles.
The Chinese sun. He told her, the Hindu Naga;
But others were Scyths, who worshipped trees and serpents.
Indian or India and also
Repeating, found again, America.
The sacred almanacs. The dates on stelae.
The cycle of Venus. The cycle of moons. The cycle
In which the sign will not return though turned
Through all eternity. Beyond the mountains
Once were those Hsiung-nu who troubled China.
The Lissu, Lutzu, west. She's always gone
To find them and to ask them, crossbow bearers,
Skillful hunters. Also known to lamas,
The mountains, colors, masks. By straits and islands.
Tombas in Yunnan, the old men dying
Like teachers in the pueblos George has seen.
Tribe to tribe the wanderers inventing,
All remembering and all transmuting.
Tahl goes with her. There no shaman's learned
A man may trust his wisdom to a woman."
And George said, "Always. A city. In the west."
And gave me one quick glance, to say, 'all right.'
"Most curious information," Senior murmured.
And Junior, "Hypnotism. Something lost.
Or if they find, then what is it that's found?"
"Our ways of living and dying," I said. "The names . . .
Your partridge . . . quail . . . won't change the fact of hunting."
"Like phoenix? Unicorn?" So Senior. Smoking.
No more the rigid figures. Stephanie spoke,
Her hands relaxed upon the table, "Learning
What we learn. They've made the world their city."
Moving toward the window, passing George,
Minna, her broad, lively face provoking
Both of us to smile, and, standing there,
Majestic, drawing curtains, "Here's a city.
I've heard that we're all here. And if we are?"

So. That. And Will brought out Robida's drawings.
I think I told you. George's current passion.
And Will's, because he likes what's out of print
For his own way of hunting what's least known.
Australian juggernauts of that old Frenchman,
Fantastic submarines toward Mozambique,
The gasmasks, airships, rifles trailing wires,
Revolving cannon, all the cartooned dream
Of what might happen, George observes, when Julie
And this, our younger, due next month will be
In their prime. But now it's come. Already.
Then what will come? And Junior saying dryly
He'd toss a coin for Trinidad, Australia,
Suitable habitats in worlds gone mad.
"Consider the kookaburra," said Will. "He's quaint.
He greets Australian dawn with raucous laughter."
"Why Trinidad?" I asked. He answered, chuckling,
"The fishes sing, the crabs eat fruit for breakfast,
The oysters grow on trees. I'll be the oyster."
And Stephanie caught his eye. And other laughter,
Somewhere there among us. And we came home.

Since that evening, George at work. Remember
The flageolet dug up in Arizona?
Then, this Monday past. And years, you know,
He's promised us that portrait. I'll be sure
More like his dragons than the usual easel.
If plastic's possible in paint, he'll find it.
But sits this morning idle on the terrace
Watching the square, the long green busses beetling.
Eyeing Alison's plants. Tries leaves in lights.
And what it's to do with flutes I don't see yet.
He's left that Chinese pipe he bought "for Julie"
Here, on my desk. It's simple to play. Her fingers
Rather too small as yet. And he'll transform it.
Like Tahl. That Chinese tale. I thought he'd dreamed it.
But found — a place, Wu Ling. And one T'ao Ch'ien
Who told it long ago, in a time of troubles.
And later — poems — "The river of floating petals"
Beyond ten thousand mountains. If George is idle,

All Judgment Fallible Except the Last

You see, I'm idle too. But no more books
Of words and words from me, for you'll be coming . . .

And as for this which troubles us, I'll wait.
We'll hear Dad's found them. Safe. They'd not expect,
I know, escaping average in disasters . . .
But much too soon to judge there is no hope.

TAHL : BOOK FOUR

CANTO III

INTO THE SEA

Beyond These Boundaries

Beyond these boundaries and only, there.
The serpent of boundaries, Tiamat. Who has bound her?
The serpent sea. No one is known not drowned there.
Within this sea the blood runs down. Whose hand
Will staunch? Whose hand will cut? A pretty torture.
Mud from tide flats festers on the land.
The sound of the sea on rocks. Like footsteps coming.
The voice on the sea goes farther. Over water.
The serpent is Tiamat. Who has found and passed her?
Beyond these boundaries and only, there.

Within these boundaries and only, here.
The gun is a present weapon. Choose your target.
The serpent is in the heart. Who found it? Here.
Within this heart the blood runs down. Whose hand
Will staunch? Whose hand will pamper? A pretty torture.
Dial on cradle. Fire graze. Judge the land.
The sound of the heart that stops. Like footsteps fading.
The voice of the heart goes farther. Season of thunder.
The gun is a present weapon. Choose your target
Within these boundaries and only, here.

Within these boundaries and always, here.
Gentleness, mercy and sufferance, wisdom and grace;
Arrogance, cruelty, ignorance, torment and malice.

Beyond These Boundaries

The heart is a present weapon. Choose your target.
The sea is preserve and oblivion. A pretty torture.
A sound from the sea on rocks. Like footsteps coming.
Always. A few. They have listened. The heart. Inquired.
A voice on the sea goes farther. Over water.
The voice of the heart goes farther. Season of thunder
From over the boundary sounding. There. And here.

Here in this country and moving from state into state, across
    boundaries,
Challenge, permission, impeding us less than the wren or the
    thrasher,
Here in July in the fragrance of boxwood and ivy, this land
As before the last treaties the green curving fields of Bohemia.
Once to say, "my land." Now to say "your land." And here in
    Virgina
Here also wars have run over, remembered, forgotten,
Lamented, by trying, forgiven, and not as the ghoul with the
    purpose
Of ghouls and the sack of a continent, Panzer's beret, the insignia
Skull with the crossbones. Coming here, Will, and together, your
    saying:
"Stephanie, if you prefer it so." Not for remand or parade,
Not for prize or diversion. And saying this wide, still veranda,
These halls and these fields. And say "ours." And not turned with
    my asking,
Having learned in these years so to ask, these uncomfortable ques-
    tions. And Walther
Said, "Farmers and cooks!" But you listen. We stand on a threshold
    and doubtful
But somehow will cross in a crossing uncertain and probable, saying
As if at our births, far apart, one same stone had been laid on our
    shadows
And somewhat to which we were born at our birth born to perish;
    and still
By our fortune permit us these years of survival. Like Tahl,
    Federico,

Much that you love me. You say so. Your liking my stories. I'll tell you
Of Florian, patron of fire in the Tyrol, beseech him:
"St. Florian, guard us. This house. Burn the house of my neighbor." I know.
It's your chuckle. But, Will. If my world's end were mountains,
Wildspitze, Mont Blanc . . .
And now I have come to some doubts of the merits of Florian, ask you
Uncomfortable questions, of you most unlike either Tahl, Federico,
And still are most like for your love, least the prize and the glory of violence,
You bring me your land and say "ours" and your friendship of princes
Uncited, except noting patina, graciousness, spirit's Vienna and Paris,
Our Prague, Budapest, once as here with the hill and the plain and the river
Between. I shall trouble you, knowing too late what I'd left but now knowing
I've seen here a bondage, a fear and an ignorance waiting releasing
As much as we may, with you by me. I've been as Tahl said, as a passenger,
Every accoutrement, never perceiving the ship could be sinking
Like any poor fishing boat fighting the trough in the Biscay. Or turning
The handrail of doors to the coffeehouse waiting the fragrance, the cream,
The vanilla, from afternoon gardens. And once as in France and the names:
Gardes Républicains. There by the canopy. Helmets. The cars
Chirring. The chestnut trees candled. The awnings, the *fleur de lis.* Names:
Les Ambassadeurs. Champs Elysées. And my mother.
And there lies her country and sinking in this second summer. July.
And he said, "month of wars." And she said, "month of freemen." July. And you read

Your Montaigne. Not Lucretius. Your Yankees play baseball. You
talk of Di Maggio
And fifty-six hits. But this morning I heard, for eight hours, on
Chungking . . .
And still you endure it, my turning so solemn. I'm not. Not so
very . . .
You were solemn indeed when you showed me the church there in
Richmond, the headstones,
The door, the four steps, the bare walls, where the burgesses gathered. I thought
"Like the breaking of icons." And hardly perceiving the altar. And
still
The center is there and the reverence aware. On this afternoon air
The fragrance of box, as in Spain in July. That's both bitter and
tang.
And if, as you say, there were chestnut trees once and a blight and
none knows
And no saving. But still here are trees. Still the oaks. The mimosa.
The willows
There by the spring house. This valley is not Bucovina, Galicia,
That are strangers to you and once neighbors to me in the school
books and nearer
Than Basil regaling me legends of rocky walled Amber, the palaces
Empty and silent so near to Jaipur. And how shall we see them with
bees
That go over the garden as Igor said cats and the field mice
survived
By the grace of the bees and red clover? And how in Virginia
More than Croatia or Schleswig, Livonia, lost in their boundaries?
But we'll not depart like the Empress Elizabeth under the cypress
Regal on Corfu. Or where? To this world which now Elsa inquires of,
And you find no harder to answer than I might, Moravia? World
Of Fortunate Isles and Dangerous Isles you remark as apart
As she'll measure a continent's sweep of the ocean; and term
Polynesian
For one and not other. And yet you say Venice and Bruges by this
fortune
Of islands so far from the map of my empires, Malay and Chinese

And the brown men and black men; and, with your cigar, in your county,
But teaching me words from the ends of the earth, as this *sago* you tell me
Gives bread from a palm tree and fed your great-uncle abroad in those islands;
And on Kaerntnerstrasse my friends, at our tailor's each spring, to remark
I'd gone out to the ends of the earth, that we summered in Spain. And I've seen
The smashed planes, the burned lorries, the blood. And passed boundaries. Here, with no sound
But our voices and those in the kitchen. And now without anger in knowing
A people can rise and the *Massenmensch* shaken, aroused, and rebellious
For evil or good, now a word lacking meaning — or dies, shall we say, before we do,
In knowing the crime and contrition lie not by a caste or canal.

And Tahl. He had dreams. Did he know the conspiracies compassed the hatred
Of all we have learned and he loved? He had dreams. Will he know
That you've found the marimba he wanted and true as a harp, and the Indian players
To follow that turn on guitars? You are patient. That turn — Federico,
You know. And you knew. If an elegy sounding the death of a hero,
The tears of a people, it is Federico; and if it is Andalusia,
It's also New York and Virginia, even Bohemia. Playing,
His coming so, playing my "son." But you also noticing when
We went for them, there at the hospital, bringing them home,
And the child with his eyes on the headlights and following strangely —
That curious dignity. Iris there, holding him, giving him over.
The lights coming toward, as George drove. The eyes followed. You watched us. I thought
Of Buck when, so often at breakfast, he sat that first summer beside me,

His hand in his hair and entranced with the long beam of light
which comes in
From the east through the window. Attention. And dignity. Why?
Must we learn
To hate, fear the dignity? Grace. As they had it. Your brother.
And Tahl.
Federico. Your brother. And Tahl, that July. It's five years. First,
Vienna.
Then Lequeitio. Their game of the bat cry in darkness to save and
discover.
And if, as you say, in Australia, the wing-spread as broad as the
height
Of a boy; and they live upon fruit and the blossoming trees and are
found
By the thousands in swamps — only mammal, true flight, the
winged bat — and are found
In the mangrove swamps. . . . You are patient, Will. Soon I'll re-
cover. But now
In this stillness, the drone of the locusts, the creak of the wagon
gone past
With the scent of the hay. And then, the crows. Rasping and mock-
ing. Recalling
The shock of the word we had known would be coming. I'd
thought long ago
And before we had inkling of China, that desolate winter I sat
With Alison watching the clouds and Gamaliel gone and I copied
The notes, many pages, for Tahl, and I found myself thinking:
And now?
When at last he'll have finished? And thought when she wrote me,
a year ago — May . . .
But having once thought he might die there in Spain or somehow
like a hero
Manning a gun and a defile. And now I see: No. And no opera
Horror and rescue. And nothing so much as the old Punic statue
Federico once talked of, unearthed there at Carthage, the pipes and
the bellows
Intact after hundreds of years, but the figure was missing and only
the fragments
To show where the shape of a man had been carved. And small
hope they survive

By a chance, as the boy that he heard there in Spain and drew out from the heap,
The blood and the tangle. She sat watching clouds. And I told her a shepherd
Once in the Tyrol had told me a soul issues out from the mouth
At the death as a little white cloud. And she smiled and said, "Stephanie,
Still in the pueblos they say that the soul is a cloud and for symbol
The smallest white breast feathers plucked from an eagle." And since, I have thought
Of the *Meno,* ". . . the soul of a man is immortal . . . and afterwards, born again,
Never dissolved." And how hear both *Requiem; Credo.* And why
After all of their searching the records, the words, the strange symbols, remains
What the air will take out in September, the words, as she says, to be heard
By the simplest translation, to move by least effort, the boundary crossing
Of language with language. But, Will, are you right in supposing he meant
In his tale of Chieh Yu, the mad drunkard advising Confucius, "Away,"
What he meant by, "Away"? To find politics "dangerous"? No.
I think he was teasing you, Will. He has strength for a love more than pity
And was not afraid. And was more than his dreams. And she said, "In this time
The heroes live all underground. And are many. Among every people."
I think that your father has heard very much when he says, "The quintet."
But I think you've heard more when you say you've reread the concerto, remarked
How Mozart compels that one reed to play more than its solo, plays on,
Plays on, may not cease through the *tutti,* is not the élite by a boundary
Marked between solo and choirs, but the music moves last integration

Of many and one. All. Together. Like prayers at the mass. And
I think . . .
And Ed said it was found near the border, the unexplored mountains, the charred
Broken plane. And he needs him so much now, with all of the
troubles, the language,
The politics, someone to move through the lines. And their waiting
her coming,
The children. Do the crows always cry so? There on the hill? Yes,
I know,
That's Jim's hill. But, Will, have you noticed? See here, in the
letter,
From Iris. Here: ". . . found near the border, the unexplored
mountains, the charred
Broken plane." They aren't sure, Will. Not sure. In the fire and
the wind and these months
And the planes sometimes found in those mountains. And Will,
now in Europe
The news. And the bodies. In Spain. And now everywhere. Will,
you are good.
And you listen. We're no more as strangers. And will be less
strangers. With years.
And I've made myself look. And I look. And I don't want to think.
And I think
Of the plane that went down in the Biscay. And covered. And
Igor. In London.
Trying to save him. But knowing him. Whole. And a man. And
not this.
Will, they don't know. They're not sure. And I look. I have
looked. They don't know.
And we'll live here with fragrance of evergreen. Here. And the
oaks. The mimosa.

TAHL : BOOK FOUR

CANTO III

INTO THE SEA

Beyond the Operating Poles of Hate and Love

Beyond the operating poles of hate and love let none profane presume.
Let none profane, with sun and moon, presume to dance beneath the sea which burns,
The strangers most profane in stranger towns attending festivals of dancing.

Let none profane presume to comprehend the fox possession: *kitsune tsuhi.*
We did not apprehend the situation of the brink beyond Walpurgis.
We thought the bed of ocean by a fable gorged the callous and malicious.
We thought that hell was passage overpassed, a lie of lamas and of parsons.
We think, we think, indeed, bad taste. Most crude. A fright for children. And a pity.
We thought: Tierra del Fuego; fire on barrens; hurricanes beyond
But on and through the Horn, the compassed route from Useless Bay, the soul's Magellan.

Let none profane presume to breach the eight hot hells, the eight cold hells and dark,
The eighty-four thousand hells by broken bailiff and the beadle bull reported:

Beyond the Operating Poles of Hate and Love

Spikes. Cauldrons. Iron clothes. The salt pits. Brine for dining at
your torment.
Clip your sinews. Cut your bellies. Pinch your livers. Gouge your
eyes. They suck.
Pull your nails. Beat your knees. Hang you by your feet, a meal
for insects.
Hack your bones. This airless tank. This running lime. Nauseate
drugs. This prick.
Insert the snake in either nostril. Kneel. The splintered mat. Your
tongue cut out.
Gravel for graves. Your head protrudes. Here. Boiling. Stewing.
Scraping. Scorching.
Drawing. Squeezing. Pecking. Scratching. Last, a surgeon. He
will take your heart.

We, profane, apart, and come so late, we may mistake. . . . We
thought
The tortures were reserved for those called damned, a lie, all continents repeating,
The uninformed, confused by bulls and bailiffs. Gallimaufry.
Laughter.
We thought that term was term. A surgeon, merciful. The fire
and dancing
Dreams by simpletons alone assumed a more than fly-by-night and
phantom.
And then we heard. And looked to find the henchmen. Gallimaufry.
Laughter.
Busy in disguises. In one function never altered. What? Through
burning oceans,
Beyond the operating poles of hate and love let none profane
presume.
The strangers are most strange in stranger towns attending at the
heart's removing.

Young man, you'll observe, if permitted survival for long in this
habit you have, I deduce,
North and south, pole to pole — and you flatter me that you consult
every Walther from London to Lisbon . . .

Into the Sea

Now here on the Sintra, observe: *Portuguesa. Lufthansa. Littoria.*
Spanish. And — British.
Observe there's no war. Your illusion. The planes unmolested.
Both legal and sane. Here in Lisbon.
Observe: Pan American. Noble Greek adjective. When we drove
out through the *Restauradores,*
You remarked the tall obelisk. Their independence. Here music.
The boulevards lighted. The dancing.
Estoril. The Casino. And since you have come here through Spain,
note the trouble we take setting straight
What your friends — perhaps you? — would disturb. Most illegal.
Supposing that women whose heads find best function
Balancing baskets from market could manage my business. We
move very easily. Others
Here crowding the streets for objecting to law and in flight coming
here for two years now this August.
You'd choose a gruff captain out hauling sardines. But not to a
fisherman, monument marbles
After the earthquake. A marquis. The citizens grateful. Now freer
than Bern or than Basel.
These lads march most happily fine in their boots down the excel-
lent avenue *da Liberdade;*
Would hardly retreat for some urchin, beret and a burro, out
peddling to cooks up an alley.

I think you are cautious but think you resemble somewhat the
young bravo you found to your interest
Keeping me occupied at the Palacio with what's long ago — in
Vienna. I find you
Amusing antagonists. You. And your Doctor and bravo who med-
dled, I hear, on Parnassus.
Permit me remark between Athens and Sparta democracy died
with the democrats' triumph.
A war? An illusion. The Spartans' best friends were in Athens at
leisure to rule over weariness.
The beauty's destroyed when the people are restless. Then let
them lie quiet at home. Cease to wander,
Obstructing the roads and requesting their deaths by a bomb and
disturbing our wires and our pipe lines.

Beyond the Operating Poles of Hate and Love

Our troops are well cared for. Their spirit most gallant. Devices
most adequate. Very intelligent.
Specialization. Decentralization. But you understand me, of course.
I have need
Of no armies except that the people lack discipline, children objecting to law, to the mind
Which is always the master — too simple to grasp I've an index not
Haushofer's now too much touted.
On file. Your simplicity. Weakness. Quite frank. You may write it.
Your words. And not mine. Will be doubted.

You have sought me in Lisbon. Perhaps Buenos Aires. Perhaps
next in Mukden. But you will forget,
Fall in love, buy your wife a new cottage. And they will be angry
with you and arrest you and save us
The trouble of finding you food in Tierra del Fuego, perhaps further
west, to dispose
Of a dancer no longer amusing as at the Palacio, writing it down:
Tungsten and copper. Not cowrie shells, bulls, or a pyx for a
prayer wheel, the bone of a narwhale?
You think: Argentina. Most quick. But a very damp winter.
Though excellent galleries. Paintings.
And also the Casa Rosada. But do not forget Patagonia. Muddy.
And cold.
Von Faufel's reports immature in accretions millennial. Assumed
you had read them. Consider.
Perhaps the reports of Tai Li are more useful? My *estancieros* will
doubt you. Suggest it.
The jest is most simple. "The Institute's *Zeitschrift*!" But, notice.
You read. A free world. As the loan
To a certain Colombo who gave you a country. The bank? Barcelona. Or shall we try China
With tungsten for surety? War, merest accident. Nuisance, of
course. On the margin of power.

Certainly. Christ of the Andes. They cast it from cannon. Most
charming. Prefer
Wolfram or skin of the wolf from the wild cordillera? Mere counter,
quick word for a currency.

Into the Sea

Once on the Amazon — rubber. The lost seringal for the clumsy at
counters and chemistries.
Several fine horses at Punta Arenas. The races. The British Club's
excellent. Come.
You might like a card to Ushuaia. And are you quite sure that
your public will care to examine
The sea lion's carcasses there by the straits of Magellan? No doubt.
Tungsten carbide has dropped.
You're informed. And quite legal. No need of your budget. Assume
that my margin is limitless. Heat,
Its resistance to heat, in the pulverized tungsten defeated, in powder
made wire. We compact
For the wealth of Yunnan. You expect me at distance. Not Denver
or Butte? The people are chalk.
Some use, to clean steel, to make castings. They laugh. Are mis-
trustful. Of me? Not at all. But of you
With your babble. Your Doctor who troubles the desert and jungle,
run out of his habitat, pouncing
On chiefs in the wilds of Tibesti. His "France versus France."
Merely marginal. I shall go hunting.
The tiger eats deer. And the deer are more docile. Annoyance in
more than the swamps of the Ganga.
The traps in the Punjab? You know them? I thought not. A tripod
with bait and a smearing of sap.
Bird lime. For those who fly out. They do not. They are caught
by their fears, by their vaunted great wits,
By their falling in love in their warrens. Their children. Their
memories, often most short. Your mistake.
"Monocled henchmen" bring gifts and not bullets. Gratitude's
gullible. Truth as I make it.

Nothing will change. You are clever, as he was, your bravo. Perhaps
you have heard he is dead?
A death's most convenient. Disposes. Perhaps you have heard? As
for taking a wife, may I urge
The classical precepts. Not folly set free. If you let her run off,
she will strangle you both
On illusions. Amusing. The bag of a century. Are you persuaded
you'll measure my index?

Cephalic? Jejune. For a Spanish fine nose and a German sharp eye,
an Italian deft hand,
A Bushido assurance, the Brahmin for caste, the Arab for wiles,
the old Mongol accustomed
To blood. And a world in one file for executives. Currency now
international. Always.
As here on the Sintra. The pilots indifferent. My henchmen grow
subtle. The stalking improves
Pour le sport. And the victim impales himself, dam on the Dnieper
— this summer. The cured system's neutral,
The people well fed and their children well coddled. The conquest is
easier. Delicate weapons.
Bombs are most barbarous. Yes. You observe. I agree. We must
play a fine hand . . . with musicians.

TAHL : BOOK FOUR

CANTO III

INTO THE SEA

Beyond the Sea

Beyond the sea the sea-borne judgment falters.
Upon the sea expect no voices after.
Beyond the sea the triumph and the failure.
Upon the sea the voices over waters.

Within the cave the darkness turns in sun.
Beyond the cave, velocity's precision.
Beyond the cave, no land from out gray waters;
Within the cave, smooth rock, the wave's roar surging.

The cave is turned more slowly than the sun.
The afternoon western message, eastward coming,
By friends examined dawn of a previous morning.
The cave, more slowly than the turning sun.

The cave is one, the rivers are many, running
Through caves, emerging, approaching the unknown sea.
The quarters are Judas branch and orchid's meaning,
Asphodel and first anemone.

Received opinion concerning the place of death:
A river, a cave, an island, a mountain: west.
The first anemone is the wind; the first
And last, the wind, believed, the living breath.

Beyond the Sea

Minstrels are best emissaries. Held,
Received opinion: forbidden molestation.
The law is very old: permit them passage.
Within the cave and darkness give this message.

Within the cave, in darkness, separation.
Within the cave, in darkness, fusion and making.
Upon the sea, the death and separation.
Upon the sea, the fusion and the making.

This is a legend. Once on Raiatea
The flood rose. The sun approached the horizon.
The fisherman's refuge, called *Toa-marama,*
Moon-tree. Flood of the moon. Flood of the sun.

Beyond the sea the sea-borne judgment falters.
Upon the sea expect no voices after.
Upon the sea the voices. Over waters.
Upon and beyond, vibration, travel of thunder.

Upon the sea the voice, come over waters:
The act is not all and the thought is not all . . .
The two trees felled and crossed in last of signs . . .
. . . And of the living who remember death
In love's regenerate. . .   . . . command: 'Atone.'
. . . Called bud of lotus, heart transformed, or orchid
Of all life's complexity — HE IS.
. . . mercy lies beyond the wrath and judgment.

Upon the sea the voices over waters:
SHELLS ON LENINGRAD. THE FALL OF KIEV.
OFFENSIVE IN HONAN. "As I observed,
Deduction orthodox in revelation;
Historical rather than mystical speculation;
Recoiled from swoon, rejected identification
Requiring *imprimis* the senses' repudiation.
Regarded *imprimis* the will, the first conversion.
In Italy. Met him." "*Sans doute.* He was the man.
Tall. Half-drowned. When, on the coast of France,
I left him, I presumed to ask his party,
Syndicate or union. He answered, 'None.'"

Into the Sea

Upon the sea the voices over waters:
"I am by nature impatient of amateur soldiers.
We must be firm with the trail of the gun. It jumps.
The shell will affect a target not announced.
They've learned at Piraeus you cannot evacuate when
We cover by air. We show them whose world. . . . again."
"He was aware of numbers always slaughtered
In closing years of dynasties. Insisted
Against neutrality. And I desisted,
Knowing myself I'd taught him contradiction,
This world's riddle, most our own creation.
Therefore I chose to carry him down the mountain."

Upon the sea the voices over waters:
"They left me a turquoise. I found it beneath the *ramada.*"
"It wasn't a trick." "About this thing in Spain."
"Your renegade!" "The scar above his ear.
We always wondered." "Igor often said,
'Of each rare species, Basil, you'll observe
Somewhat unfavorable to its survival.'"
"Whose world?" "The drill card. Here: 'Unfit for command,'
To drive the wedge, encircle, and destroy."
"The musician. Would he were my son."
With the sea's turn. The voyage of a planet.

Upon the sea the voices over waters:
AS A GENERAL RULE, THE ROUGHER THE WEATHER, THE SLOWER
THE PLANE SHOULD BE FLOWN . . . CONDITIONS OF THE WIND . . .
OCCASIONALLY UNSAFE TO MAKE A TURN
AT ANY SPEED. . . . Report of investigation:
Crash. Explosion. Doubtful identification.
The northwest reach of the river. Information
Indirect. In the present situation
Unfeasible, inquiry further. Paths. The war.
The difficulties of communication.
Neither passengers nor crew. Uncertain.
Storms particularly severe. The mountains.

Beyond the Sea

Upon the sea the voices over waters
Undying in the farthest oscillation
Of word repeated, pebble with small sound,
Wedge, encircle, none has found destroying
Wave after wave, and through and over mountains.

Upon the sea this voice across the waters:
"That's not my conclusion. I proceed
Assuming he'll come back and ask me how
Performance goes. Say: 'Well.' I hope. You see,
I know I'm very young. And still I know
He said we have to learn. He has to learn.
That's why he's gone to China. Wants to know.
You see, in this third movement, melody.
It's called *Pa Pan,* he says. And always taught,
He's heard, to those just learning music, sung
To words called 'little monk,' called *Hsiao Ho Shang.*
And in this second movement, the lament,
He says, for falling laurel leaves in autumn,
Chung Ch'iu Kuei Yüan, and here he works it in
With other elegies for crucifixion.
As here *Pa Pan* comes alternate against
The 'blues.' You'll pardon me for contradicting.
It's just I know because he told me. Not
For novelty. You've heard rehearsals. Know
It sounds more old than new. He says the heart
Does not change. Experiment's at most
To make us, all of us, articulate.
And much that was still is. As in *Kol Nidrei.*
Not as in Bruch. I doubt if you can find it,
Unless you know it. But it's in the first
And in the last. New point, he says, and still
The curve's continuous. And take these fourths.
He reaches atonality. Comes back.
To balance liberty with anarchy.
You see? Of course. He taught us that. Admit
Not many of us get it. But I've tried.
And now it's mine, to make the instruments
'Discourse,' he said. Not chatter. And we learned
The dissonance, the syncopation first,

Chromaticism, first in Bach and Mozart.
Melody's not 'Russian.' Source in common.
Tunes are hybrid, always. Sure, 'He said.'
But when you're young as I am, have to say
'He said.' I have enough to do to say
What he said. But sometimes think I'll be
Of those who learn to say. And if there weren't,
Where'd you be for orchestras and choirs?
He said I wouldn't hear from him. I haven't.
He said he'd said too much for much too long.
And wry, his mouth — like laughing . . . at himself.
This first movement. Clear and far. And yet
The fellows who competed saw it 'desert'
And lost. I hear it — well — accessible
And music, theme with theme, and time with time.
It's still not ready. Have to get it — timing —
Pull — the tension. Learn it from his songs.
The *Orpheus,* with flute. The one with gourds,
In Air. The dulcimer for obligato
In *Lincoln.* And about the vine, the voice
Unkeyed, against viola. But you're wrong.
It is not for surprise. Exploring range.
Returns on common center. But the color
Changes. Like piano to marimba.
And like guitars. He says we've been afraid
Like those afraid of something they call 'Greek'
Or 'Russian,' 'medieval,' meaning 'bad' . . .
Or dote upon the word, and so it's 'good' . . .
Ears open, unselective . . . ears tight closed.
Too hard, they think, to choose, to keep, discard,
Recover, alter, questioning the ear.
He's not afraid I'll kill it. If it lives,
He says that it will live till he comes back.
And if it doesn't, it's as well it died.
He'll always talk like that. Yes, I go in.
My number's up. Yes, when this contract's through.
You can't fix up the world the way you want.
We talked of that. This training for a war.
It's like the broadcast. If your set is bad,
You won't hear all the frequencies and lose

The fullest tone I'll make them give. He knows.
Spirituals? For that, here, in the First.
There's *Way Up On the Mountain, Lord.* The strings
Against the chorus. Here again: *Go Down . . .*
There, among the basses. But it's not
The use, but how he uses. Or perhaps,
The Fourth, *These Bones Shall Rise.* But you should not,
If I can help, be hearing it, except
As echo, in the clarinets. And not
More than the *Song of the Hearse* that moves and mocks
On the bassoon the *jota* in the Third.
The signatures aren't difficult except
This Third. But he was here, you know, to help
Our first three months. It will be just a year
When we go on the air next week. You want
More than I can give. And once he said,
'Always watch your words. Whatever's said,
The deaf take care that you're misunderstood.'
'Sacred?' Well, he'd probably just look,
And run his thumb the way he used to, rather
As if he had some bother near his eyebrow;
Or trip you gently. Like the time I said
A passage in the Händel was too brisk,
Too eighteenth century. He said he had
Some doubt 'archaic' was a 'sacred' word
And only synonym. Well, for the size,
It's not so much, you know. And I can manage.
Purcell, Vivaldi, Haydn? Who's to say?
What I learned from him, the instruments,
The interpenetrations. I'm still learning
No matter how the melody goes free . . .
And I mean his . . . and more of them he's made
Than what you call the 'folk stuff' and the 'news' . . .
There's always, underneath, the plan. Makes sense.
The modulations come. I know. And why.
And when there, in the Fourth, the baritone
Comes up, 'Thou mightiest Christ arise,' we know
What he's evaded, slipped, left unresolved,
Will end . . . and solid. And except the songs
These past two years, he'd never shape it, ending

Solid. Why I studied with him. Chose him
Because what I had heard seemed restless, haunting,
The way we felt. Was right. But this. This ends.
Solid. Not that I can understand
Why he needed that about Egyptians.
It doesn't show. Just something on his mind.
Sub-dominant, he says, is spring with autumn.
The dominant, he says, is spring with winter.
The octave, so he says, is spring with summer.
I guess that you might quote it. But he'd say,
And quiz you with his eyes, 'Unmusical.'
But what he'd mean — no absolute is caught
Except, he'd say, by what devices serve.
And 'what relates still acts, is relative.'
I'm not good at explaining. I can think
More easily with pace and key. And wish,
For all I like this chance, that he were here.
The audience? Who'd say? Some, ear for pitch,
Transitions, minor, major, who'll agree
How far is far from C sharp back to C.
And those whose pitch is relative, know shift,
But not just where and what. And no one hopes
The tone-deaf come to concerts. Take that out.
Sounds . . . well . . . like know-it-all. Sounds wrong. I don't.
That's why we like him. Just because he doesn't."

Upon the sea the voice, come over waters:
We're liaison department. We may save . . .
Know the steep dark silence . . . will not drown
But will transform and all its words be fables . . .
. . . Is our mad kind of reverence for breath,
The soul, by name you choose. . . .   . . . most dangerous . . .
. . . Which has no name but love. . . .   . . . and Tahl. . . .
    I heard . . .
The stories were wanderers' stories, a long migration.

Upon the sea this voice across the waters:
"Time goes so slowly. Is it only months?
He always did my errands. Evenings often,
Just to please me, when he set the parcels

Right there on that table, I would find
Grapes I hadn't asked him for. Or ginger . . .
Good on my old gums. He'd always find it.
Somewhere. Just say plenty on the market.
I won't forget the winter that they came.
I felt real bad. And I was sick myself.
That spring, when he'd drove off to school, she'd come
Some mornings, fix my breakfast by this window.
They were away a lot, the summer. Still
They always would come in when they came back.
'China!' I said. 'Well, mercy! It's so far!'
She tended to my fern. I hate to see it
Dying there. Like me. Just fading. Waiting.
But she could make it fresh and green as spring.
And you know what he told me? There. What was it?
Now. There's things around inside those leaves
That move, make green. She'd seen them too. That's it.
'Well, mercy,' I said. But how my mind does slip.
What would you like to know? There's lots of neighbors.
I'm not so spry and I don't get about.
Just sit. And wait. She used to like that box.
And, land sakes, I'd forgotten it was brought
All the way from China. Now, who was it?
Likely my father's cousin. Went to sea.
Yes, the view's real pleasant. Sit and wait.
Morning and night I sit here by this window.
A sea is good to watch. It always changes.
Time goes slowly. Seems like long ago
I used to see them walking out at sunset,
Out there on those rocks. And there they'd sit.
They'd always wave to me. Sometimes I think
I'll see them. I'm forgetful. And I look.
And there they'll sit. Look off. Like me. And then
They always wave. It just does my heart good.

TAHL : BOOK FOUR

CANTO IV

INTO THE THUNDER

Creation

First

. . . because that face will never be set down.
Nor hers. The countenance eludes. You come
Saying you forgot the time. You missed
Whatever countenance we'll ever see.
It may be heard again. And here's the score
If you can read it. Rather the memento,
As you say, with Iris's remarks —
The doodles there are Will's — and all the arrows,
Stephanie's, her trying hard to show me
Where the themes appear in changing keys.
I did the best I could. And here's the text.
As for my canvas, that's his head all right.
And hers. Among the leaves. They never come
Clearly. Say the motion is too swift
For this which never ceases motion, which
I've sought for all my life. I'll not destroy it.
Let it stand. I'll not say adequate —
More than once, nine years ago, in March.
And here it is September going out.

All right. It's "symbolism." Maybe learned
As much as that from him as I have learned
From her the gesture, attitude, expression

Only, always, sign for fact. I've come
To know at least that all's transcription, moving
Light with motion always to a sound.
I mean that I have lately seen the motion
In the light upon the canvas change
Always to a word. Its history
Which comes with time. The portrait will exist
As it articulates within the mind
Which did not plan the portrait. What he means —
The body's plastic and the shadow come
To second shape, like birth, within a sound.
I have not known him all my life. I found him
Unexpectedly one day with Julian
In our rooms. And then we chose our school.
Easy as that. But that's enough.

We called
And tried to reach you. Thought you'd like to come.
We had a ninth admission. We were eight.
There behind the glass, you know. Could see
The engineers, like dumbshow. And the chorus,
Orchestra upon the right. We waited.
The light to flash. And watched the young conductor.
Watched faces there below us, looking, waiting.
I found myself debating how we'd find
Device, more true than points, for a million faces
Out there, beyond, and now, perhaps on purpose,
Perhaps by accident, eyes, hands, and ears
Tuning to this hour. Light flashes. Hear
An opening full and grave. If I'd not seen,
I'd not have known. I haven't that much ear.
Which instruments, I mean. But makes me listen . . .
Iris . . . Brahms, the violin concerto . . .
To make me hear the violin come in.
Adagio. I recall it's chiefly oboe.
Bassoons and horns, then shift on bridging strings.
Same melody, but on the violin.
The way you feel when you don't know a language.
You go to effort. Greece. Or Brittany.
Feel tendons in my neck pull taut as if

They would unstop my ears. And still not sure,
Until it comes for minutes, if I hear
The violin or oboe. Queer. But this,
When I could see it there before my eyes,
In print — and in the studio — who moves,
And who does not — I know. Begins with woodwinds
Full and grave. Extends. Then higher. Far.
Sure. I was the only one surprised.
The others at rehearsals. Stephanie
Knowing every note. He'd paid attention,
Even Alfred. You know me, tied up
And this New York's a skid unless you're sharp.
But thought I knew. And didn't you? The club,
Two years ago. Well . . . cousin to the *Sacre,*
Make nervous, primitive. Say . . . chaos. No.
Not till the Third. This First. You count the bars.
Not many. Full, then far. But paced. And sure.
And then the voices. All. In canon — double —
Young Will said. You know they wouldn't miss it.
Came up especially to hear it. Words
Move in and out. Complex of sound. The text.
Hell, no. Of course I wouldn't mind. Object
If I keep at my work? Just go ahead.

IF THERE IS SOUND, THERE IS A SOURCE OF SOUND.
IF THERE IS LIGHT, THERE IS A SOURCE OF LIGHT.
WE HAVE LOOKED FROM DAWN TO YELLOW
    DUSK,
UNDER SUN AND MOON, THE COLORED LIGHTNINGS,

WORKERS IN WOOD AND STONE UNEASY WATCHING
OVER THE TRAVELING LIGHT AND TRAVELING
    STREAM.

WE HAVE LOOKED WITHIN THE MIGHTY CANYON.
WE HAVE LOOKED ON ALL BELOW THE SKY

INTO THE RAIN AND WIND, THE FOUR DIRECTIONS.

Creation

IF THERE IS SOUND, THERE IS A SOURCE OF SOUND.
IF THERE IS LIGHT, THERE IS A SOURCE OF LIGHT.

Here, let me see. The basses, under, swinging,
Chromatic, close, those lines, the rest against them.

THAT WHICH CHANGES. HE WHO DOES NOT
    CHANGE.
WE HAVE LOOKED ON ALL BELOW THE SKY,
WE HAVE LOOKED TOWARD ALL WITHIN THE SKY,
TOWARD ONE WHO WAITS UNBOUND AND BOUND
    IN LIGHT.

That's it. That word swings out and hangs. You're right.
First aria. The baritone. See. Here.
This morning's column. For the baritone.
And fair enough. That throat. That great dark face.
The word. The sound. The voice. Magnificent.

LOVE   OF GOD   FEAR OF GOD   LOVE   OF GOD
HE WHO CHANGES   HE WHO DOES NOT CHANGE

That's it. The baritone. And through the ranges.
Changing. As in faces. Look, I'll show you.
Here. This sketch. No, not the baritone.
That's Tahl, nine years ago. Now, look. The canvas.
That head among the leaves. And as it's like,
As much as it is like, it's like nine years.
No. Not exactly Gilbert Stuart. Labels.
Hell. "Surreal"? As much as say it's Giotto.
George. Or Giotto. God. It's what I say.
It's what it looks right now to me. It's like,
Well, take it in his music. Iris hears
The inner parts, the muting, shifts of time,
Transition, what goes upside down, arpeggios

Like the engulfed cathedral . . . says there's space
Finally between the sounds sunk down
And then one chord kept high and spare. And yet
It is no Breton legend and no Frenchman
Imitated. Here, I guess. Then, voices.

WE, THE NUMBERED NUMBERLESS RECALLING
WE, THE HOMELESS FROM UNCOUNTED CITIES,
OF ONE RACE AND FATHERED IN THE SUN,
OF ONE RACE AND FATHERED IN THE WATERS.

And that's the moment. Senior says they thought
There should not be the silence. Audience
Might think: gone off the air. But had his silence.
And comes back voices with the strings together.
Then lead for clarinets, but no one missing.
Stephanie says, fugue. Like something known,
Worked out, assured and like this morning there
Beyond the skylight. Merely clearness. High.
And moves without a cloud to show. We travel.

LIGHT OF LIGHT THE LIGHT IS BORN OF LIGHT.
OUT OF LIGHT THE MANY LIGHTS REVOLVING
UNMEASURED, BOUND, UNBOUNDED DISTANCE
    COMING
IN SEA UNWOUND AND WOUND, THE SPIRAL
    TURNING
THE YEARS OF LIGHT, THE LIGHT OF YEARS, LIGHT
    MOVING
BEHOLD THE COUNTED AND UNCOUNTED LIGHT
BEHOLD   UNCOUNTED   NUMBERLESS   THE SUNS

Contralto with the tenor, with the strings,
Shimmer and flash, vibration on vibration

THE SIGN OF THE LIGHT IS THE CURVE OF THE
LIGHT,
THE CURVE OF THE ARM, OF THE BRANCH, OF THE
WING.
THE STONE IS NOT STILLNESS, BUT MOVES.
THE SHAPE OF THE LIGHT IS THE SHADOW AND
SOUND

Now gouging red, the deep tones spading out
And over all, the women's voices. Right?

OUT OF THE STREAM THE OCEAN, OUT OF LIGHT.
OUT OF THE STREAM THE WIND, THE SOUND OF
LIGHT.
HE WHO IS IN SOUND, IN EVERY TONGUE.

And men reiterating. Then it comes
Drums, strings, and voices, woods and brasses, all . . .

THE TREE OF LIFE THAT IS FOREVER GREEN

It rises falls and goes. I couldn't tell. —
Restored, cut down, grown back, and falling, rising,
THE TREE OF LIFE THAT IS FOREVER GREEN
Until contralto solo takes it off
So you don't know where fall or surging stops
And suddenly she is. And what's the line?

THERE IS NO ONE WHO LIVES SAVE THERE BE SEED

But you can't find the note. You see. That mark.
The way he likes to try it. Sounds to hear,
He says, since Indus was a river — come.
But tenor after her, and on the key

THERE IS NO ONE WHO LIVES SAVE IN THE LIGHT

With those two voices coiling in your ears
Until you want to push them out. Then, six.
The leaders, men and women, conversation
Dropped against the drums and out to flutes,
The strings, the pizzicati — then, deep, rumbling

THE BREATH   THE EYE   THE EAR   THE TONGUE
WHERE   IN LIGHT   THE HEART

Repeating, "heart."

But here, here. Let me take it. I don't paint,
It seems, except your cuffs, and daub the score
That's scrawled enough already. "Modulations."
I say he modulates volcanoes. How
He does it, with that handful, I don't know.
Spurts iron-red and lapis-blue and rolls
All ochers down to purple ash; then wheels,
Gone every way at once, and grinding. Voices.
A chant off key or on some key that is,
We don't quite correlate. And so comes torrent.
Bursts. Hear roiling up. But every word.
The rhythm fast and crossing, hand beat, stamping,
And when the key comes back, not key he started.
WE ARE THESE WHO COME UPON THE SEA
WE ARE THESE WHO SUFFER IN OUR COMING
LOVE   AND FEAR   CREATING   AND DESTROYING
EVERY HEAD IS TURNED TO THE HORIZON
COMING FORTH BY DAY AND WHOLE AND SLAIN
BY LIGHT AND WIND ENJOINED WITHIN THE
    STREAM
OUR EYES HAVE SEEN AND HAVE NOT SEEN   THIS
    SEED
And this is it, on key, reciting, singing:
GIVING   RECEIVING   DIVIDED   DIVIDING   COMING
THE SWIMMERS IN THE SEA   THE LEAVES   ARE
    GROWING

THE SWIMMERS IN THE SEA   THE LEAVES ARE
  GROWING
THE CRAWLERS ON THE LAND   THE LEAVES ARE
  GROWING
THE BIRD AND SNAKE ARE ONE   THE FLOWER WITH
  LEAF
THE SWIMMERS AND THE CRAWLERS   TREES ARE
  GROWING
SWIMMING   CRAWLING   WALKING   FLYING
  WALKING
GIVING   RECEIVING   DIVIDED   DIVIDING
  GROWING
And slows and shifts, but hardly, slightly, singing:
MIGHTY AND TERRIBLE FIRE   THE BLOOD IS
  FLOWING
MIGHTY AND TERRIBLE SEA   THE BLOOD IS
  FLOWING
SO WE CAME   ARE COMING
. . . like the Indians,
Make it power with singing and repeating,
Till somewhere in the brass, trombones, with voices
Stretched against them, shouting and competing
SO WE CAME   ARE COMING   WE HAVE MADE
And there they break, but here and there are gathered
WHAT HAVE WE MADE   WE THOUGHT TO MAKE
  A CITY
HAVE SHAPED THE SOUND UPON THE MOVING
  BREATH
HAVE MARKED UPON THE STALK AND ON THE LEAF
HAVE COUNTED   FINGERS   PEBBLES   SHELLS   AND
  FINGERS
HAVE COUNTED   FROM THE FORESTS   TO THE
  STARS
WHAT HAVE WE MADE   WE THOUGHT TO MAKE
  A CITY
IN WIND   IN MOVING SEA   IN RISING FLAME
WHERE   OUR CITY   IN THE WATERED GARDEN
WHO HAS MADE THIS CITY AND THIS GARDEN
UNDER THE LIGHT   UNDER UNCOUNTED SUNS
Against the question, sound, not louder, moving

Inexorable, like someone walking, moving
Among the horns and takes them up, and calls,
And takes the flute, remarks, then violins
And plucks and gathers up. And then, by God,
I thought I heard him. There. At the piano.
Shock. And sudden. Reaching. Stephanie
Writing on the margin, "scales are tempered" —
But anyhow, piano, interrupting,
Swift — "appoggiatura" — reaching, flowing,
And talking back to tenor and contralto
IN THE HOUR OF TRIBULATION
IN THE HOUR OF DEATH AND JUDGMENT
And cut upon by bass, tremendous, lunging
HAVE THEY NOT HEARD   HAVE THEY NOT HEARD
With choir upon him as in utter space,
The instruments laid down and silenced. Once
The harp. Uncertain. Gone again. The voices:
THEIR WORDS IN ALL THE EARTH TO ALL THE
    WORLD
The women singing and the men repeating
THE FEAR   THE LOVE   THE FEAR   THE FEAR OF
    KNOWING
THE HAUGHTY HEART AFRAID   THE FLEEING
    CHILDREN
SWIMMERS   CRAWLERS   LOST ON WINGS   THE
    CAPTIVES
THE BLIND   THE DEAF   THE BRUISED
    THE BROKEN-HEARTED
THIS OUR FLESH   THE FIRST CREATED CROSS
LOST IN LIGHT AND SEED   AND WEARY GROWN
OF TEMPEST   PLAGUE   MURDER   SUDDEN DEATH
IN OUR FORTUNE   IN OUR TRIBULATION
THE WHOLE CREATION GROANING AND IN PAIN
Drifts to tenor with soprano blending,
Curious, firm and lost at once, their saying
I WILL HAVE MERCY   AND NOT SACRIFICE
To bass again. To mezzo. Baritone.
Apart. Together. All the voices singing
THEIR WORDS IN ALL THE EARTH TO ALL THE
    WORLD

Creation

WHO WILL NOT LOVE HIS BROTHER LIVES IN DEATH
Sharp. And more. Chromatic. Instruments.
They take it. Arrows. See? First chorus — theme:
IF THERE IS SOUND THERE IS A SOURCE OF SOUND
And with it second chorus. Here it is:
LIGHT TO LIGHT THE LIGHT IS BORN OF LIGHT
So going into cellos, basses, horns.
I saw the bows. The flash. They all were up.
Then saw piano coming. Tip the harp.
With all recurring, moving, turned around,
Wound in and knotted, loosened, out again
IF THERE IS SOUND THERE IS A SOURCE OF SOUND
LIGHT TO LIGHT THE LIGHT IS BORN OF LIGHT
And WE ARE THESE WHO COME UPON THE SEA
Back to his C minor where he started,
To coda not quite ending . . . Iris' scribble,
"Their words in all the earth to all the world."
But toward a chord unfinished. Saw the boy
Dipping his baton. He pulled his tie.
And then a stranger voice upon the air,
Remote, in space: "This evening you are hearing . . ."

Second

It's noon. And do you mind? We'll try the terrace.
Nothing. Just the gusts of wind. May bother,
If you keep on reading. Want to catch it.
I mean, the square. At noontime. Where the light
Cuts in here from the sea. That's why I came.
And better where he lived the past two years,
Up there along the coast. But need a city.
So, compromise. And that's a thing he knows.
He'd do what he could do — piano, harp —
But write alternative, prefer marimba.
And rather stay piano, harp, than take
Marimba in the maul of nightclub tappers.
That truth's no truth when it's a truth abused;
But truths approximate, with variations,
Survive no matter in what signs they're ordered,

He knows. And then Will found it — this marimba —
The players. Good, last night. The way he'd want.

But hear the talk last evening in the foyer,
Broadcast over. I don't mean there weren't
His friends — and honored most, old "maestro" came —
And why I think it may be heard again
For all, two years ago, his hesitations.
But others you'd expect, some faces known
And voices, their pronouncing, "He presumes
With what the poets said in Babylon."
He takes his pick of prayerbooks. "Mixing modes."
You'll give with formulas or that's no physics.
Give Bach with Beethoven or be more private,
And strangle without echo. It's no fact
Unless it's listed *anthropological* — gloss —
"Temerity," they called it. Lord, he knows.
The night he talked, the club, and then next morning
This thing came back "no go" — "It's not the music,"
He said. "Expect it 'odd.' They'd change the text."
Kept First and Third. His Second went to scrap.
Or cut. The stuff he talked at us that evening.
Still there, I think. But underneath. He said:
"It doesn't matter if it's hard or simple.
Whatever text they sing, the fact's the snag."

He may have meant, "Temerity." Write music,
Labelled *Mass* or merely *Credo.* Risk
Nothing. As he says, "They'd change the text."
He calls it "Second," means much more than "movement."
"Continuous," he says, "in exposition,
But simultaneous in meaning." Breaks
His head and mine and yours. His gravitation,
Light years, and equations, multiplying
With botany, Sun Tzu and wars in China,
Dividing by the Dutchmen in the Indies
And adds the ancestors of some old lady
Who lives, it seems, next door. It makes me swear.
Just look. And Iris counts them. Nine gray hairs.

Those gaffers in the foyer. "Over-simple,"
That's what they say. "The text is over-simple."
The music's fine. "Ingenious," so they say.
I'd not pretend to know. The First . . . I felt
Like first years out with Julian when he stopped
To show me how to draft it, sea in light.
This Second . . . feel . . . the way a child can look.
And I don't mean that's "simple." Sorry now
That I urged Iris off. She talks your language.
And we'd show off our cubs. But driving back,
Alf and Elsa, Julie's chirp for "Buck!"
Young Ed ties Iris down — but driving, managed.
The Twelfth I'll join them, see the leaves at height,
October in that country. What I meant,
This Second. Young Ed. Julie. Innocent
They look. But know their grip. And at two months
A will that you can't fool with. So, this Second.
The Chinese melody, the Negro moaning,
"They crucified my Lord," — and that's a tune —
But what he writes down under leaves you helpless,
Knowing you object, but still can't duck it,
Crawls along your blood and in you. Grip.

And I asked Minna. There's a wise old woman.
She'll out and ask. And takes it straight, the like.
She says if he so chooses with the prophets,
Psalmists or apostles, she'd not heard
A moratorium declared. She thinks
He's very likely said more prayers than most
And is more worried whether he is right.
She's right. I know him. Always wants a world
The way you feel it more than noon's reporting.
Like painters, Asiatics. In the desert,
The Indian . . . sign for color. Not apart,
The words, from what his music makes. Not "king,"
Not "lord of battle." Signals, yes. But changed.
He makes his variations. "Doesn't mean,"
He says, "change equals nothing. Transmitter sending."

If I don't paint what you'd call Whistler's river
Or leaves the way a leaf with Buddhas sitting,
I don't remove the forest or the ocean.
If Whistler shows a hand for mist, or there,
In there, upon the easel, I try leaves
Like something on a Chinese silk, I guess . . .
Hell, obvious. He wants a tenor singing
"Thou shalt love thy neighbor as thyself."
Why not? As Minna says. Or he himself:
"If they agree, they'll think it's obvious.
And if they don't, they'll think it's impudence."
The way they took it on the night I met you.
The guff about old ladies. But he'll muff you,
If you don't meet his pitch. He says, "All right.
Objections help the balance. Don't grow fat
On thinking you've outrun the opposition.
The shaman, brahman, mandarin, and pope
Recur in all economies. No hope
That they won't find our kind responsible
For what's far stronger than us all. Who holds,
Who breaks, who gathers and transforms, remain
Participate in all transfiguration."

He says the Chinese scales, the measured stones,
Were always lost or found, and no one certain
Concerning latest pitch, but found it simpler
To vow to heaven fear of alteration.
He thinks the time is coming, cults in fashion,
Once India, now for Russia, then insist
That all was wrong before, but look, behold,
"Chinese perfection! " Opposition, shrieking:
"Desecration! Flee! An Eastern custom!"
A most thin wire to balance, where he walks,
And where I earned my nine gray hairs, no doubt:
"Seeing relativities is not
Equivalent to common skepticism."

And all these years we've fought it out. He wins
This much on me. With premise, it will hold.

Creation

The signal keeps on coming, like rehearsal,
And then it comes for sure, cuts history
Between the flesh struck down and flesh and spirit
Crucified and raised again. I see it.
An argument. And if the only fact
Remained, we thought it up ourselves, it gives
Remarkable reflection on our kind.
And that's where she comes in, because she's seen
Rehearsals in so many tribes and tongues,
Recurrent in our blood. And if it came
One noon upon a hill with crosses, say
The signal will not block. I see as much.
But still . . . I block. Black out.

I like it here.
Old human kind goes home or to the drugstore.
Lunch. In sunlight. In September. Heads.
And nearer. Hands. The current. Drifts. The sounds.
The urchins row and sing. And Bess, she noticed.
Here, July and August. Said, "It's strange,
The way the words drift up. The way they chant.
"Going to a fire!" they howl. And all
Whoop off, like sirens wailing. Once she heard,
"A penny apiece! A penny apiece!" and called me.
"Listen," she said. "Like Tahl. The way he sang
For fun, that day he came, to show us how
The children sing, some streetcall that he'd heard
With you there in Chicago." Well, I listened.
And he'd hear birds. I didn't. Just hear, "Twit."
But then in Athens Alison, one morning
When we'd, the four of us, sat up the night,
Said, "Listen." And, since then, I often notice.
Like there this summer when I went for Julie,
Up at Alfred's. Heard the orioles.

I get the time all right. That's why I like it.
Plenty of shift. The Third. But have to strain
For pitch. Young Will has learned. With Senior talking.
Minna, too. Because a gentleman,

To them, has ear for music. Must have been
A stubborn customer. But mellowed. Learned.
In our own fashion. Alison and Iris,
Planning schools for Julie — they can put things —
Alison: ". . . it once was 'Holy Spirit.'
Now the term is 'aptitude.'" . . . their laughter.
Two years ago and more. There in my loft.
Was working. But the words came up. Like faces.
You know. Chicago. Day I knocked him down.

About these scales. I can't tell. Five. Seven. Twelve.
But rhythm, common, triple, other, yes.
A way of spacing. Stephanie says: "Chords
From which the third is absent." Talks of "skips"
And "flatted keynote." Bells. And that marimba.
Guitars are very old. Most, solo. Not
Fighting against the whole. But, flute. The *Talmud* . . .
Away back, when his music leaned on drums and brasses,
Jazzed bull fiddles . . . reading, "flutes are suited
Either to the bride or to the dead."
Parallel progressions? What I know,
His melodies are long, sustained, and come
Slow to start, then broken, but come back,
Long, sustained, at last. And, as in First,
You know when it's all over, it's not finished,
But waiting for the Third. And tambourines
And cymbals punctuating on the voices
With music all the time, no silence, always
Coming, sometimes like to risk your life
To hear. But then you hear it. Pulse. And always,
A wheel that turns, but this time oiled, no sound,
And yet — pulsation. Maybe like the earth
That turns and we don't hear it. Demonstrates
What Doc said once, the commonest mistake,
Our thinking "primitive" is simple. Sorting
"Tree" from "tree" to *tree;* or *shape,* abstract;
That complications simplify, but seem,
By error, complications. What Tahl means,
His scales, equations and extensions. "Rash,"
I heard them say. And, "Venturesome." Suppose,

Some rule he breaks. My oath, that he knows why.
Perhaps it's that he talked about guitars,
With WHY HAST THOU FORSAKEN ME. It comes
Fairly toward the end. He'd probably
Produce Ling Lun, Pythagoras to prove
He didn't think it up. He always means it.
Sure. Wily. Often. Year that Julian died.
In Egypt. And you know, in Spain. Comes out,
But when he's ready. As for what he makes,
No wile or guile. All credit lines. That night,
His Chilan Balam — oh, lord — Mencius — Enoch —
His Jubal through all chants for Holy Office.
Last evening, overhearing, made me sore.
They won't know Tahl. Each line he's heard from Basques
To last Jane Doe with John who came for supper.
It makes us laugh. And then he doesn't mind.
I've tried to make him sore. You can't. And yet
You'd never call him soft. He'll curse and grouse
At all damned, cruel, stupid kinds of worlds,
Or what's the more, he'll turn it on himself.
And I asked Alfred how Tahl took it. Thought
At least he'd set his heart upon that boy,
And he'd curse God and doctors. Alfred's mild,
But looked to show the idiot I am.
Till it was over, said, Tahl never slept,
Stayed there with Alison. His words most often
"Steady, girl." She'd answer, "Steady," turning,
Held against his shoulder. Elsa saying,
As if they walked an edge, but would not fall.
Well, who's to judge? You read it, if you want.
It won't take long. And then I'll have to scram.
Don't rub it in. I know. I said I wouldn't.
I guess it's habit. Class. I'd better meet it.
But if you like, run in again this evening.
Go through the rest. I'd like to. Watch the wind.
I'd hate to lose that copy. Quit it. Sure.
I like what's mine. Hang on. Instinct. Survival.
That's how it starts. Soprano. Then the flute.
We've just about the time. So. Give. I'll listen.

Into the Thunder

IN WHOM DO WE SURVIVE
THE SON OF MAN   THE SON OF GOD

LET HIM   THE SON OF GOD   COME FROM THE CROSS
ART THOU THE CHRIST   SAVE THYSELF

FROM THAT HUGE TREE ON WHOSE ENORMOUS
    BOUGHS
THE SOUL LIES   TAKES ITS REST   DESCEND
    DESCEND
DESCEND   THOU HIDDEN MOTHER   HOLY SPIRIT

WE HAVE BEEN TOLD IN MANY LANDS AND TIMES
        THAT HE WOULD COME

BEFORE THE SUNS AND SIGNS AND STARS OF
    HEAVEN
HIS NAME WAS UTTERED TO THE LORD OF SPIRITS
CHOSEN   HIDDEN   IN THE WORLD'S CREATION
IN THIS OUR FLESH   THE FIRST CREATED CROSS
TRANSFIGURED BY MUTATION IN THE GARDEN

FROM MEASURED INCOMMEASURABLE OF MOTION
FROM FIRE'S UNBOUNDED MOTION   WIND WITH
    WIND
IN SILENCE   FEAR   AND LISTENING FOR A WORD
IT IS ENOUGH   HIGH FATHER   WE ACKNOWLEDGE
LET BE YOUR NAME   BE LOVE   LET BE YOUR NAME
AND CALLED   THE LOVE A MOTHER GIVES HER
    CHILD

THOU SHALT LOVE THE LORD THY GOD
THOU SHALT LOVE THY NEIGHBOR AS THYSELF

BORN OF ONE FIRST MOTHER   ONE FIRST FATHER
FOREVER CIRCLING IN BY WALL AND STREAM
WE   THE SONS AND DAUGHTERS   KIN   AND
    CHILDREN
WE HAVE COME FROM OUT THE FOUR DIRECTIONS
EVERY LIVING SPIRIT   SEED OF SEED

Creation

THE WORD   THE SON OF MAN   THE SON OF GOD
WHO IS HE SHALL JUDGE AGAINST HIS KIN

THEY CRUCIFIED MY LORD
THEY   HIGH FATHER   CAST HIM FROM THE CITY
DEAL NOT WITH US ACCORDING TO OUR SINS

I SAW THE CROSSES ON TEN THOUSAND HILLS
BY THREE AND THREE AND THREE THE CROSSES
    TURNING

HE HAS TAKEN BREAD   THIS BODY BROKEN
THIS I GIVE   LET THIS NOT BE FORGOTTEN
HE TAKES NOW THIS CUP   TREAD GRAPES FOR
    BLOOD
HIS BLOOD IS SHED TO LIFE FOREVER LIVING
IT IS ENOUGH   THE SACRIFICE IS ENDED

THE CIRCLE IS THE LIGHT   WE STRUCK THE TREE
THE TREE ACROSS THE LIGHT IN SHADOW FALLING
THE TREE IS OF THE LIGHT   THE SIGN IS ONE
THE CIRCLE   TREE   AND SHADOW   COUNT AGAIN
AND AS IN ADAM ALL DIE
SHALL WE IN CHRIST THIS SACRIFICE BE MADE
THE SACRIFICE OF GOD   THE HEART BOWED DOWN
THE HEART HAS COME BY WATER AND BY BLOOD
AND COMING BY THE SPIRIT BEARING WITNESS
WE HAD HEARD THAT NONE HAD CONQUERED
    DEATH
LAMENT IN SPRING AND AUTUMN WITH THE
    LEAVES

Hold on, now. That's the Chinese tune. Then scale,
Then lowest tones. Then infinite, on horns.
Then up and up, a horn. Perhaps you know.
Turns Spanish. Stephanie says *flamenco.*
Whatever way he means it, when it goes,
You're off your seat and fallen upward, weightless,
Knocked back and jarred, your heart come through your teeth

WHY HAS THOU FORSAKEN ME

not noticed
Until I checked the score. There. Underneath,
A phrase that keeps on beating, low, on strings

FOR HE WHO BORE THE CROSS WENT FORTH
HE THE MAN OF SORROWS BOWED WITH GRIEF
THE PLACE WAS CALLED THE PLACE
OF A SKULL
WE HAVE LOOKED ON HIM WHOM WE HAVE
PIERCED
WE HAVE SLAIN HIM HANGED UPON A TREE
HIGH FATHER LAY NOT UP THIS SIN
TO THEIR CHARGE

Again, the muted phrase. And then, the mezzo

WHY HAST THOU FORSAKEN ME

no tears,
But flute with the marimba over hush
Like clear thin light, the cut upon guitars

IN THAT HE DIED HE DIED UNTO SIN
IN THAT HE LIVES HE LIVES IN GOD
THEY CRUCIFIED MY LORD HIS VOICE WE HEARD
FORGIVE THEM
THEY CRUCIFIED MY LORD HIS VOICE WE HEARD
I COMMEND MY FATHER TO YOUR HANDS
THIS MY SPIRIT

WE HAVE WITNESSED OF THIS SACRIFICE
SORROW IS ENOUGH
WE HAVE WITNESSED OF THIS SACRIFICE
SHALL THESE BONES RISE

And doubled, everywhere, repeating, borne
From voice to voice, the asking, "Shall these bones . . ."
"Shall these bones rise?" Tremendous. Live. And rising,
Guitars, not thin. Like noon, full blaze. Then flutes

CHRIST HAS RISEN FROM THE DEAD
AND HAS BECOME FIRST FRUITS OF THEM THAT
SLEPT
FOR AS BY MAN CAME DEATH
BY MAN THE RESURRECTION AND THE LIFE
HE WILL NOT LEAVE US COMFORTLESS
UNMEASURED MEASURED IN THE WHIRLING
TIME
IN OUR OWN TONGUES A VOICE A VOICE REPLYING
THIS WORK THE WORK OF GOD

But hear it. Vigorous. And choked. Subdued.
Then saturate with horns and trumpets. Opens
Full along the voices, like departing

WE HEARD UPON THE WIND A VOICE
SAVE US IN OUR SORROW AND OUR PRIDE
WE HEARD UPON THE WIND A VOICE
I AM THE RESURRECTION AND THE LIFE
THE SPIRIT TO THE HAND THAT GAVE IT GIVEN
SORROW IS ENOUGH
WE HAVE WITNESSED OF THIS SACRIFICE
LET US HAVE MERCY LET US GO IN PEACE

And hear it coming back on basses, cellos,
WHY HAST THOU FORSAKEN ME and flute
Brilliant, warm: THE SON OF MAN; and flute
Low and cold: WOULD COME. And space in sound,
The oboe, clarinet against bassoon
Until you think the world's rolled out and gone
Upon marimba, neither harp nor bell,

Into the Thunder

You know it's real, with gourds, and in percussion
A sound like seeds in gourds just shaken, shaken
Until the cut again, upon guitars.
But I can't tell you. I can watch that street.
And if he'd choose among the sounds it makes,
As I might choose, with light, the shape of noon,
Whatever he has chosen, it will hold,
The chorus, central — ON TEN THOUSAND HILLS.
I can't say what it does. I tell you. Like
The stones I saw out West. Of basalt. Set
In rows. To show the cone of the percussion.
The flake the blow struck off, the tool with tool.
The flake struck off. I hold it. Look. Don't know
What procedure next. Just . . . there it is.

TAHL : BOOK FOUR

CANTO IV

INTO THE THUNDER

Apocalypse

Third

I thought you'd ask when you were here this morning.
Of course it's on my mind. But Iris said,
And all the rest agreed, we wouldn't give it.
The boy who runs the show has caught the style,
I gather. Knows when talking counts or not.
And as he told Young Will . . . one interview,
And clipped that off the reel. Small chance right now
What happens over oceans and not war
Fits any news they're looking for. You saw.
They gave out he had taught and where, no mention
Even he had been in Spain, and most
The baritone — and Tahl's "discovery,"
The young conductor. News. And right enough.
As well we should not set up epitaphs,
And then we hear from Ed, and there they are
Walking in from Burma or Hsik'ang.
Not probable. That was, no doubt, their plane.
But we won't bury them before their time.
When I first heard, I thought, "That's it." But since,
Remembering Spain, the year he worked with you,
The months went by and not a sign to tell
Perhaps we ought to call a funeral,
And, as for that, gone under, year in Egypt,
Before we heard and traipsed ourselves to find him.

But won't add up. Not likely Alison
Would let him play Harun-al-Rashid walking
After his own way of learning answers.
For that, it's not just Alison. He's grown
Beyond that kind of nonsense. Had no reason
To route himself incognito. He knew
That Ed could use him. And the most he wanted,
To give what he could give where he was asked.
I will admit I hoped this trek might cure him,
Come back not thinking somehow not enough
To sit at home, write music. And it's odd.
I'd thought for years he'd jump to go off East.
And when it came, he balked. I had to argue.
"How do we know," he'd stymie, "that we're wanted?"
He'd caddy. Sure. And help stamp back the divots.
But thought they'd think we thought we knew the rules
In games they've played too long to need our answers.
But I said, "Look. There's trouble. You're in practice.
And Ed says, 'Find me someone I can trust,
And if he has an ear for what they mean
Or knows what's back of what goes on, the better.
I'll teach him what he needs of trucks and oil.'"
That's always been Ed's system. Seems it works.
Says any bloke with normal weight in brains
Can run a wheel and spring, knock ball with pistons.
What you can't give, the blueprints how to read
The wheels inside of other people's heads.
"Look here," I said. "Out there they asked for him.
And now he says he needs a fool like you.
Get going." So he went. It took some doing.
But no one here could find they'd care to keep him
Enough to stop him. So he's gone. For her
We're bothered more. But she was game to pace him.
It's likely that they're done for. But we talk
As if there were no news. It seems just decent.
Or maybe just it's easier on Iris.
She's mighty fond of Alison. We'll wait.
I've heard that's legal . . . seven years, at least.
Though Iris says, "The world's grown small," I notice
We run advertisements for persons missing.

It's where you look from, probably. Like this.
This music. What's it all about? He says,
"It's what I come to. Saying nothing proves
We can't be dumped, one boxful, in the canyon;
But doesn't prove a hundred million years
The hunch was wrong for other destinations."

I know. That's your idea. But he says no.
That's what it means if anything, our searching
The mind in space with time: no one's the same.
And each of us comes once and takes the choices.
He says, "The numbers we have learned to count,
'Analysis' . . . 'one out' gives variation
Whenever scales come close." He says he'll chance
What heart and mind composed us all can function
With plenty of "ones" in plenty of variation.
He doesn't mean for strut. You ever notice
The faces we prefer take shadows, broken
And put together? That's what makes them. Look
For something as it happens, earth and ochers,
Stand test of fires and lime, make lasting colors
But I just start from there. He starts before.
Records, he says, *Creation,* in two parts,
But simultaneous. To be created,
He says, to meet your breaking in your time,
And what you love, your fuel and your road.
He used to think as you do, button pushed,
And so you run on tracks. Though not your talk,
This coming back as your grandfather's ghost,
If that is what you're driving at. He says
That's what a microscope is good for, cuts
As much as we can cut from what we dream,
To fix an answer straighter. Doesn't harm,
So long as you don't think, to change the music
Proves, before, there wasn't any sound.
This Third. That's sound I like. That's where I start.
We took our choices. Senior says, "The First."
And Minna says, "The Fourth." But Will and I,
The Third for us. Just Stephanie and Iris,
"Second." They insist this Third is clever,

But, "not the real musicianship," though meant
To be just what it is, contrived to give
The joke, the heels kicked up, the march and squawl,
Brawl, hot, blue, dizzy, rip and pound, and wild
From on the drums to start. Then curls and snakes
And waggles, pliable, upon trombones.
Those same guitars he used to sound as calm
And curious-colored as they came that turn
Upon FORSAKEN, bodies, frets, and strings
To come on heat like all hell's concubines
Until I thought: Impaste it, oil and varnish,
And I'd be jailed for danger to the nation.
Piano woogling. Almost laughing. Trips you
To ugly clarinets. You've missed some point.
And Stephanie says some chord, three ways at once,
And intricate, he takes it, shifts. Then yell
Until you squirm. You get me — devil in him.
That spot or two, the evening you first heard him,
I guess it wasn't on his mind. He grazed it.
But had it all last night, as if the world
Gone crazy scared there won't be time enough,
Gone laky drunk and all the women willing.
But then the clarinets. And as for singing,
It sounds like nonsense, scales that hook and slide
And fast, except just twice, then brake jammed hard
To kick you forward. Won't make much — just words.
But read it speed except those brakes and clutches,
Or won't know what I mean, the coast and roll,
The tomtom, stagger, ululu, and strut,
The charivari, comic, muted trumpets,
Like hell, hooray, who cares. Some managing,
The kid half waltzing with his stick, though held.
But what ran on his face was worth the seeing.
I'm glad they wrote him up. To hold those rhythms.
Shift. Not lose. That's training. He's a good one.
Don't mind me. Like to prowl. Here. Have a smoke.
I warn you. Have to slip it with the rhythms.
And then it's not much sense without the music.

FÉAST FÉAST FÉAST FÉAST
SÁLT CLÓCK FÁLSE CLÓCK SÁLT CLÓCK FÁLSE
 CLÓCK
WĒ ARE GÓDS WĒ ARE GÓDS WĒ ARE GŌDS
HÍDDÉN HÍDDÉN HÍDDÉN HÍDDÉN
ÉVERY MÁN AND ÉVERY WÓMÁN
TRÉE IN BŪNDLE TRÉE IN BŪNDLE

You know that "blues," *I'm Too Damn Mean to Cry?*
There sits piano saying it, but twists
To tunes he's made himself to make you laugh.
And what he scumbles in before he's through,
You think it's maybe more than you had guessed.

WE MÉASURE MĀN MÉASURE KÍLL
KĪLL DÁNCE HŌLD DÁNCE KĪLL
MÁKE MÁKE BÁLL GÁME BÁLL GÁME KĪLL
BRÉAK BRÉAK BÁLL GÁME HĪDDĒN HĪDDÉN KĪLL
ÍS OF US ÍS OF US ÍS OF US
ĪS OF Ī ĪS OF Ī ĪS OF Ī

So off — on piccolo. Then tuba. That,
He used to do a lot — in his first concert —
Jeers. And strings that scrape. But now it's caught
Until your shoes start moving, thump and tap.

ÍS OF Ī ÍS OF Ī ÍS OF Ī

Recedes, approaches, pounds — and chortles — winds —

SĀCRĪFĪCE SĀCRĪFĪCE SĀCRĪFĪCE
CÍRCLE ĪN ĪN CÍRCLE ĪN ÍN
GRĒEN GRÉEN GRÉEN GRÉEN GRÉEN GRÉEN
 GRÉEN GRÉEN
RESÚRRÉCTĪON RESÚRRÉCTĪON RÉSÚRRÉCTĪON
RÉSÚRRÉCTĪON RÉSÚRRÉCTĪON RÉSÚRRÉCTĪON

You think you catch. . . . You grin. But clarinets
Sock you. Still this hushing "green," like drunk,
Like beautiful, to then no words, clear sound,
Like indigo, chrome yellow, point vermilion

LORD HAVE MERCY ON US
WHO TRAVEL IN THE AIR   ON LAND   AND WATERS
WOMEN IN CHILDBIRTH   ALL YOUNG CHILDREN
THE BROKEN FLESH AND SPIRIT   PRISONED
CAPTIVE
LORD HAVE MERCY ON US

And zingo, into pounding back zer-rum,
Bourrée, cachucha, jota, something, stamping,
And hips, and what it takes, the violins
Obscene in *pizzicati,* sneer guitars,
Who, hell, are you, zer-rum. And tamtam. Plucking

SALT CLOCK FALSE CLOCK SALT FORGOT FORGOT-
TEN
AFRAID AFRAID AFRAID AFRAID
IN CITY   IN WATER   IN WIND   IN FOREST   IN
FLAME
ANXIOUS ANXIOUS ANXIOUS ANXIOUS ANXIOUS
ANXIOUS

But take the shift. Like mountains, jerk and cut
But centered. Syncopate. And rhythm. Rhythm.
Drag out the ANX . . . and add a lick. And speed . . .
ANXIOUS ANXIOUS ANXIOUS ANXIOUS ANXIOUS
ANXIOUS
Syncopating. Buzzing. Instruments.
In stone, perhaps. Laocoön. But no.
Abstracts? Make sharp on curve. The blue toward red
Make depth. Extension. What your stomach spills
When what goes on hits close and makes you think

Those sons of *Schrecktuch* might have raped your wife,
Or, trampled Russian children, might your own . . .
Nanking . . . the war . . . yank out your heart. I say,
If you'd do that "abstract," you'd crack your skull.
They'd look and say, "Activity." Or, "Strain."
But not an angle, shadow, curve to give
Well . . . like the *Guernica* . . . that almost says.
Because it's understated. Know it's battle,
As in Picasso. But no scream. No cannon.
No bombs upchucking. Not hysterical,
But worse. As if your nerves hauled out and screwed
On pegs and scraped and bowed against trombones
That brag. And trumpets hooting. Cello moves

EXCEPT THE WILL SHALL LOVE THE MIND GROWS
VAIN

Soprano next, controlled, just this: O SAVE

And tenor answers to a horn and then
Six voices, harmony on this one line

THE WILL IS POWERLESS SAVE THERE BE GRACE

They say it's hard to sing. They practiced. Hard.
The hardest line to sing not hissed, not snarled.
But come all voices, lines, FEAST, SACRIFICE,
FORGOTTEN, BREAK, with wallow, swag and battle,
All instruments, as well guitars, piano,
With one word bucking, sometimes comes to sound,
Like cheers, rahrah, and sometimes snide . . . and leers

REVOLT

But underneath there's "Green" and shushing strings
With bass and baritone, all leaders talking
Not quite on any key but three times saying —

Into the Thunder

From Dante, Alfred says. Take melodies,
Come back to talk with flute and drum and harp

ACCORDINGLY YOU UNDERSTAND
THAT IN YOU LOVE THE SEED OF VIRTUE AND IS
GOOD
ACCORDINGLY YOU UNDERSTAND
THAT IN YOU LOVE THE SEED OF EVERY ACT
WHICH MERITS PUNISHMENT

And voices only, in full choir return

FOR THE FATHER SENT HIS SON INTO THE WORLD
NOT TO CONDEMN THE WORLD
BUT THAT THE WORLD THROUGH HIM MIGHT BE
SAVED

To final chorus, all the themes come under,
Tugging and protesting, mocking, joking,
And still they sing it out. It falls like arch
Around, above, and folding, still they sing

HAVE WE LOVED ALL SONS WHOM WE HAVE SEEN
HOW SHALL WE LOVE GOD THE FATHER
WHOM WE HAVE NOT SEEN

So flutes and oboes, violins, the tune
That's been there since the first, that's called *Pa Pan*,
And Iris says, a little monk who prays
To jump the wall and find his girl. Can't tell
If it's to laugh or cry. It skips and curves.
And while it ran, I watched the silent faces,
The restless, the complacent, the intent.
Thought, whether wave's electric to the ear

Apocalypse

Direct or shaped, augmented, shipped to distance,
Diminished and in part projected, sends
Vibration more than any ear receives,
To each as heard, makes tone, and alters meaning.
The blues and gypsy keep on dancing, pounds
The kettledrums. Up trumpets. Final chords
Like wheels for junk, and broken up, put back
As in my dragon mural. Took apart
All reptiles. Juxtaposed. My own redaction.
Like all we are, perhaps, the few old cells
Split chromosomes and shift, the like not like.
He'll change the beat on some old tune. I'll swear
It's not a tune I ever heard before.
There's more of that in this than I could catch,
So Iris says, from Second, turned, inverted.
And something, so Will says, "crab canon" — MAN,
WE MEASURE MAN. Don't know. But holds attention.

Fourth

Yes, it's late. But I don't work at night.
Can't change the light. But if I go to sleep,
Just kick me. Here, the eight of us, till morning
With Minna holding floor about this last,
Apocalypse. Up early, Iris . . . dress
And feed the infants, hustling off with Alfred . . .
Takes all day long, that drive. You find it cold?
Wind's changing. I suppose no heat. Won't count
By what the weather does. So let us freeze.
The janitors are trained to theories.
Who cares, thermometers? With shivering,
May keep awake. Don't race. It's solemn. Grave.
The way he means. Don't have him here to haunt me.
With working out the canvas sometimes think
She's here. Or he is. Sure. Illusion. Looking
Inside to see what's missing. Sometimes, weeks.
Go back to look. The heads among the leaves.
Guitar and pipe. The heads among the leaves.
The way the vines turn into strings. The hands.

All right. But try their eyes. You'd think, with paint
Slung twenty years at least — since my first snakes,
The drawing hung to dangle on the blackboard —
The thin old crawlers, harmless, from the straw
And broken branches used to lie in heaps.
I'd find them in the backwash near the pond.
Liked sunlight flowing on the coils. But Dad
Said snakes "lost customers," and, "Let them be."
And Mother scared to see me coming. Tried
To wash the motion and the light. And then
The prize. Hung on the blackboard. Trouble started.
But Dad's all right, and Mother. Thought I'd starve.
But since I don't, "O.K." But hard. They're fond
In their own way. I'll take the blame. Young Ed
Or Julie . . . talk that I won't understand,
Perhaps. Don't mind me. Half asleep. But listen.
A mighty hymn. Don't race it. And don't drag.
That's not his style. The instruments. The voices.
And, under all, one swinging mighty theme.
And no full chorus till it's FROM THE SEA.
Manhattan rising, moving, as you've known,
In mist. When from the park, or . . . over river,
Late afternoon, with every window blazing.
Slight tympani. And mostly . . . violins.
Trenchant. Then, unearthly. Strain your ears.
Returns *fortissimo.* Then, lamentation.
Goes glint on bells and horns. Most . . . violins.

WHAT HAST THOU DONE
THE VOICE OF THY BROTHER'S BLOOD
CRIES FROM THE GROUND

Wait. Marking there? Marimba. Meditation.
Not melancholy and not gay. What's that?
Alto oboe. Violins. Now. Voices.

WE HEAR THE CRY GO PAST ON YEARS OF WIND
FROM SEAS OF TOO MUCH SALT   THE HOOFS
RETREATING

FROM SEAS OF TOO MUCH BLOOD THE WHEELS
RETREATING
WE FLEE FROM SIGN IN SPACE THE SPACE IN
BOUNDS
THE ALL TO BE RECOVERED PROMISED LAND
OF FATHERHOOD OF BROTHERHOOD THE SIGN
WHOSE MERCY LIES BEYOND THE WRATH AND
JUDGMENT

THE HOUR HAS COME AND IS THE TIME THE TIME
WE SEARCH THE SPIRIT FATHERED IN THE TRUTH
WHO HAS LIVED TO SEE THE SOURCE OF LIGHT
IN THAT WE LIVE WE LIVE WITHIN THE SEA
THE LIGHT THE WATER SALT AND BLOOD OUR
NEED
BUT WE HAVE HEARD OF LOVE HAVE HEARD OF
JUDGMENT

SIGNS IN SUN AND MOON AND IN THE STARS
AND ON THE EARTH THE ANGUISH OF ALL NATIONS
MEN'S HEARTS HAVE FAILED THEM IN THEIR FEAR
AND DREAD
WHAT THINGS MAY COME MAY COME UPON THE
EARTH
IN THE BEGINNING WORD HAVE THEY NOT
HEARD
WHO SHALL SAVE US WHO WILL HUG OUR SINS
HAVE THEY NOT HEARD IN NO WISE WE BELIEVE

That's where. The melody comes flute . . . FORSAKEN.
Violas . . . RISEN FROM THE DEAD. A woman

WHICH WAS AND IS AND IS TO COME DESPISED
THE MEANS OF GRACE MOST TERRIBLE IN GRACE
WOE TO THE INHABITERS OF EARTH
A VOICE CRIES FROM THE GROUND A MULTITUDE
ALL NATIONS OF ALL PEOPLES OF ALL TONGUES
COMING COMING FROM GREAT TRIBULATION

ALL THINGS COVER A MYSTERY

One line. And Minna thinks, "Pascal." They sing
With cellos, with violas, violins.

THE DAY IS THINE AND THE NIGHT ALSO
THOU HAST PREPARED THE LIGHT AND THE SUN

Then melody. And Minna says, been sung
For years . . . and plainchant. I don't know. She says,
"Unaltered." "*A capella.*" Twelve. Small choir

GLORY BE TO GOD ON HIGH
AND ON EARTH PEACE GOOD WILL TOWARD MEN

Sure. Leave it out. You know. Until you hear
THOU ONLY O CHRIST WITH THE HOLY GHOST
ART MOST HIGH IN THE GLORY OF GOD THE
FATHER
He takes the psalm and Gloria, runs over
On instruments and massive, forceful, turns
Toward single voice. She's written, "Augustine."
You'd have to ask them, Stephanie and Iris,
Or Minna and Old Will. They know. Say, "*Cento,*
But not all *cento.* His." But seems to me
It's his, with Alison. Not his alone.

THOU WOULDST NOT SEEK ME HADST THOU NOT
ALREADY FOUND ME

I think . . . the baritone. I'm right? With bass

NOW GOD AND MAN ARE BUT ONE CHRIST

And Senior said where from. Forgotten. Brings
Twelve voices. Counted. Days he walked in Egypt,

The next. I knew. And Alfred. Jericho,
Later, wandering . . . gullies. Lines dug up,
The lines he learned, the verses. On Osiris.
AS TRULY AS GOD LIVES HE ALSO LIVES
AS TRULY AS GOD IS NOT DEAD HE SHALL NOT DIE
Then flutes. The violins. Marimba flowing
Bells. Like water flowing. Leaves. Slow. Falling

ALL THINGS COVER A MYSTERY

A second time. But now the leaders, close,

FOR GOD SO LOVED THE WORLD
HE GAVE HIS ONLY BEGOTTEN SON

Wait. Silence. Harp. And then takes off to thunder
With every sound he has, comes down to chaos,
Abyss, like stars let loose, like all to smash,
And Minna says it's "*Ragnarök.*" Perhaps
Like hurricane. Or flood. Or battle. Crash.
Then wheels, as in the First. The clarinets,
The trumpets. And percussion. Tolling. Voices.

WEST OF SUN AND MOON BRIGHTER THAN LIGHTNING
OUT OF THE SEA WE CAME HOW SHALL WE CHOOSE
EXCEPT THE WORLD BELONG TO GOD
WHOM SHALL HE FORGIVE

But rhythm changes. Like the First. Like talk.
Like controversy. Rapid. On what key . . .

IT IS NOT ENOUGH BEYOND PAIN IT IS NOT ENOUGH
BEYOND QUESTION IT IS NOT ENOUGH IT IS ENOUGH
IT IS ENOUGH THAT GOD IS LOVE

Here comes. The lamentation. Men and women,
The voices skirl and fade. I'd venture sound

He'd hear perhaps among the Basques. Or spring
And spring again he'd greet him, buy him drinks,
Old hobo with the bagpipes, stand and drone
And fling it, years at school, beneath Tahl's windows,
And I remember, came on snow, a time
Forsythia and crocus, snow on trees,
The old man with his cap. And there he'd stand
And pipe and drone. Tahl called him in and fed him.
He'd say, "The sound's not sad." I say it is.
A banshee sound if I had ever heard one.

THE NATIONS WEEP   WITH A LOUD VOICE
ALL NATIONS   THROUGH   THE WILDERNESS
IN ONE HOUR   THE CITIES   DESOLATE
UNTIL HE SLAY   THE SEA   THE COIL   THE RAINBOW
WE ACKNOWLEDGE OUR MANIFOLD SINS
IN THOUGHT   IN WORD   IN DEED
THE BURDEN   IS   INTOLERABLE

So Ragnarök repeats. You'd shut them out.
Intolerable's the word. Intolerable.
Not anguish. But a wrestling. As with death.
The Ragnarök. And once, the baritone
HE CAME TO FIND HIS OWN   BORN NOT OF BLOOD
NOR OF THE WILL OF MAN   THE BORN OF GOD
The Ragnarök gone shrill, and then, the mezzo,
THE PRINCE OF THIS WORLD COMES   AND HUNGRY
FEED HIM
BUT BE NOT OVERCOME OF THAT DARK SPIRIT
The Ragnarök come full, and then — soprano,
BEHOLD I SEE THE HEAVENS OPENED
THE SON OF MAN ON THE RIGHT HAND OF GOD
The Ragnarök, the orchestra, half chorus,
WE STOPPED OUR EARS. WE STOPPED OUR EARS AND
RAN
And always Ragnarök. But now it's driving.
Drums upon the cellos. Full choir rising,
Buttressed, fortified, the voices building,
A CITY OF THAT LIGHT FROM OUT THE SEA

OUR CITY WHICH WE BEAR OUR SHOULDERS
BURNING
OUR MUSIC WHICH WE HEAR THE THUNDER'S
WARNING
OUR LIGHT WHICH WE ENDURE THE FAR EYES
ACHING
OUR ROAD WHICH WE PREPARE IN THIS FLOOD'S
RISING
NEITHER TO THE EARTH NOR TO THE SEA
NEITHER TO THE AIR IS OUR SOJOURNING
THIS OUR CONDEMNATION AND REDEMPTION
THE TREE OF LIFE AND HEALING OF ALL NATIONS

But take it back yourself. I'm sorry. Grabbed,
Before I thought. It's your show. Go ahead.
Here. Take it. Give it out. But as rejoicing

AND I SAW A NEW HEAVEN AND A NEW EARTH
THERE IS NO MORE SEA

But orchestra returns . . . CRIES FROM THE GROUND
THE VOICE OF THY BROTHER'S BLOOD CRIES FROM
THE GROUND
Sombre, as you'd take a knife and scrape
And see it's not quite right, and scrape, goes wrong,
The color mixed and troubled. Scrape. Goes wrong,
But, under all . . . his swinging, mighty theme
Which comes and keeps on coming till it comes
From orchestra to single voice, that man,
The baritone, alone, magnificent

I WILL BE HIS FATHER HE MY CHILD
FIRST AND LAST BEGINNING AND THE END
THE MOVING SOUNDING LIGHT AND BEING LIGHT
GOD OF GOD LIGHT OF LIGHT WHO MOVES
WHOM WE HAVE SOUGHT FOR IN THE WILDERNESS
THOU MIGHTIEST CHRIST ARISE
THOU MIGHTIEST CHRIST ARISE
THOU MIGHTIEST CHRIST ARISE
THE WORD OF LIFE

By God, you really took that, man. Your voice.
That's what I noticed first, the night I met you.
No wonder you could run your crazy army.
You're loud enough to swerve a bullet coming.
But that's not how he does it. Gives it plenty.
But not to shout. The orchestra comes firmly
With every chord. Authentic. Harmonies
Play close, but sure. And headed where you want.
No hanging off. And nothing brag or rumpus.
Asserting. But it's not to shout the roof off.
Just sure. And nothing missing. With the chorus
Thanks and glory . . . MIGHTIEST CHRIST ARISE
MIGHTIEST CHRIST ARISE . . . THE WORD OF LIFE.
If they were listening somewhere, that scant million
They estimate as "talking to yourself," —
A million is enough, for me to paint them.
They knew when this was over. There's no doubt.
We knew. I watched to see. You'd fairly draw
That handful of us pulling in the breath
And out. Attention. Finished. Trouble is,
The sounds that sound full harmony . . . a sadness.
A close all right. But does not close. It aches.
As if the sound went on. Like us. We talked.
Back here again. We'd watched the crowd move out.
The packing instruments. The folding pages.
We'd thought we'd ask the boy . . . but had his friends;
They rushed him off to his own celebration.
We kept it high and gay. Were glad to have them,
Stephanie and Will. And always good
With Alfred, Elsa. Like old times. And then,
Senior, earnest. All of us debating.
He says, "Not contradiction." Says, "Extension."
The "scholarship," "emotion," and "the dance,"
The rhythms, figures, all the keys; he said,
"He makes the Fourth true recapitulation."
And Stephanie agreeing. Minna, then,
As if we were, the lot of us, her children,
Needed teaching, minutes here explaining
Apocalypse, tradition, what he means,
Essential tragedy of all we've known

And only triumph. Other answer . . . none.
And there it knocked us. Those hours, half-forgotten
They were not here. Aren't here. And what's the use?

Within one space to draw a million faces?
One hundred thirty million? Years? And aeons?
Say I don't know. And they're not here. They're gone.
We don't know where. I ought to stay awake.
But . . . god . . . I can't. Perhaps I'm growing old.
A laugh. But can't burn nights. Not now. Oh, Lord . . .
Take off that grin. It's my own jaw to break
With yawning. And I lay awake last night.
When Iris has ideas, she'll have them out . . .
Like Tahl. She'd keep inquiring, was she right,
Means present, past, and future always moving,
Generations, union and mutation,
Modulation, dying, always living,
Fighting, always knowing and not knowing,
Until there "is no sea," the end of time.
And I was yawning then, as now. Could think
Just pictures. I could see him years ago
At his first concert when, that night, I asked him
Why talk to idiot children. See him standing
Waiting in the wings there, waiting sign.
He said, "It's not what's said. A child won't judge . . .
Not word. Except in act. The act is word.
There's more than sound and light in our perception."
Kept dozing off. And half in dream. The time
We started off from Athens, just we three,
Iris, Alison, the two beside me,
And I knew Iris was the woman. Still,
I'd have her in the corner of my eye,
That head, this Alison. I'd watch her turning
For one more look at him in coming dawn.
Kept dozing off. But always Iris' voice,
The other bed, a murmur through the dark,
Until she said, "I wonder how he looked?"
I heaved myself to clear my ears. Her voice,
Quiet through the dark, "Like him? Like both?"
An hour, perhaps a minute, till it clicked,

Till I knew whom she meant. The child. To sleep
Fighting with the canvas and at once
Both in the wings and jammed against the wheel
Driving, driving, driving. And their faces.
Faces. Alison and Tahl. I'd turn,
And where I turned, they looked. You see it is
What I can't catch, the smile that's not quite smiling
And what's alike in those two pairs of eyes.
Not color. Not the harebell blue that darkens
With lashes down, her eyes. Not "depth" or wind
Or more than wind, the crease and pucker, shadow
That gave him even those first years I knew him
The seaman's look, the weathering. Not mocking.
Not still. Not "thoughtful," merely. Something said.
Sad. Or good. To mean, "is well." A light
Not rendered and not hiding. Plain to see.
Good night. Perhaps I'll find it. Something hidden.
Good night. He said, ". . . the particles of sound."
I see her head. "The particles of light."
Good night. Perhaps I'll find it. Something hidden.

TAHL : BOOK FOUR

CANTO V

THE YEARS ALSO HIDDEN

Now

Now. Do you know of whom I speak?
I have searched long to find a face.
At times we trust. And you I trust
Of these, long promised, gliding down.
We'll guide you. We shall take the town.
You will move north. We shall move west
And south. "Watch sharp. Until the death,
There's space to move. But watch," he said,
"The time." And I? We have no names.
But once in Spain were freemen. Once
In France, again in deserts, beaten,
Afraid of thirst and whips and ties,
The heavy rails across the sands.
But when I fled last year, I sought.
I asked. Among your people coming.
The great ships opening. The planes.
Now here, this southern coast of France,
You knew us. *Nuestro! No fascista!*
We said this. You I trust. You know our meaning.
You know I do not lie. We have no names.

But do you know of whom I speak?
And once I had a father, known.
Physician. I once seventeen . . .
And younger . . . when he died. I saw . . .
Your father told you what they did.

The Years Also Hidden

The merciful, the wise . . . were slain.
His son escaped. And fled from Spain.
From holes the view distorts and hard
To judge a distance. Spew of shells.
I saw us burn from burning bullets
At seventeen. The legs. The arms.
On ground you hide your face from planes,
But listen for the rasp of tanks.
They laughed against my father's saying
Infection. Far away! In China!
We ate the filthy bread. We whispered.
In France, the motorcycles. Fled.
Antwerp. Paris. Stalingrad.
The times reverse. Escaped, I see the turn.
I guard you. As he guarded me in Spain.

You know of what I speak. We learned.
They also learned. We would not lie,
One creature, chloroformed and stretched
Upon our mountains. They had brought
The tools to prove. New scalpels. When
We moved and spoke, they would not stop.
Performed the operation. Laughed.
You learn. How men will stumble. Slip
When hit. And women also. No?
In England. Not your country. No.
How much to learn. We also heard
Of those who died at Almería.
I had not seen, along the Tagus,
Elms. The walls at Tarragona.
We saw. We crossed our country. Broken.
Groped toward freedom. Spring . . . in France.
And trapped. Like criminals. I speak
With difficulty. Be so kind . . .
I try to think of China or Japan
When you were seven; I was ten. How long . . .

You know of what I speak. To throw
Grenades, steal guns, the parts, the clamps,
The spindles, sockets. Pins will foul,

Will break. Not you supplied, come down
With ammunition necklace, knife,
Grenade, and gun inspected, oiled.
But you tonight, without us, lost.
Expand. Withdraw. Maintain the circle.
The wind, oblique or gusty, turns
The shell. We lack the lens and card.
Direction. Once El Alamein . . .
And then. . . . Keep contact. Mobile. Lunge.
Each knows some part of battle. Told,
Sevastopol. But Stalingrad . . .
But we were children in Madrid.
The bolt against the trunnions tight,
Or aim will fail. Or test a fuse,
How long it burns. And who explodes.
Our ambush is this world. From every nation
Nosotros y ellos, here — as once in Spain.

You do not know of whom I speak?
"Uncertainly, faultily, check with the heart."
Our courtesy to strangers once:
"Your name? Your parents? And your province?"
But now we do not ask. He asked
To see my wound. He seared his knife.
It was not deep. In flesh. He cut.
He bathed and hid me, that cold night.
Not warm as here, with stars to watch.
Night noises are deceptive. Once
I thought Achilles noble. Sulk
And brag? To judge. But doubtful. Wait
For years in pens and holes and drink
The grease of leavings. I had seen
My blood run on his hands. I'd seen
My father's blood . . . before. He stood
Unarmed, my father. And he said
Starvation, ignorance, and fear were sad.
He'd worked. They had his record. He is dead.

You know of what I speak. They stuck
As butchers stick. . . . You know. You speak

Our language. But your friends have doubts.
Us they call the bandits. Yet
Must trust. Each man decides. Himself.
Could burst a tank with pitched grenades.
But wiser, wait. The guns improve.
Guns. Bubbling sound. "Although we gauge
Our principles, there still remains
One factor in the span of time —
'Uncertainty' — will not," he said,
"Remove." Not test by name. But test
By eye and hand, by heart and act.
Your friends are very strange. They joke
So much. "Sure! Moscow!" How reply?
Whoever hates because the blood
Runs under darker skin or formed,
The flesh, to variant of his own,
I've heard a court near that Red Square will judge
The hater guilty and condemned . . . for crime.

And did I know his name, you say
You do not think you'd know him. No.
But you must ask . . . for a musician
Who fought in Spain. That night we lay
Between the glistening boulders. Pulled
The splinters out. I said, "Physician."
His fingers. Deft. But he said, "No.
I once was called 'musician.'" So.
Inquire. And greet him. Good! First signal.
We move toward liberation. Yes,
Your friends are good. Well trained. We'll move.
But two more flares to wait. He lay
In cold beside me. And I wept.
For I was only seventeen.
My friends who died, their bodies heaped
About the gun. He'd heard the moan.
Alive. All night he held me. Talked.
Hidden. Talked to shield the pain.
"Before the Hindus slew Dravidians,"
He said, "the crime. The blood cries from the ground."

Now

You know of what I speak. The slope,
The beaten zone, to judge the column
For enfilade. Must judge the wind.
Through mountains, best detached, small groups.
You must not waste the ammunition.
Save oil and soda ash. Watch rust.
Traverse. Cross-level. Target moves.
And best to memorize a map.
Bivouac in river bends.
Most dangerous, the hostile flank.
Be sure. Maintain communication.
The principles remain. The change
Is in location. Cover approach.
They come in the name of the people. Watch.
They come in the name of God. Watch sharp.
The heart. The act. When great Christ took
The whip, He struck the thieves in temples.
The sword He took but once . . . struck treason.
Those who comprehend are of one nature.
Look! The second signal. That green flare.

I wish to know a reason. Now.
This night as not before. I seek
The reason. From my self of self.
My father said, "Behold the great.
Let each man read the great of old."
I looked. I saw the sulk and pride.
My comrades said, "Behold the small.
The small are good." I looked. I heard
The quarrels, treacheries, and lies.
But when I lay beneath the heap,
I feared to die. Cried out. And why?
He heard my voice. I saw his face
Wet with snow. His back was strong.
The bodies heavy. Noise was loud,
More loud than this tonight. The noise
Much louder, in the cold. He came
From seas of noise and snow, he came
In crack and thud. Among the squeals.

Most terrible, the squeal. No sound of planes
Since snow came on. But shells. Within the zone.

I wish to know a reason. Time
Is brief. Please listen. Who are they?
Who delight in oppression. Their fornication
With guns. With guns. They kill the children.
They torture the women. They laugh. They burn.
They kill physicians. They kill the kind.
They kill the wise. And laugh. They like
The music of shrieking women and children.
So. We must have reserves. You know.
Must guess the enemy's intention.
They move. Unless we have reserves,
We cannot meet their next location.
You know. A flexible plan. You land.
You find us or do not. Proceed
On general principles toward target.
Defense in depth, you find us. Good.
Must raise the bore. Judge angle. Fire
Beyond the mask. Take elevation.
We rectify. Traverse. Uncertain target
Beyond the mask. Take aim. We range the earth.

The time now is brief. The last flare will come soon.
Make ready. And when we have passed from this wood,
I shall not speak further. In silence. Now. Listen.
Even that night, when we moved, we were sure
The forces were east. Not enough to know where,
To pass through the zone. Through the cones. Through the cold.
Rigid against the damp boulders. Thin snow.
The slope raked with fire. And the dead as they fell,
The snow on the crook, the snow filling up
The wide hanging mouths, the naked wide eyeballs.
My pain. We must freeze. Or must move. In the pit
The scant oil smudging out. Now. Less thunder. I whimpered,
A child I was, seeing my blood on his hands.
He listened. The noise rolling off. Knotted coat
And with rope from his waist and he bore me so, bound
At his shoulder, a child. And I clung to his head.

And we crawled, his arm under my body and lifted
Or holding us down. It was bitter. Now drizzle. And ice.
From heap to next heap for a cover. The dead. And I died
In the cold. And woke up in a river. And screamed.

The flare! We now move. But listen, my friend.
He swam with me. Winter. A river. Who knows
What happened? He dragged me on shore. And we lay
And I saw the great blood on his shirt. It welled up
And it froze. And the snipers were everywhere. There,
On the river, they struck him. He swam with me, bound
To his shoulder. He held up my head. And I died
On that shore. But they found us, our own. In the stall
The litter boys quick. And we lay there together . . . on straw.
And he could not speak. For his wound. . . . And toward morn-
ing. . . . This war. . . .
I might have asked why . . . and heard answer. I slept.
The orderly said, "Shipped him east." I was healed.
I fought on the Ebro. And back to Figueras. But find him.
Greet him. And tell him I live. But may die very soon.
I shall die and not know. I have fled. Have escaped.
But for what? Ask him that, if he lives. We survive.
He had wounds near his lung. He is strong. I am strong.
But had frozen there under the dead. I have lived.
I have lived to come back. Was not frozen or drowned. For what
reason?
Look there! On your belly now. Quiet. *Nuestros!* The planes.

TAHL : BOOK FOUR

CANTO V

THE YEARS ALSO HIDDEN

After

Who lives to mark the boundary of sound
May come on pastures of the unicorn,
May come on first of orchids in that garden
Which first gave breath, the witness of survival,
Which is refreshed by light upheld on thunder
Beyond this sea, the first and final ocean.

Who lives within the boundary of ocean
Lives troubled ever by recurrent sound
Of many names, the particles of thunder.
Who hears the legend of the unicorn
Compels to question by what vast survival
He reappears, seeks rest in this world's garden.

Who tends the orchid, treasure of his garden,
Will fear the sterile wave, the coming ocean;
Compels to question by what strange survival
The rarer species still return, the sound
Of hooves reported, fleet-foot unicorn
Among the trampling bulls in this world's thunder.

Who will inquire the substance of the thunder
Remarks the fire-scarred tree within the garden.
Who has deduced the substance of the ocean
Rejects the rumor of the unicorn.

After

Who will inquire the substance of the sound
Knows that which never is has no survival.

Who knows in pain contingence of survival
Compels to question scar of fire and thunder
Which quakes the active ear, the self-same sound,
The sound of death and life within the garden.
Who knows in love contingency of ocean
Will tend the orchid, guard the unicorn.

Who loves may comprehend the unicorn;
Who loves will guard the orchid's rare survival;
Contingent in the histories of ocean
Beneath the tree whose roots still feed in thunder
Within the sign, the first and final garden
Discovered first in light transmuting sound.

Who loves the unicorn will fear the thunder.
Who seeks survival searches for the garden.
Who drowns, the ocean bears. We hear the sound.

AUTHOR'S POSTSCRIPT

TAHL has been growing through the thirty-three years of my own life and, more especially, through the thirteen years since July 1931 when I first asked myself in what obscure ways "civilization" survives periodic catastrophes in human experience. The story has grown by a process familiar in the history of the arts, the projection of the commonplaces of experience into another "real" world. Questions concerning meaning in human life are specifically dated for me in the death by drowning at the age of eighteen of my close friend and constant childhood companion, Graham Brinnick. My inquiries into our behavior as "political animals" began, simply enough, in the circumstance of being one of the first women appointed to the editorship of the magazine at Tufts College where men have always largely outnumbered women students; the procedures and party conflicts of that minor issue provided my first active encounter with the machinery of social adjustment. My study of the great period in Greek literature and philosophy, with Dr. William F. Wyatt, gave me my major discipline and first active aspiration toward the creation of a symmetrical and truly "composed" long poem in which the narrative, dramatic, and lyric possibilities of poetry might accomplish a valid integration. The underlying design in Tahl's own experience, the human tradition now in the making from the conscious reunion of the Western and Eastern worlds, expressed in Tahl's own life by his voyage toward China, is not completed in Tahl's own experience; but, like the "carriers" of the past, he has made a way, has left clues and signals, toward those partial achievements which have been and continue to be the heritage of the whole family of mankind — achievements which have been and continue to be our best hope.

Jeremy Ingalls

October, 1944 — *Chicago, Illinois*